Italy Chooses Europe

Italy Chooses Europe

F. ROY WILLIS

New York OXFORD UNIVERSITY PRESS 1971

HC
305
.W48

Copyright © 1971 by Oxford University Press, Inc.
Library of Congress Catalogue Card Number: 75-83024
Printed in the United States of America

To Jane and Clare

Preface

Italy has been largely neglected in studies of European integration. Indeed, its unflagging endorsement of every move that would further the political and economic unification of western Europe has come to be taken for granted. British statesmen, rejected in their suit of Europe by an imperious French President, fly at once to Rome to have their wounded pride assuaged and to be told that Europe still desires them. The Italian capacity for staging prosaic events like the signing of a treaty establishing an economic union as pageants radiant with emotional appeal has made Italy the ceremonial heart of the European Community. But too often the economic heart of the Community has been taken to mean the steel factories of the Ruhr, the farmlands of the Beauce, or the coalmines of the Campine. A study of Italy's participation in European integration, however, is in many ways more revealing of the difficulties and the rewards of the process of European integration than that of its less complex partners.

Italy possessed in abundance the factors that should have made it difficult for it to participate—backward agriculture, protected industry, overpopulation, unemployment, underdevelopment, atrophied bureaucracy, anachronistic education, wartime destruction, social and regional antagonisms, and a huge Communist party. Fully aware of these problems, Italy's governments, almost without hesitation, took Italy into Europe, and the result, in the balance, was far more than they had hoped to achieve. By 1970, no study of the European Community could afford to ignore the steel of Taranto, the automobiles of Turin, or the fruits of the

Conca d'Oro. From a first period of confusion, when, as Italians said, they were uncertain whether they were the biggest of the small powers in EEC or the smallest of the big, they had established their big power status.

Yet Italy could only participate successfully in European integration if it solved, or at least began to solve, its internal problems. A workable political system had to be constructed in place of Fascism; an industrial system had to be created that would expand in spite of Italy's poverty in natural resources; reform in agriculture had to solve deep-rooted social and economic problems; overpopulation, unemployment, and underdevelopment all had to be tackled as one problem; a modus vivendi had to be found between capital and labor. Europeanism implied not only an alignment in foreign policy but internal change as well; and for this reason, a study of Italy's commitment to Europeanism illuminates not only the character of the integration movement but also the national history of postwar Italy.

The first part of this book, "The Process of Choice," describes the various decisions by which its leaders defined Italy's new role in Europe. It is complete in itself, and can be read alone by those who want a brief description of Italy's position in European integration. The second part, "The Choices Determined," analyzes the internal factors that determined the form and effects of those decisions. It is intended to be of use to students of Italy who wish to establish the importance of integration in the country's postwar development and to students of integration who would like to have a national case-study for comparative purposes. For these reasons, I have deliberately limited my focus and my documentation to Italy, assuming that the reader has knowledge both of the international context, such as the events of the Cold War, and of the role of the other five partners in the European Community.

I was able to profit from the great richness of Italian source material that was made available to me by the kindness of innumerable Italians during the four visits I made to Italy in working on this book. I am particularly grateful to the Guggenheim Foundation for the fellowship that enabled me to spend the academic year 1966–67 in Rome, and to the research fund of the University of California for support of visits to Italy in the summers of 1965, 1968, and 1969. I would like to express my thanks for unstinting

PREFACE

help from officials of the Banca d'Italia, the Banco di Roma, the Banca Nazionale del Lavoro, IRI, Finsider, ENI, Fiat, Olivetti, Montecatini-Edison, Confindustria, Confcommercio, Coltivatori Diretti, Confagricoltura, Unione Italiana delle Camere di Commercio, Movimento Europeo, Giovane Europa, Consiglio dei Comuni d'Europa, CISMEC, Centro Internazionale di Studi e Documentazione sulle Comunità Europee, ETFAS and the office of the Piano di Rinascita in Cagliari, the Ministry of Foreign Affairs, and the Information Service of the Presidenza del Consiglio dei Ministri. Much material was made available to me by the officials of the labor unions, CGIL, CISL, and UIL, and by the political parties, especially the SPES office of the Democrazia Cristiana, the PSU, PLI, MSI, and the Centro Studi di Politica Economica of the PCI. Parts of this manuscript have been read by Drs. Mario Bandini, Alberto Benzoni, Gian Giacomo dell'Angelo, Attilio Logato, Pietro Merli Brandini, and Raffaele Porfidia, who should not, of course, be held responsible for its contents, but whose comments were invaluable. For their continual help and encouragement, I should like to thank Dr. Gianfranco Speranza of the Press and Information Service of the European Communities, and Altiero Spinelli, director of the Istituto Affari Internazionali in Rome and the doyen of Italian federalists.

Finally, I should like to acknowledge with great appreciation the kindness of the following people who took time from their busy schedules to answer my questions and to share with me the insights that come from close personal acquaintance with the complexity of decision-making in the process of European integration:

Ajello, Aldo. Chief editor, *Mondo operaio*, PSI.
Albonetti, Achille. Delegate to Spaak Committee and Val-Duchesse conference; author, *Euratom e sviluppo nucleare*.
Arena, Romolo. Head of Servizio Rapporti Internazionali, IRI.
Badini-Confalonieri, Vittorio (PLI). Undersecretary for For. Affs. 1955–56.
Baduel Gloriosa, Fabrizia. Head, Office International Affairs, CISL.
Bandini, Mario. Director, Istituto Nazionale di Economia Agraria, Rome.
Benvenuto, Camillo. Director, *Il Lavoro Italiano*, UIL.
Bobba, Franco. Delegate to Spaak Committee and Val-Duchesse

conference; former Director General, Economic and Financial Affairs, EEC.

Boni, Piero. Member executive committee, CGIL; member of Economic and Social Committee.

Cattani, Attilio. President executive committee OEEC, 1952; Director General of Economic Affairs in Ministry of Foreign Affairs, 1955–58; chairman Cattani committee, 1962.

Chiti-Batelli, Andrea. Parliamentary secretary to Italian delegation in European Assemblies.

Crijns, Leo. Problems of Labor office, in General Directorate of Social Affairs, EEC.

De Marzi, Guido. President, Istituto di Tecnica e Propaganda Agraria, Rome.

Dusausoy, Fernand. FEOGA office, General Directorate of Agriculture, EEC.

Ferlesch, Giuseppe. Director General, Commercial Agreements, Ministry of Foreign Commerce.

Gazzo, Emanuele. Director, Agence-Europe, Brussels.

Geldens, Jean. Free Movement of Persons office, General Directorate of Social Affairs, EEC.

Gronchi, Giovanni. President of Italy, 1955–62.

Guazzaroni, Cesidio. Vice-General Director, Economic Affairs in the Ministry of Foreign Affairs, Rome.

Guéron, Jules. General Director, Research and Training, Euratom.

Guerci, Antonio. Director, Publicity and Press, Olivetti Co.

La Malfa, Ugo (PRI). Minister of Foreign Commerce, 1946, 1951-53; Minister of Budget, 1962-63; Secretary-General PRI.

Levi Sandri, Lionello (DC). Member of Commission, European Communities.

Lombardo, Ivan Matteo. Minister of Industry and Commerce, 1948-49; head of Italian delegation to EDC negotiations.

Macchia, Angelino. Counselor for social affairs and emigration, permanent Italian delegation to the European Communities.

Martino, Edoardo (DC). Member of Commission, European Communities.

Martino, Gianfranco. Assistant Secretary General, Associazione Italiana per il Consiglio dei Comuni d'Europa.

Masera, Francesco. Central Co-director, head of Servizio Studi Economia Italiana, Banca d'Italia.
Meriano, Carlo. Head of Segreteria Tecnica del President, IRI.
Merli-Brandini, Pietro. Member of General Council of CISL; member of Economic and Social Committee, EEC.
Morandi, Luciano. Ufficio Studi, IRI.
Morganti, Giovanni. Ufficio Studi, IRI.
Mosca, Ugo. Director General, Economic and Financial Affairs, fairs, EEC.
Munzi, Ugo. European Social Fund office, General Directorate of Social Affairs, EEC.
Murgia, Ivo. Secretary-General, Giovane Europa.
Nicolai, Mario. Secretary, Commissione tecnico-economica nazionale per i fornitori di bordo, Confcommercio.
Olivi, Beniamino. Head, Spokesman group, EEC.
Pacciardi, Randolfo. (Unione democratica per la nuova repubblica). Minister of Defense, 1948–53.
Pavan, Monsignor Pietro. Professor, Lateran University; expert, Second Vatican Council.
Pella, Giuseppe. Minister of Finance, 1947–48; Minister of Treasury, 1948–51; Minister of Budget, 1951–53, 1960–62; Premier, 1953–54; Minister of Foreign Affairs, 1957–58, 1959–60.
Porfidia, Raffaele. Head, Ufficio Studi, Finsider.
Roscani, Bruno. Editor, *Rassegna sindacale;* CGIL.
Sandri, Renato (PCI). Member Foreign Affairs Commission, Chamber of Deputies.
Santero, Natale (DC). Senator, Member of European Parliament.
Scelba, Mario (DC). Minister of Interior, 1947–53, 1960–62; Premier, 1954–55.
Sertoli, Giandomenico. Director, European Investment Bank.

Contents

I THE PROCESS OF CHOICE

1. The Chimera of the Resistance View of Europe, 1943–1945 3
2. Italy Enters the Atlantic Alliance, 1945–1949 12
3. From Consultative Federation to Sectoral Integration, 1949–1954 30
4. The Economic Miracle and the *Rilancio Europeo*, 1954–1958 53
5. Italy and the European Community, 1958–1968 72

II THE CHOICES DETERMINED

6. The Economic Geography of Italy: Industry 103
7. Italy's Economic Geography: Agriculture 119
8. Overpopulation, Unemployment, and Emigration 150
9. The Problem of the South 160
10. The Industrial Decision-makers 178
11. Pressure Groups in Industry and Agriculture 202
12. The European Policy of Italian Labor 221
13. Christian Democracy and Its "Currents" 252
14. Opponents and Allies of Christian Democracy 286
    Notes 321
    Bibliography 356
    Index 367

Tables

Italian Trade with EEC Partners   74
Agricultural Zones (map)   facing page 120
Working Population by Economic Sector   140
Proportion of Selected Italian Agricultural
Exports taken by EEC Countries   144
Largest Industrial Companies   190

I
The Process of Choice

1

The Chimera of the Resistance View of Europe, 1943–1945

The Italians have long felt that they were responsible for the only successful efforts to unite Europe, namely for the Roman Empire and the Catholic Church; and they have always taken pride in the noble plans for a united Europe expounded by their thinkers and statesmen, from Dante to Mazzini. Even those who wanted to unite Italy as a nation-state, from Machiavelli to the Risorgimento, saw Italy only as part of a wider European community.[1] In the years between the two World Wars, however, several of Italy's intellectual leaders, especially after the triumphant beatification of militant nationalism by Mussolini, reformulated the demand for a European federation in a more cogent, contemporary, and urgent appeal, and these ideas were taken up during the holocaust of World War II by many members of the Resistance who saw in them the sole hope of ridding Europe of the diseases of nationalism and war.

On January 5, 1918, the great Liberal economist and future President, Luigi Einaudi, wrote a letter to the editor of the *Corriere della Sera*, in which he demanded that the states of Europe renounce their national sovereignty, just as the states of America had done by their federal Constitution. "Beside the United States of America," he wrote, "we ought to set, in close association, the United States of Europe, while waiting to see the birth at a later moment of human progress of the United States of the world."[2] Many of the Italian political exiles took up these ideals, though with little popular success. Count Carlo Sforza, a well-known diplomat, and a member of one of Italy's noble provincial families, devoted much of his great energy to popularizing the cause of European unification since, he said, "in the face of the other non-European communities that are emerging, [Europe] is discovering that the ideas and feelings which every European holds in common have greater value than the ideas and feelings that divide them."[3] Luigi Sturzo, the founder of the Catholic political party, the Partito Popolare Italiano, used his People and Freedom Group in London to promote closer ties with European Christian Democrats and to oppose nationalist excesses in all parts of the world.[4] The first political movement to take European federation as its major theme was, however, the Giustizia e Libertà group, formed in Paris in 1929, and led by Carlo Rosselli until his murder in 1937. Rosselli's ideas of a modernized socialism, which would be free of the ideals of class war and would seek a reconciliation of the European peoples in a European federation, appealed to individualistic politicians and intellectuals, including the fiery Professor Ernesto Rossi, and the future leader of the Northern Resistance, Professor Ferruccio Parri. The Giustizia e Libertà leaders founded the Action party in 1942, and they carried into the party the ideal of "a European federation of free democratic states within the framework of still broader world collaboration." After the collapse of the Action party in 1946, its members brought into the parties to which they dispersed this ideal of Europe that Rosselli had preached.[5]

Ernesto Rossi had been arrested in Italy in 1930; and during his thirteen-year imprisonment he and prisoners of similar persuasion read and discussed all the writings on constitutional history that they could lay their hands on, especially those dealing with the formulation and implementation of the American and Swiss federal constitutions. On the prison island of Ventotene, Rossi and two friends, Altiero Spinelli and Eugenio Colorni, drew up a "Manifesto for a free and united Europe," which urged that political parties should not be judged primarily by their internal programs, but by their attitudes toward European unity. In 1943, the group was finally able to engage in active proselytizing. Colorni, who had escaped from imprisonment, began an underground newspaper called *L'Unità Europea*. Following the overthrow of

Mussolini in July, the political prisoners were released from Ventotene; and at a congress in Milan on August 27, the federalist group, which included Spinelli, Rossi, and Colorni, founded the Movimento Federalista Europeo (MFE), and approved six political theses, in which they argued that European federalism had to be achieved during the period of disorder that would follow the end of the war. The federalists themselves would give up their original idea of becoming a separate political party seeking social reforms as well as federalism, and would work with all forces favorable to a European federation, "from the Communists to those strictly liberal."[6]

Following the conclusion of the armistice between Italy and the Allies in September 1943, the Germans seized control of Italy to the north of Naples, and the federalists, like the political parties that had also surfaced during the preceding two months, went underground, or fled to Switzerland. *L'Unità Europea* was still published, though at infrequent intervals and with a very small circulation. A couple of Spinelli's earlier pamphlets were issued in Rome, while in Switzerland Rossi and Einaudi prepared two longer statements in support of European unification. Rossi's little book, *L'Europe de demain,* presented the political arguments in favor of unification. The primary aim of such a federation, Rossi argued, would be the prevention of war. Even so-called peace was nothing more than "international anarchy," in which national governments frustrate the spontaneous demand of their citizens for decentralization of power. The solution was an international juridical order with a federal police to enforce it. Europe, as a spiritual unit in which the people have "in common a certain way of living, feeling, and reacting to major questions . . . [and] the same conception of family life and the relationship between the different social classes," was the natural area in which to create a new Federation of United States.[7] The economic reasons for uniting were presented by Einaudi in *I problemi economici della federazione europea,* in which the arguments later to be presented in favor of the creation of a European Common Market were previewed—larger markets, increased competitivity, freedom of movement of labor, most productive use of capital. A small state, Einaudi argued, adopts a philosophy of scarcity, limiting production, forbidding new investment, restricting consumption. A federated state adopts a philosophy of abundance, and, of especial importance to Italy, the richer members find it to their advantage "to equip economically and to raise to their own level the territory and the inhabitants of the poorer states. . . . Commerce does not prosper on the misery of others and on theft at the expense of one's clients."[8]

Meanwhile, the federalists concentrated their activity on coordinating views with the federalists in the Resistance Movements in other countries and on persuading the Italian political parties to adopt a federalist plank in their programs. Largely through Spinelli's initiative, representatives from Italy, France, Denmark, Norway, Holland, Poland, and Czechoslovakia, and several anti-Nazi Germans, met in Geneva between March and May 1944, and drew up a Draft Declaration of the European Resistance Movements, which called for a Federal Union, responsible to the peoples and not to the governments of Europe, with its own army and judicial system. The Resistance Movements represented "bound themselves to consider their respective national problems as particular aspects of the European problem as a whole." Three months later, the Italian federalists wrote to their French counterparts that federalism had ceased to be a utopian movement and had become a practical reality in "the resistance of the European peoples to Nazism. Thanks to the resistance movements, we have at last discovered the solidarity that unites the free peoples of the continent."[9] In the Resistance Movement the Italian federalists felt they possessed a unique instrument for preventing the resurgence of those conservative forces that would attempt to reconstruct the national states.

The federalists knew, however, that the Resistance was not an apolitical force, rising spontaneously from the reaction of peoples to Nazi occupation of their countries, but was created and led by political parties. By 1945 they were congratulating themselves that they had persuaded every political group except the Communists to accept federalist views. Many leading federalists, like Spinelli, Rossi, and the historian Aldo Garosci, joined the Action party, which was by far the most vigorous supporter of their theses. Einaudi joined with the progressive northern wing of the Liberal party in persuading the conservative majority to recognize that "the unitary organization" of Europe was "inevitable."[10] The Christian Democrats recognized at once that the teaching of the Church espoused the creation "of confederal organisms with continental and intercontinental ties" and the loyal collaboration of Italy in the "European Community."[11] Even the Socialist party had recognized the ideal of a Europe united through the ties of its Socialist parties. The federalists were therefore extremely disappointed when they found, within a year after the end of the war, that none of their hopes had been realized. Both international and internal political circumstances had been against them.

When Marshal Badoglio finally accepted the Allied armistice terms, on September 8, 1943, Italy lost whatever independence of action in foreign policy it had enjoyed under Mussolini. Within a few days the whole of North and Central Italy, including Rome, was taken over by the Germans, and they set up Mussolini as ruler of the so-called Salò, or Italian Social Republic, although he was given no real powers. In the South, the Allied Command gave the king and Marshal Badoglio rule only over an insignificant patch of Puglia. Roosevelt and Churchill made it clear that the further increase of autonomous powers for the Italian government was dependent upon the contribution Italy would make toward defeating the Germans. When the Badoglio government declared war on Germany in October 1943, Italy was granted the status of "cobelligerent," but the nucleus of a foreign office being created at Brindisi was given little freedom of action. Italy had fallen into the Anglo-American sphere of influence. Stalin realistically accepted the fact that the presence of the Anglo-American armies in Italy gave them preponderant power in the treatment of Italy; and, when the leader of the Italian Communist party, Palmiro Togliatti, returned to Italy from exile in Moscow in March 1944, it was to declare his party's intention of collaborating with the monarchy and the Badoglio government. A *coup d'état*, he wrote later, would not only have destroyed the Communists, but the country itself. The only attempt the Soviet Union made to increase its influence on Italian affairs was to recognize the Badoglio government and take up direct diplomatic relations with it.[12]

The British and Americans were far from agreed on the form of government they would accept in Italy, or on the powers they would grant to it. While Churchill favored retention of the monarchy but opposed a rapid restoration of Italy as a military or economic power, Roosevelt and his representatives in Italy seemed ready to jettison the monarchy and to press for more generous treatment of Italy, both politically and economically. At every stage, however, the British resisted American demands for an increase in Italian autonomy, and only slowly were these powers handed over. The six anti-Fascist political parties that had joined together in Rome in September 1943 as the central Committee of National Liberation were permitted to take a share in the cabinet in April 1944 only when they accepted Badoglio as premier and dropped their demands for radical social change until the end of the war. The United States opened diplomatic relations with Italy in 1944, but Britain still did not. The powers of the Allied Control Commission remained virtually unchanged, however, and the partisans in the North themselves agreed in December to accept the authority of the Allied Military Government when that area would be finally liberated, in return for the Allied promise of arms and money. Allied controls continued throughout 1945, with increasing strength. Sforza's appointment as foreign minister was vetoed by the British; Northern Italy remained under Allied military control until December 1945; the British refused to hand back any of Italy's colonies; and only after vigorous Italian protests did the British and American governments compel the Yugoslav armies to withdraw from Trieste.

Thus, in the crucial period following the close of the war, the period that the federalists had looked to as their great opportunity for uniting Europe, Italy was subject directly to the control of outside military forces. Looking back on the failure of the hopes of Ventotene, Spinelli commented: "In the first elaboration of a plan of action, there was the belief . . . that Europe would continue to be the center, and an autonomous center, of the political life of the world. America would return across the ocean . . . , Russia behind its borders. . . . The reality of 1945 and of the following years was instead completely different. Europe became merely a passive object of American power and Russian power that had divided it and were occupying it."[13] Under Anglo-American controls, therefore, the national life of Italy was reconstituted; and the federalists were forced to wait and see whether those political parties that had so cheerfully declared their devotion to European union would be able, and willing, to further that cause in Italy alone. Here again they were disappointed.

The political parties, ignored in most matters of foreign policy by the Anglo-American authorities, devoted themselves almost entirely to the struggle over the shaping of the reconstructed national state. The primary goal of the Italian Communist party (PCI) was to capitalize upon its popularity as the principal contributor to the Resistance in the North to create a nationwide organization, both among the workers of the cities and among the discontented peasantry; and it succeeded so well that by 1945 it had 400,000 enrolled members.[14] Warning his followers not to give the British the opportunity to repeat in Italy their repression of the Communist uprising in Greece, Togliatti attempted to establish direct Communist influence through participation in the government, especially in the work of economic reconstruction and of judicial administration, and to weaken the power of the middle classes by destroying their political basis through the new Constitution, their social position through the purge, and their economic position through economic reforms. With a display of intransigent nationalism on such issues as the peace treaty or the colonies, and by demands for a neutral position between the United States and Russia, the Communists succeeded in hiding for a time their alignment behind the dictates of Stalinist foreign policy. The federalists could hope for little more from the Socialists (Partito Socialista Italiano di Unità Proletaria). The moderate wing of the party, led by Giuseppe Saragat, which was firmly committed to the ideals of European unity, was in a minority, and had, in any case, accepted Unity of Action Pacts with the Communists. Moreover, in 1943-45 the main concern of the Socialists was for the rapid socialization of Italian society, beginning with the dispossession of the great monopolies and proceeding to the nationalization of the major means of production. The power of these two parties was affirmed at the elections for the Constituent Assembly in 1945, when the Communists polled 18.9 per cent of the vote and the Socialists 20.7 per cent. The only other party that was able to build a mass following, the Christian Democratic party (DC), was inclined to treat its Europeanism at this time as a declaration of benevolence rather than as a binding program. It was in the process of building a powerful political machine based upon such representatives of the Catholic Church as the local clergy and the lay Catholic Action society. But its greatest concern was to preserve the structure of the state and the existing economic and social system against a revolutionary challenge from the Left; and in the tough, dedicated leader from the mountains of Trentino, Alcide De Gasperi, it found a statesman of genius to lead it to political hegemony. Its ally, in blocking the purges, guaranteeing freedom of action to the employer class in the work of reconstruction, and curbing the excesses of the local committees of national liberation, was the Liberal party (Partito Liberale Italiano, PLI). The PLI, however, was dominated by a coalition of great Southern landowners and conservative businessmen, who appealed very little to the country as a whole; and although the party contained such persuasive "Europeans"* as Luigi Einaudi, and genuinely believed in the future creation of a united Europe based on liberal principles of economics, its primary concern at the end of the war was its internal struggle against the forces of the Left, in defense of the existing forms of society. The Republican party (Partito Repubblicano Italiano, PRI) had a hundred-year history of supporting federalism; and its able leaders, such as Randolfo Pacciardi, were determined to seek internal federalism by grant of autonomy to the local regions of Italy and a wider federation at the European level. They were, however, concentrating their efforts on the ouster of the monarchy, and, by refusing to compromise, even to the extent of entering the wartime coalition governments, they were unable to exert any serious influence. The so-called Democracy of Labor party (Partito Democratico del Lavoro) was a tiny, heterogeneous party of mildly social democratic inclination, whose only importance lay in the willingness of all the other parties to serve under its leader, Ivanoe Bonomi. The party had little popular support, and by 1946 it was dead. The one party that the federalists felt was genuinely promoting their cause was the Action party. This small group of intellectuals had an articulate program, combining agrarian reform and land redistribution, a moderate socialization of industry, and local and European federalism. As individuals, its leaders were to make important contributions to Italian development during the whole postwar period—Manlio Rossi-Doria as an agrarian reformer; Riccardo Lombardi as the economic theorist of the Socialist party; Ugo La Malfa as the Republican minister who intro-

---

* Throughout this book, the word "Europeans" will be used, as is common in Europe today, to denote supporters of European integration.

duced the first liberalization of trade and, later, the proposals for national economic planning (programmazione); Altiero Spinelli as the prime mover of the federalists; Ferruccio Parri as the idealistic premier of the first postwar government. But the Action party was too diverse and impractical. It lacked an "idea-forza"* that could move the masses, as Paolo Emilio Taviani commented after its demise in 1947.[15]

In a sense, the failure of the Action party was the failure of the federalists. Their program was sound, their leadership of high caliber; but neither their program nor their leadership was suited to the circumstances in which Italy found itself at the end of the war. The two parties that had plumbed the reality of the postwar situation, the Christian Democrats and the Communists, each with its own "idea-forza," were aware that they were engaged in a duel for control of the nation-state of Italy. Foreign policy for them became an instrument for furthering their internal aims: for preserving or overthrowing the class structure, for strengthening or weakening the forms of industrial or agricultural ownership and production, even for safeguarding or jettisoning a particular set of cultural or moral values. The federalists had failed to realize that the ideal of European unification had to grow from internal forces inside Italy and could not be imposed upon Italy from without. The mere consciousness of the "idea of Europe" was not enough to make Italians ignore their immediate problems within the existing national framework. A more practical approach was needed for the realization of European union.[16]

The only concrete achievement of the federalist movement in these early years was a result of their recognition that Italy itself must eventually renounce part of its national sovereignty in order to enter a European community. Mostly through the work of Parri and La Malfa, a group of federalists in the Constituent Assembly inserted into the Constitution Article Eleven, by which Italy "consents, on conditions of parity with other States, to the limitations of sovereignty necessary for a system that would secure peace and justice among Nations." Italy, in short, was free to renounce part of its national sovereignty should an organization ever be created to which it could pass those powers; but in the postwar chaos the prospects for such an organization being created seemed very dim.

---

* An ideal of great attractive power, such as, in Taviani's view, Christianity or Marxism.

2
Italy Enters the Atlantic Alliance, 1945–1949

To the surprise of most advocates of European unification, acceptance of the privileges and burdens of membership in an Atlantic community proved to be a prerequisite to creation of a European union. Economic necessity was a major factor in compelling Italy to commit itself to the American bloc in the Cold War; even so, the choice was not primarily economic, but political in the broadest sense—a value judgment passed upon a political system. The decision to join the American bloc was based upon the conviction that the set of values the Resistance Movement had labeled "European" could only be safeguarded by joining other West European states in an alliance with the United States of America. Recognition of the Atlantic Alliance as the bulwark of European values led, as corollary, to the belief that those values no longer existed in the area of eastern Europe under Communist control. "The West has not only the right but the duty," Luigi Salvatorelli wrote in 1949, "to state its own diverse conception in opposition to that of the East. . . . More than any antithesis of capitalism and anticapitalism, convictions of conscience and the highest values of the spirit are in conflict."[1]

Membership in the Atlantic Pact thus involved a redefinition of "Europe" as an area restricted to the non-Communist countries. This decision was taken in Italy only with the greatest reluctance; and it was some time before the more enthusiastic Europeans could be persuaded that such a redefinition was a necessary precondition to progress toward a federal union with any real powers.

EUROPE FORGOTTEN: THE YEARS OF NATIONAL RESTORATION, 1945–1947

"The project of creating this European federation . . . has no chance of realization," Premier Bonomi declared at the very end of the war. Two years later, the federalists were ruefully admitting that he had been correct. "To measure how much we have slipped back in these two years alone," Ignazio Silone told a group of militant federalists, "it is enough to remember the almost unanimous fervor that the idea of a not distant political unification of Europe then excited in the resistance movements. . . . Today in our country there is a widely diffused feeling of disorientation, a depressed sense of the quality of life, a sterile bickering on secondary or unreal questions."[2] Yet this very disillusionment was a measure of the federalists' lack of realism in those years. In the immediate aftermath of the war, Italy's predominant need was a period of recuperation—to build a new political system after twenty years of Fascism, to reconstruct the economy from the ruins of the war, and to regain a position of equality internationally. Only when these tasks had been completed could Italy think again about Europe.

The last chance for a major political renovation in Italy was lost with the failure of the government of Ferruccio Parri (June–December 1945). Parri's five-party cabinet was dominated by the left-wing parties (Communists, Socialists, and Action party) who were demanding that "the wind from the North" sweep away both the political and the economic power of the conservative classes and assert the dominance of the industrial and agrarian masses. But Parri was unequal to the struggle. Inexperienced as an administrator, he was paralyzed by quarrels within his government, interference by the Anglo-American military government, opposition by the bureaucracy, and the need to get the economy working at once. His partisan forces had disarmed; the local committees of national liberation were deprived of their powers by the Allied forces; the workers' administrative committees, set up to share in the running of the factories, were ignored. The appointment of De Gasperi's first cabinet (December 1945–July 1946) symbolized the restoration of the pre-Fascist state, and the end of hopes for a radical renovation. Italian democracy was to pick up where its development had been interrupted by Mussolini's March on Rome.

De Gasperi combined political flexibility with uncompromising morality. His political talents proved essential in holding together the wide variety of men and opinions that a common Catholicism had linked in the Christian Democratic party; and they enabled him to use the Communist and Socialist parties as governmental allies only as long as he needed them to draw up the Constitution and to ratify the peace treaty. His morality, deriving from a Catholicism that was neither fanatical nor exclusive, gave him the cathartic quality of a great political leader. In his life, he once said, he had followed two principles, "Involve yourself totally. Never half involve yourself in something. . . . And keep your word."[3] Backed by the whole apparatus of the Catholic Church, possessing the impeccable credentials of a moderate who had suffered for his resistance to Fascism, De Gasperi was able to carry through a program of conservative restoration with widespread popular support. He ended the purge trials of ex-Fascists, ousted the last representatives of the Resistance from public office, reorganized the police, and forcefully suppressed any violent demonstrations. He took no stand on the future of the monarchy, however, and accepted its rejection in the referendum of June 1946 with equanimity. The elections for the Constituent Assembly, held concurrently with the referendum, gave the Christian Democrats 35 per cent of the vote and a first mandate for his policy.

During his second ministry (July 1946–January 1947), formed with the Communists, Socialists, and a few Republicans, De Gasperi kept the Ministry of the Interior for himself, so as to be personally responsible for the restoration of order.[4] The uneasy coalition with the two left-wing parties lasted through De Gasperi's third cabinet (February–May 1947). De Gasperi was determined to keep the coalition in force until the Catholic Church's favored position, established in Mussolini's Concordat with the Papacy, had been made an integral part of the Constitution, and until the peace treaty was signed. The Communist party afforded him the crucial votes on the Constitution in March; and both Communists and Socialists supported the signature of the peace treaty in February. In May De Gasperi announced that he was remodeling the political coalition composing his government, and he resigned. When he presented his new government, the Socialists and Communists had been dropped and the new cabinet had a frankly conservative composition.[5]

The second task of the postwar governments was economic reconstruction. Through wartime destruction about one-third of the country's wealth had been lost. Seventy-five per cent of the railroads were in ruins; the merchant marine was almost nonexistent; all forms of public works needed reconstruction, which would require vast expenditure; agricultural production was down to 60 per cent of the prewar level; industrial production was down by a third. And the ruined economy had to provide for the needs of a rapidly increasing population, whose pressure was made worse by the lack of emigration during the wartime years, by the arrival of refugees from the former Italian colonies, and by the demobilization of the armed forces.[6]

From 1945 to 1947, the government was concerned exclusively with fighting hunger and economic paralysis.[7] Immediate American aid was invaluable. Minimum public services and sustenance was provided in the occupied areas by the military government and later by direct aid from the American Federal Economic Administration. Then, between 1946 and 1947, the United Nations Relief and Rehabilitation Agency (UNRRA), funded mostly by the United States, provided $417 million in grain, coal, and raw materials. In all, before the beginning of aid under the Marshall Plan in 1948, the United States had supplied grants and loans to Italy of $1.6 billion.[8] This enabled the government to maintain a minimal standard of living and to get industrial production moving again. By the end of 1947, Italian production was approximately at the level it had been in 1938. Most factories were in operation. With aid from UNRRA and the Ministry of Agriculture, farmers undertook the repair of buildings and the reconstruction of herds. The transportation system was again in working order. The government's choice of means for carrying out its economic policy was, however, to have lasting influence.

Under Parri there had been a six-month period of confusion, coinciding with the "great fear" of the business classes that the reforming government would carry out a wholesale attack on big industrial companies. Parri's plans, however, were vague and impractical, and they were easily blocked by the Christian Democrats and Liberals. In De Gasperi's first cabinet, control of economic policy was exercised by Epicarmo Corbino, the minister of the treasury, who favored a laissez-faire policy. There was a little government interference in the economy. The state attempted propulsive action in vital sectors by allocating materials or by direct investments, and it extended its activity both to state-owned and to private companies. It compelled companies to maintain redundant workers on their payrolls to alleviate unemployment. But the philosophy underlying most governmental economic action was to "remedy the shortage of goods, and especially of foodstuffs, by encouraging a flow of goods to the market rather than by accentuating government intervention."[9] Price controls and rationing were abolished, thereby ending most of the black market. The export trade was returned to private hands in 1946, and foreign exchange controls were eased. Almost no measures were taken to curb the huge companies that dominated such sectors as chemical, electrical, or automobile production. State intervention in the economy was primarily used to safeguard troubled industries, felt to be of national importance, like heavy engineering, and to provide the infrastructure of roads, irrigation, and so on, to make private industry and agriculture more profitable.

The third task was to bring Italy back to a position of international equality. Although the Italians had contributed small forces to the Allied armies in Italy, and the partisans had helped clear North Italy of the Germans, co-belligerence had won Italy little influence. The Soviet Union, remembering the Italian contribution to the German attack on Stalingrad, was insisting on a share of reparations from Italy, supporting Yugoslavia in its demands on the Istrian peninsula and Trieste, and even suggesting that part of Libya would make a suitable colony for Russia itself. The British government had no sympathy for the revival of Italy: "We have no need of Italy just as we had no need of Spain," Churchill told the House of Commons in 1945."[10] General de Gaulle had sent French troops into the Val d'Aosta; and the French government maintained its claim to the province and to a strip of the Riviera coast until September 1945. Both Roosevelt and Truman showed great sympathy for Italy; but they were usually willing to bow to British pressure. Nevertheless, after those early contacts with the Americans during the last months of the war, no Italian statesman could ignore Italy's dependence on American good will. As early as the Yalta Conference, in February 1945, Roosevelt had pressured Churchill to encourage the recovery of Italy, and to help it again take a position of international responsibility, while at the Potsdam Conference, the Americans had been responsible for the decision to give precedence to the Italians in the coming peace settlement.[11]

At the Paris meeting of the Council of Foreign Ministers in September 1945, however, De Gasperi was coldly received. Yet in one of his most effective speeches he succeeded in winning the friendship of Secretary of State James F. Byrnes. For the first time, he spoke as "the protagonist of a new, federated Europe." Italy was prepared to make sacrifices in the name of European solidarity, he said, to help construct a better world; and, to bring home to the Council that he was the representative of a new, democratic Italy, he referred briefly to his own sufferings under Fascism. "I too finished up in prison; and my newspaper at Trento was set on fire and destroyed. Like so many Italian and Slav anti-Fascists, inside and outside Italy, thousands of democrats, without distinction of nationality, had to live as exiles."[12] In an impulsive and highly appreciated gesture, Byrnes rose from his seat and shook De Gasperi's hand as he strode out through the ranks of silent delegates.[13]

During the next year, the punitive attitude toward Italy lightened. The French reduced their claims on the Alpine border. Italy was permitted to retain control of the South Tirol, which it had acquired in 1919. Trieste was made into a Free Territory, with the city itself under Anglo-American occupation but in fact administratively linked with Italy. But no Italian pleading could persuade the Allies to return its African colonies of Libya, Eritrea, or Somaliland. Both the Trieste and colonial issues provided an unfortunate stimulus to Italian nationalism, fanned by the right-wing parties and even at times by the Communists; and, when the peace treaty was presented to the Italian parliament for ratification in July, orators from all sides of the Chamber assailed it in terms of outraged nationalism. Even the distinguished elder statesmen Benedetto Croce and V. Emmanuele Orlando expressed their dissatisfaction with highly dramatic appeals for rejection of the treaty on moral grounds. De Gasperi and his new foreign minister, Count Sforza, in the Chamber and Luigi Einaudi in the Senate, struggled to present the treaty as a sacrifice that had to be made by Italy to get the occupying troops out, as a move to regain a position of equality in international relations, and, above all, as a contribution to understanding among the European nations. Acceptance of the peace treaty, coinciding with the ouster of the Communists and Socialists from the government and completion of the first phase of economic reconstruction, marked the end of a period in which Italy had had no opportunity to seek a role in the process of uniting Europe because of its status as a defeated enemy power. From mid-1947 on, it became imperative for Italy to use its new-found independence to shape such a role for itself.

MARSHALL AID: THE ECONOMIC REWARDS OF ATLANTICISM

Until the signature of the peace treaty, De Gasperi had attempted to maintain the appearance of neutrality in the growing confrontation between the United States and the Soviet Union. But even before Secretary of State George C. Marshall, in June 1947, offered large-scale American aid to the countries of Europe, De Gasperi had been forced to align Italy with the American bloc. By its punitive attitude in the peace negotiations the Soviet Union had shown itself to be no friend of Italy, whereas the benevolence of the United States had been proven by the grant of economic aid, at first with no political strings attached. From the beginning of 1947, however, the American attitude changed. Quarrels with the Soviet Union in the occupation of Germany, the forceful establishment of Communist control in the countries of eastern Europe, the revival of the Communist guerrillas in Greece—all this had convinced the American government that it had to intervene directly to prevent the further spread of Communist influence. In February 1947, Truman, in offering aid to Greece and Turkey, laid down the Truman Doctrine, stating that the United States would aid any country threatened by Communist aggression from without or by subversion from within. And when De Gasperi had visited the United States in January, he was informed that continuance of aid to Italy was dependent upon maintenance of a stable democratic system at home; and it was implied that the

American government regarded the activities of the Italian Communists and their fellow-traveling Socialists as very close to internal subversion.[14]

The American government, however, was only demanding something that De Gasperi was already resolved upon. He had always regarded the Communist and Catholic faiths as inexorably opposed. There had been constant conflict with the Communists even during the period of governmental coalition. By 1947, pressure from the Center and Right within his own party and from the Vatican for a break with the Communists and the Nenni Socialists had become so strong that the ouster could not be long delayed. De Gasperi resigned on May 13, and at the end of the month he formed his fourth cabinet, with only Christian Democrats and three "independents"—Sforza as minister of foreign affairs, Einaudi as minister of the budget, and Cesare Merzagora as minister of foreign commerce. He had thus made his first major commitment to the American alliance, by ending the anti-Fascist alliance born in the Resistance.

The new government therefore felt it had the right to seize upon Marshall's offer of aid a week later. Italy's interest in the proposal was threefold—to regain a position of equality in international affairs, to use the proposed organization on the lines suggested by Marshall for the furtherance of the economic cooperation of Europe, and, above all, to move from reconstruction to a more positive program of economic expansion.

Sforza was delighted to bring Italy back into the mainstream of international negotiations. "This was the first favorable opportunity," he wrote later in his memoirs, "to rise again in dignity to take our place amid the nations of Europe."[15] Hence, the attempt of the British, French, and Russians to formulate the European response to the American offer without consulting Italy infuriated him. He attempted to bring Italy into the diplomatic maneuvering by thanking the American people directly in a radio message, and he ordered Italy's principal ambassadors in Europe to demand immediate Italian participation.[16] Only after the Soviet Union had refused to participate, and had forbidden any East European country to do so, however, was Italy invited to attend the plenary conference in Paris sponsored by France and Britain. Italy's return to international diplomacy was thus to take place under very unfavorable auspices. To accept the invitation to Paris was to admit that Europe was already divided into two blocs—an American bloc of the fourteen powers attending and a Soviet bloc of the eight that were not. Sforza himself attempted to ignore this implication, urging that "the door be kept open to all the East European states that might eventually want to join," and to the states bordering the Mediterranean as well. But few Italians really believed that Italy could remain neutral while receiving Marshall aid. Hence the battle over acceptance of aid turned into a conflict over alignment with a bloc dominated by the United States.

From the time of their ouster from the government, the Communists had made obstruction of the Marshall Plan one of their major goals. In the fall and winter of 1947, they provoked huge demonstrations, spearheaded by members of the Communist-dominated trade union, the Confederazione Generale Italiana del Lavoro (CGIL). In parliament, they argued that the Marshall Plan treaty's goals of individual liberty, free institutions, and national independence meant only acceptance of American goals: "By free institutions is meant capitalist institutions, by individual liberty the freedom of economic enterprise . . . by real independence acceptance of the foreign policy of the United States, especially toward the Soviet Union."[17] The Socialists opposed the Plan no less vehemently, as a danger to Italy's neutralism. The supporters of the Plan, comprising Saragat's Social Democrats (PSLI), who had just broken with the Nenni Socialists, and all political groups from the Christian Democrats to the extreme Right, held that alignment with the United States was a necessity, given the character of Communist expansion abroad and the threat to Italian social institutions from Communism at home, and that acceptance of American aid in no way implied a change in the direction of Italian foreign policy.

The elections of April 18, 1948, were fought principally on the theme of support for or opposition to the Marshall Plan.[18] The Christian Democrats, aided by massive support from the Vatican and the United States, by suspicion of international Communism after Communists seized control of Czechoslovakia in February, and by the widespread fear of internal disorder and left-wing revolution, were swept to an overwhelming victory. With 305 seats in the Chamber, they possessed an absolute majority. Although De Gasperi welcomed into his fifth ministry the three minor democratic parties (PSLI, PRI, PLI), he felt justified in regarding the election results as a mandate to continue the basic foreign policy begun in May 1947, of which friendship for the United States and the union of western Europe were the cardinal principles.

Indeed, American intervention in western Europe had, in the view of De Gasperi and Sforza, provided the opportunity for union. "We do not have the right not to unite," Sforza told the Paris conference on July 12. "If we do not succeed, it could be that this glorious Europe, which has guided the world with the force of the spirit, would again become what it was six thousand years ago, a poor, small, insignificant peninsula of Asia."[19] To give the lead, he announced at the end of the conference, France and Italy had agreed to negotiate a customs union that would be the first step toward the economic integration of Europe; and a month later, the Italian government proposed the creation of an international consortium for the utilization of the hydroelectric resources of the Alpine chain and realization of an "inter-European customs union."[20]

The Franco-Italian customs union was negotiated between September and December 1947, and a protocol approving the institution of such a customs union was signed by the French and Italian foreign ministers in March 1948. Further detailed planning was to follow before the union would be consummated in a treaty. With the replacement of Georges Bidault as French foreign minister by the dedicated European Robert Schuman in July 1948, Sforza felt that the chances of beginning the union of Europe with an "organized and permanent understanding between our two countries," were very near.[21] In private letters to Schuman in August and December, Sforza called for the linking of "one hundred million Latins" to make possible the later admission of Germany to the European community: "The union of our countries will be the real beginning of the union of Europe."[22] Yet the two ministers, although they created lasting personal bonds of friendship and trust, went about the formation of a customs union in the wrong way, by not consulting the industrial groups, a mistake repeated two years later at the time of the negotiation of the European Coal and Steel Community. When the business leaders of

Italy and of France realized that a customs union implied the end of protection and a freer movement of labor from Italy into France, there was an outcry from the employers' federations, who claimed that neither country was ready for so radical a step;[23] and in 1949 French business interests finally persuaded the National Assembly not to ratify the treaty.

In 1948, however, encouraged by his talks with Schuman, Sforza ignored the unwillingness of Britain and the Scandinavian countries to write any form of economic or political integration into the Marshall Plan treaty. "The Italian government for its part," he wrote to Schuman in August, "is convinced that one must arrive at the reality of a European union or federation by proceeding in successive steps, beginning with foundations of an economic kind . . . in order gradually to reach forms of political, economic and social collaboration." He proposed that the Organization for European Economic Cooperation, which had been set up in 1948 to distribute Marshall aid among the sixteen countries participating in the Plan, be given a permanent character, and that it should form a political committee for common examination of international political questions and a European Court of Justice.[24] He spelled out these proposals in a memoradum to the members of OEEC on October 27. OEEC, he suggested, should be attended by cabinet ministers who would work to create a "concerted economic policy": "We are ready for any limitation of our national sovereignty on one condition: that the others do the same."[25] For all its farsightedness, Sforza's proposal did not have the results he had desired. OEEC did continue to exist after the end of Marshall aid, but as an increasingly technocratic body; and his proposal for a political committee was embodied in the foundation the next year of the ineffective Council of Europe.

The Italians had failed in their efforts to turn OEEC into a nucleus for European union. The main importance of Marshall aid for Italy was that it provided the backing for the economic policy imposed by Einaudi, the minister of the budget from February 1947 to May 1948. With the promise of Marshall aid, Einaudi felt safe in carrying out the stringent measures necessary for restoring the value of the currency, even though they would temporarily restrict production and employment. In September 1947 he imposed high reserve requirements for the banks, raised the discount rate, and cut the Treasury's power to draw upon advances from the Bank of Italy. "The central idea was to keep Italy within the orbit of the free market economies, relying upon private incentives to achieve renewed growth and increased competitive efficiency"; and it succeeded.[26] Without achievement of price stability and a sound lira, home production would have been hampered by a fluctuating currency, which in 1947 alone had lost half of its purchasing power, and exporters would have continued to lose their overseas markets through ever-increasing prices.[27] Victory in the "battle for the lira," bought as it was with a year's minor recession, gave Marshall aid a suitable economic environment in which to produce its intended results.

Interim aid from the United States in the winter of 1947 provided $176 million in food and raw materials, while the Marshall Plan itself, operating in 1948–52, provided a total of $1,519 million in grants and $96 million in loans.[28] Industrial revival was facilitated by American provision of raw materials and sources of power, while the regularity of supply made possible the abolition of a whole series of governmental economic controls, such as the governmental assignment of coal and petroleum and the strict regulation of use of gas and electricity. This freeing of internal economic life was accompanied by a liberalization of foreign trade, which proved to be one of the most significant economic steps of the period.[29]

Italian exporters had already, in 1946, been given virtual freedom to export most industrial and many agricultural products without governmental controls, and they had been given special exchange privileges to facilitate their operations. In the sweeping measures of 1951, the minister of foreign commerce, Ugo La Malfa, put an end to almost all quantitative controls over industrial imports. Combined with membership in the European Payments Union, which was founded in 1950 and permitted the settlement of debts among the OEEC countries on a multilateral instead of a bilateral basis, the liberalization measures threw the Italian economy open to the advantages and perils of European economic competition.[30] American aid and the liberalization measures enabled the most efficient (and usually the larger) Italian companies to profit from the reviving European market. Between 1948 and 1953, Italian imports from Europe rose from 23 to 48 per cent of the country's total imports, while exports rose from 46 to 57 per cent.[31] A form of economic interdependence, if not of integration, was in fact being created within OEEC, and it was serving to reinforce within Italy the dominance of the more dynamic companies.

Meanwhile, the Italian government was attempting to use "counterpart funds"* as a means of tackling the structural problems that affected the weaker sectors of the economy. The existence of over a billion dollars in counterpart funds enabled the sixth De Gasperi ministry (January 1950–July 1951) to begin a moderate program of reforms. The permanent economic depression in the South was tackled through the foundation of the Cassa per il Mezzogiorno (Fund for the South), a totally new body with enormous funding ($1.6 billion, half of which was covered by counterpart funds). The Cassa was to further agricultural reform by building dams, aqueducts, roads, and farms, while it was to provide, through ports, communications, and so on, the infrastructure for industrial development. Other major irrigation works were carried out with the aid of counterpart funds, while two agrarian reform laws, one for the Sila region of Calabria and a second for a wider area of the South, provided funding for the confiscation of great estates and the redistribution of the land among the peasantry. New housing programs provided over 800,000 rooms in 1948–51.[32] Finally, funding was made available to those branches of industry controlled by the government through the Istituto per la Ricostruzione Industriale (IRI); and Marshall aid made a major contribution to the modernization of the Italian steel industry.

In the area of European integration, however, the Marshall Plan achieved little. Sforza's grand schemes for economic cooperation were forgotten. American remonstrances in favor of greater unity of the member nations were ignored, though not by the Italians. OEEC had been compelled to let the recipients of aid go about their national programs in their own ways. Only in the eas-

* The Italian government was required to sell to its citizens the goods supplied and paid for by the United States. The money it received in its own currency, called "counterpart funds," was to be used, with American permission, in Italy itself for large-scale projects aiding the revival of production, including projects for the improvement of the economic infrastructure.

ing of international trade through liberalization and financial cooperation had some progress been made. Altiero Spinelli was already warning the United States by December 1948 that it had forgotten the lesson of its own history: that "a league of sovereign states is, by definition, incapable of making a reasonable and functioning economic program." Why, he asked, had America not demanded as a precondition for aid "the creation of an effectively federal European political power, endowed with the means suitable for making a common monetary, customs, military, and foreign policy for Europe as a whole?"[33] Yet, from the standpoint of Italy's future in Europe, the Plan had a major significance. It had prepared the country economically for entry first into the European Coal and Steel Community and, later, into the Common Market, by restoring the productive capacity of its largest private companies and of some of its public companies. Without the dynamic economic machine created at this time Italy could never have entered a European economic union.

THE ATLANTIC PACT: THE PRICE OF ATLANTICISM

Few Italian politicians showed any desire in 1948 to follow up acceptance of American economic aid with participation in a military pact, either with other members of OEEC or with the United States. Even the most unyielding opponents of Communism felt that its danger to Italy was not external, but internal, and that it should be met by a strengthened Ministry of the Interior and by economic revival. Moreover, opposition to membership in a military alliance directed against the Soviet Union was enormously strong. The extreme Left could marshal large workers' demonstrations and strikes in opposition to any commitment to the United States. An even larger group, ranging from the Socialists to the parties on the extreme Right, were demanding a policy of neutralism. The people as a whole were war-weary and suspicious of any military obligations. Politicians like De Gasperi and Sforza were well aware of these feelings, and proposed to respect them as long as possible.

In March 1948, when Britain, France, and the Benelux countries signed the Brussels Pact, by which they formed a defensive military alliance called the Western European Union, directed formally against Germany but in reality against the Soviet Union, they showed no interest in Italian participation; and the Italian government made no effort to join.[34] Many forces, however, were pushing Italy toward military involvement with the other Western powers. The primary factor was the attitude of the United States government. Ambassador Tarchiani in Washington noted in March that the American government was displeased with the "agnostic" attitude of Italy toward the Brussels Pact, and at "our shilly-shallying between East and West."[35] In September 1948, the State Department informed the Italian embassy that it hoped Italy would join the military alliance of the United States, Canada, and the Brussels Pact powers that was being negotiated, and that this hope had "the value of an official wish." Even then, however, De Gasperi and Sforza procrastinated: and it was only on January 6, 1949, that Sforza officially informed the United States government of Italy's wish to join the Atlantic Pact.[36]

The change of mind was due in part to the pressure of the diplomats, who had warned of the peril of diplomatic isolation, and of the Italian General Staff, who were arguing the urgent military necessity of such collaboration and especially of American aid for rearmament. De Gasperi and Sforza had also become convinced that to remain out of the Atlantic Pact would destroy their ties to the other West European states and would therefore endanger the prospects of European union. This argument took several forms. The most practical was the fear that the isolation of Italy would "not only deprive us of any guarantee [of security], but would exclude us from the great currents of production and trade," and would prevent Italian emigration to the West European countries. In the longer run, however, the military security offered by the Atlantic Pact was held to be the necessary barrier behind which the powers of Europe would be able to unite. As Luigi Salvatorelli pointed out, the Pact's supporters thought there was a direct connection between the Atlantic Pact and European union. "On one hand European union increases the solidity of the Pact, while the Pact supplies the union with the necessary shield behind which it can survive and develop. On the other hand, the union assures . . . the independence of the European states which, associated together, will constitute an entity capable of autonomy in face of the United States."[37] Thus, the argument became circular.

The Communists were held to be the opponents of European union because union would prevent their advance into western Europe; the supporters of European union had therefore to support the Atlantic Pact, as a defense against the opponents of European union. "The hostility shown to the Atlantic Pact," Sforza pointed out, "comes from those who fought the Marshall Plan and European union and who hate federalism."[38]

With the coming of the Atlantic Pact, it became important for Italy to prove through concrete advances toward federal union that the military alliance was defending a Europe that had begun to unite. At the Hague Congress of May 1948, when the major European federalist organizations met to discuss the coordination of their goals and efforts, the Italian delegation had enthusiastically endorsed the proposal of creating a European parliament, even though it would be based upon the national parliaments. The five Brussels Pact powers, however, proceeded alone. Compromising between the British desire to avoid any infringement on national sovereignty and the French desire to give the Assembly a consultative role and representative character, they drew up proposals for the creation of a Council of Europe, consisting of a Committee of Ministers and a European Consultative Assembly. The Assembly was to be named by the national governments and consulted by the Committee of Ministers.[39] During this stage of the negotiations, Schuman persuaded the five that Italy should be the first nonmember of the Brussels Pact to be invited to join the Council.[40] Italy, together with Denmark, Norway, Sweden, and Ireland, accepted the invitation of the Brussels Pact powers to come to London in March 1949 for the final drafting of the Statute of the Council of Europe; and at once Italy threw its support to the French in their efforts to make the British cede the new Assembly some real powers. Nothing was achieved, however; and the statute approved on May 5 provided for little more than an impotent debating chamber. Sforza, nevertheless, remained hopeful. As he told the Chamber of Deputies during the ratification debate: "Today there is the Council of Europe, tomorrow there will be an effective European union; today, there is a committee of ministers, tomorrow there will be a supernational organ of government; today there is a consultative assembly, tomorrow there must be a true and proper European parliament."[41]

With the concurrent creation in 1949 of the North Atlantic Treaty Organization (NATO) and of the Council of Europe, the debate inside Italy over the two creations merged, as the Italian government had intended them to do. Both the Communists and the Socialists attacked the two institutions for the same reasons. They held that NATO and the Council of Europe were simply diverse ways of maintaining the division of Europe into two blocs and of increasing the subordination of the West European states to American hegemony.[42] The Christian Democrats supported ratification of both the treaty and the statute, and they were joined by all the members of the governmental coalition. It was, however, the former Action party leader, Ugo La Malfa, spokesman for the Republican party, who made the strongest defense of NATO as an impetus to Europeanism. Europe was being constructed, he argued, through OEEC, the Brussels Pact, and the Council of Europe, which were for him "the re-creation of a western European civilization. . . . ERP* and the Atlantic Pact are the means to the goal of the reconstruction of western Europe."[43] The Statute of the Council of Europe was overwhelmingly approved by the Chamber on July 13, and the Atlantic Pact on July 20, 1949.

Amid the chorus of self-congratulation raised by the governmental parties, the federalists again sounded a sour note. According to Altiero Spinelli, "Just as it is not possible, not even with ERP, to restore the health of the European economy without first creating a European state, so it is not possible, not even with the aid of an Atlantic Pact, to create a European army without having first founded the European federal state"; and "the Council of Europe is still not European unity, and cannot guarantee the peace, security, liberty, and well-being of Europe, unless there develops a federal European state."[44]

The federalists, however, were professionally pessimistic in their role of goad to recalcitrant governments. The decisions of 1947–49 had been a prerequisite for Italian participation in future efforts to unify Europe. Internally, the end of the experiment of coalition government by parties with opposing goals had made possible a coherent foreign policy based upon Atlanticism, Europeanism, and anti-Communism. Economic policy had given to the large private companies and to certain sectors of the public companies

---

* The European Recovery Program, i.e., Marshall aid.

the propulsive role in the country's economic development; and the "take-off" into sustained expansion of these industries had been supported financially with Marshall aid. The erection of the military shield of NATO did have the effect of restoring the independence of western Europe, because it helped end the fear of internal Communist subversion aided from outside and lessened the temptations of neutralism which had implied a kind of nationalistic isolationism. Finally, the very shortcomings of the organizations that were supposedly furthering the unity of Europe taught a lesson for the future. The European states had still to create a community to which its members would be willing, in their own self-interest, to cede part of their cherished sovereignty. The European Coal and Steel Community proved to be just such an organization.

3
From Consultative Federation to Sectoral Integration, 1949–1954

The Italians had no part in conceiving or preparing the two major proposals of 1950 for the advance of European integration: the Schuman Plan for the pooling of Europe's coal and steel industries and the Pleven Plan for the creation of a European army. But they had been eagerly awaiting just such moves. By 1950, the Italian supporters of a united Europe had given up all hope of using OEEC as an instrument of integration, and were already deeply disillusioned with the character of the Council of Europe. The foundation of a new state of West Germany had made it urgent to readmit the Germans into the community of European peoples, as De Gasperi and Sforza had been urging for years. The proposals made by Schuman and Pleven implied to Italians a new geographical concept of Europe, with Britain and the Scandinavian countries excluded and West Germany included; the experiences of OEEC and the Council of Europe, whose roles as instruments of integration had been largely vetoed by the British, had prepared the Italians for this transition. At the same time, the proposals involved a new approach to the method of integration, the so-called functional or sectoral approach, by which concrete steps toward the end of national sovereignty were to be made in specific, restricted areas in which material advantages could immediately be seen. Here too, the Italians, disappointed by the total lack of response to the Resistance Movements' schemes of federal union, were ready to experiment. In organizations that were essentially Franco-German in character, the Italians were ready to participate enthusiastically.

ITALY AND THE SCHUMAN PLAN

The disillusionment of the Italian supporters of European union was profound and bitter by the spring of 1950. Since 1947, when the movement was thoroughly reorganized in Italy, the federalist movement had made great progress. Spearheading the drive for support was Altiero Spinelli's Movimento Federalista Europeo, which showed considerable genius in popularizing its message. The MFE, for example, had asked every candidate in the 1948 elections to declare whether he would favor a European federation if elected, and had received a predominantly favorable response. The other federalist organizations representing political or economic groups were also well supported. Christian Democrats had joined the Nouvelles Equipes Internationales; Socialists, the Socialist Movement for the United States of Europe; and some Liberals and businessmen, the European League of Economic Cooperation. The Council of the Communes of Europe was active in pressing for a European federalism that would permit a decentralization of national power. In the two houses of the Italian parliament, there were many members of the Parliamentary Group for European Union, the one in the Senate presided over by former premier Ferruccio Parri and that in the Chamber by Enzo Giacchero. This Group, which numbered 100 senators and 235 deputies, attempted to orient the foreign policy of Italy toward European federalism, especially through close consultation with the government, whose members frequently attended the group's meetings. Opinion polls showed that there was a widespread public awareness of the concept of the United States of Europe, and strong interest in an organization that would increase emigration possibilities for Italian labor and aid the country's exports. As early as 1948, an organization promising these benefits was favored by 71 per cent of those questioned.[1] This widespread popularity of the idea of a United Europe—even one-third of the Communists questioned said they were in favor—increased the disillusionment when the aim was not achieved. The Marshall Plan was not the main object of criticism, since its material benefits were indisputable, whether or not it was contributing to unification. It was the Council of Europe that dramatized the lack of progress and the reasons for it.

The Italian parliament had sent a large and optimistic delegation to the opening sessions of the Council in August 1949. But by the sixth day, Lodovico Benvenuti, the spokesman for the Parliamentary Group for European Union, was begging the Council delegates to remember that the man in the street was "not unduly interested in questions of pure theory like that of the 'functional approach,'" with which the British were delaying proceedings.[2] During the next year, the refusal of the British and Scandinavian delegations to consider any attempts to endow the Assembly with real powers, or to turn the Assembly to the formulation of common policies for the member countries, infuriated the Italian delegates; and the exasperation that brought the first Assembly president, Paul-Henri Spaak, to resign in disgust in 1951 was fully shared by the Italian delegation. "Our Assembly, as things are, is divided into federalists and non-federalists," Benvenuti commented in 1951. "The Council of Europe will never create a united Europe. It will do excellent things. It will do anything except create a united Europe."[3]

The reappearance of a German state provided the incentive to action. When the Federal Republic was formed in September 1949, most Italians looked upon it with the same distrust and foreboding as the French did. The German occupation of Northern Italy after the armistice of 1943 had aroused great hatred. The Germans had brutally murdered hostages, tortured prisoners, and shipped thousands of young men to Germany as forced laborers. Even Sforza, in a secret letter he had sent to Schuman in August 1948, had justified the link of France and Italy as "the only thing that will prevent the return one day of the aggressive madness of the Germans."[4] The Italians had watched with trepidation the rearguard action fought by France to prevent the restoration of a powerful Germany—its attempt to hold on to the Saar, to water down the powers of the reconstituted central government in Bonn, to supervise German coal production. With the formation of the Federal Republic, the Italians had to come to terms with the appearance of a new German state of almost fifty million people, with the greatest industrial potential of any European country.

On May 9, 1950, Robert Schuman proposed a plan that seemed to combine the establishment of permanent international controls over German war industries with the inclusion of Germany in a supranational European union. He thus offered both assurance to Italians who feared German military resurgence and hope to federalists for a beginning of European union. "Europe will not be created in one blow," Schuman began. "It will be made through concrete achievements that create from the start a solidarity in practice." The elimination of the centuries-old opposition of France and Germany was a prerequisite for the coming together of the nations of Europe. To begin that reconciliation on "a limited but decisive point . . . the French government [proposed] to place the whole of Franco-German production of coal and steel under a common High Authority, in an organization open to the participation of the other countries of Europe." By placing these two industries that are basic to war production under a common authority within a unified plan of economic development, Schuman claimed, the interdependence created would make "any war between France and Germany not only unthinkable but materially impossible."[5] Although Britain quickly decided not to participate, West Germany and the Benelux countries at once agreed to begin negotiations for participation in the Schuman Plan. Sforza's first consideration was of the meaning of the Franco-German agreement. He desperately wanted the reconciliation of the two to succeed, but he feared at the same time the establishment of a Franco-German hegemony in western Europe. For both reasons, he thought that Italy must participate. The presence of Italy in the Community would lessen French fears of Germany, and would at the same time ensure that Italy would not suffer by being left outside. His second consideration was the contribution that the Schuman Plan would make as "the first serious attempt to have a supernational authority in modern Europe," a goal that he ordered the Italian delegation to the preliminary discussions in Paris to keep foremost.[6] The head of the Italian delegation to the talks that opened in Paris on June 20 was Paolo Emilio Taviani, a leading professor of economics from the University of Genoa and one of De Gasperi's most trusted lieutenants among the younger Christian Democrats. Taviani was clear on his priorities—"faith in democracy, in social evolution, in the unifying destiny of free Europe and in the conviction that, without European solidarity and integration, the way would be opened to the success of Soviet totalitarianism."[7] In short, Taviani was prepared to throw Italy's full support to Schuman's proposals for predominantly political reasons.

The negotiations on the Schuman Plan went through three main stages: an initial brief session in June 1950, when the French constitutional proposals were discussed; a second, detailed period of drafting of both the constitutional and economic provisions of the treaty, from July through October; and a final stage in November–December, when the text of the treaty, with several major gaps, was prepared for submission to the governments. From January through March 1951, the occupying powers in West Germany negotiated a plan for the deconcentration of the German coal and steel industry with the government of Konrad Adenauer which they regarded as the minimum prerequisite for their acceptance of German participation in the Schuman Plan. The delegates then reassembled in Paris and initialed the draft treaty on March 19. The six foreign ministers, meeting in April for three days of tough bargaining, finally filled in the gaps in the draft treaty that concerned the size and voting procedure of the High Authority and the future of the Saar. The treaty was signed on April 18, 1951.[8]

The Italian delegation accepted the constitutional proposals of the French without much demur. The European Coal and Steel Community (ECSC) created by the treaty was to be administered by a High Authority of nine members, eight of whom were to be appointed by the governments and one co-opted by the other members. The High Authority was to be supported by an independent income from receipts of a tax of up to 1 per cent of the coal and steel production of the Community. A Special Council of Ministers was to coordinate the action of the High Authority and the national governments, and was given veto powers over certain actions of the High Authority. In voting on certain matters, the Italians were forced to agree that a majority must include one state producing 20 per cent of the Community's total value of coal and steel, that is, either France or Germany. But in the assignment of seats in the Common Assembly, which had the right to force the resignation of the High Authority if it disapproved of its annual general report, the Italians were given the same number of seats as the French and Germans—eighteen out of seventy-eight.

The Italians also accepted the economic principles that Schuman had spelled out in his original proposal. A common market for coal and steel was to be created by the abolition of all customs duties and quantitative restrictions that were preventing the free movement of these products among the six ECSC members. The High Authority was to abolish the restrictions imposed by discriminatory transport rates. But the working of the free market was to be modified by the action of the High Authority, so as to ensure "the continuity of employment," "the rational distribution of production at the highest possible level of productivity," and the readaptation of regions depressed through the working of the pool. The Italians, however, demanded the further extension of these principles and the adoption of special transitional measures to safeguard Italian industry. The most important omission from Schuman's original proposal, in the Italian view, was free movement of labor within the two industries. As Taviani explained later, in the ratification debate, the Italian delegation had argued that labor was one of the factors of production and that "the Community, and the resulting unified market, should be extended to the labor force in the coal and steel sectors." After initial opposition from the other delegations, the Italian position was accepted, and it was established as Article 69, which abolished discrimination by nationality in employment in the coal and steel industries of the Community. Second, the Italians pressed for a free market in scrap, since the extensive use of electric furnaces in Italian steel production made Italy more dependent upon scrap supplies than any other ECSC member. They were satisfied with the provision in the treaty that the Community's scrap supplies and imports should be made available to any member of the ECSC without discrimination, through High Authority action.[9] Third, Taviani demanded that the Community include Algeria, then a French possession, from which the Italian steel companies were purchasing most of their supplies of iron ore. Neither France nor the other partners were willing to accept this demand, and instead, at the meeting of De Gasperi and Sforza with Premier René Pleven and Schuman in February 1951, the French guaranteed to supply Italy with large quantities of Algerian iron ore for the coming five years at fair prices, a provision that seemed to many more favorable to Italy than opening the Algerian market to the whole Community. Finally, the Italians joined with the French in insisting that strong anti-cartel provisions be written into the treaty (thereby disconcerting the Italian industrialists, who had initially believed their delegation would be defending a "liberal" interpretation of the treaty). The result was that strong controls over ententes and concentrations were established by Articles 65 and 66, which, Taviani claimed, gave the treaty "a decidedly interventionist orientation . . . [and] there is something socialistic about interventionism."[10]

Taviani also succeeded in gaining special safegard measures for the weaker sectors of Italian production. To permit the completion of the modernization of the Sulcis coal mines on Sardinia, Sulcis production was to be subsidized by ECSC. Italy was permitted to maintain customs duties on coke imported from other members for five years, in order to carry through a modernization of the Italian cokeries that might suffer from increased German competition. Finally, customs duties could be maintained on steel imported from the Community, at levels reduced gradually over five years, to enable the IRI Sinigaglia Plan for modernization of steel production to be completed.

During the year that elapsed between the treaty's signature and its final ratification in June 1952, Italian political and economic groups engaged in a vigorous debate on its value and implications. Both the Communists and the Socialists attacked the Schuman Plan as another aspect of America's growing hegemony in Europe. Economically, the spokesmen of the far Left argued, the creation of a common market for coal and steel would result in the destruction of the tiny Italian coal and steel industry and the conversion of the whole of Italy into a depressed area. What the South was to Italy, Italy would be to Europe—the "Mezzogiorno d'Europa." This pessimistic view of the character of Italy's steel industry was shared by the Italian employers' association, Confindustria, probably under the influence of the smaller steel producers of Lombardy.[11]

The coalition parties supporting the Plan laid their emphasis upon the political value of the new Community. "It is well known," Giuseppe Pella wrote in 1954, "that the Italian Government immediately supported this initiative for its political significance above all."[12] All saw ECSC as the nucleus for a future union of Europe; and all agreed with more or less enthusiasm that a more united western Europe would be better able to meet the challenge of Communism. De Gasperi and many Christian Democrats insisted upon the "Christian solidarity" that underlay the new union, upon its contribution to the prevention of war among its members, and upon its appeal to the young.[13] The Liberals insisted upon the Community's function as a safeguard of political and economic liberty; and they demanded that the Community not be permitted to become an instrument for intervention in the economic system on an international scale, an intolerable form of distortion that they trusted their German partners in particular to oppose. The Social Democrats, on the other hand, felt that the formation of the wider European Community opened the way for socialization on a broader scale. With such broad political advantages expected, the Plan's supporters tried to play down the economic consequences of joining the pool, since they did not expect the results to be immediately favorable. Although they all admitted the theoretical advantages of larger markets, they were aware that the Italian coal industry would never be able to compete with the Ruhr, and would probably have to be phased out of existence eventually. They realized that the alleviation of the scrap shortage by ECSC would not solve the long-term problems of supplying raw materials to the steel industry, that the ultimate solution would be to shift to pig iron produced from rich iron ores, and that the ECSC countries could not supply this type of ore. But the greatest fear was whether the principal steel companies within IRI had the ability to meet Community competition. For this reason, Taviani, in the ratification debate, emphasized the advantages to the engineering industry of access to cheap steel from the other member countries: "The eventual suffering of the steel industry—due, for example, to a big fall in the price of steel—is bound to be compensated for in advance by an expansion of the engineering industry, due to the same large reduction of costs."[14] Only Finsider, the steel-making branch of IRI, did not share this fear. By locating new steel plants along the coast at "tidewater," the IRI Sinigaglia Plan had solved the problem of access to cheap raw materials, both coal and iron ore, while by setting up integral cycle plants for carrying out the whole process of steel-making from cokery to strip-mill, it made large-scale, economical production possible. Provided that the Sinigaglia Plan was carried out, Finsider felt it would be able to fight off the competition of imported steel; and since most of its production would for the foreseeable future be sold inside Italy, it would not be faced with the problem of forcing its way into new markets where the cost of transport would weaken its competitiveness in price. But only Finsider had this confidence. The other steel companies were worried. Thus, Italian politicians nobly prepared themselves for a sacrifice on the altar of European political unity, without realizing that the sacrifice would be far smaller than they secretly expected.

The European Coal and Steel Community proved to be neither a disaster nor a great economic benefit to Italy, as can be seen by considering each of the major products that fell within the Community's control.

The action of the High Authority in abolishing discrimination in transport rates and in controlling the prices of Ruhr coal gave a stimulus to imports of coking coal from Germany; but within two years, especially as a result of the falling cost of maritime transport, Italian steel producers found it more advantageous to buy American coal than German. By the 1960's, German coal accounted for less than 5 per cent of Italian coal imports. Italy's only significant coal-producing region, Sulcis on Sardinia, whose high-cost production of poor-quality coal was a burden on the rest of the country, was greatly aided in its readaptation program by the High Authority. At first, half of the working losses of the Sulcis mines were covered by payments raised by a levy on the production of the German and Dutch mines, a sum that reached $2.4 million in the first ten months alone.[15] When the readaptation programs put 1000 miners out of work, the High Authority paid them a gratuity and resettlement allowance; and by 1961 $2.3 million had been assigned to aid 5530 Italian miners.[16] The modernization program was finally completed by the 1960's, when output per man was five times higher than in 1953. By then, however, there were only 1800 coal miners at work in the whole of Italy. ECSC therefore had little effect upon Italy's coal supplies. Its main significance was that it helped underwrite the cost of closing down most of the Sulcis mines and of making the remaining coal mines viable.

The poor quality of the iron ore of French Lorraine made it uneconomical to import it into Italy; and, since there were no other sources of ore inside the Community, Italy continued to import most of its ore during the 1950's from the French possessions of Algeria and Tunisia and from Sweden. In the 1960's, however, Italy participated in the development of mines of high-quality ore in Mauritania, Labrador, Liberia, and Goa. The only influence of ECSC was in the encouragement it gave to the companies of the member countries to cooperate in the search for and development of these new mines. The only iron ore in Italy, at Cogne in the Val d'Aosta and at Piombino on the Tuscan coast, continued to be produced for local use, with a minimal amount of layoffs of workers caused by modernization programs.

The one direct consequence for Italy of the foundation of ECSC was that it helped provide the Italian steel industry with vitally needed scrap during the 1950's. Owing to the predominance in Italy of the use of the electric furnace for the production of steel, Italy used a far higher proportion of scrap to pig iron than did the other countries of ECSC, and needed to import up to 700,000 tons a year. The Community helped stabilize a notoriously volatile market by introducing the principle of equality of access of all Community members to the scrap produced within the Community, and by setting up an equalization fund, by which its price, when imported into the Community, was brought down to the Community price, with subsidies obtained from the tax on that purchased inside ECSC. In this way, it was possible for Italy to purchase scrap from the United States with the aid of subsidies of 80 billion lire from the Community equalization fund, while increasing its supply on a regular basis from German and French sources.[17] Scrap was the only product in which there was a major increase in Italian trade with the other members of ECSC.

During the five-year transitional period in which Italy was permitted to maintain tariffs on steel imported from the Community, Finsider was able to complete its modernization plan and to reduce the prices of Italian steel products to a level competitive with those of the major producers of ECSC. The primary effect of the common market for steel was to accelerate the reconstruction and development programs already begun, by Finsider as well as by some of the private companies, such as Falck.[18]

The changes in Finsider's organization, especially the concentration of production in the three huge coastal steel plants at Cornigliano, Bagnoli, and Taranto, brought Italian steel production up from 3.6 million tons in 1952 to 15.8 million tons in 1967. From 1956 on, the country's exports and imports of steel products were roughly in balance, and represented approximately one-tenth of total production. The market for this vast increase in steel production was in the expanding Italian economy, which would have supplied itself from the other ECSC countries had Italy's own producers not been able to match the competition in both quality and price. The existence of ECSC was therefore a continual stimulus to Italy's steel producers to meet the needs of the Italian market, but only to a minor extent did it stimulate Italian producers to seek export openings in the Community or enable Italian manufacturers to replace home-produced steel with better or cheaper products from the Community.

Only a few of the smaller iron and steel companies collapsed as a result of the increased competition within ECSC, and their failure was probably due as much to the pressure of the big Italian companies as it was to the effect of the common market. By 1962, the High Authority had made available credits of $9.7 million to aid 13,650 steelworkers who had been put out of their jobs, mostly in the areas of Genoa, Brescia, and Piombino; and it helped finance regional reconversion studies for Liguria, Piombino, Brescia, and Umbria.[19] The majority of the smaller steel plants were forced into further specialization, and they generally proved adept at finding their place in supplying the needs of their local markets. The Italian steel industry therefore adjusted rapidly and with comparative ease to the coming of ECSC.

Most of the other measures taken by the High Authority to implement the treaty had surprisingly little effect on Italy. Although the Italian delegation had laid great emphasis on the need for free circulation of workers, few Italians in the coal and steel industries emigrated. The number of Italians employed in the steel industry of the five ECSC partners rose from 15,000 in 1954 to 25,000 in 1961, but those employed in the coal industry fell from 47,428 in mid 1955 to 36,709 in 1962.[20] The creation of a "Community Work

Card" and the conclusion of an agreement on the Community-wide extension of social security for migrant workers aided the Italian laborer only to a minor degree. The increased openings in the steel industry of ECSC for migrant Italians had almost no effect in relieving unemployment at home. The High Authority's action on concentrations and ententes affected Italy only slightly, and very few applications for sanction of concentrations were presented by Italian companies. Italy was at first concerned that the High Authority should succeed in breaking the monopolistic control of Ruhr coal sales exercised by the Gemeinschafts-organisation Ruhrkohle (GEORG); but by 1963, when the High Authority finally settled the problem by authorizing two sales agencies, the Italians had already shifted their purchases to the United States. In general, the Italian steel companies were satisfied that the High Authority had not become more interventionist, and that it had not degenerated into an unresponsive technocracy.

Thus, Italy's experience of the influence of sectoral economic integration did not have any conclusive effects. Italy had remained on the periphery of the common market for coal and steel. It was no longer cut off by autarkic policy from the rest of Europe, but rather, it was isolated by the economic rationale of raw material supplies and of markets. A completely different form of integration would be needed to make Italian participation in a political community of Europe seem inevitable.

THE NEGOTIATION OF THE EUROPEAN DEFENSE COMMUNITY

The invasion of South Korea by Communist forces from the North in June 1950 would hardly seem to be a suitable stimulus to the advance of European integration; but within three months some Europeans were attempting to use it for that purpose.

The Italian government had immediately denounced the invasion and declared its support for American aid to South Korea; and, after some hesitation, a hospital ship was sent to Seoul as a symbol of that support. Moreover, in September, when Secretary of State Dean Acheson demanded that the NATO Council agree to German rearmament within an integrated European force, to relieve the military burden being carried by the United States, Sforza's response was unequivocally favorable. Unlike Schuman,

De Gasperi and Sforza felt that a disarmed Germany was likely to become a second Korea; and they saw at once that Italy would be greatly benefited by German rearmament. First, as Sforza declared to the press, he had demanded that the defense of western Europe should be advanced from the Rhine-Moselle line to the Elbe, thus providing a firmer guarantee for Italy's eastern borders "up to the flatlands of Croatia."[21] Second, Sforza explained, in a private letter to De Gasperi, "in a typically empirical way, [Acheson] was almost creating Europe without saying so. . . . You would have imagined that everyone would have seized upon the proposition, moved and excited. Nothing of the sort."[22] The Pleven proposals of October 1950, suggesting the formation of a European army in which small German contingents would be mingled, and which would thus avoid creating the separate German divisions that Acheson had originally proposed, was also welcomed by Sforza, who thought the Plan "brilliantly resolved and composed the disparity of views between us and Paris on the whole German problem."[23]

In February 1951, De Gasperi and Sforza used their meeting with Pleven and Schuman at Santa Margherita to reach closer agreement on the strategy the two countries would adopt in the formal negotiations on the European Defense Community (EDC). The four convinced federalists had little problem in agreeing, in De Gasperi's words, that "the structure of the European army could become a permanent basis for the United States of Europe," and that the two countries would take every opportunity in the future to reach preliminary agreement on future steps toward this goal.[24] While the long, serious meetings produced little detailed agreement on the European army, they did have the very important result of creating lasting bonds of sympathy between De Gasperi and Schuman that enabled them to work almost instinctively in harmony for the next three years. Both were men of the invasion frontier, De Gasperi from the South Tirol, Schuman from Lorraine; while De Gasperi had grown up under the Austro-Hungarian Empire in the last years of Francis-Joseph, Schuman had been a citizen of the Second Reich of William II. Both were devout Catholics who had struggled through the interwar years to create Catholic political parties, and were imprisoned at the hands of the Fascists or the Nazis. Finally, both had come to the conclusion that the sufferings of Europe, and of their own native provinces not least, were due to an exacerbated nationalism that could only be exorcised through the creation of a European state. The European army, for which neither De Gasperi nor Schuman had much enthusiasm, was to be the expedient by which political integration could be accelerated; for, in their view, a European army could only obey the orders of a European government.

On February 15, Schuman opened the Paris conference on the European Defense Community, which was attended only by France, Germany, Italy, Belgium and Luxembourg, although Holland joined later and five other countries sent observers. Schuman himself presented the draft proposals, but they evoked very little enthusiasm. According to Taviani, the head of the Italian delegation for the opening negotiations, "The Germans were cold and offended, the Dutch skeptical, the Belgians indifferent and almost ironical; the English and the North Americans, there as observers, were waiting for the French to be convinced of the practical impossibility of their plan." Only Taviani's firm intervention prevented the proceedings from lapsing into silence.[25] Very little was achieved by July, when the conference went into recess, because each of the future partners was beginning to realize not only the extent of the internal opposition to an integrated army but also the enormous technical difficulties and financial burdens of the new Community. In a statement drawn up in June, just before Sforza resigned as foreign minister, the Italian Foreign Ministry expressed fear that the political ties of the Defense Community would make Italy economically vulnerable to the power of France and Germany by breaking its ties with the United States and Britain and raised the possibility of going slowly toward a wider European grouping that would include England.[26] This pessimistic view was supported by Pella, at the Ministry of Finance, on the ground that Italy's financial burdens would increase in EDC, owing to the need to raise the pay of Italian soldiers to the same level as those of the other countries. The army, meanwhile, was urging upon De Gasperi the technical difficulties of integrating six national armies, and asked him to procrastinate in the negotiations, although the Republican minister of defense, Randolfo Pacciardi, who was an enthusiastic federalist, was insisting that the Defense Ministry change its distrustful attitude toward the European army.

De Gasperi, who took over the Ministry of Foreign Affairs himself after Sforza's resignation, was well aware of the widespread opposition to EDC that existed even within the bureaucracy and army.

He had, however, committed himself fully and stubbornly to federalist ideals, and he was beginning to see the European Defense Community as the edifice that was to crown his life's work. Under federalist persuasion, he appointed Ivan Matteo Lombardo, one of the most vigorous Europeans in the Social Democratic party, as head of the delegation to the EDC talks.[27] In October, however, Pella's fears momentarily triumphed in the Italian cabinet; and Taviani was dispatched to Paris to propose that the Community's budget be severely restricted, and that the army units be federated, rather than integrated at the level of very small groups. The plan was at once rejected by the French, who saw it as a subterfuge for creating a national German army; and the Italians thereupon resumed their support of the French position on military integration and made their main effort the creation of a European Political Community to oversee the military.

On December 10, 1951, De Gasperi warned the Council of Europe of the need for "a central organization, in which the wills of the various nations can come together to gain fresh decision and worth in a higher union . . . a joint, elected, deliberative body, with powers even of decision and control, confined to those spheres which are governed in common, and exercising its authority through an executive 'College,'" and having a common budget.[28] The next day, at the meeting of the foreign ministers of the six, De Gasperi proposed that the EDC treaty should contain a clause sanctioning the creation of a European political authority, a proposal that Lombardo had already made to the Paris conference. De Gasperi's proposal was accepted, and it became Clause 38 of the EDC treaty. These two days in Strasbourg probably mark the high point of Italy's influence on the European integration movement. For De Gasperi had thrown his great moral prestige behind the European federation, and had done so more decisively than any other European leader. "Italy is ready to transfer wide powers to a European Community, provided that it be democratically organized and give guarantees of life and development," De Gasperi had told the other foreign ministers, a statement that went further than any other European head of government had ever dared.[29] In that meeting and a further one held in Paris on December 27–30, De Gasperi, strongly supported by Adenauer, was able to bring the ministers to agree that the EDC Assembly, elected by the national parliaments, should have the task of drafting a federal statute for the six members of the Defense Community within the following six months.

During the first five months of 1952, the EDC negotiations moved more quickly in Paris, while the foreign ministers met on several occasions to iron out major difficulties. During the meeting of the Atlantic Council in Lisbon in February, the size of the German military contribution—twelve divisions—was decided. After a considerable struggle, Pella and Pacciardi were able to get their future partners to agree that Italy would not have to raise its defense expenditures.[30] In Paris, on May 9, the delegates concluded their work on the EDC treaty, leaving to the foreign ministers the decisions on the thorny problems of language in the European army, length of military service, and duration of the treaty. Taviani represented Italy at the meetings in Paris on May 19 and Strasbourg on May 23, during which he had to threaten the withdrawal of Italy from EDC in order to win for Italy voting strength on a par with France and Germany, rather than with Belgium and the Netherlands, during the transition period. On May 27 in Paris, De Gasperi signed the treaty for Italy. Apart from its security aspect, he told the Italian journalists present, it had two preeminent advantages—it was bringing definitive peace to France and Germany, and it was making possible "the necessary evolution to a vaster and deeper political and economic community."[31] Finally, on September 10, De Gasperi joined with Schuman in proposing that an enlarged ECSC Assembly, rather than the future EDC Assembly, should be given the task of preparing a constitution for a European Political Community (EPC).

The pre-eminence that De Gasperi had achieved was suitably recognized two weeks later, when he traveled to Aachen to receive the Charlemagne prize for his contribution to European unification. When he returned from the ceremony, De Gasperi showed his family the medallion he had received, with the seal of the city on one side and the head of Charlemagne on the other, and instructed them: "Put this decoration, and only this one, on the cushion that will be carried at my funeral."[32]

CASTLES IN THE AIR, 1952-1954

Rapid progress toward elaboration of the EPC statute was made by the enlarged ECSC Assembly, now called the Ad Hoc Assembly, with the federalists taking the primary role. A study committee, under the presidency of Spaak, with Benvenuti, Calamandrei, and Spinelli representing Italy, prepared working papers for a federal constitution for Europe; and it presented nine draft resolutions with comments to the Ad Hoc Assembly. Spinelli was ghostwriting many of the motions presented in the Assembly, but the Italians found themselves continually fighting to preserve the supranational character of the new Community against those who wished to reduce it to a confederation. When the draft treaty for the European Political Community was completed in March 1953, and approved by the Assembly by a vote of 50 to 0 with 5 abstentions, the federalists were still dissatisfied; but they were prepared to fight for ratification rather than lose what had been achieved.

During the six months the Ad Hoc Assembly was at work, the EDC treaty had already begun to run into difficulties. Although it was clear that the parliaments of Belgium, the Netherlands, and Luxembourg would ratify without any difficulty, Chancellor Adenauer was faced with enormous internal opposition to German rearmament, from the Socialists, the Protestant Churches, many labor leaders, and most young people. In France, opponents of German rearmament joined with the Gaullists and right-wing deputies who opposed the fusion of the French in a European army; and each of the four premiers who served between 1952 and 1954 felt it necessary to demand new concessions for France in the functioning of EDC in order to make ratification by the French National Assembly possible.

In spite of many efforts to satisfy these demands, the chances of EDC's ratification declined rapidly. The death of Stalin in March 1953 and the subsequent relaxation of international tension gave renewed popularity to the slogans of neutralism in western Europe. In Germany, French procrastination and displays of anti-Germanism, coupled with the French refusal to return the Saar, were provoking growing resentment. In France, the new Foreign Minister Bidault displayed much less interest than Schuman had in the cause of European integration; and the French struggle in Indochina helped postpone presentation of the EDC treaty to the French Assembly. Only with the formation of the ministry of Pierre Mendès-France did a French premier have the courage to present the EDC treaty for ratification. Meanwhile, in Italy itself the prospects for ratification of EDC were little more favorable.

The elections of June 7, 1953, proved a personal disaster for De Gasperi. The Christian Democrats campaigned on the record of their achievements during the preceding five years—land reform, the Cassa per il Mezzogiorno, the restoration of order, the beginning of the economic boom, and their contribution to European integration. The Communists and the Socialists criticized all these supposed achievements, presenting land reform as a political palliative, emphasizing the widespread poverty revealed by a recent parliamentary inquiry, comparing that poverty with the wealth of the "monopolies," and portraying the DC's contribution to European integration as work toward a clerical, capitalist Europe, subordinated to the economic and military power of the United States. EDC in particular was singled out as linking Italy to West Germany's irredentist claims on the Oder-Neisse territories and preserving the Cold War atmosphere in an era when the Soviet Union was seeking to ease East-West tensions. The disaffection of many former DC voters reduced the party's representation in the Chamber from 304 to 216, putting an end to its absolute majority; and De Gasperi failed to persuade the minor center parties to join his ministry. His eighth cabinet, composed of Christian Democrats alone, was rejected by the Assembly on July 28.

With the ouster of De Gasperi, Italian government policy lost its consistency. The struggles of the currents within the DC itself, the constant bargaining for the formation of a governmental coalition, the frequent changes of personnel in the principal ministries, all tended to increase the incoherence, or rather the stasis, of government. While Europeanism remained the cardinal principle of the DC's foreign policy, it became a general belief rather than a practical program. Italy's lead in the integration movement had been an ephemeral gesture. The caretaker government of Giuseppe Pella, invested in August to keep current administration functioning, was unwilling to handle the thorny issues of the European Defense or Political Communities. Pella himself, who was combining the offices of premier and minister of foreign affairs, was in fact deeply distrustful of the economic implications for Italy of EDC, and inclined toward the right-wing view of the need to maintain the traditions of Italy's armed forces. Pella dropped a bombshell on September 13, 1953, when he proposed a plebiscite in both zones of Trieste and made it clear that he regarded a solution of the Trieste problem as a prerequisite to Italian ratification of the EDC treaty. In the aftermath of his speech, the British and Americans declared their willingness to return Zone A of Trieste to Italy; Tito warned the Italians to stay out; and Pella sent troops to the border area, provoking Tito to do the same. Although both sides pulled back in a few days, the incident created a flurry of outraged nationalism in Italy which was scarcely consonant with Pella's proclaimed Europeanism and encouraged the right-wing parties to a renewed criticism of EDC. It was in this overheated atmosphere that De Gasperi and a large group of Italian federalists attended the second Congress of the European Movement at the Hague in October. But this time both De Gasperi and Schuman were out of office, and their appeals for more rapid progress toward ratification of EDC had little effect. When the foreign ministers of the six met a month later they agreed to procrastinate on EDC.

In January 1954, the DC forced Pella to resign, and he was replaced by Mario Scelba, the most outspoken defender of the policies of De Gasperi and the old leader's choice for premier. Scelba's Europeanism, fervently sincere, was tightly linked to the anti-Communism he had displayed with great effectiveness during his years as minister of the interior. Scelba was determined to have the Chamber ratify the EDC treaty, as he promised in his investiture speech on February 18; and on April 6, he formally presented the treaty to parliament.[33] At the same time, he coupled his foreign policy with a program of internal social reforms that won him the adherence of the Social Democrats. Of the other members of the governmental coalition, the Republicans were enthusiastically favoring ratification "in the conviction that the European Defense Community, through the vast and complex demands for unity of action that it implies, is destined to be converted rapidly into a supranational political community," while the Liberals were expressing a rather more muted acquiescence. Although there were rumblings of discontent among the right-wing Christian Democrats, Scelba probably had the necessary votes for ratification. Nevertheless, he ignored the demands of the federalists that Italy ratify in order to put pressure on the French National Assembly, and decided to wait for the French to act first, even though the Foreign Affairs Commission of the Italian Chamber approved the treaty by a large majority on July 31, 1954.

In the middle of August, French Premier Mendès-France presented a new series of demands for modification of the EDC treaty, by which he hoped to get the French Assembly to ratify. When he presented them to the other five foreign ministers in Brussels on August 19-22, he received a very cold reception. The Italian representative, Attilio Piccioni, one of De Gasperi's longtime collaborators from pre-Mussolini days, was given the news, at the very beginning of the conference, that De Gasperi had died suddenly at his home in the mountains of Trentino; and it was a universal belief among his closest friends that it was the imminent failure of the EDC that had killed him. In one of his last letters, De Gasperi had decribed his anguish to Amintore Fanfani, who was then the political secretary of the DC:

> If the news that arrived today from France is true, even half true, I believe that the cause of EDC is lost and any start toward European union delayed for years. . . . You can scarcely imagine how my suffering is aggravated by the fact that I have neither the strength nor the opportunity to raise my voice, at least to relieve our country of its share in the responsibility for such a misfortune. . . . This whole project [of Mendès-France] is inspired with extreme distrust toward those nations that are called today to a common defense; and here is the most bitter disappointment.
>
> How can one hope, with feelings like these, either now or ever, to build Europe?[34]

Thus, the conference presented the spectacle, to be repeated only too many times in the Common Market later, of a France grimly isolated and immovable, facing the united and increasingly irritated opposition of its five partners. On August 22, 1954, the meeting broke up in failure; and on August 30, the French National Assembly rejected the EDC treaty. Most Italians were outraged. "The vote of the French Chamber is sheer madness," Randolfo Pacciardi commented. Mendès-France "left the decision on the fate of Europe to a hundred Communist deputies," wrote Don Sturzo. "France has not hesitated to stab western Europe, and to weaken its Atlantic policy," said *Il Tempo*. "After four years of insidious and dilatory moves, presenting projects that could not be realized in order to delay the most necessary decision, always proposing new formulas and new conditions, . . . France has assumed the responsibility for torpedoing the democratic experiment of Adenauer and for reinforcing the American tendency to isolationism. It would be criminal folly if it were not the product of senility and lassitude."[35] Most disheartened were the federalists, who had sustained their greatest blow. "The epoch of Europeanist governments ended on August 30," wrote Spinelli. "The words Europe, union, and such like are nothing more than dust in the eyes of the stupid."[36] Yet this attitude was far from universal. The Communists and Socialists rejoiced. According to Nenni, "the vote of the French Chamber does not surprise me; it fills me with satisfaction."[37] The neo-Fascists saw the defeat of EDC as the opportunity for Italy to begin a new foreign policy based upon friendship with Germany and Spain. But, far more important for the future, those governmental leaders who had been lukewarm to EDC seized the chance to call for alternative solutions of a more traditional kind. The EDC formula was "worn out," Fanfani declared, and a dialogue between the continents was needed. "New formulas suggested by the circumstances" would have to be found, Pella claimed. Many Italians were therefore ready for the new formula that the British Foreign Secretary Anthony Eden had dreamed up in his bath one Sunday morning—to broaden the Brussels Pact organization to include Germany, and, as an afterthought, Italy.[38]

ANOTHER STEP BACKWARD: WESTERN EUROPEAN UNION

Eden made a lightning tour of the European capitals in early September, to explain how he proposed to broaden the Brussels Pact organization into a mutual defense agreement "of the Locarno type" in order to find a solution to the problem of rearming Germany. In Rome he found the Italians resigned to the lack of supranationalism in his plans. Where the right-wing parties were still hostile to Britain because of its wartime attitude, the Social Democrats and Liberals were correspondingly cheered by the prospect of British involvement in Europe. All were convinced that the French had to be persuaded of the good sense of rearming West Germany, by provision of armaments controls that would reassure them.

At the London conference of September 28–October 3, 1954, attended by the six ECSC powers, Britain, Canada, and the United States, Italian Foreign Minister Gaetano Martino played the role of mediator. New to international diplomacy, Martino had not gone through the bitter confrontation with Mendès-France that had permanently soured the French premier's relationships with Adenauer and Spaak. Martino spoke English, French, and German; his Sicilian courtesy, his mastery of detail, and his commitment to the ideal of European unity made him immediately influential among more experienced diplomats; and, while restricting himself to the search for compromise solutions, these often on procedural matters, Martino was able to prepare the sound personal relationships that were to be of greater importance the next year when, in his native Messina, the foreign ministers of the six ECSC powers sought to revive the process of integration. At London, Martino agreed to the admission of Germany and Italy to the Brussels Pact and of Germany to NATO, and to Italian participation in the establishment of an Armaments Control Agency that would supervise the level of armaments of the six as well as the ban on German possession of atomic, biological, and chemical weapons. Thus, within six weeks of the defeat of EDC, he returned to Rome with a substitute proposal that would re-create an autonomous German army and make only the most superficial concessions to the sentiments of the Europeans.

Italian reception of these Agreements, which were drawn up formally in Paris at the end of October, was quite calm. The most convinced supporters of integration, like La Malfa and Pacciardi, continued to bemoan the loss of EDC and the death of supranationalism, and the federalists of the MFE denounced the new Agreements as "the abandonment on the part of the European governments of the policy of European unification."[39] A few Christian Democrats objected to the rearmament of Germany in any form; but two prominent members who attempted to force a three-month postponement of consideration of the Agreements were shortly afterward expelled from the party. The Communists and Socialists continued to denounce WEU for rearming a Germany still dominated by the great Nazi trusts;[40] but neither group attempted full-scale obstruction in the Chamber. The majority of EDC's supporters decided to treat WEU as a small but significant advance toward European integration, the best that could be hoped for in the situation provoked by the rejection of EDC. As Taviani wrote in *Il Popolo:* "It represents a little progress—perhaps too little—on the road toward integration. . . . It is not necessary to dress in mourning thinking that all future progress of Europe toward unification is henceforth impossible. Far from it!"[41]

The ratification debates, in the Chamber from December 13 to 23, 1954, and in the Senate from February 24 to March 11, 1955, took place with a minimum of disturbance. In supporting the Paris Agreements, the Christian Democrats were joined not only by their governmental partners, the Republicans, Social Democrats, and Liberals, but also by both groups of monarchists. Even the neo-Fascists (MSI) supported the government, for the first time in the postwar period. The Agreements were approved in the Chamber by 355 to 215, and in the Senate by 139 to 82. For all the oratory spent in proclaiming the economic, cultural, and social character of the Western European Union and its contribution to attracting Britain into Europe, the Paris Agreements had almost no effect on Italy. Yet another assembly had to be attended by the indefatigable parliamentarians; one more council of ministers was to meet to achieve almost nothing. The one important consequence of the Agreements was the restoration of the sovereignty of West Germany and its participation in NATO; and Sforza had announced Italy's willingness to support these moves as early as September 1950.

4

The Economic Miracle and The *Rilancio Europeo*, 1954–1958

Italy did not go through the months of disillusionment with Europeanism that afflicted France and, to a lesser degree, Germany, in the aftermath of the defeat of the European Defense Community, the resignation of Jean Monnet as president of the High Authority of the European Coal and Steel Community, and the conclusion of the Paris Agreements. Indeed, the attempt to present the Western European Union as a contribution to Europe's unification was probably sincere, if self-deluding. The governmental parties continued to call for a revival of the impetus to integration that had been blunted by the French Assembly. At its National Council on November 3, 1954, the Christian Democratic party renewed its pledge of "an active foreign policy directed to the acceleration of the processes of European integration, which is a guarantee of international peace and of the economic development of the Italian nation."[1] The Social Democrats continued to proclaim their belief that the essential principles of Italian foreign policy, alignment with the West against the Soviet bloc and the "unity of western Europe as an instrument of peace," had not changed with the acceptance of WEU.[2] The Liberals were emphasizing the need for total economic integration as a substitute both for sectoral integration like ECSC and for military or political integration. The Republicans were rumbling with impatience for a new beginning. The volatile Ugo La Malfa reminded the government that at the beginning of 1953 the Dutch foreign minister, Johan Willem Beyen, had presented a plan for an economic union of the six ECSC countries: "This plan abandoned the idea of European economic integration realized by sectors and conceived the plan of a great economic community, through the creation of a vast and complete common market. . . . The establishment of a political community would have to be accompanied by concrete steps toward the fusion of the interests of those countries in the economic field. The fusion was to come gradually. It would have to apply to the national economies as a whole and not to their individual separated sectors."[3] Here, in brief, was the proposal for the future European Economic Community (EEC) that the Republicans were determined not to allow to die.

Beyen himself had come to the conclusion that the moment was ripe for revival of his plan; and, after concerting his views with those of the foreign ministers of Belgium and Luxembourg in April 1955, he called for the meeting of the ECSC foreign ministers to consider a Benelux memorandum based upon his original plan. On May 20, the memorandum, which called for sectoral integration for electricity, atomic energy, and transportation, and for a total customs union of the six, was presented to the other foreign ministers. Martino decided to gain both nostalgic and political advantage from the conference, and invited the foreign ministers to meet in Messina, where he was born and still held the position of rector of the University, and where, coincidentally, a hard-fought election to the Regional Assembly was taking place. He also decided to submit an Italian memorandum that would emphasize the Italian government's determination "that the common market should not be limited to several sectors, no matter how vast and important, but should cover the whole of economic and social life of the countries concerned, without neglecting the social or the labor fields." Because of the Italian government's experience in the various European organizations—and its memorandum was principally the work of the young diplomats trained in OEEC—the Italian memorandum urged that sectoral integration "does not lead easily and rapidly toward general integration"; that the general economic integration should be gradual; that its effects should be moderated through a "readaptation fund" for retraining workers and modernizing or converting factories; and that the ultimate goal should be to "favor a policy of expansion and investment." Here were several of the key ideas that guided the Italian delegation throughout the long negotiations of the Treaties of Rome: to seek total integration, including agriculture as well as industry, a Community social policy, freedom of movement of labor, a readaptation fund, Community sources of capital, and safeguards for the country's underdeveloped regions.[4]

THE NEGOTIATION OF THE TREATIES OF ROME, 1955–1957

Coverage of the election campaign in Sicily drove the Messina conference off the front pages of the Italian newspapers, so Martino's idea of reaping any internal political advantage from the conference was a failure. From the Italian point of view, this was probably the only shortcoming of an otherwise thoroughly satisfactory meeting.

The conference at once took on the character that was to mark the later negotiations: a dialogue, and often a duel, between the French and German delegations, with the Italians supporting the Benelux powers in their pressure for integration, while safeguarding essential Italian interests. The French delegation, headed by Antoine Pinay, the conservative businessman and politician, was far more enthusiastic about sectoral integration, especially in atomic energy, than it was about general economic integration; and it agreed to the establishment of an Intergovernmental Committee, under Belgian Foreign Minister Spaak, only when the Committee's task was limited to studying the methods for realization of the Benelux proposals, rather than negotiation of a treaty.[5] The French were satisfied with the recommendation that the Intergovernmental Committee study integration of atomic energy, conventional energy, and transport; the others with recognition that "the constitution of a European common market, excluding any right to customs and any quantitative restrictions, is the objective of their action in the economic field." The Italian government in particular was gratified by the enumeration among questions to be studied of all the demands listed in its memorandum—harmonization of monetary policy, safeguards against economic disruption, a readaptation fund, a European investments fund, free movement of labor, and common social policy.[6] As Martino commented, "At Messina, we did not only express wishes and display preferences, but we adopted precise decisions concerning the development of common institutions, the progressive fusion of the national economies, the creation of a common market and the gradual harmonization of our respective social policies."[7] After the disillusionment of the preceding winter, that was an enormous advance.

The Intergovernmental Committee of experts, soon renamed the Spaak Committee, met in Brussels on July 9, 1955. The Italian delegation was chosen largely by Ambassador Attilio Cattani, who was then director-general of economic affairs at the Ministry of Foreign Affairs, and he picked his men mostly from those who had served under him previously at OEEC. The group included Roberto Ducci and Achille Albonetti; Franco Bobba, who had been an assistant to De Gasperi and had taken part in the ECSC negotiations; and, as political head of the delegation, the Christian Democratic deputy Lodovico Benvenuti. The predominant characteristics of the delegation were its youth—Albonetti was only twenty-eight—and its Europeanism. And it acted with almost no supervision from Rome. Both in the Spaak Committee and in the treaty negotiations that followed, the Italian view was formulated by this handful of young officials who enjoyed far greater decision-making power than the other nations' delegates. At the time this was a great advantage, in view of the technical character of the discussions; but, as Bino Olivi has pointed out, it also "presents pregnant proof of the inadequacy of the political and administrative structure of the Italian State" to carry on prolonged negotiations at the European level.[8] By October, the experts had rejected the proposals for sectoral integration of conventional energy and transport; and on the Common Market and the community for atomic energy (Euratom) they had prepared voluminous reports that were contradictory and over-cautious. At that point, Spaak changed the character of the work groups, centralizing all decisions in a six-member political committee composed of the heads of the delegations; and in April 1956 he succeeded in persuading them to accept the Spaak Report unanimously.

The Spaak Report was divided into three parts—The Common Market, Euratom, and "Sectors Requiring Urgent Measures" (energy, air transport, and post and telecommunications). The principal interest of the Italian delegation was in the Common Market, and the Spaak Report satisfied almost all their demands. The main features of the Common Market had already been laid down in the Benelux proposal to the Messina conference—the elimination, on a gradual basis, of all customs barriers between the member states; free competition unhampered by state intervention or by monopolistic controls by individual companies; free movement of workers and capital; and safeguard and readaptation measures. The Italians, under the instructions of the director general of the Ministry of Foreign Commerce, Dall'Oglio, had fought the French when they wanted to retain any form of quota, but had joined them when they insisted upon the inclusion of agriculture in the Common Market. Above all, however, the Italians were responsible for the long section of the Report entitled "The development and full utilization of European resources," the key to which would be the establishment of an Investments Fund endowed with large resources for carrying out vast projects of European interest. The common duty and interest of all member states in developing the depressed areas of the Community was justified on the basis of the lessons of Italian unification. "As was shown by the experience of Italian unification after 1860, and also by that of the United States after the war of secession, the divergence [between regions] can grow in aggregate if the fundamental conditions for the development of production are not immediately created by public bodies, through the construction of roads, ports, means of communication, public works for drainage, irrigation, and land reclamation, and with the creation of schools and hospitals."[9]

The Euratom negotiations were more clearly a Franco-German dispute, with the Italians determined to gain access to the technical knowledge and training facilities of their partners and, if possible, to locate part of Euratom's future research facilities in Italy. All delegations agreed that Euratom should encourage common access to fissionable materials, found common installations, and facilitate the exchange of atomic knowledge. The French, however, insisted that military as well as peaceful uses of atomic energy should be permitted in the Community, while the Germans objected to giving the new Community a monopoly on fissionable materials. On the first point, the Italian government sided with the French; on the second, they procrastinated.[10] In the Spaak Report, agreement was achieved by leaving open both major questions.

Spaak presented the Report to the governments on April 21; and the foreign ministers of the six met to consider it on May 29–30, 1956. The choice of the meeting place caused the Liberal deputy, Francesco Colitto, to wax lyrical: "So in the enchantment of Venice, on the serene island of San Giorgio Maggiore, in the palace of the abbots of the old Benedictine monastery . . . between a cloister of Palladio and the canal of the Giudecca, in a severe luminous chamber, which one reaches by climbing the majestic staircase by Longhena, decorated . . . by the statues of 'Prudence' and of 'Justice,' there met the ministers of foreign affairs of the countries which signed the Messina 'resolution.'"[11] Not only was the setting Italianate; the results of the Conference were eminently pleasing to Italy.

The foreign ministers agreed to "adopt the proposals of this report as the basis for negotiations for the elaboration of a treaty instituting a general Common Market and a treaty creating a European organization for atomic energy." The treaty negotiations were to begin in Brussels in June under the presidency of Spaak. Each of the delegations had, however, pointed out its essential preoccupation about the character of the two future Communities. The French had demanded a satisfactory treatment of agriculture, safeguards against economic disruption caused by the Common Market, and association of their overseas territories, this last a particularly unwelcome proposal for Italy at a time when the French army was becoming mired down in a vicious war in Algeria. The Germans pressed strongly for the conclusion of a Common Market in industrial goods, and for the avoidance of interventionist tendencies in either Community. The Italians paid little attention to Euratom, but Martino made three specific requests concerning the Common Market. It should aid completion of the recently approved ten-year plan for Italian economic development; it should regard exchange of manpower as an important means of placing resources in common; and it should open tariff negotiations immediately with nonmembers.[12]

The delegations reassembled in Brussels with little change of personnel. Benvenuti remained head of the Italian delegation;

but Bobba and Ducci ran most of the day-to-day negotiations. In Rome, an interministerial committee, set up to follow the negotiations, was composed of representatives of the major ministries concerned with the content of the two treaties, and of the main industrial confederations (Confindustria, Confcommercio), agricultural confederations (Coltivatori Diretti, Confagricoltura), and of the non-Communist trade unions (CISL, UIL). This committee met fairly regularly, at intervals varying from a week to a month, with delegates from Brussels returning to Rome over the weekends to report to them. This interministerial committee proved important, partly because of the occasional suggestions it made for the negotiations but even more as "a first nucleus of people in Italy who understood the problems of EEC."[13] Nevertheless, the Italian delegates in Brussels continued to negotiate "without a formal mandate" from the government, enjoying the same freedom of action as they had had in drawing up the Spaak Report; and only in February 1957 did the premier, Antonio Segni, hold two short cabinet meetings, restricted to the ministers of the economic sectors, for a brief discussion of the progress of the delegation.[14] Since the members of the Italian delegation were trained in the De Gasperi era of Europeanism, and frankly admitted their continuing belief in those ideals, one can see in the work in Brussels De Gasperi's continuing contribution to the cause that had dominated his last years of life.

The work of the conference was divided between two committees, one for Euratom and one for the Common Market, with a directing and supervising committee coordinating their work and a committee of heads of delegations taking the final political decisions. At times, knotty problems were submitted to special meetings of the foreign ministers or even heads of governments. The institutions of the two new Communities were defined with relative ease. The Common Market was to have a Commission of nine members, Euratom a Commission of five. The Common Assembly of the European Coal and Steel Community, increased in size from 78 to 142 members, was to act for all three Communities, as was the ECSC Court of Justice.[15] A Council of Ministers, composed of one delegate from each member country, was to coordinate economic policies and to have final say on a large number of the decisions of the Community organs. Its voting procedure was to change at each stage of the implementation of the treaty, so as to reduce the veto powers of any one member. An advisory Economic and Social Committee, composed of representatives of industry, trade unions, the professions, and consumers, was to give its opinions to the Commission, mostly on long-term planning.[16] Italy's main demand, equality with France and Germany, was met with the grant of equal membership in the Common Assembly (36 members), and the Economic and Social Committee (24 members), equal weight in the Commission when voting was by qualified majority (4 votes), and equal payment of the Community levy for administrative expenses (28 per cent).[17]

In negotiating the Common Market treaty, the six delegations quickly agreed to adopt the timetable indicated in the Spaak Report for the abolition of customs duties within Community, namely in three four-year stages, with a reduction of 30 per cent during each of the first two stages and complete elimination of customs in the third stage, but with provision for acceleration of the timetable or for its extension to a maximum of fifteen years. "This seemed reasonable and sufficiently prudent," the Italian government pointed out, "even for those sectors or those industries in each of the six countries, which, because they had a less competitive structure, would have to improve or be converted in order to operate in that new and vaster market."[18] The internal freedom of movement of goods was held to require the erection of a common external tariff, to prevent a member with low tariffs reexporting at a profit to high-tariff members of the Community goods it had imported from "third countries"—countries outside the Common Market. In the dispute over the height of the external tariff, the Italian delegation joined the French in demanding the highest possible protection—"more for motives of political character than out of desire for a healthy economy," Ducci commented.[19] The delegates compromised by permitting a large series of exceptions for specific products to the general rule that the tariff level was to be set at the mathematical average of tariffs in force in the six on January 1, 1957, especially the products on the so-called List G, a particularly sensitive group of raw materials and specialized manufactured goods that the members regarded as uncompetitive but of vital national interest. For the Italians these products included sulphur, cork, iodine, bromine, lead, zinc, boracic products, and silk, most of which provided employment in the depressed regions of the country.[20]

The customs union also implied total abolition of import quotas; and here the Italians led the battle to compel the French to agree to their progressive elimination in parallel with the customs reductions. As a corollary, however, the Italians were forced to recognize that they would have to modify the action of some of their favorite revenue-raising state monopolies, in tobacco, salt, and quinine.[21] All agreed that a country with balance of payments problems could impose restrictions on trade with nonmembers and to a lesser degree on members, or enact protective measures for regions or industries in economic trouble. Again, for Italy this meant protection for sulphur, lead, zinc, chemicals, and silk.[22]

On agriculture, the Italian delegation had difficulty in formulating its own position, because the views at home differed so violently. Some members of the government felt agriculture should be excluded from the Common Market, as it was from OEEC; and they were sympathetic to the British proposals for a Free Trade Area in industrial products. The agricultural unions, Confagricoltura and the Coltivatori Diretti, expressed great fear of the lack of competitiveness of Italian agriculture, and demanded safeguards and financial aid to make possible the needed structural changes in land holding, labor supply, and productive methods. The minister of agriculture, Emilio Colombo, and the director general of the Ministry of Agriculture, Paolo Albertario, were both convinced Europeans, however, and they directed the delegates in Brussels to support the Dutch in their demands for the full integration of agriculture.[23] The end result was a compromise, recognizing that agriculture must be within the Common Market, but that it must have a very different form of organization from that for industry. The section on agriculture in the treaty was both general and procrastinating. It laid down the goals of the agricultural policy—increased production, a higher standard of living for agricultural workers, stable markets, security of supply, and reasonable prices. The policy was to respect "the particular character of agricultural activity deriving from the social structure of agriculture," that is, the family character of European farming and the disparity between regions; and it was to be applied gradually. The methods envisaged by the treaty were common rules of competition; common organization of markets, including adoption of minimum prices; and long-term contracts. The policy was to be drawn up following a Community agricultural conference, and implemented by the end of the transition period.[24]

It proved impossible to invent a timetable for the introduction of the other features held to be essential to the Common Market. The free movement of workers was considered necessary for the solution of the problem of unemployment in Italy; but only the Germans showed any interest in receiving an increased number of Italian workers. Italian interests were eventually satisfied with a requirement that there should be free movement of labor by the end of the transition period, to be guaranteed through regulations of the Commission and facilitated by machinery for continuing social security protection and for bringing together worker and employer. The treaty also called in extremely vague terms for free movement of services, such as insurance and banking, and of capital; but neither the Italians nor the other delegations thought this would be a serious question during the early years of the Community. After another long struggle to draw up the treaty's provisions on transport policy, the French and Germans demanding that their system of running their nationalized railroads at a loss be extended to the Community, and the Italians and the Dutch opposing the idea, the negotiators left to the Council and Commission the task of formulating a common transport policy.[25]

Each of the delegations made several demands for special treatment of their particular national problems. The French and the Belgians, for example, demanded that their overseas territories be given a preferential trade association with the Community, and that the six share in the financing of a development fund for those territories. The opposition to these demands was so great, especially as the Germans and Italians were very unwilling to appear to be financial accomplices of a moribund French colonialism, that only in February 1957, at a special meeting of heads of government and foreign ministers in Paris, was agreement reached. The compromise was that the overseas territories would be associated provisionally for five years only, after which a new form of association would be negotiated. The development fund was to be $581 million, but the Italians, who had raised the cry that they had their own Africa in the South of Italy, were to contribute only $40 million. Moreover, $5 million was to be returned to Italy for use in Somalia, which had been placed under Italian trusteeship in 1950.

Italy's other requests met less opposition. First, the Italian delegation demanded a special "Protocol concerning Italy," attached as an appendix to the treaty. In this protocol, the six powers recognized that the ten-year plan for the economic development of the depressed regions of Italy and for the elimination of unemployment was in "their common interest," and they agreed that the Community should use all measures provided in the treaty to aid the Italian government in completion of this program. The Community institutions were ordered to give special consideration to "the effort that the Italian economy will have to bear in the coming years, and the importance of avoiding the arising of dangerous tensions, especially concerning the balance of payments and the level of employment, tensions that could compromise the application of the Treaty in Italy." Here the Italian government had at the very minimum the guarantee that in dealing with the South or with unemployment it would have the right to demand special, and perhaps discriminatory, treatment within the Community.

Second, as part of the social policy of the Community, the six agreed to institute a European Social Fund. The Italians argued that the depressed regions of the Community, especially Southern Italy, Sicily, and Sardinia, would be the first to feel the increased competition, and that the Fund should therefore have the double objective of relieving the distress caused by increased unemployment and of making the unemployed, retrained and relocated partly at the expense of the Fund, available to labor-hungry parts of the Community. The Fund was to pay half the expenses of retraining workers, resettling them where jobs were available, setting up vocational training centers, and subsidizing the unemployment pay of workers temporarily suspended during factory reconversion. The national governments were to carry out these measures, and to pay the other half of their cost. The share of the Italian government in financing the Fund was set at only 20 per cent, with the French and German governments each paying 32 per cent. At the time of the negotiation it was thought that the countries with the greatest number of unemployed would profit most from this Fund; but it was realized later that there was a fallacy in this reasoning, namely that those countries were the least able to afford to pay half of the re-training, especially to enable the worker to move to another country of EEC. On the other hand, the Italians did succeed in persuading the others that it would be impossible to differentiate between unemployment caused directly by the Common Market and that due to other causes, and "to include within the Fund's jurisdiction the phenomenon of unemployment independent of its cause and its form."[26]

Third, the Italian negotiator Bobba struggled hard and successfully to change the character of the investment fund that the Spaak Report had proposed. He demanded that the large-scale investments of the Community for economic development of depressed regions, modernization and conversion of industrial enterprises, or major projects of community interest, should be made through a Bank rather than a Fund, and that the Bank should be an autonomous legal entity, responsible to its own Council of Governors composed of finance ministers of the six and to a Board of Directors composed mostly of businessmen and bankers. Although it was not officially stated, it was understood that the president of the Bank would be an Italian. At first the figure set for the Bank's funding was only $50 million, but Bobba and Ducci, after a great deal of argument, were able to get it raised to $1 billion, with France and Germany each providing $300 million and Italy $240 million.

The grant of Italy's three demands—the "Protocol concerning Italy," the European Social Fund and its special treatment of Italy, and the establishment of financial machinery for aiding the Italian government—persuaded the Italian delegation that they had negotiated a treaty that would not only satisfy the moral exigencies of Europeanism and the economic imperatives of modern productive conditions, but would also provide direct international help in the solution of long-standing national problems. Italy, in short, seemed to be receiving far more than it was giving.

In the negotiations on the Euratom treaty, three major disagreements kept progress at a snail's pace for months—military use of nuclear energy, the monopoly of fissionable materials by the

Community, and the Community's financing. And again the Italians acted as mediators between the French and the Germans. The first problem was settled by restricting Euratom to peaceful uses of nuclear energy, while the six agreed not to make military use of nuclear materials for five years. The question whether Euratom should have a monopoly of fissionable materials, as proposed by the French and bitterly opposed by the Germans, was finally solved by Achille Albonetti. Albonetti proposed that, rather than give Euratom direct control over supply and pricing of fissionable materials, each member of the Community should have the right to obtain fissionable materials where it wished, on condition that the materials be made available at the same price to any other member who wished to purchase them. This scheme would be implemented by a Community Supply Agency with a right of option on all materials produced in the Community and of monopoly on imports into the Community. Thus, each country would be free to obtain its materials where it wished at a price it wanted to pay; but the principle of Community equality of access to these materials would be preserved without developing a strongly interventionist bureaucratic organization. The Germans wanted to keep the financing of the Community quite small, but the Italians supported the French in seeking a large budget. It was finally agreed that the Community should be given a budget of $215 million during its first five-year period for scientific research, with Italy contributing 23 per cent and France and Germany each 30 per cent.[27]

The two treaties were signed with great ceremony on the Capitol Hill in Rome on March 25, 1957, with Premier Segni and Foreign Minister Martino representing Italy. The main stages of the *rilancio europeo*, the relaunching of Europe, had all enjoyed the not negligible advantages of an Italian setting—the Messina resolution, the Venice Conference of 1956, and the Treaties of Rome. Though negotiations had taken place in the damp northern winters of Brussels, the sentimental meaning of the re-creation of Europe could best be felt in Italy. As Segni pointed out, "it was not without deep significance that the treaties . . . should be signed in Rome, in this city that, even through the mouths of illustrious foreigners, has been recognized as the cradle, the seat of that great European civilization that these treaties themselves aim to advance in its economic development in order to make it take again its political importance in the world." In Italian eyes at least, the new Europe would be the continuation of Rome—of the Republic and Empire, of the Christian Church, and of the Holy Roman Empire.[28] During the next few months, however, Italy suddenly woke to the fact that historical revivals could have serious economic consequences.

THE APPRAISAL OF THE TREATIES OF ROME, 1957

Since there was never any doubt that the Italian parliament would ratify the Treaties of Rome, a searching appraisal of their probable consequences began almost immediately after their signature. The prognosis was generally encouraging.

By 1957, Italy was beginning to show incontrovertible evidence of an economic boom almost more miraculous than that of West Germany. In 1949, the level of prewar production had been surpassed, indicating that the period of reconstruction was over. During the 1950's, the gross national product increased at about 6 per cent a year; industrial production doubled; agricultural production rose by a quarter. This extraordinary growth was achieved without inflation and with a steadily improving balance of payments.[29] Unemployment was cut by more than half, and new jobs were created for over two and a half million workers.[30] Foreign trade more than doubled.[31] In short, it was the economic miracle that made possible Italy's entry into the Common Market, and not the Common Market that brought about the economic miracle.

The bases of this economic boom were fairly clear by 1957. American economic aid had culminated in the $1.6 billion of the Marshall Plan.[32] The laissez-faire policy of the De Gasperi ministries helped the great companies, like Fiat and Montecatini, grow to the necessary magnitude for entry into European-wide competition. Einaudi's stabilization of the currency had provided an essential basis for economic development by helping to reduce the agitation of the labor unions for higher wages, encouraging the accumulation of savings and the employment of investment capital, and keeping Italy "within the orbit of the free market economies."³³ The effect was seen in the maintenance throughout the 1950's of a reinvestment rate of 19 to 23 per cent of gross national product. The trade liberalization measures, supplemented by a farsighted policy of making foreign currency available to companies engaged in foreign trade, were regarded by industrialists and politicians alike as proof of Italy's lead in bringing western Europe to closer economic integration and of the benefits of freedom of international trade.³⁴

Even direct state intervention in industrial production, through the state companies of the Istituto per la Ricostruzione Industriale (IRI) and of the Ente Nazionale Idrocarburi (ENI) contributed to the adaptation of the Italian economy to modern competitive conditions. Through IRI, the Italian state was able to sponsor vast programs of industrial renovation, such as the Sinigaglia Plan for Finsider, and enormous infrastructural investments in public works, such as the building of the autostrada network. Through ENI and its component companies, the country was able to take advantage of the rich natural gas discoveries in the Po valley, which supplied 18 per cent of Italy's energy needs by the end of the 1950's. And ENI had started to find and exploit petroleum deposits elsewhere in Italy. During the 1950's Italy enjoyed a spectacular "triumph over her stultifying shortages of energy," and this was attributable in part at least to ENI.³⁵

Power, however, was the only new natural resource that Italy was able to discover. The secret of the economic boom was that Italy became "a humming factory for the conversion of raw materials into finished goods."³⁶ Since Italy possessed very few raw materials, and produced those few, like Sicilian sulphur, well above the world price, Italian manufacturers bought their raw materials all over the world, wherever they were cheapest, and brought them into Italy by sea: coal, iron ore, scrap, copper, timber, rubber, cotton, wool, textile cellulose. Imports of raw materials accounted for 40 per cent of the country's $1 billion in imports in 1955. The genius of Italian business was that it concentrated on those products where the skill of the designer could be combined with the low cost of labor to produce finished products that appealed to the increasingly affluent consumers of western Europe and North America, while it avoided those products that required either rich internal resources in raw materials or high scientific technology, both of which Italy lacked. The lead in this process was taken by the larger companies. By the opening of the Common Market in 1958, Fiat exported 157,000 automobiles and trucks, almost half of its total production, with the EEC countries buying half of these exports.[37]

In all large-scale industry in Italy, there was more or less enthusiastic recognition that the Italian government had come to grips with the problem of creating the large economic areas necessary for modern business. More pragmatic approval was extended by a large number of dynamic, small and medium-sized companies that saw a chance for enhanced profits and rapid growth within the new Community with the removal of their greatest enemy, discriminatory tariff barriers. These companies were grouped in several key consumer industries—light engineering, textiles, and shoes and other leather goods. In these products, the fine Italian sense of consumer needs, the ability to change direction rapidly, and, above all, the capacity to produce good-looking products at a low price without heavy capital investment were major assets. Throughout the 1950's, companies in these lines of production surged steadily ahead under the direction of a large group of self-made entrepreneurs; and these companies joined the larger companies in welcoming EEC.

Italian industry, however, contained many problem sectors which it was the avowed aim of the Common Market either to cure or to kill. The most obvious of these were the heavy engineering and shipbuilding companies, many of which were controlled by IRI;[38] and the private companies in the sectors of machine tools, electrical engineering, and silk and cotton textiles. But it was the very small companies, regardless of products manufactured, that feared the new competition most. According to the 1951 census, 27 per cent of the work force was employed in firms with ten employees or less, and 15 per cent in artisan shops of one or two workers. Lacking capital, specialized equipment, sales facilities, and advertising, these small concerns seemed likely to disappear, and their owners and employers to join larger companies.[39]

With the important exceptions of the very small firms and of specific sectors of large-scale production, Italian industry was therefore favorable to the institution of EEC and felt that it was sufficiently advanced to meet competition and to profit from new openings.

The attitude of Italian agriculture was much more guarded. The most beneficial results, Italian agricultural experts felt, would be evident in the Po valley, which had advantages not found in most of Italy: level, well-irrigated land; a permanent, moderately well paid body of skilled farm workers; large local markets; high capital investment and good management; and concentration in suitable lines of production, especially meat and dairy products, rice, fruit, and vegetables. In this area, there was almost unqualified support for the Common Market. Openings for the sale of the Mediterranean fruits and vegetables produced in such coastal plains as the Conca d'Oro behind Palermo made these small but highly productive regions almost as enthusiastic for EEC, although the reduction of population pressure on the land through EEC's stimulus of expanded industrial openings was felt to be necessary. The fears of the remaining area of the country, and of the very small and very large proprietors, were twofold: the competition of the producers in the rest of EEC and in countries that might be associated with the Community, and the difficulty of carrying out the necessary changes to make Italy's agriculture competitive. France, with ideal climatic conditions, increasing mechanization, and efficient farming units, was producing ever larger surpluses of wheat, beef, wine, fruit, and vegetables and selling them at the lowest prices in EEC. Holland, too, was maintaining its traditional production of beef and dairy products. The association of the French and Belgian overseas territories threatened competition with Italy's Mediterranean products. The competitors, in short, were already prepared to invade the Italian market, while the weaker Italian producers would need enormous and time-consuming changes to meet the competition. To remedy the overpopulation of the land, industry would first have to expand, and greater opportunities for emigration would have to be found in EEC. Governmental encouragement of the regrouping of fragmented properties would be required for the restoration of pasture and forest in the mountain areas, just as it would also be required for the establishment of the medium-sized farms desired in the more favored areas. A shift from cereal to livestock production would demand capital investment in herds, investment in refrigeration and packing facilities, and new educational facilities for training farmers in the new techniques. Expanded fruit and vegetable production would require a vast governmental apparatus for classification and supervision of quality controls, as well as a widespread replanting program in many parts of the country. Finally, the social conflicts between landowner and sharecropper and between employer and wage-laborer would have to be eased. Most sectors of Italian agriculture looked toward the Common Market with great misgivings because many of these conditions seemed unlikely to be met.[40]

The ratification debates in July in the Chamber and in the Senate in October simply reechoed these hopes and fears. Indeed, so well worn were the arguments by then that the sessions attracted an extraordinarily small number of deputies—only twenty-two turned up on July 19! The debate centered on the fine Report of the Special Commission appointed by the Chamber to study the treaties, written by the future European Community commissioner, Edoardo Martino (DC), and on a much less incisive minority report, written by the Communist Giuseppe Berti.[41] For once, as Bino Olivi has pointed out, the Communists "were not up to the task and were even, contrary to their normal habit, poorly informed and in the end very bad prophets."[42] The Communist president of the main labor union, the CGIL, had proved the uncertainty in Communist ranks by coming out in favor of EEC in 1957; but he had been quickly called back into line, and the attitude taken by PCI and CGIL was an outmoded, Stalinist interpretation. They spoke of EEC as the instrument of the United States in the Cold War and a means for the hegemony of West Germany in Europe. The Socialist party, which had pulled away from the PCI after the suppression of the Hungarian uprising, explained through its leading economic spokesman, Riccardo Lombardi, that it approved the principle of European economic integration. In the case of a new industry like atomic energy, it would ratify the creation of the new organization of Euratom. It would give its benevolent abstention on EEC, while waiting to be sure that right-wing liberalism was not predominant in the Community.[43] As expected, the Social Democrats warmly supported the treaties, while the Liberals, through Giovanni Malagodi and Gaetano Martino, welcomed the lack of interventionist features in the new Community. Ugo La Malfa for the Republicans gave the most brilliant speech of the debate, an impassioned appeal to move even further toward supranationalism.[44] The monarchists supported the treaties, Roberto Cantalupo explained, because "national values will be neither submerged nor destroyed, but instead will be the determining factor in the union of the historic traditions, moral values, and all the civil, philosophic, political, juridical, and economic patrimony of Europe."[45] The neo-Fascists were favorable for the same reasons. "We do not believe it possible to substitute the sordid economic patriotism of Europeanistic citizenship for national feelings," Augusto De Marsanich declared. But "the states are carrying out the integration of the European economy, without obliterating the nations that compose Europe. So, they are constructing European integration on the basis of the national principle."[46] The Christian Democrats presented a united front, with the new foreign minister, Pella, arguing cogently for the economic good sense of the treaties.[47] The EEC treaty passed the Chamber by a favorable vote of 311. One hundred and forty four Communists voted against, and 54 Socialists abstained. All parties except the Communists voted in favor of the Euratom treaty. The parties voted in exactly the same way when the Senate ratified the treaties on October 9, 1957. In an oddly uninterested way, the Italian parliament had helped revive the impetus to unite Europe.

5
Italy and the European Community, 1958–1968

The first decade of the Common Market was the greatest period of economic prosperity in all Italian history. The gross national product rose from $41.9 billion in 1958 to $71.6 billion in 1968 (in constant 1968 dollars), a growth of 71 per cent for the whole period, equivalent to an annual growth of 5.5 per cent. Per capita annual income rose from $805 to $1358, which, though still low in comparison with the income of the other EEC members, was a considerable reduction of the gap between them.[1] The increase of Italy's trade with EEC countries was even more startling, rising more than 500 per cent. At the same time, the economic and social transformation of Italy accelerated. The contribution of agriculture both to employment and to the national income decreased rapidly. The number of people living in large cities increased dramatically, as the emigrants from the countryside found work in Italy itself instead of abroad; and the flow of emigrants from Italy was cut by half. It became possible at last to make concerted efforts on a large financial scale to tackle Italy's age-old problems—the South, agriculture, education, bureaucratic reform, and income distribution. In the experiment of the "Center-Left" governments, the Christian Democrats attempted to come to terms with the reforming aspirations of the Socialist party, while the Communists shifted from a policy of obstructionism on European matters to one of critical collaboration. It is impossible to define exactly to what degree EEC was responsible for the vast changes in the character of Italy that occurred in the decade of 1958–68; but the pressure of EEC was felt in almost every change of these years, and nearly always in a positive way.

ITALIAN INDUSTRY AND THE COMMON MARKET

The most immediate effects of EEC on Italy were produced by the progressive elimination of customs barriers among the six; and, as was the case with the other member countries, Italian industry frequently anticipated the effects of the customs union, carrying out the necessary readaptation, investment programs, or mergers before rather than after the increased competition was felt or the new markets were opened.

Following the first 10 per cent tariff reduction (based on national tariffs existing on January 1, 1957) that was implemented on January 1, 1959, most Italian companies welcomed the automatic character of the reductions. During 1959 alone, EEC's share of Italy's exports rose from 21 to 27 per cent, giving evidence of an important shift in the country's pattern of trade.[2] The larger Italian companies, though not the industrialists' federation Confindustria, were thus quite ready to support the acceleration of the timetable of customs reduction implemented through the additional 10 per cent tariff cuts of December 1961 and July 1962, especially since, by the agreement of March 1960 on the level of duties on the sensitive products of list G, some of the high-priced raw materials Italy produced, such as sulphur and lead, were to be isolated for six years while the European Investment Bank helped programs of modernization, and others enjoyed relatively high tariffs at the Community level.[3]

Italy and France had applied the highest tariffs in EEC in 1957, and it might have been expected that they would see a far larger increase in imports than exports as a result of the abolition of customs duties. Italy, for example, had applied a tariff of 35 to 45 per cent on automobiles, 31 per cent on washing machines, 20 per cent on refrigerators, and 18 per cent on woollen cloth, while German tariffs on the same products were only 17 to 21, 10, 5, and 13 per cent, respectively. The expected increase in imports from EEC countries did occur, as can be seen from Table 1;[4] but there was an even greater increase in exports. The character of Italian exports once again underscored the vast change in the nature of the

Table 1. Italian Trade with EEC Partners
(in millions of dollars)

	Imports 1956	Imports 1968	Exports 1956	Exports 1968
France	$165.0	$1,162.1	$142.1	$1,280.5
Germany	395.7	1,827.1	291.4	1,902.8
Belgium-Luxembourg	67.1	321.1	47.3	422.8
Netherlands	70.2	398.9	44.1	473.0
EEC Total	698.0	3,709.2	524.9	4,079.2
World		10,252.6		4,079.2

Italian economy that was in progress. Agricultural exports steadily declined in importance as the Italian consumer bought almost the whole of national production and satisfied his remaining needs with continually increasing imports. The export of Italian raw materials rose, but almost exclusively in petroleum products, while the imports of raw materials—one-third of all imports—and of semi-finished industrial goods fed the insatiable transforming industries that spearheaded Italian economic development. By 1968, the Italian producers were the greatest exporters within the Common Market in several fields of industrial production, especially clothing, shoes, domestic electrical appliances, petroleum products, cement, artificial and synthetic fibers, textiles other than cotton, and canned foods; and they held second place for exports of metalworking machines, textile machinery, building materials, ceramics, plastics, leather goods, and alcoholic beverages.

The Common Market had thus accelerated the evolution that had characterized the economic miracle of the 1950's. Still in the forefront were the great companies that had formerly enjoyed virtual monopoly of the Italian market. With the ending of customs protection within EEC, and with lower protection by the Common Market external tariff against imports from third countries, such companies as Fiat or Montecatini were exposed for the first time to competition inside Italy from companies of the same size or larger. They reacted by starting large programs of investment and reorganization, based upon thorough reviews of their productive and marketing possibilities.[5] The most outstanding example was the Fiat automobile company, which showed that the way to success lay in large-scale investment programs, rationalization of production, efficient and aggressive sales organization, and appeal to the consumer through good design, novelty of product, and low price.[6] The rapid penetration of the Community markets by the chemicals and plastics of Montecatini and Snia-Viscosa, the typewriters and business machines of Olivetti, the ceramics of Pozzi, and the tires of Pirelli was the result of similar tactics.

The secret of the smaller though equally successful producers of domestic appliances, clothing, and shoes was less one of major reorganization than of a constant flexibility that enabled them, with the minimum of capitalization, to cater to the changing desires of a Community-wide clientele. So rapid and widespread was the increase of sales of Italian refrigerators in France that the French government imposed a 12 per cent import duty on them in 1962, and was upheld both by the Commission and the Court of Justice on the ground that the imports were causing serious difficulties to the French refrigerator industry.[7] But the consumers continued to buy Italian models. Italian manufacturers had produced only 67,000 refrigerators in 1953; they produced more than three million in 1967. In the 1960's the same companies turned to the production of washing machines, with the same startling success; and in the mid 1960's, with the same ingenuity, the electrical appliance companies began turning out dry cleaning machines, opening up a new, untapped market.[8] With the Common Market buying half of the Italian refrigerators exported and two-thirds of the washing machines, its influence in the expansion of the industry was second only to that of the expanding market at home.

The effect of EEC upon the weaker sectors of Italian industry was far less disastrous than had been expected.[9] The number of companies going into bankruptcy, rather than increasing, dropped by half between 1957 and 1963, and did not reach the 1957 level even during the recession of 1963–65. Even the smaller companies had found it necessary and profitable to increase their capital investment in new machinery of better quality, and some of it could be bought from the other EEC members. The artisan trades, which had feared the consequences of EEC, more than doubled the number of their employees during the first four years of the Common Market, and, what was more remarkable, the heads of 40 per cent of these firms were under thirty-one years of age. In short, the artisan trades had known a boom that was attracting many of the younger people of initiative; and their success in the export trade was evidenced by an expansion of exports 50 per cent higher than the national average.[10]

In Italian heavy industry, the two sectors suffering the greatest difficulties were heavy engineering and shipbuilding, which were dominated by companies within IRI. In both cases, the EEC Commission objected to the aids granted by the Italian government as a falsification of competition, thereby, the Italian government felt, increasing the problems of those sectors. The Court of Justice upheld the Commission's demand that Italy end the system of granting "reimbursement" equivalent to an export subsidy on engineering products; but the Commission later reversed its stand to permit a Community-wide system of subsidies to shipyards. The pressure of EEC did, however, force a complete reorganization of IRI's shipyards in 1966, with improved results in productivity.[11]

To the generally glowing picture of widely diffused industrial progress in the decade 1958–68, the recession of 1963–65 contrasted sharply; and it provided a test case of the value of Common Market to one of its members during the unaccustomed experience of falling production. In the fall of 1963, the Italian economy, which had expanded almost continually since the early 1950's, began to show signs of inflation, a worsening balance of payments, falling industrial production, and increasing unemployment. The primary cause of this recession was held to be a sudden rise in wages of 16 per cent in 1963, compared with an increase in gross national product of only 4.8 per cent, which, by reducing the profit margin, cut the incentive to private investment in plant and machinery; and the deflationary measures in the early months of 1964 by the Italian government, including reduction of credit and restriction on borrowing abroad, probably worsened the decline in output and employment.[12] In August 1964, new antirecession measures were applied, including a special tax on manufactured goods and on personal wealth.[13] Public investment was substantially increased in 1965, and private investment was encouraged by the end of the special tax on automobiles and the end of controls on purchasing on credit.[14] But the most effective aid to Italy during the recession was provided by the Common Market. According to OECD, "one of the most striking features of the cycle was the extent to which a very rapid growth of exports of goods and services replaced deficient domestic demand."[15] While imports were falling, Italy succeeded in 1964 in increasing its exports to Germany by one-quarter and to Benelux by one-third. By the spring of 1964, a large deficit in the balance of payments had been converted to a surplus. The 1963–65 recession was primarily an internal Italian phenomenon, and the ease of access to markets that were not suffering economically was the major factor in enabling Italy to avoid the worst effects in unemployment that the recession would otherwise have produced and to shorten the period of its impact. By 1966, it was clear that Italy was embarking on a new economic boom.

During its first decade of operation, the Common Market had thus proved enormously valuable to Italian industry. But far from being satisfied with what had been achieved, the Italian industrialists desired a more rapid realization of the missing features of the economic union, such as common monetary and fiscal policies, and the beginning of political union. The success of the customs union strengthened this desire. In 1958, the politicians had attempted to convince the industrialists that economic union was needed for political reasons; in 1968, the industrialists were urging the politicians that political union was necessary for economic reasons.

THE LONG STRUGGLE FOR A COMMON AGRICULTURAL POLICY

The one sector for which the Community succeeded in working out a common policy during its first decade was that of agriculture. The enormous difficulty of improving the productive conditions of Italian agriculture gave Italy a vital interest in the eight-year-long formulation of this policy.

From the start of the discussions at the conference of Stresa in July 1958, the Italians demanded that the policy achieve two ends: first, increase of production through a Community system of market regulation for the various agricultural products, based upon a common price within EEC and upon protection against imports from third countries, and, second, improvement of the structure of Italian agricultural production. Representatives of the agricultural unions, the Confederazione Nazionale Coltivatori Diretti and the Confederazione Generale dell'Agricoltura Italiana, and of the Ministry of Agriculture consulted frequently with the EEC Commission during the two-year period during which it was preparing its proposals for the common agricultural policy; and the Italian government was able to make preparations for implementation of its five-year "Green Plan" for agricultural improvement in close coordination with the Community planners. The Green Plan, passed in 1961, which provided for state intervention to aid in farm consolidation, mechanization, rural education, increased livestock rearing, and stable prices and markets, was directly influenced by the prospects of greatly increased competition for the Italian market from the farmers of northern Europe through EEC's establishment of a common agricultural policy.[16] The "Mansholt Plan," as proposed to the EEC Council of Ministers in June 1960, therefore caused little surprise or immediate concern in Italy.

The Commission's proposals were twofold. Structural reform of agriculture was to be encouraged by Community advice to national governments, coordination of national planning, and establishment of a European Fund for Structural Improvement in Agriculture, to be financed by the Community. Market organizations with common Community prices were to be set up to regulate the sale of all the major agricultural products of the Community, especially cereals, meat, eggs, poultry, fruit and vegetables, dairy products, and wine. To bring prices within the Community gradually together, a system of levies was to replace customs duties and quotas; within the Community, the levies were to be gradually abolished, while on imports from third countries, the levies were to move gradually toward a Community level. These proposals were turned over by the EEC Council to a Special Committee for Agriculture, in which Italy was represented by several of its most experienced and European-minded negotiators, including Attilio Cattani from the Ministry of Foreign Affairs, Paolo Albertario from Agriculture, and Giuseppe Ferlesch from Foreign Trade. Although the Committee quickly accepted the principle of levies as the basis of the new policy, each national delegation made specific demands. The Germans, for example, claimed that export subsidies by most of its partners were falsifying the market. The Italians wanted to keep their transport rebate paid to exporters of fruit and vegetables. After a fifteen-hour meeting of the Council of Ministers on December 19–20, the Italians were permitted to retain their subsidy; and their representatives, Rumor and Colombo, thereupon agreed to a compromise resolution that accepted the levy system and directed the Commission to prepare proposals for market organizations of pork and cereals by May 1961 and of sugar, eggs, and poultry by July.[17]

As directed by the Council, the EEC Commission presented its draft regulations in May–June 1961, and they were discussed by the Special Committee during the summer. In October, the Council of Ministers began a long, exhausting series of discussions that culminated in the first agricultural "marathon" negotiation of January 4–14, 1962. The products under consideration comprised more than half of EEC's agricultural production, presented enormous difficulties of organization, and brought the interests of several Community members directly into conflict. The negotiations were dominated by the French, who were determined to force open the German market for its surpluses of cereals and livestock and to gain Community financial support for exports outside EEC. The Italian ministers probably made a major error in policy by assuming that Italy would remain a net exporter of agricultural products, whose interests were similar to those of France, rather than an importer, which it shortly became, whose interests were closer to Germany.[18] Undoubtedly the impatience of the Italians, especially of Colombo, to make progress toward a political union by implementing the economic union, played its part, especially since the French had refused to accept passage from the first to the second stage of the treaty timetable in January 1962 unless agricultural agreement was reached.[19]

The purpose of the decisions taken in the marathon was to create a common market in agricultural goods during a transition period ending in December 1969. By then, most agricultural products were to circulate freely and were to be sold at a Community-wide price; levies on imports from third countries were to establish preference for Community farmers; and an agricultural fund was to finance structural improvement of EEC farms. To begin preparation for this common market, an extremely complicated series of regulations was adopted. First, marketing organizations were set up for several major products. For cereals, which were regarded as the basic product whose treatment would influence most other agricultural products, the farmer was to receive a guaranteed price. At the end of the transition period, the Community would fix "target prices" which would be the base prices in whichever marketing center of the Community had the least adequate supplies. If prices fell to the "support price," about 5 to 10 per cent below the target price, the Community was to buy the surplus to force up the price. Protection from outside would be provided by levies on imports, set to raise the cost of imported cereals to a "threshold price," which would be the target price less the cost of transportation to the region of the Community with the least adequate supplies. The key to the system was thus the choice of target price. Since Italy was the country with the highest cereals price, its cereals producers, like those in Germany, were demanding a high Community price level, to avoid the competition of low-priced cereals from more efficient producers, such as France. But it was in the Italian national interest to seek a lower Community price, to stimulate the conversion of Italian farms from grain to livestock rearing, to discourage the efficient EEC producers from concentrating more heavily on cereals to the even greater disadvantage of the Italian producer, and to avoid the expense of subsidizing the exports to third countries of the surpluses which the efficient producers would be encouraged to grow.[20] The problem of price proved so difficult that the Council postponed consideration of it until the following year.

Slightly different forms of market organizations were adopted for the other products discussed. For pork, eggs, and poultry, levies on imports from outside the Community were to be imposed when the price fell below a minimum, called the "sluicegate price." The products that most concerned the Italians were, however, wine, fruit, and vegetables, since they hoped to export large quantities to the north, and to profit from their Mediterranean climate to become the "garden of Europe." An impetus to production of better quality wines in Italy was provided by the decision to register all vineyards, including types of vines planted, by 1963. Both Italy and France agreed to import up to 150,000 hectolitres of wine, while Germany established a quota of 1.2 million hectolitres, much of which would come from Italy. Only at the end of a hard-fought struggle on the last day did Italy gain some satisfaction on fruit and vegetables. Customs duties were to be abolished by 1968, and quota and minimum-price systems more rapidly. The alignment of prices was to be achieved by quality controls, while customs duties were still to provide protection against third countries; but no financial responsibility was assumed by the Community at that time. Since fruit and vegetables were the major source of revenue for the Italian farmer, and his largest export item, it seemed satisfactory at the time to have abolished the obstacles to trade with EEC.

To finance the agricultural policy, the six agreed to establish a European Agricultural Guidance and Guarantee Fund (Fondo Europeo di Orientamento e Garanzia Agricolo, or FEOGA), with two functions—to guarantee the producers the receipt of the Community price for their products and to aid the structural adaptation of agriculture. The Fund was to pay refunds to farmers who exported their surpluses outside the Community at the world price; it was to intervene to maintain the Community level of prices within EEC; and it was to devote one-third of the amount that was spent on guaranteeing Community prices to structural reform. The Italians supported the Germans in their refusal to accept the French demand that the income of the Fund be derived from the levies on Community imports; and Italian representatives and members of the Commission came into the private Franco-German meetings to help iron out the difficulties, which were threatening the whole negotiation.[21] The final compromise was to derive the Fund's income from national contributions during the transition period, with the actual amount decided annually and partially weighted according to the amount of a country's imports from outside the Community. During 1962–65, the share of the national contribution fixed in relation to imports, which was in effect a penalty to be paid for buying outside the Community, was to rise to one-fifth of the Fund's income. During this period, the Fund was to cover only part of the expenses of export refunds and structural reform—one-sixth in 1962–63, one-third in 1963–64, and one-half in 1964–65. Agreement was purchased by procrastination, therefore, and a new tough negotiation was inevitable in 1965. No one realized in 1962 how explosive that issue would become.

There was general satisfaction in Italy with the results of this negotiation; and most observers felt, with *Il Messaggero,* that "France and Italy will receive the greatest benefits from this diplomatic battle."[22] It was in an overly optimistic spirit that Italy paid out to the Community $22 million for the agricultural policy during the first year of operation, 1962–63, and it was chastened to find that it received back less than 5 per cent of that sum.[23] This result, Italian leaders felt, was due to the fact that the principal product affected by the financial regulation, cereals, was not an Italian export; and they looked impatiently for the inclusion of the remaining agricultural products within the common policy. The Germans were still unwilling to move quickly, however, especially on beef and dairy products, which composed two-fifths of their agricultural production; and it took an ultimatum from French President Charles de Gaulle to get the negotiations moving again in the fall of 1963. Since de Gaulle had refused to participate in the Kennedy Round of tariff negotiations in January 1964 unless the market regulations were largely completed, the EEC Council undertook a second "marathon" on December 18–23, 1963. For beef, it was decided to extend Community protection to EEC farmers by application of levies on imports when Community products fell below a sluicegate price, a system already devised for pork. National prices were to be aligned with an EEC orientation price by 1970, although member countries could intervene to support their home product when prices fell 93–96 per cent below the orientation price.[24] For Italy, Community preference in beef sales was regarded as a stimulus to production only in the long run; in the immediate future, no member but France could satisfy its needs, except by large imports of meat and of cattle for fattening, so that duties were likely to be kept low and levies not applied.[25] Milk and dairy product prices were to be aligned by 1970. During this transition period, levies on imports from member countries were to be reduced by a fixed sum in comparison with imports from third countries, in order to establish Community preference. Italy allied with France in demanding that the producers of butter and olive oil receive Community support. Against strong Dutch objections, it was agreed that a tax of 22 lire per kilogram should be imposed on vegetable fats used for margarine, the income being used to compensate producers of butter and olive oil for lower national prices. Italian producers expected to receive about fifty billion lire.[26] Ferrari Aggradi and Colombo made their strongest plea for Community protection of rice, of which Italy was by far the largest producer. Most rice consumed in EEC, however, was either imported from Asia and processed in the Netherlands or Germany, or imported from the United States, at what the Italians regarded as a "dumping" price. Italy's partners accepted the Italians' request, imposing levies on imports from third countries. Now, as *Corriere della Sera* remarked, the Dutch and the Germans would have to shift their preference to "the rice of the Lomellina, of the Valtellina, and of the Vercellese."[27] With the conclusion of these agreements, more than 95 per cent of EEC's agricultural production had been regulated; and Italy looked with hope to an increase of its exports to EEC of fruit and vegetables, wine, rice, and olive oil, and of expansion of livestock production to meet national needs. Crucial to the success of the whole agricultural policy, however, was the price level established for the Community, which would be dictated by the decision on the price for cereals.

In 1964, the pattern of the previous year was repeated. General de Gaulle again laid down an ultimatum, linking continued French participation in EEC and in the Kennedy Round to conclusion of the agreement on a cereals price. The Germans remained recalcitrant in their opposition to lowering the German cereals price; but finally, in a new marathon negotiation, agreement was reached early in the morning of December 15. In this negotiation, all partners were in agreement that the Italians had gained the most.[28] Agriculture Minister Ferrari Aggradi succeeded in having Italy's contribution to FEOGA reduced from 28 per cent to 18 per cent in 1965–66 and to 22 per cent in 1966–67. Fruit and vegetables were to be guaranteed automatic protection against imports from third countries. Tobacco was to be brought under EEC's responsibility. In the central question of pricing, the Community price of soft wheat was set a little below the Italian price, while hard wheat (durum), which was almost exclusively produced in Southern Italy, for the manufacture of pasta, was guaranteed a minimum price supported by EEC subsidies.[29] Finally, to compensate cereals producers in Italy for loss of revenue, FEOGA was to contribute $131 million in 1967–70 to Italian producers, while the Germans would receive $280 million.[30] The almost universal enthusiasm for the agreements in Italian political and economic circles was due to the feeling that its partners had finally realized that the moment had come to do something for

Italy. "Bravo, Ferrari Aggradi," Confagricoltura commented, with unwonted enthusiasm, "Today we have to say that you won your battle."[31]

In reality, however, the battle was only just beginning. In March 1965, the Commission, in presenting its proposals for the financing of FEOGA during the remainder of the transition period, shocked the French government by proposing a revolutionary increase in the powers of the European Parliament and of the Commission itself. To cover the expenses of the Fund, the Commission suggested that all industrial tariffs and all agricultural levies should be paid directly to the Community, and that the administration of these funds by the Commission should be supervised directly by the European Parliament. The Commission was claiming control over an anual revenue of more than $2 billion, or about one-eighth of the total revenue of the individual states, which would have made it, in de Gaulle's words, a "major independent financial power." These proposals, combined with the recommendation that the common market in both agriculture and industry should be achieved within two years, provoked the greatest crisis in EEC's history. In the crucial meeting of the Council of Ministers on June 28–30, the Italians played a major part in provoking the French into boycotting future EEC negotiations.

The Italian delegation, headed by Foreign Minister Fanfani, strongly supported the Commission's effort to create a supranational federal authority through its proposals of March; but Fanfani requested complete reconsideration of the financial contributions to FEOGA, on the ground that Italy's share was still unjustly large. He proposed that the method of financing should be settled for only one or two years and then reviewed, rather than be fixed through 1970, as the French desired.[32] The French, backed by the Belgians, refused this temporizing stand, and they offered to cover part of the share that Italy and Germany would be required to pay into the Fund. In the last hours of discussion, the Council split between the French, who wanted an immediate decision on one matter only, agricultural financing, and the other five, who wished to take up all the Commission's proposals. Fanfani called in vain for approval of the "prudent Italian position that would have made it possible to avoid immediate consideration of the Community's own resources or of the powers of the European Parliament," and the meeting broke up in anger.[33] The next day, the French cabinet declared that their partners had broken their agreement to settle the agricultural financing by June 1965, and that it had "decided to recognize the economic, political, and juridical consequences of the new situation." Within a few days, the principal French representatives had been withdrawn from Brussels; the French ministers ceased to take part in the EEC Council of Ministers; and the French experts attended only routine meetings at the Common Market headquarters in Brussels. De Gaulle had decided to have his own way by paralyzing the working of EEC through the policy of the "empty chair."[34]

In Italy, the reaction to France's new effort to bludgeon its partners into agreement was one of resignation to the need for seeking an understanding with France, because of the proven value of economic integration and because Europe could not be constructed without France—"Men pass, France remains."[35] Throughout the seven months when France's chair was empty, Emilio Colombo assumed the role of intermediary between the Community and the French. In October, as president of the Council of Ministers, Colombo was authorized to invite the French to attend a meeting of the Council of Ministers in Brussels, at which the Commission would not be present.[36] But the French government did not reply, preferring instead to engage in bilateral talks with the Italian ambassador.[37] In November, the five powers again authorized Colombo to communicate with the French government; and, at a meeting he held with French Foreign Minister Couve de Murville in Rome in December, agreement in principle on French participation in a foreign ministers' meeting of the six powers was reached. When General de Gaulle was reelected to the presidency of France, he apparently felt again able to act from strength; and shortly after the election the Italian ambassador in Paris was told that the French had agreed to an "intergovernmental meeting" with the five other powers, not in Brussels, but in Luxembourg.

In Luxembourg, on January 17–18, 1966, the French ignored the question of agricultural financing and instead attacked the powers of the Commission and the Treaty of Rome's provision for majority voting in the Council during the third stage of the treaty. At this meeting Italian pliability gave way to German firmness, with the five grouped behind Foreign Minister Gerhard Schröder in opposition to the French demands. When the meeting resumed on January 28–30, the French and the other delegations became more conciliatory; and a face-saving compromise was reached. The six powers agreed to attempt to seek unanimity on decisions where "very important interests of one or more partners are at stake," noted that "the French delegation considers that when very important interests are at stake, the discussion must be continued until unanimous agreement is reached," and that "there is a divergence of views on what should be done in the event of failure to reach complete agreement." Colombo accepted the compromise with great reluctance; he objected not only to the French unilateral declaration of their determination to ignore majority rule, but especially to the preference given to national over Community interests, which, he said, was a "sword of Damocles" hanging over EEC. The reduction of the Commission's independence, both real and ceremonial, was equally distasteful, as was the ignoring of the question of increased powers for the European Parliament. News that the French would return to full participation in the Community was greeted in Italy with relief mixed with bitter resentment of de Gaulle. But, as *Mondo Agricolo* pointed out, although the six had merely registered their disagreement, "the Community mechanism was again rolling . . . raising in the first place the agricultural problems that have been in suspense in Brussels since last July."[38]

On May 9–11, 1966, in a fifth marathon discussion, the six reached agreement on agricultural financing. The Italian delegation had found itself under renewed pressure from the agricultural unions to get a more equable settlement for Italy than they had done previously. According to Confagricoltura, "Italian agriculture could have expected much more than it received from entry into the European Economic Community if only [its representatives] had acted with greater prudence and knowledge of the problems. . . . While Italy cheerfully accepted the regulation of sectors on which it should have been defensive, such as cereals, milk or meat, it failed to obtain the return concessions that Italian agriculture was expecting in the sectors, for example, of fruit and vegetables, tobacco, etc."[39] The Italian delegation, headed by Fanfani and the agriculture minister, Restivo, therefore demanded Community approval of regulations for products of special interest to

Italy, including fruit and vegetables, olive oil, rice, tobacco, and wine; a financial subsidy for tobacco; an increase in the funds of FEOGA devoted to "orientation"; and a reduction of Italy's contribution to no more than 20 per cent.[40] Once again, most of Italy's specific demands were met. After July 1967, when FEOGA was to be financed half from agricultural levies and half by direct national contributions, the Italian share of those contributions was to be only 20.3 per cent. FEOGA could spend up to $285 million on its guidance section, and was permitted to increase its share of the cost of projects financed from 25 to 45 per cent. Temporary subsidies were to be granted to Italian olive oil, fruit and vegetables, and tobacco. Social and regional policies were to be advanced in harmony with agricultural policy. With these specific concessions, the Italian delegation agreed that the common market for both agricultural and industrial products should be complete by July 1, 1968, the dates of free circulation of various agricultural products being dependent upon the beginning of their marketing year.

Most of the remaining decisions necessary to complete the common agricultural policy were taken at a sixth marathon negotiation on July 21–23, 1966. The remaining market regulations, for fruit and vegetables, sugar, and olive oil, were of interest primarily to Italy, a fact that probably made it easier for Agriculture Minister Restivo to demand satisfaction similar to that Italy's partners had received from the earlier regulations. For fruit and vegetables, which constituted 25 per cent of the value of Italian agricultural production and 70 per cent of its exports, the Italians complained that the regulation adopted in 1962 had established Community preference, but that Italian exports to third countries were growing faster than they were to EEC. After Dutch objections were finally overcome, the Council decided to spend $60 million for price support and structural improvements in fruit and vegetables during the following three years, with $40 million going to Italy; and producers' organizations were to be subsidized by FEOGA and the national states. If a "serious crisis" occurred, the member states themselves could intervene to buy up surpluses. For some products, including certain fresh fruits and preserves, export refunds could be granted. For sugar, to avoid overproduction, a guaranteed price was established only for a fixed production quota, that for Italy being set at 1.23 million tons, or approximately the level of Italian consumption, while a seven-year transition period was allowed for alignment with the Community price. For olive oil, the normal Community system of guaranteed prices, levies on imports, and export subsidies was to be applied. Italy thus succeeded in obtaining Community support for its special products equivalent to that already obtained by France and Holland for cereals and milk products.[41] Finally, the Council settled common prices for milk, beef, rice, sugar, olive oil, and oilseeds at a level usually only slightly below the high prices of the Italian market. With these decisions, which covered both the market regulation and the price level of most of the Community's agricultural production, the common agricultural policy was virtually complete.

During the next two years, it became possible to glimpse what the effects on Italian agriculture of participation in the common agricultural market were likely to be. The prognosis was not particularly favorable. The introduction of common prices and market regulations produced only a slight improvement in Italian exports to EEC countries. Results were especially disappointing in the vital sector of fruit and vegetables, and Italian producers charged that their partners were ignoring Community preference and were blocking Italian imports by abuse of such measures as quality controls. The high cereals price encouraged an unwanted increase of production of wheat in Italy, thus adding to the Community's surplus and discouraging the shift from cereals production to livestock rearing desired by Italian agricultural authorities. Competition with northern European dairy farmers at Community price levels prevented a large increase in the size of Italian dairy herds. It appeared to Italian farming groups that the policy was designed to suit the farmers north of the Alps, with corresponding damage to the interests of the farmers of Mediterranean Europe, whose agriculture was entirely different. Moreover, the measures taken through the Orientation Section of FEOGA to help bring Italian farms up to the competitive level of northern Europe were too small in scale and too poorly financed to make anything more than a superficial impression on the deep structural problems of Italian agriculture. The first decade of the Common Market thus saw a worsening of the financial position of the Italian farmer in comparison with that of all other groups in Italian society. The farming organizations reacted by joining the industrialists in demanding that EEC move beyond the stage of a mere customs union and begin the unfinished business of creating a genuine economic union. One Europe, the Italian farmers felt, could still help heal the division of the two Italies—the Italy of the fields and the Italy of the cities.[42]

TOWARD SOLUTION OF THE PROBLEMS OF
UNEMPLOYMENT AND THE SOUTH

In 1958, the Italian government had presented the Treaty of Rome as proof of the decision of their northern European partners to assume through the European Social Fund part of the responsibility for two of Italy's most basic and interrelated problems, unemployment and the underdevelopment of the South. Ten years later, the Fund's Italian administrator found that, in financing the Fund, Italy's partners had taken "the first timid steps toward a more extensive and profound solidarity among the peoples of Europe."[43] Progress was slow but encouraging.

Obviously, the beneficial effects of the economic expansion stimulated by EEC were felt by the Italian worker. Real wages rose 55 per cent in 1959–66, reducing the gap between Italian wages and the highest wages paid in the Community (in Luxembourg) from 100 per cent to 40 per cent. Unemployment was reduced from over one million in 1959 to a low of 426,000 in 1963, although during the recession of the mid 1960's the number of unemployed drifted back up to around 800,000, an unemployment rate of about 4 per cent. The expansion of employment opportunities in the industrial cities enabled about 300,000 peasants to leave agriculture annually—they either moved into the Italian cities or emigrated—and it helped raise the number of emigrants from the South to the rest of Italy from 340,000 in 1951–56 to 605,000 in 1956–61 and to 713,000 in 1962–66.[44] Increasing opportunity at home thus made the expected boon of greater emigration opportunities within EEC a brief though important consideration. Italian emigration to EEC countries had been large since the end of World War II. What EEC did provide were more secure and fairer conditions of work for the emigrant, as a result of new

Community regulations in 1961 and 1964, and Community preference for Italian workers over emigrants from third countries. After a large increase in emigration in 1960–62, the number of emigrants dropped sharply, and in years of prosperity the excess of emigrants over persons returning was minimal.

Unfortunately, few Italians learned any advanced industrial skills while they were working in the Common Market countries, and fewer still found jobs where they were able to use the particular skills they had acquired when they returned home. The Italian government and the labor unions felt that in the long run Italy had the worst of the bargain: they raised and educated workers for their partners, but in return their partners did little to carry on the technical training that the workers needed. It was partly for this reason that the Treaty of Rome had provided for the creation of a European Social Fund for the retraining and relocation of workers. To be eligible for aid, a worker had to be unemployed for six months, suitably retrained and sometimes relocated, and then employed in a new job for six months. At the end of that time the member country could apply to EEC for one-half of the costs of his training and relocation. Italy's contribution, 20 per cent of the total for the Community, amounted to $16.05 million in 1960–68, and in this case, unlike that with FEOGA, it received back more than it paid—$27.22 million. With this moderate sum Italy was able to retrain 203,310 workers and to resettle 340,037, principally because the Italian government paid only about one-tenth per worker of what, for example, the German government paid. The system had considerable shortcomings. The Italian government could have received much more if it had felt able to finance its half-share of the cost of the program for more people and if it had been less cautious in its applications for aid; and it almost entirely ignored the provision in the program for aid in reconversion of factories. Dissatisfaction with the extent of the Fund's activity made the Italian government the principal proponent of the new plan for the Fund proposed by the Commission in June 1969. The plan would increase expenditures from $9 million to $250 million annually and vastly broaden the scope of retraining programs.[45]

EEC's direct contribution to the solution of the problem of the South was far less than most Italians had expected, but its indirect contribution, through the stimulus of economic growth in the rest of the country, was enormous. A large part of the funds paid by FEOGA to Italy for structural reform in agriculture was used in the South. The majority of the workers retrained with the contribution of the European Social Fund were from the South. And the $500 million loaned to Italy by the European Investment Bank were spent on projects within the area of the Cassa per il Mezzogiorno, and especially in the zones of industrial development like Taranto, Latina, and Gela. Continuing emigration from the South to the Common Market countries helped relieve the pressure of population growth during the first five years of EEC's operation. But the main contribution to a solution of the South's difficulties was made by the Italian economic miracle, which was stimulated by the process of economic integration. In the period between 1945 and 1968, the South consumed almost exactly what it produced, and thus it was unable to accumulate any investment capital from its own resources. As Pasquale Saraceno has shown, the huge investments carried out in the South, notably since the foundation of the Cassa in 1950, had to be drawn from the resources produced by the rest of the country, and, to a minor extent, by its EEC partners.[46] By 1968, for the first time, Southern economists were beginning to recognize that the eighteen years of effort to make the South as economically viable as the rest of the country were succeeding; and that the gap between the South and the North was being closed. The statistics for the period 1950–67 showed several basic changes in the economic structure of the South. The percentage of the population employed in agriculture had fallen from 55 to 36 per cent; 1.4 million new jobs had been created in industry in the South itself; per capita income in the South had risen from 230,000 lire to 530,000,* at an annual rate of 5.1 per cent, reducing the gap between Southern and Northern income by over 7 per cent. All this had been achieved while the process of industrialization of the South was just beginning. It was predicted that in the decade of the 1970's the need for workers in Italy and the Common Market would exceed the numbers available, with the result that 1.4 million Southern farmers would leave agriculture. This exodus would help solve the problems of unemployment and underemployment in agriculture and make possible a more rational use of the agricultural land of the South. The

* At 1967 prices.

Southern labor force would continue to divide between those finding work in the South, where industrialization would have to be continued to relieve the population congestion in the North and the consequent pressure on the infrastructure of the Northern industrial triangle, and those emigrating to the Northern Italian cities and EEC. Thus, the redistribution of population between industry and agriculture and between South and North raised the possibility that the gap between North and South might be eliminated by 1980.[47] While attempting to unify Europe, the country's leaders would thus have achieved the unification of Italy.

THE DISAPPOINTMENT OF EURATOM

The value of Euratom seemed so obvious to most Italians in 1957 that the Socialist party had decided to cast its first pro-European vote of the postwar years in favor of the creation of a European Atomic Energy Community. By 1969, Italy felt that Euratom had been a resounding and expensive failure, from which the poorer members of the Community had suffered most.[48]

During the early years of Euratom, Italy appeared to be profiting significantly from the Community's operation. The government was elated when Euratom accepted its offer of its newly constructed nuclear research center at Ispra, near Lake Maggiore, as the major common research center of the Community.[49] Euratom participated financially in many programs of nuclear research of the Italian atomic energy agency and of private industry, including, for example, projects for a rapid or third-generation reactor and for the development of nuclear propulsion for merchant ships. Euratom also contributed 4 billion lire toward the construction of a nuclear power station of American design at the mouth of the Garigliano and another 2.5 billion toward a power station near Latina. The norms for protection against radiation for nuclear workers developed by Euratom were applied in Italy in 1964. Finally, Italy shared in the common market for nuclear material. At the end of the first five-year program, the Italian government calculated that, whereas Italy had paid 27 billion lire into Euratom, the Community had invested 28 to 29 billion lire in Italy.[50]

As early as 1961, when the second five-year program was being formulated, the Italian government began to share in the grave doubts expressed by its partners on the way Euratom was functioning; by 1963, the six governments were officially discussing the "Euratom crisis," and by 1969, they appeared ready to scrap the whole organization.

The main criticisms of Euratom were that it had given up trying to create vast projects on a Community scale with Community-wide participation; that it had made major errors in its technical choice of programs to support; and that the very need for a Community organization in nuclear energy had been exaggerated, since, as early as 1960, it was clear that there was a glut rather than a shortage of nuclear materials.[51] The bitterness of the Italian government was documented in the Report on Euratom presented to the Senate by Foreign Minister Fanfani in 1967. Italy, he pointed out, was only receiving back from Euratom 66.8 per cent of what it was paying in during this second five-year program. Yet the benefits originally expected from Euratom were not being received. "Euratom no longer corresponds, in its present structure, to today's pressing needs," Fanfani concluded. "We believe that Euratom is destined to disappear in its present form."[52]

TOWARD A MORE GENUINE UNION

While wrestling with the problems of creating an economic union of the six EEC powers, the Italians never forgot their original aim of creating a political union of all western Europe. Their efforts were, however, to be constantly frustrated, at times by the behavior of the countries they wished to invite into the Community, more frequently by the attitudes of their partners.

The key to the enlargement of the Community was, in Italian eyes, the admission of Great Britain, but only on condition that Britian accept the responsibilities imposed by economic integration and the desirability of political integration. In the stormy negotiations within the OEEC intergovernmental committee in 1957–58, during which the French firmly opposed the British attempt to persuade the six to set up a Free Trade Area with the other members of OEEC, the Italians supported France's intransigence. Since the German and Benelux delegations were ready to pay a high price for agreement with Britain, the support of Italy, as Bino Olivi has pointed out, prevented the isolation of France, and helped defeat the first serious challenge to the Community's aspiration to unity.[53]

In spite of their deep suspicions of General de Gaulle's attitude toward Europeanism, the Italian government continued to follow the French lead as long as its aim seemed to be the strengthening of the Community. It enthusiastically supported the acceleration proposals of 1960 and the concurrent demand for formulation of a common agricultural policy, and accepted the French proposal of November 1959 that the foreign ministers of the six meet quarterly for discussion of "the political aspects of the activity of the European Communities as well as other international problems."[54] In the summer of 1960, however, de Gaulle announced that France was proposing the creation of an "imposing confederation" in western Europe, the pillars of which, he said in September, would be the states. Regular cooperation was to be organized through specialized intergovernmental bodies for political, economic, cultural, and defense matters, and discussed in periodic meetings of an assembly of delegates from the national parliaments. Once again the Italians tried to mediate. In the summit conference of the six heads of government in Paris of February 10–11, 1961, Fanfani worked hard to bring the Benelux representatives to accept a compromise with de Gaulle, by which a Study Commission was to make "concrete proposals for the meetings of the Heads of State or Government and of Foreign Ministers, as well as for any other meeting that might appear desirable" and to "study other problems of European cooperation, particularly those relating to the development of the Communities."[55] The report of the Study Commission, presided over by the French delegate Christian Fouchet, was adopted at a second summit meeting in Bonn on July 19.[56] The six agreed to "hold, at regular intervals, meetings whose aim will be to compare their views, to concert their policies, and to reach common positions, in order to further the political union of Europe, thereby strengthening the Atlantic Alliance"; and they instructed the Fouchet Commission to draw up "proposals on the means by which a statutory form can be given as soon as possible to the union of their peoples." Among the governmental parties in Italy, the decisions of the conference roused great enthusiasm; *Il Popolo* even called it "a fundamental stage in the construction of united Europe." Moreover, Italian *amour propre* received a nice boost with the agreement that a European University, "to whose intellectual life and financing the six governments will contribute," should be created by Italy at Florence.* Only two weeks after the meeting in Bonn, the British government added to Italian elation by declaring that it intended to open negotiations with the six for full membership in EEC. For a brief period, it seemed that Italy's greatest hopes would be realized—French agreement to political union, British membership in the economic union.

At first, the British decision had little effect on the work of the Fouchet Commission, which gave favorable attention in November to a French draft treaty instituting a union of the states, even though it contained no supranational features nor even any link with the existing Communities. On January 15, 1962, however, the French delegation suddenly presented a new text considerably less acceptable to the Europeans, especially as it again infringed upon EEC by bringing economic matters within the purview of the political union. An atmosphere of distrust at once permeated the meetings of the Fouchet Commission and the tense foreign ministers' meeting in Luxembourg in March. At this point, Fanfani again attempted to mediate; and, in his meeting with de Gaulle at Turin, he felt that he had persuaded the French President to accept a more collaborative attitude toward NATO and the Euro-

* The European University was originally planned as a scientific institution created by Euratom; but as early as September 1958 the Italian government offered detailed plans for the creation of "a great European university, . . . conceived as a fundamental driving force in the integration of our continent" and comprising not only scientific studies but European cultural studies too. In December 1958, Fanfani proposed that the University be at Florence, and in 1960, after the Councils of Ministers of EEC and Euratom had provisionally approved the choice of Florence, the Italian government paid 250 million lire for the Villa Tolomei on the edge of the city. Following the Bonn decision of July 1961, the Italian government set up a committee to study the organization of the European University, and in September 1963 it approved a draft law for the creation of the University. In 1963–64, an intergovernmental conference presided over by Cattani created two working groups to draw up a convention on the participation of the other EEC members and the first programs of study. Owing, however, to quarrels among the EEC members as to the character of the University, especially to French unwillingness to finance the creation of an institution devoted to furthering "Europeanism," and to disagreements among academics in Italy itself as to the goals, the negotiations were broken off in 1965. At the summit conference in Rome in 1967, the six agreed to study the project once more.[57]

pean Community. In fact, when he met Adenauer three days later, Fanfani found himself in the odd position of persuading the Chancellor to work along with de Gaulle. "Do you think, Mr. Chancellor," Fanfani asked, "that the European political community can arise, already perfect and armed from head to toe, like Minerva from the head of Jupiter?" "None of us has a Jupiter's head," Adenauer retorted.[58] Italy's position as intermediary seemed to be further recognized with the substitution of Cattani for Fouchet as president of the Study Commission, and it was the Italian proposals that were presented to the meeting of the six foreign ministers in Paris on April 17. The Italians had made two mistakes, however. They gave the Belgians and the Dutch the impression that they had joined the already existing duo of France and Germany in presenting the smaller EEC members with an ultimatum; and they ignored the demand made by the British government in April for full participation in the talks on political union. Thus, the Italian delegation could only watch impotently when Spaak and Luns, the Belgian and Dutch foreign ministers, refused to proceed further with the political negotiations until a decision was made on British membership in EEC. After the dramatic exchange of visits of Adenauer and de Gaulle in July and September 1962, which spotlighted de Gaulle's ambition to create preferential ties with Germany, Fanfani told the British that Italy would not participate in any further discussions on political union until the question of Britain's EEC membership was settled.

The Italians' increasing frustration with de Gaulle caused them to look with greater impatience for a successful end to the negotiations with Britain. Britain appeared more than ever a necessary democratic counterweight to the autocratic behavior of the French President. "Britain represents in the most eminent way a great democratic civilization," wrote the Social-Democratic leader Saragat, "and the countries of western Europe have everything to gain from more intimate contact with it."[59] Of Britain's loyalty to the Atlantic Alliance there could be no question, while de Gaulle's attitude to NATO was disturbingly truculent. But British entry to EEC had also a strictly economic appeal to the Italians. They wanted to see the Community expand to the north, to countries whose markets and products would complement rather than compete with those of Italy, especially since the favored commercial relations with the former French and Belgian colonies and with Greece, and the opening of negotiations with Turkey and Israel, seemed to be linking EEC with regions that were in competition with Italy alone among all the EEC partners. The Italian delegation to the Brussels negotiations with the British therefore sought once more to expedite the discussions by playing the role of practical-minded intermediary—avoiding both the dogmatic intransigence of the French delegation and the overeagerness to compromise of the Benelux representatives. At the end of the first phase of the negotiations (October 1961–April 1962), it was Roberto Ducci (who had already taken an important part in drawing up the Treaty of Rome), who helped get serious discussions started. He isolated the major problems at issue in the report of the ministers' deputies, presented on April 12. The second phase of negotiations (May–August 1962) devoted largely to problems of British Commonwealth preference, opened with discussion of an Italian proposal, the Colombo-Ducci plan, for a temporary extension of Community preference to the Commonwealth countries. By August, agreement had been reached on treatment of Commonwealth industrial products; but when Colombo attempted to mediate the sharp disagreements over Commonwealth temperate-zone agricultural products he had no success. In the third phase of the negotiations (October–December 1962), devoted to a discussion of British agriculture's adaptation to the common agricultural policy, the Italians found themselves caught between the stubborn British refusal to give up their system of deficiency payments on entry to EEC and the French unwillingness to consider any other alternative, and they had to settle for the procrastinating device of appointing a fact-finding commission.

On January 14, 1963, President de Gaulle declared in a press conference that the British, because of their distinctive ways of life, of production, and of trade, were not yet ready for entry into the European Community; and, at the end of the month, the French forced the six to break off the negotiations with Britain. This peremptory action provoked enormous resentment in Italy. Budget Minister La Malfa suggested that Italy should seek special ties with Britain and the Benelux countries.[60] In February, the Italian government joined the Dutch in refusing to sign the new convention with France's former colonies, as a symbolic rebuke to de Gaulle. And the British prime minister and foreign secretary were given an effusive welcome when they visited Rome on February 2–3.[61] Within a short time, however, a more sober reassessment led to the conclusion that Italy could not afford to paralyze EEC, or to seek preferential ties with countries outside it. Italian economic interests demanded that the market continue functioning, even though it be through a process of tough bargaining on mutual concessions, as proposed by German Foreign Minister Gerhard Schröder in April. From 1963 on, therefore, Italian policy followed three principles: to achieve the greatest possible economic integration within the existing structure of the European Communities; to continue pressing for political integration, notably by supporting the fusion of the three executives and the direct election of the European Parliament, and by occasionally reviving plans for political union; and by reiterating at frequent intervals its desire for the admission of new members to the Community.

The futility of these hopes was underlined, however, when de Gaulle interrupted the spate of self-congratulation among the Germans, Italians, and Benelux countries, following the Luxembourg agreement of February 1966. He informed them that, after stripping Commission President Walter Hallstein of his carefully cultivated ceremonial functions, he wanted Hallstein fired from his job with the Commission, presumably because of his attempt, in the crisis over agricultural financing in 1965, to increase the independence of the EEC Commission from the national governments. The occasion for Hallstein's ouster was to be the merger of the Commissions of EEC, ECSC, and Euratom, which had been finally agreed upon by the six governments in 1965 and ratified by the national parliaments a year later.[62] Whereas the Europeans, who had been calling for this merger since 1959, had regarded it as a measure for strengthening the Community administration, de Gaulle obviously intended the enlarged Commission to become what he had always denounced the former executives for being, a body of faceless technocrats, deprived of any political authority and subservient to the national governments. In May 1967, the German government persuaded de Gaulle to allow Hallstein to head the new Commission for six months, but this compromise was so personally insulting to Hallstein that he refused to stay on, and thereby consolidated the Gaullist victory. The summit conference in Rome on May 29–30, 1967, which the Italians had hoped would achieve real progress toward political unity, thus turned into a mockery. At the beginning of May, British Prime Minister Harold Wilson had roused great hopes in Italy with his announcement that Britain intended to apply a second time for EEC membership; on May 14, de Gaulle had destroyed those hopes with a new, barely veiled veto. It was still a No, wrote *Il Messaggero*, even if it was hidden in a bouquet of flowers and not hurled like a paving stone, as it had been in 1963.[63] Throughout the two days of the summit conference, de Gaulle strode like a gigantic monarch through the flag-bedecked palaces, enjoying the diplomatic precedence accorded him as the only visiting head of state. Behind him trailed the heads of government of his five EEC partners; and, far behind all the minor members of the national governments, came the members of the Community executives, spurned in the ceremonials and frequently almost lost in the crowds. The forced optimism of governmental circles carried little conviction in face of the symbolic snub handed the European Community. The French agreed to discuss political union "provisionally," to allow British application for membership to be discussed by the Council of Ministers, and to implement the fusion of the Commissions on July 1, 1967; but most observers felt that these decisions had little value. Even Pope Paul VI, when de Gaulle visited him for a private audience at the end of the conference, felt it necessary to remind the President that "if the nineteenth century saw nationalities become conscious of themselves and form states, the twentieth century—if it does not want to move toward new catastrophes—must see those states join closer in a fraternal understanding."[64]

Thus, after the excitement of the summit conference, Italy relapsed into a state of resignation; it had little hope of strengthening or broadening the European Community, at least as long as de Gaulle remained President of France. It did name deeply committed Europeans to the new Commission—Lionello Levi Sandri, Guido Colonna di Paliano, and Edoardo Martino. In 1969, under the pressure of the Socialist party, the Chamber and Senate, who, to avoid nominating Communists to the European Parliament, had, since 1958, refused to replace even deputies who had died or were not re-elected to the Italian parliament, renewed the Italian nomination of members to the European Parliament; and it created a revolutionary precedent by naming not only members of the governmental coalition but seven Communists and one representative from the Monarchist and one from the neo-Fascist party.[65]

The more active of the remaining federalist groups, the Italian Council of the European Movement and the Council of the Communes, continued to agitate for greater powers to the European Parliament and British membership in the Community. But only the economic aspects of the Community received much attention. As Altiero Spinelli pointed out at the beginning of 1967, Italian foreign policy "has lost its supranational compass bearing without, however, acquiring a national one. This intellectual uncertainty explains in the final resort its inertia and its vagueness."[66]

The first decade of the Common Market had brought enormous economic benefits to Italy. Yet the original ideal that had taken Italy into Europe, the belief in a political union that would safeguard the values of European civilization, seemed to most Italians farther than ever from realization.

II
The Choices Determined

6
The Economic Geography of Italy: Industry

At the end of World War II, Italy was one of the poorest countries in Europe. It lacked almost all the raw materials and sources of power necessary for industrialization. In most sectors, a few large companies exercising semimonopolistic controls dominated a restricted home market that had been isolated from external competition by the autarkic policies of the Fascist regime. The labor movement was internally feuding and in a state of quasi-warfare with its employers. The South and the islands of Sicily and Sardinia were in a permanent economic depression, with per capita income barely 40 per cent of that in the North. Agricultural production had been insufficient to feed the population even before the war.

How could such a country consider integrating its economy with the advanced industrial countries of northern Europe, thus exposing itself to unrestricted competition with some of the most productive countries in the world? Did Italy possess, or would it be able to discover, the natural resources, the supplies of energy, and the industrial and commercial capacity that would enable it to meet the challenge and profit from the opportunity of European economic integration?

ITALY'S INDUSTRIAL RESOURCES

Italy possesses few of the raw materials traditionally considered necessary for industrial growth. Its geological evolution was particularly unfavorable to the creation of those subsoil deposits that encouraged the industrialization of England, Belgium, and Germany. In only five products—sulphur, lead, zinc, mercury, and aluminum—was it self-sufficient.[1] Italy's coal and iron ore deposits were particularly poor. It had only one coal deposit of any size, Sulcis, on the island of Sardinia, which produced about one million tons annually, but the coal was of poor quality and production costs were high. It was useless for coke and therefore for steel production, and was used mainly for thermoelectric power production.[2] The only advantage enjoyed by the Sulcis coal was its local market, in Sardinia and along the Tuscan coast. From the national point of view, the Sulcis mines were a liability rather than an asset. Small deposits of iron ore were located at Cogne in the Val d'Aosta, on the island of Elba and the Tuscan coast nearby, and on Sardinia.[3] Nevertheless, even during the period of Fascist autarky, one-quarter of the ore needed was imported, and by the 1950's one-half was imported, even though 70 per cent of the Italian steel was made from scrap. The ore mines had helped in the foundation of an Italian steel industry, but they were insufficient for any major industrial expansion.[4] From the national rather than the local point of view, Italy's shortage of mineral resources indicated the need for new and secure sources of supply.[5]

Shortage of coal made Italy one of the pioneers in the development of electricity; and the very first power station in Europe was opened in Milan in 1883. In the early twentieth century, the waters of the Alps were harnessed; and the acquisition of the South Tirol in 1919 was followed by establishment in the Dolomites of some of the largest hydroelectric stations in Europe.[6] In 1938, electricity production was so highly developed that it provided 30 per cent of Italy's power requirements. This was especially important, since the introduction into Italy in 1905 of the electric furnace for the making of steel had made it possible to cut down the amount of imported coke needed. Nevertheless, there were clear limits to the quantity of hydroelectricity that could be produced. The water supplies in the Alps and Apennines were divided into many small basins and relatively expensive to exploit; and by the 1950's it was felt that almost all economically feasible sources of waterpower had been harnessed. The electrical companies thereupon turned to thermal power stations, which accounted for one-fifth of the Italian electricity production by 1954. The thermoelectric stations were able to use the Sulcis coal and natural steam deposits; but the main fuel envisaged was natural gas.[7]

Natural gas had been discovered in the 1920's, but it had not been exploited, because it was assumed that separate extraction would jeopardize the adjacent oil deposits. Serious development of the gas deposits only began in 1944, with the discovery of enormous fields of natural gas at Caviaga, 25 miles from Milan and thus ideally situated for industrial use. By 1950, further exploration by the state petroleum company (AGIP) and by many private companies revealed that Italian natural gas was an enormously important new source of power, and one of great richness and versatility. Large fields were opened up in the Po Delta and in the upper Po valley near Milan, while smaller fields were found in the Marches, Basilicata, and Puglia, and on Sicily. The proportion of the country's energy needs covered by natural gas rose from 0.1 per cent in 1938 to 11.6 per cent in 1960.[8] The exploitation of natural gas was thus a major stimulant to Italy's industrial progress and to confidence in the ability of Italian industry to meet the competition of those countries of Europe which had always previously enjoyed superior energy resources.[9]

The shift away from coal was further accentuated by the development of the petroleum industry. No major oil deposits were found in Italy itself until the 1950's, when a small oil field was discovered in the Abruzzi and a larger field at Gela on the southeast coast of Sicily. The state petroleum company concentrated on developing Italy's oil refining capacity, which reached 5.5 million tons by 1955, and on seeking new sources of oil in Iran, Morocco, Somalia, the Sudan, Libya, and Egypt, to free Italy from reliance upon the great foreign companies that dominated the oil industry of the Middle East. Throughout the period following World War II an increasingly large proportion of Italy's energy needs came from petroleum products, their share rising from 23 per cent in 1949 to 55 per cent in 1964. The continent-wide abandonment of coal as the major energy source placed Italy in a position of greater equality with its industrial competitors in availability of cheap sources of power.

MAJOR ITALIAN INDUSTRIES

Italy was a latecomer among the industrial powers. Not until 1956–57 did the number of people employed in industry surpass that in agriculture.[10] Between 1861 and 1914, the construction of a railroad network over the whole country provided a basis for future economic growth; the textile industry pioneered in the introduction of the factory system and mechanization; and, under the stimulus of the railroad and shipbuilding boom, an iron and steel industry and an engineering industry were founded, as well as small cement and chemical industries.[11] The Fascist regime favored those industries that contributed directly to war preparation, such as steel, chemicals, and rubber; but controls over investment, high protective tariffs, and uneconomical development of Italy's raw materials stunted industrial growth and held back modernization of the economy. The destruction inflicted on the country during World War II, amounting to one-third of all Italy's wealth, was felt particularly by the steel, electrical, shipbuilding, and chemical industries. At the end of the war, production of the mines was one-third that of 1938, production of the metallurgical and engineering industries one-sixth, and production of the textile and chemical industries one-tenth.

The Iron and Steel Industry: Two major factors dictate planning of steel production: the high cost of transport of the raw materials and the economies to be achieved by integration of the processes of coking, pig-iron production, steel production, and rolling in one plant, as a result of which heat losses are minimized, scrap produced in the rolling mill can be re-used, and by-products, such as gas, can be sold. In Italy, the high cost of coking coal dictated the use of electric furnaces, while the poor quality of Italian iron ore compelled the wider use of scrap through the Thomas converter and the electric furnace. After the war, however, the state holding company, IRI, which controlled the country's largest iron and steel companies through its sector holding company, Finsider (Società Finanziaria Siderurgica), adopted a new approach to iron and steel development in Italy. In IRI's view, the future growth of the industry was to depend upon imported iron ore of high quality, and home-produced scrap was to be left for the smaller companies. Most steel was to be produced in a few, very large, integrated plants.[12]

In 1950, Finsider President Oscar Sinigaglia, in the plan named after him, resolved the problem of the high cost of transport of raw materials to Italy by locating integrated steel plants on the coast at "tidewater," where they could use cheap sea transportation; huge new freighters could be used for importing coal and iron ore and for exporting finished products. Coastal location of the plants even encouraged the use of the ore of Elba, while capitalizing upon the accessibility of almost every part of Italy to some seaport on the Mediterranean or Adriatic coasts. The greatness of Sinigaglia lay in his proving that a country with little coal or iron ore of its own could produce steel at prices competitive with those countries of Europe possessing coking coal, like Germany, or iron ore, like France.

The Sinigaglia Plan proposed to continue the emphasis on iron ore rather than scrap and to concentrate mass production in three integrated plants: one at Cornigliano, another at Piombino on the Tuscan coast, and a third at Bagnoli near Naples. A new Thomas furnace was to be constructed at Bagnoli. The remaining plants of Finsider were to specialize in particular steel products.[13] The success of the Sinigaglia Plan was dependent upon large capital investments, which were obtained mostly from reinvestment of profits, issuing of new shares, and Marshall Plan funds. Modernization programs were also undertaken by second-rank companies, such as Falck in Lombardy and Fiat in Turin, and by many smaller ones. By 1954, $75 million had been invested in the twenty-one largest steel companies and steel production had risen to 4 million tons. Steel prices in Italy continued to fall during the decade following implementation of the Sinigaglia Plan.[14] The enormously important change in the competitive position of the Italian steel industry was proved by the fact that the price of Italian Siemens-Martin steel dipped below that of Germany in 1962 and below that of France in 1963;[15] and this superiority was enhanced by the completion in 1965 of IRI's integrated steel plant at Taranto, which utilized the newly invented basic oxygen furnace.

The Engineering Industry: The engineering industry originated in Italy with the great railroad boom that lasted from 1861 to the end of the century, with the transition of shipbuilding from wood to steel after the 1880's, and especially with the invention of the automobile. By 1914, although the industry was still in its infancy, some of the great companies were already in operation—Fiat, Lancia, Romeo, and Isotta-Fraschini in automobiles, Olivetti in typewriters, Ansaldo of Genoa and Breda of Milan in heavy engineering. During the Fascist period the industry was diverted from its natural development by the policy of autarky and war preparation, and a vast reconversion was needed after 1945. The postwar Italian government recognized that this industry was of primary importance to all Italian economic progress, gave it a large share of American aid, and intervened directly to favor its reconversion from war production and its rapid expansion. By 1951, the industry was employing 920,168 people, equivalent to 22 per cent of all industrial employment, and its production, valued at 568 billion lire, was 18 per cent of the country's total industrial production.[16] Even more important was the role of the engineering industry in Italy's export trade. In 1926 only 6 per cent of Italy's exports were in engineering products; these rose to 18 per cent in 1950 and to 35 per cent in 1965.[17] In short, after World War II, the engineering industry became the most important branch of Italian production, in numbers employed, in contribution to the export trade, and in capacity for future expansion.

The most important branch of the engineering industry was in the production of motor vehicles. The automobile industry was dominated by the Fiat company of Turin, which accounted for over 90 per cent of all production, especially of mass-produced, low-priced cars, while the remaining companies concentrated on luxury, specialty cars, such as the sports cars of Alfa Romeo or the limousines of Lancia. By 1957, the Italian automobile producers were accustomed to regarding the home market as their own preserve, protected as they were by duties of 45 per cent or more.[18] The expansion of sales in Italy seemed to promise unlimited possibilities, in view of the low rate of "motorization" at the end of the war. As late as 1950, there was only one motor vehicle for every 82 inhabitants. With the rapid industrial development of the 1950's and 1960's, this changed to one for every 15 in 1962. But the amount of motorization varied widely throughout the country: Basilicata, in the extreme South, for example, had only one motor vehicle for every 59 people. There remained great potential for expansion, if the efforts to raise the economic level of the Center and South were successful. The automobile industry catered to the growing Italian market very successfully, with small economical cars; in 1962, over one-half of the cars produced in Italy were 1000 cc. or less.[19] These cars, designed with flair for style and marketed abroad with imagination and drive, became one of Italy's most important exports, accounting in 1955 for 28 per cent of all Italian export trade.[20] In facing the possibility of opening this protected Italian market in return for unhampered access to the markets of western Europe, the Italian automobile industry was bound to have great misgivings. In 1957, the last year before the opening of the Common Market, Italy imported only 5400 cars and exported 119,123. There would clearly be a large increase in imports, if only to satisfy the Italian consumers' desire for variety. The gamble was whether increased sales to the five EEC partners and the growing size of the home market would compensate for the loss of a share of Italian purchases.

The gamble paid off very rapidly. Large-scale investment in new models of automobiles, establishment of service facilities abroad, and aggressive marketing, coupled with highly successful reorganization of production facilities, enabled the Italian automobile companies, and especially Fiat, to sweep the European market. West Germany alone increased its imports of Italian automobiles in larger numbers than Italy's total imports.[21]

A similar situation prevailed in the light engineering industry, where Italian ingenuity and quality of workmanship made remarkable advances in the postwar years. Before the war, Italy had been known for the typewriters and calculating machines of the Olivetti company and the sewing machines of the Necchi company. Both industries received large financial support, especially from Marshall aid funds, and were able to resume and modernize production rapidly.[22] Typewriter production rose from 70,678 in 1947 to 864,536 in 1965; sewing machine production rose from 88,668 in 1947 to 477,031 in 1965.[23] These well-established products were rivaled in importance in the 1950's by new industries catering to the increasingly affluent consumers of western Europe and the United States. After the war it took the domestic appliance industry about twelve years to meet foreign competition in cost and quality; but from the late 1950's Italian products began to conquer the European markets, undercutting both French and German manufacturers in their home markets. A vast range of products were developed, including electric stoves and irons, vacuum cleaners, razors, toasters, fans, and the staples of the industry, washing machines and refrigerators. By 1965, Italy was the second largest producer of domestic appliances in the world, surpassed only by the United States. In 1954 Italy imported 7.3 billion lire worth of appliances and exported only 1.7, a decade later it was exporting appliances for a value of 45 billion lire more than it imported.[24] Of these exports, three-fifths were refrigerators, 900,000 of which were exported. Thus, at the time of the conclusion of the Treaty of Rome, the domestic appliances industry was ready to embark on the conquest of the European market. This industry, which within six years was to surpass the production of Germany and France and, indeed, to drive many foreign appliance companies out of business, was overwhelmingly enthusiastic about the abolition of barriers to its expansion into western Europe.[25]

Support for integration was also expressed by the aeronautical industry. Built up by Mussolini, it had ceased production upon the Duce's fall in 1943; and during the period of reconstruction through 1949, only minimal financing was made available for the renovation of the aircraft factories. In fact, the government decided that, in view of the high development costs and the restricted Italian market, Italy could not afford to maintain a national aeronautical industry. Rather than rely on purchases abroad, however, it was decided that small and medium-sized planes should be produced under license from foreign manufacturers, principally for the needs of the air force. Agreements were made with French and German companies for collaboration in production of aeronautical materials and for exchange of licenses. Although the industry had filled orders valued at about 147 billion lire and was employing 9000 people by 1958, it was perhaps more conscious than any other branch of the Italian economy of the inadequate size of the Italian market, of the insufficiency of research and of funds on a national scale, and of the benefits of close cooperation with other advanced industrial countries. While the most beneficial collaboration had been with the United States and Great Britain, fruitful beginnings had been made in the formation of a French-German-Italian aeronautical industry. In this small but technically important industry, the Common Market found some of its most convinced advocates.[26]

The two branches of the engineering industry most disturbed by the prospects of integration were the shipbuilding and heavy engineering sectors, both of which were in constant difficulties throughout the postwar period. Whereas Italy was prepared to equip its civilian fleet with British, American, and French planes, it was determined to build its merchant ships in Italian shipyards and its generators, turbines, and rolling stock in Italian factories. In spite of vast subsidies paid by the state to maintain its shipping lines, shipyards, and heavy engineering companies, at the opening of the Common Market little had been achieved to make these sectors viable. The shipping companies were costing the government 20 billion lire a year in subsidies, and the shipbuilding program, begun in 1954, received 75 billion a year in state aid. The heavy engineering sector of IRI lost 75 billion lire in the first decade after the war. These forms of state intervention, the deliberate sustaining of industries not economically viable and the accompanying subsidization of maritime transport, were directly counter to the basic philosophy of an integrated Community. As expected, the EEC Commission objected to the subsidies as a falsification of competition, and it demanded their abolition, although it later withdrew its opposition to the shipbuilding subsidy. As a result, a reorganization of both industries was undertaken. This succeeded in reducing their losses, but it did not eliminate them.[27]

Thus, the major part of the engineering industry spearheaded Italy's drive to profit from the opening of EEC, which came just at the moment when the more dynamic companies in the sector were finding the Italian market too small for them.

The Chemical Industry: The third most important branch of industry, and the one destined to have the greatest postwar expansion, was the chemical industry. Even at the time of the 1951 census, it employed almost 200,000 people. The Italian chemical industry, like that of the other industrialized countries, had gone through three historical phases. Before World War I, it had played only a subsidiary role to coal and steel, concentrating on the traditional products of sulphuric acid, copper sulphate, and phosphatic fertilizers.[28] In the 1930's, the industry expanded through the development of nitrogenous fertilizers. In the 1950's, an enormous expansion took place with the production of synthetic resins and plastic materials used in making synthetic rubber, man-made fibers, and various plastic substitutes for metal or wood. This development was closely tied to the exploitation of the by-products of the petrochemical and natural gas industries.

In the postwar years, production of the traditional industrial chemical products increased steadily but slowly; and it became clear that, although these products remained of basic importance to Italy's industrial development, they were not likely to experience any revolutionary expansion. Production of sulphuric acid, needed for innumerable industrial processes, from metallurgy to dyestuffs, attained the prewar level of 1.2 million tons by 1950, and almost doubled during the following twelve years, to reach a level close to that of the United Kingdom and greater than that of France.[29] Other inorganic products, like caustic soda and calcium carbonate, used in various industrial processes, increased at about the same unspectacular rate. The synthetic products, like nitric acid and synthetic ammonia, particularly those that could be made from natural gas, were greatly expanded to meet the demand for nitrogenous fertilizers.[30] Prewar production of nitrogenous fertilizers, 109,000 tons, was exceeded in 1950 and had increased sixfold by 1962.[31] After 1950, production exceeded the needs of Italian agriculture, and Italy became an increasingly important exporter. It was, however, in the production of plastic materials that Italy once again found the ideal field in which to profit from ingenious development of its few natural resources.

Production of plastics in Italy became important only during World War II, and its major expansion came after 1955. Before the war, the most important products had been those made from regenerated cellulose, such as rayon and acetate, which had been used as artificial fibers, replacing wool or cotton. After the war, however, synthetic resins were produced: by polymerization, such as polyethylene, or by condensation, such as polyester, or by the most recent process of polyaddition. The introduction of these new processes revolutionized the chemical industry, and indeed the whole industrial system, by making possible the substitution of vast numbers of natural materials, from wood and iron to silk and rubber. The Italian chemical industry realized immediately the enormous importance of these new products to a country that was so poor in raw materials, and huge investments were made to prepare for the opportunities ahead. This evolution was greatly aided by the rapid and imaginative expansion of the Italian petroleum industry, and especially of the petroleum chemistry sector, which provided much of the raw material for plastics.[32]

The chemical industry was therefore one of the strongest branches of the Italian economy; and its attitude toward integration in western Europe was positive. It depended very little upon Italy's neighbors for raw materials. Its greatest needs were cheap electricity for nitrogen production, which was obtained from the Alpine hydro-electric stations; natural gas, from the Po valley deposits; petroleum, which came largely from the Middle East; and sulphur, of which Italy possessed an abundance. The home market for industrial chemical products expanded steadily with the over-all economic growth; agricultural reform, often state-financed, required ever-increasing supplies of fertilizers; and the vast increase in purchase of consumer goods gave enormous impetus to the production of plastic materials, whether for automobiles, typewriters, refrigerators, or clothing. Prices and quality of Italian chemical products compared favorably with those of the chemical industries of France and Germany, and there was little fear that the Italian producers would be ousted from their home market. Integration opened wider possibilities for export to an industry that was producing far more than the home market could consume.

During the first decade of EEC, Italian chemical production increased 312 per cent, a far larger increase than any other sector of Italian industry and any other chemical industry in the Community. Its exports of plastics and man-made fibers accounted for the major increase in its trade with EEC, although the expanding Italian market and increases in trade with third countries provided an even greater stimulus. The merger of the

Montecatini and Edison companies in 1966, for the express purpose of achieving a company large enough to compare with the great chemical companies of Germany and the United States, gave Italy the eighth largest company in the world, outside the United States.[33]

The Textile Industry: Italian textiles were famous throughout Europe in the late Middle Ages and Renaissance, and, indeed, wool paid for many of the great artistic achievements of the Florence of Lorenzo de' Medici. Only in the late nineteenth century, however, was the industry mechanized, the lead being given by the cotton factories of Piedmont and Lombardy, and by silk manufacture, which reached its height in the early 1900's. By the time of World War I, most of the great textile companies had been founded, such as Lane Rossi at Biella in Piedmont, and Marzotto and Kössler Mayer at Prato in Tuscany.[34] With the concentration on cellulosic fibers in the Fascist period, especially through the rayon production of the Snia-Viscosa company, the industry was able to compensate for the declining importance of wool and silk production and to maintain its working force (650,900 employees in 1951) and its important role in Italian export trade.[35] The industry suffered relatively little damage during the war, and was able to profit in the early postwar years from the great demand for textiles and from the slow revival of its principal competitors in Japan, Germany, Britain, and France.

After a short period of prosperity, however, the industry entered a period of extreme difficulty. Both external and internal factors threatened its continued progress. Traditional markets for Italian woolen and cotton cloth were closed, as many countries in the Middle and Far East and Latin America developed their own textile production and, indeed, began to drive Italian products from those countries that still remained importers. The revival of German, French, and British textile production in Europe, and especially the lightning growth of Japanese production, even challenged the Italian producer in his home market and forced him to lower prices to meet this competition. Italy, moreover, was dependent upon imports for its basic raw materials, cotton and wool. Competition with artificial fibers struck particularly at the silk industry, and compelled the producers to concentrate on the luxury market in western Europe. Internal problems were even greater. First, Italians used relatively small amounts of textiles, owing to the warm climate and the low per capita income. The industry's growth therefore depended upon exports and upon the rising standard of living at home. Second, the industry was only to a minor degree run on a factory basis. The 1951 census showed that of the 413,700 clothing workers, only 50,000 worked in factories, 150,000 were artisans working at home, and the rest did piecework in their homes on goods farmed out to them by the manufacturers. Not only was uniformity of quality difficult to obtain, but this "cottage industry" form of production represented a social problem of exploitation that the left-wing parties were determined to end. Third, as Vera Lutz has pointed out, the rise in labor costs in the textile industry (accompanied as it was by greater foreign competition) led to a reduction of the size of the labor force in textiles and to the abandonment of part of the manufacturing equipment, especially in the cotton industry, as surplus. By reducing employment, especially among women, raising the wages of those still employed, and increasing the capital ratio per worker, the textile industry in particular and all Italian industry in general failed to share the increment in national income with the underemployed or unemployed, who would have spent a significant share of their new income on textiles.[36]

The textile industry was thus in a state of crisis when it came to face the prospect of European integration. For those sectors of the industry already in decline, notably linen, jute, and silk, it offered neither increased competition nor much prospect of wider markets.[37] The cotton industry, which had over a quarter of a million employees in the early 1950's, and was the most important branch of the textile industry, had seen its exports dropping rapidly after 1953. Its reaction had been to begin a modernization of plants and concentration of production, which had helped reduce costs and increase its competitive position. Maintenance of moderate prosperity in the future, however, was regarded as being dependent exclusively upon greater consumption at home, and especially in the South. The woolen industry, on the other hand, whose exports had been hampered by the protectionist policies of western European countries and which felt itself increasingly competitive as a result of conversion from artisan and piece-work to factory production, welcomed the opening of outlets in neighboring countries, especially West Germany.[38] In the decade following the opening of EEC in 1958, Italian cloth again began to win worldwide fame.[39] While Italy could increase its exports of woolen fabrics of good design and high quality, total production could only be expanded slightly, in comparison with the enormous possibilities open to the man-made fiber industry. This newest branch of the Italian textile industry, concentrated in thirteen large companies with only twenty-two factories among them, was able to compete successfully with the highly advanced industries of France and Germany. By 1965 Italy was the fifth largest producer in the world of cellulosic and synthetic yarn; exports of man-made fibers exceeded imports for a value of 95 billion lire; its favorable balance with the EEC countries alone was 18 billion lire.[40] Introduction of mass production into the clothing industry enabled it to profit from the challenge of wider European markets. Exports rose from 24 billion lire in 1960 to 76 billion lire in 1965, with West Germany the principal client.

The textile industries were almost symbolic of the reaction to economic integration. Old, anachronistic branches found their decline accelerated; artisan production declined in favor of mass production in factories; Italian exports prospered where technological ingenuity, quality of workmanship, and understanding of consumers' taste could remedy the lack of raw materials and of a broad industrial base.[41]

Cement and Construction Industries: An efficient cement industry is basic to a country engaged in postwar reconstruction and rapid economic expansion. Through modernization of prewar factories and construction of new ones, the industry reached its 1938 level of production of over 6.5 million tons by 1952, doubled that figure by 1959, and tripled it by 1962.[42] But both imports and exports throughout the postwar years were negligible, and the progress of the industry was clearly tied to the amount of building and public works that the progress of the economy made possible. This was especially true of construction in the South and the Islands, where the greatest possibility of expansion lay. Both housing construction and the creation of an industrial infrastructure in the South were directly related to the wider economic markets offered within EEC and were to be partly financed through the European Investment Bank by the member countries of EEC. The cement industry was therefore interested in European integration indirectly, for integration provided the stimulus to the extension of building activity and hence to increased cement purchases.

The construction industry, with over half a million employees, played an important role in the general level of production and of employment. In the immediate postwar years, its major task was the repair or replacement of war-damaged homes, estimated at 10 per cent of all Italian housing, or some six million rooms. War damage, however, had only accentuated the already existing housing shortage caused by obsolescence of buildings, reduced housing construction in the interwar years, and total suspension of construction during the war.[43] Only by 1951 had Italy returned to the abysmally low prewar figure of one room for every 1.3 inhabitants (compared with one room for every 0.87 in Great Britain); and in the South there was only one room for every 1.7 inhabitants. Government housing programs and the vast investments in housing of the land reform programs and of the Cassa per il Mezzogiorno gave great stimulus to private building activity.[44] Between 1946 and 1950, 1,175,089 rooms were constructed, in 1951–59 another 11 million, and between 1960 and 1967 a further 9 million. By 1961 there were only 1.1 inhabitants per room in Italy; but there still remained an enormous need for housing in the South and the Islands and in the mushrooming industrial cities of the North and Center.[45]

The expenditures on public works, such as roads, railways, dams, and drainage, were about two-thirds of those on housing in 1955. These vast investments, with their enormous impact upon the general economic development of the country, were the direct outcome of planning priorities established by the government—postwar reconstruction from 1945 to 1948; new construction under coordinated planning for the whole country from 1948 to 1950; and economic development plans from 1951 on, to end the imbalance between the different regions of Italy and to raise the living standards of the poor. The prosperity of the construction industry was to a large extent dependent upon the success of these plans, which in turn were drawn up in relation to specific conceptions, held by government leaders and the economists who advised them, of the impact of economic integration upon Italy. The industry was therefore deeply concerned with the possible benefits of European integration upon the general prosperity of Italy, which dictated the level of housing and public works construction, and with the development programs adopted by the government in relation to European integration. Insofar as it believed that integration would benefit the whole of the Italian economy, the construction industry favored it; but it saw no direct benefits for itself in the process.

To sum up, the response of Italian industry to the coming of economic integration was dictated by the extent to which it had succeeded in overcoming the fundamental difficulty of the lack of natural resources at home. Certain branches of industry, such as iron and steel, freed themselves from the fear of competition from other European countries by finding new sources of raw materials and new methods of production. Other industries, most notably the light engineering, chemical, and man-made fiber industries, overcame the lack of home resources by developing, with great technical ingenuity and often fine aesthetic ability, products whose value depended principally upon the value added in the process of manufacturing. Within the industries favoring European integration, one group saw only the indirect benefit in the over-all growth of the Italian economy stimulated by integration, while another group, composed mostly of consumer-oriented industries, believed that the Italian market was too small for them and hoped to find new outlets in western Europe. Integration was feared by a third group of Italian industries—shipbuilding and heavy engineering, among others—that had not overcome Italy's natural inferiority in resources. For them, the loss of a protected home market posed a major threat. It was, of course, the purpose of integration to encourage the dynamic branches of industry and to allow the decadent to decline. Yet this process could not be easily undertaken, for to allow certain old, established industries to disappear would exacerbate both the problem of unemployment and the difficulties of the South. In Italy's case, the logic of integration could not be followed inexorably.

7
Italy's Economic Geography: Agriculture

Although Italy's ability to profit from the economic integration of western Europe was ultimately dependent upon the capacity of its industry to meet the challenge and exploit the opportunity of trade with its new partners, the evolution of Italian agriculture played an equally important, if very different, role in conditioning Italy's response to integration. The central question was whether Italy's agriculture could be transformed sufficiently for it to assume the economically rational character dictated by Italy's soil and climate, labor resources, potential markets at home and abroad, and concurrent industrial expansion, either before or upon entry into an integrated community. This transformation, however, involved the solution of some of the most deep-rooted problems of Italian society—abuse of the land, unwise choice of agricultural production, structural difficulties of ownership and management, overpopulation, shortage of capital, inadequate education, and regional imbalance. Progress in all these areas was a prerequisite for successful adaptation of Italian agriculture to European integration.

TOPOGRAPHY OF ITALIAN AGRICULTURE

As every tourist knows, Italy is predominantly a mountainous country; and one of the most useful classifications for an understanding of its agricultural problems is the division between areas of mountain, hill, and plain. Mountain zones (above 600 meters in height) cover 35 per cent of Italy's land surface, and hill zones (between 200 and 600 meters) another 42 per cent. Less than a quarter of the land is level, and, surprisingly enough, as late as 1956 the level land, or plain, accounted for only one-fifth of the area under cultivation.[1] This extraordinary situation had been brought about by the pressure of population from the mid-seventeenth century on, when more and more of the hill and mountain area was brought under cultivation for wheat. In the century following the unification of Italy, an area of over one million hectares was brought under cultivation, much of it in the mountains.[2] The result was widespread deforestation, plowing up of pasture, reduction of livestock and thus of natural fertilizer, and extensive erosion. In the South, the cultivation of much of the mountain and hill areas thus worsened the already treacherous physical conditions, increasing the number and scale of the floods, landslides, and droughts that are still recurrent tragedies today.

The mountain and hill areas are by no means alike in their character or problems; and it is useful to consider the regional division of Italy into nine agricultural zones, as classified by the National Institute of Agrarian Economy (see map opposite).[3] This division is especially important, since, as Vera Lutz has pointed out, it throws light "on something more than the economic disparities among Italy's farming population: it helps to explain the regional pattern of her industrial development as well."[4] Italy's natural boundary in the North is the great semicircle of the Alps, sweeping from the Tyrrhenian coast near Genoa to include such great peaks as Mont Blanc, the Matterhorn, and the Gran Paradiso group, and ending near Austria in the sharp crags of the Dolomites. This Alpine zone (Zone I) had a little arable land, where wheat, potatoes and grapes were grown, but was mostly devoted to livestock and forestry carried on by small farmers who owned their own land.[5] While scenically superb, agriculturally the area was extremely poor, holdings excessively fragmented, and the standard of living low. The lower slopes of the Alps that merge into the edge of the Po valley and the northern tip of the Apennine chain to the east of La Spezia (Zone II) were relatively prosperous because the small land-owning farmers could devote themselves to market gardening and sell their produce in the large industrial cities near by. The regions of Tuscany, Umbria,

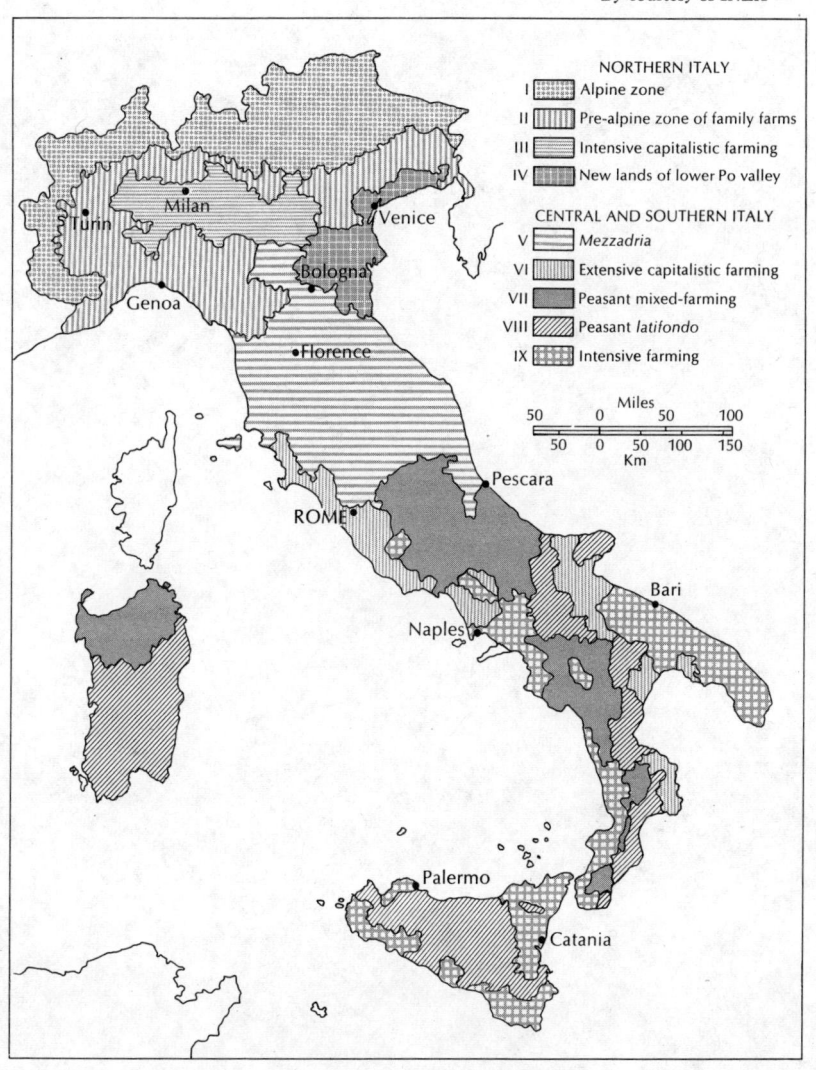

Agricultural Zones

and the Marches (Zone V), dominated by the Central Apennines, are mostly mountain (27 per cent) and hill (68 per cent). Still retaining the placid beauty of a Fra Angelico painting, this region had a prosperous mixed agriculture, based on wheat, grapes, olives, and livestock, up to the past decade. The basis of this prosperity was considered to be the system of mezzadria contracts, by which the peasant farmers shared the produce in agreed proportion with the landlords. Most of these contracts were of many generations' standing, but the mezzadria relationship came under severe attack after the end of the war, and a large number of peasants left these holdings.[6] The agricultural problem was worse in the mountain areas, where many peasants lived an isolated, poverty-stricken existence and survived by subsistence farming.[7]

In the South, less than one-fifth of the land is classified as plain, while 35 per cent is mountain and 46 per cent is hill.[8] The agricultural situation, however, was far worse than in the mountain and hill areas of the North and Center because population pressure and the lack of alternative employment forced the peasantry to bring a far greater proportion of the mountain and hill area into cultivation. In fact, almost one-half of the Southern mountains were cultivated at the beginning of the 1950's, with pitifully poor results.[9] The form of agriculture in the Southern mountains and hills must, however, be further subdivided. The simplest zone to identify lies in the higher stretches of the Southern Apennines, the Gargano Massif, and the Sila mountains (Zone VIII), where the peasants engaged almost exclusively in subsistence farming on plots too small to provide an adequate livelihood. This form of farming also dominated the northern coast and all of the interior of Sicily, and most of Sardinia. Also easily distinguishable, for the very contrast they offer to the poverty of the mountain regions, are the fertile coastal lands of Puglia, northern Calabria, the Campania, and Sicily (Zone IX). In this favored region, olives, grapes, almonds, and especially the highly important cash crops of winter and early spring fruit and vegetables, which could be sold in the North of Italy and the rest of Europe, were grown by independent farmers. These farmers, however, were far too numerous for the small plots they owned. Finally, there was the area of the great estates (latifondi), often, before the land reforms of the 1950's, owned by absentee landlords, and still devoted to "extensive" agriculture—cereals, sheep, and some cattle. This area, the "bare Mezzogiorno," must also be subdivided. The more productive area, known as the "capitalistic latifondo" (Zone VI), although worked by very large numbers of small farmers who owned or leased tiny plots, also was worked on a capitalistic basis in large and medium-sized farms employing wage-labor. Most of Lazio, the region around Rome, the Campania north of Naples, Puglia around the cities of Foggia and Taranto, the western tip of Calabria, and the Metaponto plain of Basilicata made up the region. The area of the "peasant latifondo" (Zone VII), where the large estates were leased in extremely small plots for cash or under sharecropping arrangements, was principally the huge mountain region of the Abruzzi and Molise, western Lazio, Basilicata, and southern Campania. The northern section is the more rugged, and its symbol is the bagpipe-playing shepherd of the Abruzzi, whose annual Christmas incursion into the streets of Rome reminds its citizens of the persistence of a primeval poverty barely two hours' drive from the capital. The southern section is that area of treacherous clay hillsides, malarial valleys (although the malaria was eradicted after 1945), and hilltop villages that was more effective as a place of exile for Mussolini's opponents than any jail, as Carlo Levi has testified in his moving *Christ Stopped at Eboli*.[10]

The Po valley is the only region of Italy where there are large areas of level land for farming. The upper Po valley in Lombardy (Zone III), where reclamation and irrigation has been practiced for almost a thousand years, was distinguished from the rest of Italy in many ways. Wage-labor was used on 40 per cent of the land; workers were trained for specialized tasks and given annual contracts and fairly high wages; capital investment was high. Cattle-raising was a major agricultural activity, accounting for 20 per cent of Italian cattle and one-third of milk production. Most of Italy's rice was grown in the section of Novara and Vercelli; and, through a highly efficient rotation of crops, wheat and corn were alternated with soil-enriching plants for pasture. The upper Po valley was thus the most productive, most technologically advanced area of all Italian agricultural zones, with the greatest possibility of expansion and of profit from integration in a wider

European market.[11] The lower Po valley (Zone IV), comprising the Venetian plain and the Plain of Emilia and Romagna, was only brought into cultivation through vast reclamation projects begun in the 1880's, and is often referred to as the "new lands" of the Po.[12] As a result of the great capital investment involved in working these lands, most of the farms were large, and worked by day laborers (braccianti); but land reform in the 1950's introduced a number of smaller proprietors. Social unrest was caused by the excessive size of the labor force, which resulted in widespread underemployment. The main crops were wheat and corn, sugar beets, hemp and flax, vegetables and tomatoes.

The development of Italian agriculture, and its role within an integrated European agricultural market, was greatly influenced by the topographical divisions just described. A complete reconversion of the mountain areas was imperative. The cultivation of cereals had to be stopped almost entirely in those areas, and the land had to be returned to forest and to natural pasture that could support increased numbers of livestock. In 1964 it was calculated that two-thirds of the inhabitants of the mountain regions of the South would have to leave, and this figure was fairly applicable to the mountain areas of the whole country.[13] It was only in 1952, with the Fanfani "Law for Mountain Areas," that the state provided large-scale financing to aid reforestation and livestock-breeding, to control erosion, and to encourage tourism.[14]

The hill areas also required reconversion to make their agriculture economically competitive. A distinction has to be made between the hill areas where cultivation was "extensive," that is, devoted to cereals (most of Zone VII and VIII), and the "intensively" worked hills (Zones II, V, and IX), where fruit trees and mixed farming predominated. In the former area, more than half the workers would have to leave, mechanization and consolidation of holdings would have to be introduced, and pasture area would have to be increased. In the latter area, there would have to be a reduction of costs and better access to markets, and efforts would have to be made to improve production of specialized products, such as Southern fruits, Sicilian vegetables, and flowers.[15]

Finally, the areas of plain, while presenting their own special problems, would be those in which the greatest expansion of production could be expected. In the traditionally "intensive" farming areas, particularly in the upper Po valley in Lombardy, greater capital investment, mechanization, and reorganization of the distribution system could increase productivity and enable the area to profit from the opening of new markets in EEC. There would be little change in the work force or in the products cultivated. Much the same was true in the few extremely fertile zones of plain in the South, where vegetables and citrus fruit production would be expanded. The relatively small parts of the plain devoted to cereals would have to reduce production costs and introduce a variety of cereals other than wheat. A very difficult situation existed in the reclamation areas of the plain, that is, in the Po Delta, in the Tuscan Maremma, and in about 7 per cent of the arable area of the South.[16] All these areas had in common the continued need for vast government planning and financing, reorganization of ownership through the land reform programs, and large-scale organization of cooperatives for provision of services and for sales.

The creation of a satisfactory standard of living for the Italian agricultural population therefore involved a mass exodus from agriculture to other occupations; the conversion of the mountain areas to forest and pasture; the reduction of cereal-growing in the hill areas, with greater concentration on mixed farming; and the concentration of agricultural production in the highly fertile plains, both in the traditional areas of intensive farming and in the newly irrigated lands.

THE CHARACTER OF ITALIAN AGRICULTURAL PRODUCTION

Cereals: In 1956, 53 per cent of Italy's arable land was devoted to cereal production, although cereals accounted for only one-quarter of the market value of agricultural production.[17] By far the most important was wheat, which had been protected by government tariffs since 1887 and had been especially encouraged by the Fascist "battle for grain" and by compulsory poolings of all wheat production from 1936 on.[18] The decision to continue the wheat pool into the postwar years, first to safeguard the food supply and later to keep up the price paid the producer, helped prolong the excessive concentration on wheat. Production rose from an average of 69,934,000 quintals in 1948-51 to a peak of 98,145,000 in 1958. At that point, the government attempted to force a shift from the production of soft wheat to the production of hard wheat, which was more difficult to grow, more nutritious, and, until recently, the only grain suited to pasta manufacture. Production fell for two years, but by 1965 it had climbed back up almost to the level of 1958. Although the total area devoted to growing wheat had fallen from 5,117,000 hectares before the war to 4,274,634 in 1968, there had been an increase in production per hectare from 14.9 quintals in 1948-51 to 22.4 in 1968. This was brought about by better seeds and fertilizers, and deeper plowing.[19] For rye, barley, and oats, a situation similar to that of wheat prevailed, although one healthy sign was an increase in the growing of barley and oats for livestock feeding.[20]

The situation of other kinds of cereals was by no means so critical, since they were localized in areas where conditions were favorable. Rice, for example, was grown almost exclusively in Piedmont and Lombardy, where the waters of the Po could be used for flooding the fields. The area under cultivation steadily increased through 1954, when production exceeded demand at home and cheaper foreign produce cut into foreign markets. The government intervened to cut down acreage and to maintain prices through a pooling of all production.[21] Production was eventually stabilized at about 6 million quintals. There was little prospect that Italy could compete with the low-cost production of the Asian countries, and therefore Italian producers looked to the European Community to establish preference in EEC. Corn (that is, maize, or granturco) was also a product of Piedmont and Lombardy, but was also grown extensively in the Veneto region, where it was made into "polenta," a local form of corn pudding. The introduction of hybrid seeds after the war raised production enormously without any increase in area under cultivation. Until 1963 Italy was the largest producer of corn in Europe. Since a large proportion of the corn crop was used for animal feed, the increasing importance of livestock production could be expected to stimulate further corn production.

At the time when the member governments of the EEC were discussing the establishment of a common market for cereals and a Community price (1960-64), an important debate was going on in Italy over the future course to be followed in cereal production. At one extreme were the supporters of continued emphasis on wheat production. They argued that wheat would remain the basic food in Italy for many years and that home production should not fall below consumption; that technical progress was making possible a reduction in the area devoted to cereals; that a high grain price was a necessary support to the farmer; and that large areas were not suitable for conversion to livestock production. At the other extreme were those who proposed buying much of the cereals needed abroad at the low world price, thereby ending the uneconomical production of wheat and making livestock feeding economical. The view of the government and its economic advisers was that, with the rise in productivity per hectare on the fertile land, the reduction of area under cereal cultivation should be accelerated, particularly in the million hectares of mountain land under grain. Livestock production should rise by 33 per cent. Farm revenues should be increased, not by enforcement of a so-called "political price" for wheat, but by reduction of costs and orientation of production toward market demand.[22] These principles were adopted in the first agricultural plan, the Green Plan of June 1961, which provided large funds to aid the conversion from cereals to livestock, and they were carried on in the Second Green Plan of 1965.[23]

Until this program was well under way, the excessive importance given to cereal production was a major deterrent to Italy's approval of the integration of European agriculture. In 1964, the French price for wheat was 2000 to 3000 lire per quintal below the government-supported price in Italy. With the abolition of the wheat pool, which was required after the establishment of a common agricultural policy, and the establishment of a Community cereals price, many Italian cereal producers expected to be driven out of production, with a consequent worsening of the problems of unemployment and regional imbalance. On the other hand, many economists feared that a high community price would perpetuate the concentration on cereals. Solution of the problem of cereal production was therefore basic to the entry to Italian agriculture into a common agricultural market.

Livestock Production: For Italy to achieve a high level of livestock production, several major changes had to occur. A general rise in personal income as a result of successful industrialization had to provide the consumer with the necessary cash to improve his diet by shifting from cereals to meat and milk products. Conversion of land planted in cereals to fodder crops in natural or irrigated pasture, erection of new farm buildings, and the acquisition of herds would require large capital investments and a reduction in the size of the agricultural population. Technical education would be needed, especially in the South, to enable the peasants to make the shift from the fairly simple process of growing wheat to the far more complicated one of raising livestock. The distribution system would have to be completely transformed, to cut costs and to balance supply and demand; and production costs would have to be cut, in order to make it profitable for a farmer to raise livestock.[24]

From 1948 on, economic boom made possible the beginning of the desired shift to greater consumption of meat and dairy products. Annual meat consumption rose from 19 kilograms per person in 1952–53 to 38 in 1967–68. Milk consumption rose from 49 to 68 kilos, and cheese from 6 to 10 kilos.[25] These figures were, of course, still extremely low compared with those of other western European countries. With continuing economic progress, however, the Italian consumer could be expected to emulate his better-fed neighbors, although he had little prospect of overtaking them. The prospect of growth in Italian meat and dairy product consumption was a further justification for a rapid expansion of livestock production.[26]

The increase in fodder crops, which, in addition to large imports, was necessary for raising more livestock, proved to be one of the most difficult problems to solve. Measures to cut wheat production and the flight of many farmers to the cities enabled much mountain and hill land to revert to pasture; but, because of poor climate and soil in most of Italy, the yield in grass and other fodder crops was low. To compensate, large supplies of mass-produced animal fodder high in protein and carbohydrates, notably hybrid corn, would be needed, since in 1954 it was calculated that there was a deficit in animal fodder of about one-ninth of the total needed.[27] By 1965, with 10.3 million hectares devoted to fodder, compared with 9.5 in 1953, production had risen from 341,937 quintals to 414,140.[28]

Construction of farm buildings was aided by the land reform agencies and the Cassa per il Mezzogiorno and by a series of government credit measures. In 1957, a small fund of 5 billion lire was made available to develop livestock production. There were no customs duties imposed on animals imported for breeding purposes, and minimum prices for meat were instituted in 1959. Technical assistance and professional instruction, which had fallen badly from the high level they had had at the turn of the century, were slowly improved in the postwar years through both government and private action.[29] During the 1950's there was a marked change in both quantity and quality of livestock, with significant increase in the numbers of dairy cattle and pigs.[30] Nevertheless, livestock production failed to keep up with the increased demand at home, and throughout the postwar years imports of meat products were needed more and more. By 1962, Italy had become as large an importer of meat and animal products as Germany, and had no possibility of covering more than half of its deficit by increases in home production.[31]

Thus, the prospects for rapid development of Italian livestock production were good, because of increasing demand, government pressure to shift from cereal to livestock production, and the greater suitability of livestock rearing to much of Italy's agricultural areas. However, this increase in production could be halted by the opening of a common market for livestock within EEC, if Italian producers were unable to meet the competition of other member nations. The opening of the common market for livestock was therefore an important stimulus to much needed improvements in rural education, to land improvement and structural reform programs, and to greater capital investments in livestock production.

Milk and Other Dairy Products: Consumption of milk and other dairy products had always been low, and so a great expansion could be expected with the postwar rise in incomes. Production increased constantly, but it failed to keep up with demand. Throughout the postwar years, imports of milk and butter exceeded exports by increasingly large amounts, and in 1958 for the first time imports of cheese exceeded exports. There was clearly an important home market for increased production. Italian production could only be increased through solution of great technical problems, however. The quality of Italian livestock had to be improved through importation of selected breeding animals; but this process was very long and arduous. Although the dairy farms of Lombardy could compete successfully with the highly organized dairy industries of Holland and of France, in the rest of Italy the poor quality of Italy's cattle, as well as unsatisfactory sanitary and hygienic conditions, restricted production and raised costs.[32] Greater technical aid from the state and improved agricultural training and education were needed. Finally, the South lagged far behind the North in livestock rearing. Although there was a slow but fairly steady increase in the amount of animal fodder and in the number of animals produced in the South and the Islands, the North and Center produced more than three-quarters of the total fodder and maintained just under three-quarters of the total livestock in Italy.[33] In spite of some improvement, the hostile character of the land in the South and the Islands, and even in parts of the North and Center, was the greatest opponent of agricultural conversion.

Throughout the 1960's, the Italian dairy industry slumped, because Italian producers did not find it profitable to try to meet the growing demand for dairy products, owing to their own high costs of production and the lack of any state subsidy and price support similar to those enjoyed by other western European countries. In 1962-63, Italian milk production was sharply reduced, and producers began to cut the size of their dairy herds. While a rise in prices reversed this trend, the incident was sufficient to show the precarious margin within which the Italian producer worked. Competition within EEC could easily throw Italian producers back into crisis and, by precipitating a new reduction in dairy herds, run counter to the basic aim of all postwar Italian agricultural policy. Italy was therefore interested in gaining time to carry through the needed improvements in production methods and in receiving Community aid to do so.

Fruit and Vegetables: Whereas beef and dairy production interested the North above all, the production of fruit and vegetables was of major interest to the South. From the EEC point of view, it was the one sphere in which Italy played a predominant role.

Until the beginning of the 1950's, Italy was assured of primacy in citrus fruit production. Geography and climate seemed to have given it the role of Europe's supplier of oranges, tangerines, and lemons, for its sole prewar competitor, Spain, sent its whole supply to the United States market. For a brief period after the war, Italian citrus fruit was again in great demand; but by 1950 the Italian producer was in serious trouble. Competition from the renovated orchards of Spain and the new groves of Israel, Tunisia, and Algeria, as well as from Brazil, Chile, and the United States, was driving the Italian producer from his traditional markets.[34] Against the high-quality, homogeneous, and carefully packaged products of his competitors, the Italian producer could only offer a vast variety of badly packaged products of uncertain quality. This crisis was particularly dangerous because it struck at the poorest areas of the country, where unemployment was already great; the Islands and the South produced 99 per cent of the lemons, 95 per cent of the oranges, and 98 per cent of the tangerines.[35]

The necessary remedies were, once more, expensive and slow. The lack of uniformity in the types of fruit could only be solved by reduction of the large numbers of small holdings and by new plantings in the orchards. But the biggest problem lay in the distribution system. Some 550 companies handled the distribution of citrus fruits, from the purchase from the farmer to the final sales, and 400 of these companies were in Sicily alone. Many small middlemen operated as well, with inadequate transportation, packaging facilities, and storage, causing damage to the product and loss to themselves and the farmers. There was poor information on the needs of the importing countries, and too often the bulk of the citrus crop was exported at low prices at the height of the season.[36]

In this situation, the opening of a common market for citrus fruit seemed a godsend to Italy, for it was the only large-scale producer within the Community. The citrus producers therefore welcomed EEC, but fought vigorously against the conclusion of association agreements with France's Mediterranean territories or former colonies, such as Algeria and Tunisia, and later demanded defense against citrus imports from newly associated countries, such as Greece. Fear of Spanish agricultural competition was an important factor in making the Italian government oppose that country's association with EEC. Widening of the Community to include Britain and the Scandinavian countries was regarded as a necessary opening of more northern markets to the Mediterranean products of Italy, as well as a recompense for admission of other Mediterranean countries to the Community.

Before the war, the three centers of Italian non-citrus fruits were the Alto Adige area, the area around Ferrara, and the coastal plain of Campania; but while these regions retained their primacy, fruit growing expanded throughout the country in the postwar years, and technical improvements greatly raised productivity. Of the wide variety of fruits grown, four expanded at an exceptional pace—peaches, pears, apples, and table grapes—while the traditional dried fruits, such as figs and prunes, were in decline. By the mid 1950's, in spite of growing home consumption of fresh fruits and the development of an efficient canning and bottling industry, about one-sixth of Italian fruit production had to be exported, West Germany being by far the largest customer.

The Italian fruit producer would profit from the opening of the agricultural common market, but only if he met several important conditions. Methods of production in the South and the Center had to be brought up to the high technical perfection of those in the North; better refrigeration facilities had to be constructed; and higher and more uniform standards had to be observed in the production, selection, and packaging of the fruit. The prospects for expanded exports were enormous, and the possible profits very high.[37]

Only 6 per cent of the Italian vegetable crop was exported. This situation was caused by a great increase in home consumption of fruit and vegetables; by the failure of Italian producers to meet the uniform quality standards required by importers; and especially by the failure of the distributors to profit from the long growing season in Southern Italy to supply the European markets with early spring vegetables. Prospects for expanded sales at home and abroad were good for the more delicate vegetables, such as peas, asparagus, artichokes, and tomatoes, while consumption of potatoes and cabbage declined. The tomato industry in particular had great prospects of growth, since Italy produced 85 per cent of the tomato crop in EEC.[38]

In spite of these difficulties, the Italian fruit and vegetable producers had a great stake—indeed, the major interest of all Italian farmers—in the opening of wider markets in Europe. Italy's soil and climate was perfectly suited to the production of all types of fruit and vegetables at the times of year when they were most in demand north of the Alps. Large numbers of workers were employed in this sector—750,000 in 1955—so that its influence in reducing agricultural unemployment was very important. The contribution of the sector to Italy's balance of trade was vital, since fruit and vegetables accounted for 13 per cent of all exports in 1955. Finally, the fruit and vegetable trade played an important part in the income of the South: in 1964, of all Italian production, the South and the Islands produced 52 per cent of the potatoes, 56 per cent of the tomatoes, 72 per cent of the artichokes, 57 per cent of the cauliflower, and virtually all of the citrus fruits.[39]

Industrial Crops: Italy had two important industrial crops—sugar beets and tobacco. The continual increase in consumption of sugar in the postwar years was the principal factor not only in stimulating greater production of sugar beets in the traditional area of the Veneto and Emilia, but in encouraging its spread to other parts of the country, including the South. By 1955, the area under beet cultivation was double that used prior to World War II; and until 1960 production exceeded the home demand for sugar. From then on, however, between one-quarter and one-third of Italy's sugar supply was imported, to satisfy the demand that had risen from the prewar 7 kilograms per person per year to 25 kilos by 1964–65.[40] The difficulty of the Italian sugar producer was thus not the lack of a home market, but his inability to produce at costs comparable to those of other European countries. The Italian soil and climate are unfavorable to the growth of sugar beets, as the dry summers cause a reduction of the sugar content of the beet. The great variety of soils and climatic conditions throughout Italy where the beets were grown had prevented the development of seeds most adapted to Italian conditions. In 1964–65, Italian production was only 50 quintals of sugar per hectare, compared with 67 in France and 82 in the Netherlands. Prices were correspondingly higher—1191 lire a quintal in Italy compared with 1123 in the Netherlands and only 807 in France.

Yet the world price for sugar was less than half the French price! The Italian sugar beet producer was therefore concerned with maintaining a high price for sugar in the Community, so that he would not be driven out of production by the French producer. But because high prices for sugar would impose an unacceptable financial burden on the Community as a whole, since the export of surplus production at the world price had to be subsidized by the Community, the Italian producers pressed for the application of national quotas on the area to be devoted to sugar beet production. At the same time, they demanded national and Community aid to improve the yield and lower the production cost of Italian sugar. Italy was thus in the paradoxical position of defending high prices and reduced production of sugar, while, as the only member of EEC with a deficit in production, it should, logically, have been importing the surplus production of other members.[41]

Tobacco cultivation began on a large scale in Italy only in the twentieth century, with the development of various plant types suitable to the different regions of Italy. Production, intended largely to cut the financial burden of tobacco imports, increased from a prewar high of 425,000 quintals to 903,000 in 1959, to satisfy the growing needs of Italy's smokers, who boosted their consumption from 785 grams per person in 1948–49 to 1147 grams in 1960–61 and total consumption from 36 million kilograms to 59 million.[42] The market for tobacco was falsified by the State Monopoly, however, which bought all tobacco produced at guaranteed prices and contributed a large share of the profits to the Italian state.[43] This situation, though burdensome to smokers, was very satisfactory to the tobacco producers, who had no interest in seeking markets abroad or in opening the Italian market to competition. The Monopoly tended to maintain a sector of agriculture in need of modernization; and the tobacco producer allied with the Italian government in demanding that a Community agricultural policy maintain this state of affairs on a Community basis.

Two Problems—Wine and Olives: Italy made one-quarter of all the wine consumed in the world. Even so, the winemakers had problems. Unlike France, Italy imposed no controls upon the production of wine, such as restriction to particular geographical areas, prescription of type of grape to be planted, or government authorization to plant; nor did it follow the French example of paying vineyard owners to allow land planted in old vines to go out of cultivation.[44] As a result, under the stimulus of exports and of rapidly growing consumption of wine at home, an impressive increase of wine production took place throughout the country; but this production lacked quality control and thus lacked the commercial advantage of recognized labeling practices. Nor was quantity coordinated with demand. During the first postwar decade, the wine producers found little difficulty in selling their products, and production by 1955 had reached 58 million hectolitres, compared with 38 million before the war. In 1956, however, when production hit a record for the preceding half-century, 63 million hectolitres, some 5 to 6 million could not be sold. In 1958, with production even higher (68 million hectolitres), wholesale prices tumbled 28 per cent; and in five of the next eight years production exceeded 66 million hectolitres. Wine production would be in crisis, the Coltivatori Diretti predicted in 1958, whenever production exceeded 54 to 55 hectolitres.[45]

At the opening of the Common Market in 1958, Italian winemakers were therefore facing a crisis of overproduction. Several factors promised relief. The Italians continued to consume more wine. Per capita consumption, which had risen from a prewar figure of 85 litres a year to 95 by 1952, reached 125 litres in 1965. Exports expanded at a very high rate, from 905,000 hectolitres in 1950 to 1.5 million in 1958 and 2 million in 1965. Yet even this amount was relatively small compared with total production of 69 million hectolitres; and Italian producers were determined to develop new markets in western Europe. To profit from free competition in the wine trade within EEC, and to increase exports to third countries, several basic changes had to be made in the system of Italian wine production and marketing. First, order had to be brought into the confusion of Italian productive methods, by installation of a vineyard register, an annual declaration of volume yield and of stocks, and, above all, some form of government supervision over the demarcation of the region of production of quality wines. The Italian government and agricultural groups had recognized this need but, unlike the French, had made little progress in implementing the necessary laws when the European Community turned in 1961 to the organization of the market for vine products. Once these measures had been taken, the production of quality wines, for which there was a large market, would have been encouraged; fraud would have been made more difficult; and measures could be taken for adjusting production to demand. A more difficult problem was reducing costs of production while raising quality. The abandonment of about 10 per cent of the poorest quality vineyard land by the flight of the farmers to the cities in the 1960's had to be followed by further transfer of production from the hills to the plains, where productivity was greater and grape quality better. Cooperatives of wine producers were needed on a larger and more efficient scale. New production each year had to be regulated on the basis of the declaration of stocks remaining from previous years. The Italian producer demanded aid in making these changes, both from his own government and from the European Community.[46]

The regional variations in wine production in the postwar years emphasized the importance of general economic factors as well as the suitability of land, the "vocazione delle terre," to quality wine production. The greatest expansion occurred in Veneto, which had excellent cooperatives, and whose best wines—Bardolino, Valpolicella, and Soave—enjoyed proximity to the markets of the big Northern Italian cities and to Germany and Austria. Those around Trapani in Sicily expanded production, largely because of the popularity of Marsala, the dessert and cooking wine, and because the small proprietors of the region found conversion from wheat to grapes tripled their income. The growth of the population of Rome stimulated production of the light white wines of the Castelli Romani in the nearby hills of Lazio, where the main occupation of some 270,000 people was in wine production.[47] Wine production in Tuscany and Umbria, whose Chianti and Orvieto wines were perhaps the two Italian wines best known abroad, remained fairly stable. Several regions were in difficulties, however, and for totally different reasons. In the Campania around Naples, in spite of the suitability of the soil and climate to grape-growing, the wine industry was stifled by local monopolies, lack of credit facilities, and lack of cooperatives. In Puglia, with one-quarter of Italy's vineyards, the traditional markets in northern Europe for low quality wines, used as a base for sparkling wines or brandies, had been reduced by the development of concentrated musts.

Most surprising of all, however, was the reduction of vineyards in the Piedmont area, which not only produced Italy's best table wines—Barbaresco, Nebbiolo, Grignolino, and the pride of Italian wines, Barolo, as well as the sparkling wines of Asti—but had an efficient cooperative organization and easy access to the markets of the industrial triangle of Turin, Genoa, and Milan. It was the very proximity to this area that made it easy and tempting for the farmers to abandon their vineyards and to find better paying employment in the cities. It was doubtful whether new markets in northern Europe would have much influence in saving the Piedmont wine industry.[48]

The plight of the olive cultivator provoked an unusually biting condemnation in the annual report of the president of the Coltivatori Diretti in 1958. Italy, he pointed out, was the world's major olive producer, with 160 million olive trees, many of which were hundreds of years old; yet Italy did not produce enough olive oil to satisfy even home consumption. The reasons were obvious: "For many, olive cultivation is still an unguided activity, subject to great losses from parasites, from unseasonable cold spells, from thoughtless pruning and harvesting." Modern methods could raise production to 300 to 400 kilos of olives a tree, but the Italian average was barely 8 kilos![49] More suitable lands had to be planted in olive groves, and those existing groves worth renovation had to be defined. Only through these reforms could Italy hope to produce the high-quality oil needed to open up new export markets and to meet the competition of other vegetable oils and of animal fats. Barely 30 per cent of Italian oil was of sufficiently high quality to be worth exporting, however, and only about half could be classified as "fine quality." The oilseed products, such as peanut or safflower oil, had conquered half of the Italian market for oils by 1960, and their use was increasing far faster than that of olive oil. In western Europe, however, only between 5 and 10 per cent of vegetable fat needs were covered by home production. The Italian olive oil producer was worried not by competition from within EEC, but from outside. The problem of olive production was therefore to make it more uniform, of higher quality, and of lower price; and a double stimulus to do this was fear of competition from other vegetable oils and the prospect of lucrative markets at home and within EEC for high-quality products.

From the Community point of view, the Italian olive oil problem had two possible solutions. On the one hand, the problem could be regarded as specifically Italian, and the Italian government could be permitted to maintain national protection against olive oil imports from third countries, against other vegetable oils, and even against animal fats from within the Community, a solution in conflict with the purpose of integration. On the other hand, the Community could accept full responsibility for a common market in all animal and vegetable fats and oils, and agree to take financial responsibility for the renovation of Italian olive oil production. This was the method eventually adopted, to the gratification of the Italian producers.[50]

STRUCTURAL PROBLEMS OF ITALIAN AGRICULTURE

For Italian agriculture to achieve its optimum character in relation to the country's economic and social needs and to its opportunities within an integrated European community, it would not be sufficient solely for the changes in land use and in choice of crops already outlined to be carried out. Major changes would be needed in what is called the "agricultural structure" (strutture agricole)—that is to say, in the pattern of land-ownership, in the organization of the individual farms as working units (imprese agricole), in the forms of land tenure, and in conditions of labor-hiring. As Professor Corrado Bonato pointed out to the Coltivatori Diretti in 1967, the ideal, which Italy was far from achieving, would be a farm "with the optimum combination of productive factors, operated by a professionally trained and dedicated entrepreneur who, with adequate information services at his disposal, would be in a position to make informed choices either with regard to the quality and volume of production or with regard to the quality and quantity of the productive methods to be used. A farm of this kind would be in a position to produce at the minimum cost, other things being equal, and is characterized—at a given situation and time—by a certain optimum size."[51]

The Fragmentation of Agricultural Ownership: In 1947, Italy was the unenvied leader in western Europe in the number both of extremely small properties and of extremely large ones. Holdings of less than 5 hectares accounted for 31 per cent of all the land in private hands, while there were an astounding 5 million properties of less than half a hectare (one hectare being 2.47 acres). At the other extreme, properties of 100 hectares or more accounted for 26 per cent of the land, and these were owned by only 21,300 people.[52] Many of the small properties were the result of the subdivision of land among a farmer's sons, and in some cases the original property continued to be worked as a unit. Many of the others were owned by city-dwellers, to whom it represented a small source of additional income, or by day-laborers, who supplemented their meager earnings with the produce of these scraps of land. No one could make a satisfactory living by cultivating only one portion of land of less than five hectares, although many tried. The existence of these tiny property holdings was a great burden on Italian agriculture because they were rarely brought through leases into consolidated, viable farming units. "In the regions in which small or minute properties predominate," Alessandro Silj concluded, "the chances for any farm to organize production rationally, to make use of modern techniques, and, in short, to increase productivity . . . are little or none."[53]

Government action was directed against the large properties, however, for obvious political and social reasons. While many large properties in the upper and lower Po valley were efficiently organized and highly capitalized working units, the latifondi of the South were worked "extensively," with few laborers, to produce low yields of cereal crops, were subdivided into many small, inadequate farms, and leased to unskilled peasantry, or were simply neglected. When land reform was finally enacted in 1950, it was applied mainly in the area of "capitalistic latifondo" in the South: 759,000 hectares were expropriated, and by 1960 618,000 had been redistributed to 109,000 families in units averaging 5.7 hectares in size.[54] The result was a diminution of the total number of large properties in Italy, and a corresponding increase in the number of small properties. Unfortunately, the reform did not increase the number of medium-sized farms of between 40 and 50 hectares, which most European agrarian economists consider to be the healthy size for a family farm in Europe.[55] Other measures also helped increase the number of small properties. The Law in Favor of Small Peasant Property, passed in 1948, which was accompanied by the foundation of the Fund for the Formation of Small Peasant Property, and followed by a series of similar provisions, enabled the peasantry to acquire more than 800,000 hectares by 1958.[56] Most Italian economists agree that these measures, however necessary socially, were not justifiable in purely economic terms; and as early as 1957 the Coltivatori Diretti, the voice of the small peasant proprietor, admitted that the structure of Italian agriculture was not "in harmony with the goals of the European Common Market" and that "the pathological aspects characterizing peasant property in Italy are alarming."[57] Fragmentation, accompanied by "dispersion" of holdings, that is, the cultivation by one farmer of widely scattered pieces of land, while a problem in all parts of the country, was at its worst in the poorest, most overpopulated sections.[58]

Structural Deficiencies of the Working Farm: According to the agricultural census of 1961, the first ever held in Italy, there were 4.27 million farms in Italy, composed of 15.65 million separate pieces of property. Only 1.7 million farms were on one consolidated piece of property; 2.28 million were made up of 2 to 10 pieces of property, 174,368 of 11 to 20 pieces, and 68,452 of 21 or more pieces! The phenomenon of "dispersion" had reached fantastic proportions.

Consideration of the main three forms of farm enterprise will help explain this disturbing situation. By far the most predominant type of farm enterprise was that run by the coltivatore diretto, the working farmer, who, with the help of his family, cultivated land that he either owned or leased. The average size of these farms was only 3.8 hectares, but they covered almost exactly half of Italy's cultivated land, and provided the worst problem for agricultural reformers.[59] Capitalistic farms run with wage-labor and sharecroppers, averaging 28 hectares, covered 35 per cent of the land, and provided the one sector of Italian agriculture whose productivity could rival that of the best farms of northern Europe. Finally, 12 per cent were share tenants (mezzadri) who were supplied with farmland and buildings by a proprietor who usually shared in the provision of livestock and received under contract a fixed proportion of the year's produce, usually one-half (lowered to 47 per cent in 1948). This form of enterprise was predominant in Emilia-Romagna, the Marches, Tuscany, and Umbria.

From the structural point of view, the crying need in the 1960's was to solve the problem of the coltivatore diretto, by creation of consolidated working farms of an adequate size with the necessary financial and technical backing.[60] The trend indicated by the census, toward farms composed of land partly owned by the farmer and partly leased, was healthy, as this was proof of the farmers' own attempt to create a viable working unit; and the Green Plans of 1961 and 1965 provided large funds to enable farmers to own their land. The major factor that promised an early solution, however, was the movement of the rural population to the cities, with the corresponding fall in the number of workers engaged in agriculture and the freeing of land for consolidation into adequate farms. The Italian Statistical Institute's statistics show that the number of workers engaged in agriculture in Italy dropped by almost half between 1931 and 1964, while during the same period the total Italian population increased from 41 to 52 million (see Table 2).[61] By the mid 1960's a third of a million people were leaving the land each year. Thoughout Italy the spectacle of abandoned holdings in the midst of fragmented farms that were still being worked provided dramatic evidence of the structural problem, as well as of the way it could be solved. Consolidation of holdings into viable economic units was possible at last, particularly in those areas of mountain and hill where climatic and soil conditions dictated a small working population engaged in "extensive" agriculture and forestry.

Government and EEC aid would have to be on a very large

Table 2. Working Population by Economic Sector
(Size in Thousands, and Percentages)

	1931 Size	%	1951 Size	%	1964 Size	%	1968 Size	%
Agriculture	9,356	51.0	8,261	42.2	4,967	25	4,218	22.1
Industry	5,730	31.0	7,075	36.1	7,996	41	8,005	46.1
Total Working Population	18,341		19,577		19,581		19,035	

scale, however, and would have to take into account many social problems arising from the rural exodus. The majority of those leaving the land were the young and skilled, the women, and the children. Many of those who abandoned tiny parcels of land refused to sell them, but preferred to keep them unworked as a personal insurance against the loss of industrial employment. The change was far less marked in the South, where fragmentation was at its worst and productivity of agriculture was lowest. In 1964, 54 per cent of the population of Basilicata, 46 per cent of the Abruzzi-Molise, 45 per cent of Puglia, and 44 per cent of Calabria were in agriculture. In the South and the Islands, 38 per cent worked in agriculture, compared with 24 per cent in the Center and only 19 per cent in the North. While change was feasible, it would be far from easy.

The Dispute over Agrarian Contracts: Disputes over mezzadria in the first decade after the war concerned the nature of the contract between proprietor and farmer, but, as Professor Mario Bandini pointed out as early as 1952, these disputes were really caused by the fact that the relationship itself had become an anachronism.[62] The usual form of mezzadria, which dated back to the thirteenth century, was the lease by a farmer and his family of a complete farm unit, with farmhouse, outbuildings, and livestock (which the farmer might have a share in providing).[63] The annual produce was customarily divided in equal parts between the farmer and the landowner, although much cheating occurred at the time of the division. At its best, the system gave the peasant a pride in land his family had held for generations; and it was encouraged by Mussolini, who felt it brought social stability to the countryside. The need for reform had been recognized at the end of the nineteenth century, but all reform projects had languished in parliamentary committees. During the war, however, the termination of mezzadria contracts, whose length had previously been fixed by the Civil Code as one year, was not permitted, and the postwar governments simply carried on this ban during the long battle over formulation of a new mezzadria policy.

The mezzadri were well organized, particularly by the Communist trade unions, and their vote was a major reason for the

Communist predominance in Tuscany, Umbria, and the Marches. Opposition to their demands for longer and more secure contracts and for a greater share of the produce was strong, however, in the right wing of the Christian Democratic party and in all the parties of the Right. It was led by Confagricoltura, the union of the larger landowners. As a result, all efforts at reform were blocked in parliament. De Gasperi succeeded in 1948 in raising the peasant's share of the produce to 53 per cent; but only in 1964 did the Center-Left government of Amintore Fanfani abolish sharecropping altogether. By this law, no new mezzadria contract could be made and no old contract renewed. When a contract expired, the landowner would be compelled to sell the land, with the mezzadro given first choice at buying. The government would provide low-interest loans to enable the peasant to buy the land and to stock it with animals and seed, and he could appeal to the local agricultural agent to arbitrate the purchase price.[64] By the time the law was passed, however, the mezzadria problem had changed its character. The rural exodus had been very great in the mezzadria areas. By 1964, the problem was to keep the peasant on the land with material inducements to rival the appeal of the cities, rather than to safeguard his right to hold the land; and in the hill and mountain areas, land vacated by the mezzadri was often combined in large farms employing hired labor. In the 1960's, therefore, the mezzadria problem was well on its way to solution, and could not be said to be a major disadvantage for Italy in the common agricultural market of EEC. Where the mezzadro bought his land, however, he did add to the problem of the inability of many coltivatori diretti to run viable farms; where he abandoned the land, he raised an entirely new problem for Italy—that of good agricultural land left idle for lack of farmers.[65]

The Problem of the Hired Farm Laborer: Hired farm laborers comprised more than a quarter of the total agricultural population during the 1950's. Of this group only about 32 per cent were classified as permanent workers (salariati), even though a man had to work only 150 days a year to enter this class. Many of the permanent workers were employed in the North, in skilled jobs, were paid wages comparable to those in Northern industry, and jealously fought any effort to link their wage structure to that of the temporary or day laborers. The situation of the day laborers—the braccianti—who had nothing to offer but the strength of their arms, was pitiful. Those workers, who numbered a million and a half in 1959, were employed mostly at peak periods of the year, at wages below even the legal minimum.[66] They were forced to spend innumerable hours waiting around in the village square for the chance of employment, or filling their hours of unemployment by foraging in the mountains or fields for brushwood, or for a scrap of food to feed their families. Their plight is best described in their own words, in the heartbreaking pages of Danilo Dolci's *Poverty in Sicily*.[67] This underemployment represented a terrible waste of manpower; the OECD calculated that, in 1958 alone, 1.7 million day laborers did the full-time work of only 517,803 workers.[68]

The flight from the rural areas did not solve the problem of the braccianti. In spite of a total reduction in the agricultural population by at least 300,000 workers every year, the number of hired laborers available varied little;[69] and even in the 1960's, when actual labor shortages were being felt in the North and Center, the South and the Islands still had a vast excess of manual workers seeking agricultural jobs. The problem of the hired laborer therefore had two major facets. On the one hand, there was the necessity to link into one wage system the two pools of labor, the permanent workers and the day laborers. On the other, there was the need to solve the total economic problem of the underdevelopment and overpopulation of the South, which was the only solution to the plight of the braccianti.

THE IMPACT OF EEC ON ITALIAN AGRICULTURE

The extent to which implementation of EEC's common agricultural policy affected Italian agriculture can be estimated by consideration of increases in the Community's share of Italian agricultural trade; changes in the character of Italian agricultural production; and reforms in the nature of the Italian agricultural structure. However, because the agricultural common market has been fully functioning only since 1968, judgments of its effects can be only of the most provisional kind.

By 1968, a slight increase in the proportion of Italian exports of agricultural goods taken by the Common Market countries had occurred, but imports from EEC countries remained at approximately the same proportion of total agricultural imports. Between 1956 and 1967, Italian exports to EEC rose from 132 billion lire to 286 billion, while exports to the rest of the world rose from 196 billion lire to 315 billion. During the same period, imports from EEC rose from 116 billion lire to 350 billion, while imports from the rest of the world increased from 393 billion to 1,196 billion.[70] As had been expected, Community preference was most marked in the sector of fruit and vegetables, although, as can be seen in Table 3, the proportion of certain fruits and vegetables bought by EEC countries actually declined, especially that of citrus fruits.[71] Most Italian producers felt that the increase in their exports to EEC was disappointing, and that the common agricultural policy had failed to give them the competitive advantage for which they had hoped.[72]

The effect of the Community price structure and of the market regulations upon individual products was felt by the agricultural confederations to be ineffective, or even damaging, to the reorganization of the crop choice of Italian farmers. The price for soft wheat, the key to the whole pricing structure, had been set high for the Community as a whole, but lower than the Italian price. Contrary to expectation, this price did not bring about a major

Table 3. Selected Italian Agricultural Exports
Taken by EEC Countries
(Percentage of total exports)

	1958	1967
Rice	13%	42%
Tomatoes	80	70
Potatoes	40	70
Onions	60	70
Apples	70	70
Apricots	40	15
Pears	63	68
Peaches	74	67
Oranges	39	28
Wine	30	47
Tobacco	48	85

reduction in Italian production and the much desired shift to livestock production. Instead, in the four years following establishment of the Community price in 1964, while the area devoted to soft wheat fell by 8 per cent, production increased by 5 per cent; and similar effects were seen in the production of hard wheat.[73] Between 1965 and 1967, Italy produced for the first time 2 million quintals of wheat more than it consumed, thereby adding to the growing Community surplus of wheat which was one of the principal financial burdens created by the common agricultural policy. The Community's desire to encourage the growing of forage cereals (barley, oats, maize, rye) by setting the price high had the effect of encouraging Italian production; but its far more important result, in view of the inadequacy of home production, was that it discouraged imports, since the high price, combined with the excessive costs of shipping through Italian ports, made it uneconomical for Italian livestock producers to seek to increase their forage supplies and thus the size of their herds.[74] In short, the cereals price within EEC helped bring about a slight reduction in the area under cereals within Italy, and encouraged the more efficient producers to increase the total production both of wheat and of forage cereals. While the situation was satisfactory to the growers of cereals, it was contrary to the long-term goal of Italian agricultural policy of shifting from cereal to livestock production. The increase in the production of rice through large investments and increase in acreage, on the other hand, was welcomed by producers and government alike, since the Common Market countries were absorbing the surplus at prices that completely satisfied the Italian producers.[75] As had been foreseen, the Common Market had proved a boon to the highly capitalized rice growers of the Po valley.

The opening of the common market for beef had little effect on Italian livestock production. Italian producers felt that the price of beef had been set too low to encourage an increase in production by their high-cost producers or to compel a shift away from purchases from third countries to purchases from other Community members. A higher price, combined with a greater allowance for the transport cost from France to Italy, would both encourage domestic production and increase purchases from within the Community.[76] Yet in the period 1958–68, Italian beef production had increased by little more than one million quintals, compared with an increase in imports of three and a half million.[77] Price and market regulation within the European Community could do little unless it was accompanied by drastic structural changes in Italian agriculture that would enable the Italian beef producer to profit first from his home market.

The Community regulation of the pork market proved much more favorable to the creation of Community preference. Italian imports of pigs from EEC members rose in 1958–67 from 29 to 54 per cent of total imports; but the Italian pig raiser, unlike the cattle farmer, was able to increase his production quite rapidly, and to hold imports to 10 per cent of national consumption.[78]

The support extended by the Community to producers of milk and dairy products brought about a chronic state of overproduction in the Community as a whole, and this had extremely unfavorable effects in Italy. The financial burden was very great, owing to the cost of subsidizing the exports of every country except Italy and of keeping up the home price of butter. The Italian farmer could not compete effectively with the Dutch or French producers of the rich northern European meadowlands, and, compelled to reduce his prices to the Community level, he was discouraged from further expansion. The Italians also complained that the Community policy was intended to favor the consumption of vegetable fats rather than butter, even at the cost of subsidies to the butter producers. Italy, alone among the six in devoting most of its milk to cheese, rather than to butter or milk powder production, was therefore discriminated against, until the EEC Council of Ministers adopted protective measures for Italy's Parmesan cheeses. The Italians, in protesting the Community's discouragement of butter consumption, had also objected that low prices for vegetable oils would discourage olive oil consumption. The Community solution, making deficiency payments to the olive oil producers rather than raising the prices of vegetable oils, was felt to be a temporary expedient; and, although the deeper problems of the quality of the oil and of the efficiency of the production methods of the Italian olive growers remained unsolved, the farm federations continued to press for higher prices of margarine and vegetable oils in order to favor consumption of butter and olive oil.[79]

Finally, Italian producers of fruit and vegetables and of wine, who had expected an enormous stimulus from the opening of the Common Market to their exports, were disappointed with the results. The fruit and vegetable producers felt that the quality controls had been left largely in the hands of the importing countries by the EEC authorities and that, as a result, Italian products were frequently discriminated against;[80] but they also complained that the necessary improvements in quality and in methods of production could only be achieved if associations of producers were more effectively encouraged by the governmental authorities in Italy itself. As for the Community attempts to regulate the wine market, the failure to take Italian interests into account was, according to Confagricoltura, "a true and genuine scandal."[81] The Community's desire to limit acreage and to impose strict labeling controls was felt to be another form of discrimination against the mass-produced inexpensive wines of Italy; and as late as 1969 the Italians were still fighting dourly in Brussels to gain recognition of wine as a mass product that should receive consideration similar to that of milk or wheat.

Insofar as any conclusion could be drawn from the early functioning of the common agricultural policy, little beneficial effect upon the redimensioning of the choice of crops in Italy seemed to have been achieved. Cereal production was growing at an unwanted rate. Livestock rearing was lagging behind, both for the production of beef and of dairy products. The fruit and vegetable producers and the wine producers had not enjoyed the stimulus of a much wider market. Only the rice producers were pleased with the benefits of EEC.

Moreover, the whole program had been very costly to Italy, with the great proportion of its contributions to the Guarantee Section of FEOGA going to support the farmers of France. Between 1962 and 1968, Italy had paid into the Guarantee Section $232 million more than it had received; and, even though it received $147 million more from the Orientation Section than it contributed, its total deficit with FEOGA was $85 million. For a poor country like Italy, this was absurd.[82]

This unsatisfactory situation was in part caused by the deficiencies in the Community organization of the agricultural markets, but in part it was the result of the structural weaknesses in

Italian farming, which the Agricultural Fund was intended to improve.[83] The Italian government had been spending enormous sums for agricultural improvement since the end of the war; and, in comparison, the $269 million in aid extended by FEOGA's Orientation Section was quite small.[84] The three basic principles underlying the orientation program were to reduce costs and increase productivity of each worker through consolidation of properties and irrigation; to increase sales by improvement in quality and marketing of such products as fruit and vegetables; and to improve livestock rearing and wine and olive production by programs of a "mixed character" involving improvements in both production and marketing.[85] For example, in 1967, of the 152 requests for aid approved by the Commission, the 59 Italian projects approved included construction of a harbor silo at Cagliari in Sardinia, a fruit and vegetable cooperative near Ravenna, and an abbatoir for pigs at Potenza.[86] But these small-scale projects acted as mere palliatives. By 1969, the Community authorities were coming to accept the opinion consistently expressed by Italian agricultural leaders. As Alfredo Diana, president of Confagricoltura, pointed out in October 1969:

> In agriculture we tried to speed up the process of integration: reaching the single market, reaching the common prices, without tackling what ought, to our way of thinking, have been the primary policy to follow, that is, without tackling the policy of the real and genuine structure of agriculture. Common prices were dreamed up for agricultural products; it was imagined that a common agricultural market could exist, independent of advances, independent of progress in all the other sectors. It was a great mistake.[87]

The Community's emphasis upon the free circulation of agricultural goods at common prices and on maintenance of Community preference through market support and export subsidies had failed to touch the structural weaknesses of Community, and especially of Italian, farming.

A special survey conducted by the Italian Statistical Institute (ISTAT) in December 1967, following Community criteria, showed that only a small beginning had been made since the census of 1961 in meeting the problems of fragmentation of ownership and structural deficiencies of the working farm. Since 1961, the total number of farms had dropped by 416,000, or by 10 per cent. More than half of these had been cultivated by working farmers, the coltivatori diretti, and their exodus helped raise the average size of the farm worked by the remaining coltivatori from 3.79 to 4.29 hectares. Almost half of Italy's farms were thus still of a size considered by the Community authorities to be inadequate for efficient production. Worse, the survey showed that 30 per cent of Italy's farms were still less than one hectare in size! The problem of the coltivatori diretti was thus far from solution. There were some moderately encouraging signs: the number of farms worked by sharecroppers fell by 116,000, from 11.7 to 5.3 per cent, indicating that the institution of mezzadria was finally disappearing; and the number of farms worked by hired labor, which were in general the most efficient, increased by 7000, denoting a modest increase of from 7.6 to 8 per cent of all Italian farms.[88] These changes, even though accompanied by a reduction in the working population in agriculture, were proved to be insufficient by the low increase in productivity and in total production and by the increasing gap between rural and industrial income. In 1965, for example, agricultural production increased by 3.6 per cent, in 1966 by 0.3 per cent, and in 1967 by 5.4 per cent.[89] The average yearly wage in agriculture rose from 311,000 lire in 1957 to 912,000 lire in 1968, while the income in other activities rose from 617,000 lire to 2,154,000 lire. In short, while agricultural income, which originally was only half that of other professions, tripled in 1957–68, the income of the other professions rose even faster.[90]

The dismal conclusion to be drawn, at least as of 1968, was that neither Italian governmental measures nor the first years of operation of the Community agricultural policy had solved the deep-rooted problems of Italian agriculture. The gap between rural and industrial Italy was growing steadily wider, to the increasingly violent anger of the rural classes.

8

Overpopulation, Unemployment, and Emigration

The success of Italy's industry and agriculture within an integrated Europe was threatened by two vast burdens that weighed upon the whole country—a population that was too large for the country's resources and was rapidly increasing; and a sharp division in economic achievement and prospects between the North-Center and the South.

OVERPOPULATION

For at least fifteen years after the war, the primary interest of most Italians in a European federation was the hope of finding an outlet for the emigration of large numbers of their excess population. Most economists held that about half a million Italians should emigrate each year if the long-standing unemployment problem was ever to be solved; and, with the restriction on emigration to North and South America, begun at the end of World War I, they felt that openings for emigration to the neighboring countries of western Europe must be found.

The reason normally given for this overpopulation was simply the combination of a high birth rate and a falling death rate. The American economist George Hildebrand, however, holds that neither the Italian birth rate nor even the natural rate of increase of the population was particularly high, and that the unemployment problem was economic rather than demographic, the result of the failure to create jobs rather than of an excessive population growth.[1]

It is true that, in the period since 1924, the growth rate of the population has declined rapidly, to only 9.8 per thousand in 1965. At that time, too, the birth rate was lower than that of the United States—18.8 per thousand compared with 19.4 per thousand. The Catholic Church's teachings on birth control were evidently being ignored.[2] But two factors made the demographic problem of continuing relevance. First, the population had grown enormously in the century after unification. In 1861, the Italian population was 26,128,000, with a density of 85 inhabitants per square kilometer; a century later it was 50,695,000, with a density of 168 inhabitants per square kilometer, making Italy one of the most densely populated countries in the world. Italy, in fact, was badly overpopulated by 1924, in relation to its available resources. Even though the population growth fell to what economists consider acceptable limits, the economy still had to provide for that earlier and excessive population growth.

Second, the regional figures of population growth reveal that the limitation on population growth was exclusively a phenomenon of the North-Center. By 1965, the excess of births over deaths in the North-Center had dropped to 6.4 per thousand, while in the South it was 13.4 per thousand. For most of the postwar period, the Southern rate of increase was more than three times that of the North-Center, and better medical care for infants was certain to increase the rate of population growth in the South even further. Pressure of population growth hit the area of the country where employment prospects were least good.[3]

UNEMPLOYMENT

Discussion of unemployment is made extremely difficult by the lack of reliable statistics, or, indeed, of commonly accepted definitions of unemployment. The two principal sources are the quarterly sampling taken by ISTAT, the Italian Statistical Institute, from September 1952, and the figures of the Ministry of Labor, based upon the registrations in the labor exchanges, which consistently run higher than the ISTAT figures. Finally, there are the figures of the censuses, taken every ten years, which differ widely from ISTAT's quarterly sampling, in that they give a far smaller working force. To this problem is added the task of evaluating the extent of underemployment in agriculture. Any conclusions about the relative extent of unemployment from one year to the next are therefore fairly reliable, while estimates of total unemployment are approximate at best.

The first ISTAT sampling, of September 1952, gives a good starting point for consideration of the character of Italian unemployment. Total unemployment was about one and a half million, about 11 per cent of the work force. In the South, the working population constituted only about 32 per cent of the total population, while in the North-Center it varied from about 43 to 47 per cent. This disparity was undoubtedly an indication of the departure from the South of many of the working population in search of jobs in other regions or abroad, and of the higher number of women employed in the North-Center than in the South—25 per cent compared with 11 per cent. The rate of unemployment in the South was only slightly higher than that in the North, although certain areas there had high unemployment rates. Catania, in Sicily, for example, had 11.2 per cent unemployed. This equality of unemployment was, however, not real, since a large proportion of the South's so-called working population was underemployed, either helping on family farms or working for a few days each year as braccianti. About 43 per cent of the unemployed were those just entering the labor force, unsuccessfully seeking their first jobs. Of these, the proportion who had only finished elementary school or who were illiterate varied from 43 to 54 per cent according to the province sampled; more than a quarter of a million semiliterate teenagers were seeking jobs without even the minimum of necessary schooling.[4]

In 1953 two reports were published by parliamentary commissions appointed to examine unemployment and poverty in Italy. The situation they revealed was startling, even to those who had demanded the investigations. The reports documented the incredible deprivation that unemployment and underemployment caused. The commission on poverty declared that 11.7 per cent of Italian families were totally destitute and a similar number were in need. Over 2.8 million families were living more than two to a room, 232,000 were living in cellars or attics, and 92,000 in caves or lean-tos. Medical examinations of sample members of the unemployed showed large numbers to have poor sight, hearing, and teeth, to be underweight and shorter than normal, and to have developed psychological reactions of fatalism and passivity as a result of their unemployment.[5] The well-publicized hearings and reports of these commissions gave urgency to the government's first major attempt to solve the country's unemployment problem, by the Vanoni Plan, presented to parliament by Budget Minister Ezio Vanoni in 1955.[6] To deal with unemployment during the ten-year duration of the plan, it was calculated that it would be necessary to create four million new jobs to meet the natural growth of the population, the shift from agriculture to industry, and the existing unemployment. Emigration of 800,000 workers per year and the continuance of an unemployment of 700,000 workers were assumed. To provide the new jobs, real national income would have to increase at a rate of 5 per cent per year, through higher productivity, a larger work force, and especially higher investment by both state and private enterprise. The plan called for closing the gap between North-Center and South by maintaining a growth rate of 8 per cent in the South, and by increasing its share of the national income from 21 to 28 per cent. To make this possible, half the public investment in the three "propulsive sectors"—agriculture, public utilities, and public works—as well as in housing, would be made in the South.

The introduction of the Vanoni Plan coincided with negotiation of the Common Market treaty (1955–57) and with a new peak of unemployment in Italy. Great pressure was therefore exerted by the Italian negotiators of the treaty to persuade their future partners not to interfere with the implementation of the Vanoni Plan and to open up immediate outlets for the emigration of the Italian unemployed.[7] The Special Protocol concerning Italy, annexed to the treaty, recognized that successful realization of the Vanoni Plan's goals of "curing the structural imbalance of the Italian economy . . . and creating new jobs to eliminate unemployment" was in the "common interest" of all EEC members. Vittorio Badini Confalonieri, the under secretary for foreign affairs, even claimed that "the realization of the Vanoni Plan thus implicitly becomes a duty not only for Italy but for the six Community countries,"[8] while Premier Giuseppe Pella explained that Italy's partners would have the advantage of access to labor in Italy during the Common Market's labor shortage, although the country's economic experts were trying to discourage the idea that "opening the frontiers could free a massive emigration of Italian workers and eliminate unemployment in a flash."[9]

The first decade of operation of the Common Market showed the economists' caution to be justified. First, the Vanoni Plan was never fully implemented, because of opposition within the governmental coalition and the government's failure to compel private industry to follow the scheme. Although the gross national product rose even faster than envisaged by the Plan, increasing 5.5 per cent annually, the failure of the Vanoni Plan was obvious. There was still disparity between the growth rate of the North-Center and the South and an increasing contrast of living standards, and, especially, persistent unemployment in the South. Second, the Common Market provided a great stimulus to Italian industry at a time when it had completed the preparations for an economic "take-off" into sustained rapid development. Reconstruction was completed in 1948, but, in the decade that followed, Italian industry had made almost no contribution to the reduction of unemployment, in spite of its continuous economic progress. What increase in job openings had occurred had been offset by the increase in the labor force and by the movement out of agriculture. Professor Hildebrand has shown that the persistent unemployment cannot be attributed to the "classical case of economic development with unlimited supplies of labor." According to Hildebrand, the reasons were a temporary bulge in the labor force after 1945, composed of demobilized soldiers, refugees, and returning colonists; the legal ban on internal migration until 1961; the movement out of agriculture; and the low demand for additional workers as a result of the wage boosts won by unions in the advanced sector of industry, the introduction of labor-saving machinery, and the consequent rise of productivity per man.[10] Italian business, in short, had placed economic growth ahead of reduced unemployment, and had been strongly supported in this attitude by the governmental anti-inflationary policies and by the trade unions' preference for higher wages over more numerous jobs.[11] There is little indication that the attitudes of management or of labor changed after 1958. Yet from that point until the beginning of the recession of 1963–65, unemployment was decisively reduced, from 1,662,000 in 1957 to 426,000 in 1963.

Up to 1962, emigration, especially emigration to the Common Market countries and to Switzerland, was far more important in reducing unemployment than was the increase of employment inside Italy. In 1958–62 inclusive, unemployment fell by 1,057,000, during which period 715,000 emigrated. Of these, 323,157 emigrated to the Common Market countries.[12] In 1963, emigration dropped sharply, falling to only 56,000, but unemployment continued to fall, and it reached the lowest point in the postwar years, 426,000. After the recession struck in 1963, emigration increased only slightly, and as a result unemployment again climbed upward, to 673,000 in 1966.

We can conclude, therefore, that Italian industry did not begin to absorb the youths entering the labor market and the workers leaving agriculture, as well as part of the pool of unemployed, until 1963—at least to any significant degree. But from this point on, emigration became only a minor relief to unemployment, since workers felt that openings were available for them in Italy itself. Even during the recession of 1963–65, emigration remained small, and the loss of expansive power within the Italian economy was at once translated into an increase in the numbers of unemployed. Italian industry was thus compelled to realize that it had the primary responsibility for solving Italy's excess of labor. The excuse of an outlet to Europe no longer existed. The one lasting factor that could eliminate unemployment was the extension of the use of labor by an expanding home industry; and the long-term significance of European integration was to help maintain that expansion.

EMIGRATION

Emigration was an important factor in Italian economic development primarily in the years up to 1962; and the most powerful reason for it was demographic pressure from the South. This Southern pressure dictated Italian patterns of emigration, both external and internal. Whereas before World War I most of the emigrants from Northern Italy went temporarily to neighboring European countries, Southern Italians went permanently overseas. In spite of desperate efforts by the postwar Italian governments to find outlets for Italian emigration, the number emigrating overseas each year reached a maximum of 145,614 in 1954, after which it fell steadily to only 41,984 in 1964. The great majority of these emigrants were from the South, and only a few returned to Italy.[13] The pressure of the growing population of the South was by no means siphoned off by this small overseas emigration. Three results followed: emigration on a greater scale to the countries of Europe; emigration from the South to the North-Center; and continuing high levels of unemployment.

The growth of Italian emigration to the countries of western Europe was one of the most important features of postwar Italian development. Italian emigration to the countries of EEC had been firmly established even before the formation of the Coal and Steel Community in 1952. By 1961, over one million Italians had migrated to France, Germany, and Benelux, and just under half a million later returned. In the early postwar years, most emigrants went to the Belgian coal mines, or took up industrial or agricultural work in France. With the beginning of the German economic boom in the 1950's, increasingly large numbers moved to West Germany, and in 1960 it became for the first time the major recipient of Italian migration within EEC.

European emigration, which predominated from the mid 1950's, was of a different character from that of the earlier migrations overseas. Very few Italians intended to seek a permanent home in the other countries of Europe, although a few who married foreign girls or settled their families with them actually did so. Most Italian workers sought a job for a fixed period of time, with the intention of returning home on completion of their contract. Some received technical training which enabled them to find jobs in Italy on their return. The group of Italians living in European countries was constantly changing its composition, and the Italian government found itself directly involved in finding jobs, acting often as an intermediary between the foreign company and the Italian worker through the local labor exchanges in Italy. It assumed responsibility for the nature of the contract, for the Italian's living conditions abroad, for the equal grant of social security benefits, for such rights as equal access to public housing and schools, and even for representation on foreign trade unions. This change in the character of Italian emigration directly influenced Italy's attitude toward a European federation. The establishment of a federation was regarded as a guarantee of unchallenged outlets for Italian labor. The rights of Italian workers abroad could be safeguarded, and a position of equality with the workers of the host country could be demanded as a legal right. And, in times of economic crisis, the Italian worker could not be sent home, thus reducing the unemployment of native workers, as was consistently the practice of the Swiss government.[14]

There was a major increase in Italian emigration to the Community from 1960 to 1962. In 1963, however, more jobs became available in Italy itself, and not only did the number of emigrants fall, but far greater numbers of workers began to return. In 1966, the excess of emigrants to the Community over returnees was only 3000, compared, for example, with 88,000 only five years earlier. The great flood of workers into the Community therefore occurred before their conditions of work and residence were improved by the two important Community regulations on freedom of movement of workers, Regulation 15 of August 16, 1961, and Regulation 38/64 of March 25, 1964, which ended national preference in employment but established Community preference, recognized the emigrant workers' right to bring his family and secure education for his children, and even gave him the right to serve on workers' elected bodies.[15]

The priority given to Community workers over migrants from nonmember countries was an advantage almost exclusively for Italy, which was particularly necessary in view of the growing numbers of workers from Spain, Portugal, Greece, Turkey, and North Africa being employed in France and Germany. Community preference gave the Italian worker greater freedom of choice in the location and type of work he could accept in the Community; few Italians were still willing to go down the mines, for example. Some EEC officials even began to fear that the need to give Italian migrant workers better conditions than was given to those from nonmember countries would make the Italian worker less attractive to employers and might in fact jeopardize the openings for Italians. However, the impact of EEC upon Italian unemployment had been significant. Between 1958 and 1966, the number of workers and family members of Italians in the Community increased by 386,000. Community regulations eased the bureaucratic problems of migration, established preference for

Italian workers, and undoubtedly made migration more feasible and more attractive to Italians. But the prospect for the 1970's was for a rapid decrease in the number of Italians migrating to the Community. The gap between Italian factory wage levels and the highest wages in the Community had been reduced by 60 per cent, making the financial incentive to migration far less. The annual increase in Italy's active population was expected to fall at a time when the growth of the economy was increasing manpower needs. Italy, in short, was expected to have less need for emigration outlets within the Community and its workers less inducement to leave.[16] Free movement of labor would be what the authors of the Treaty of Rome had envisaged, a necessary accompaniment to the readjustment of industrial and agricultural production to favor those branches where greatest economic benefit was obtained.

More important even than emigration to Europe was the move of Southerners to the North-Center of Italy itself, under pressure of the overpopulation of the South. The census of 1951 showed that almost one million of the 29 million people living in the North-Center had been born in the South, while only 219,000 people born in the North-Center were living in the South. During the following decade, more than 1,800,000 Southerners left the South. It is difficult to say exactly how many of these moved to the North-Center, since ISTAT only began registering internal migrations in 1955. However, from 1955 through 1961, 802,165 more people moved from the South to the North-Center than the reverse, even though there was the beginning of an appreciable movement of Southerners returning to find work in the developing regions of the South.[17] By the early 1960's, several very important trends had become clear. First, Southern migration to the North-Center was greater than Southern migration abroad—it varied, from eight times to forty times greater—which indicated not only that the attraction of overseas emigration had almost disappeared, but that openings in Italy were preferred over those in the neighboring European countries. Italy was likely to see both a lessening of the interest in employment within the European Community and a large-scale return of those emigrants who had moved to other European countries. This return of workers, some of whom had received technical training and experience abroad, would prove of great benefit to Italian industry, but it would also provoke considerable problems for the labor-poor countries, especially Germany, where they had been working. As Francesco Compagna points out, "the transalpine migrations of a seasonal character are recuperable, that is, they constitute a kind of reserve for the Italian labor market just as the Italian labor market has constituted and still constitutes a reserve for a Europe with full employment."[18] Second, migration to the North-Center was absorbing over 30 per cent of the South's natural increase in population, contributing in an important way to the phenomenon Italian observers were beginning to call the "Southernization" of Italy. Southernization was in fact a double process. Not only was the population born in the South accounting for a greater percentage of the total Italian population (it increased from 37 per cent in 1931 to 39 per cent in 1951), but the percentage of Southerners living in the North-Center was also increasing. Third, the Southern migrant established himself whenever possible in a large city. Rome was the choice of about one-fifth of Southern migrants, followed closely by cities of the provinces of Piedmont and Lombardy, especially Turin and Milan. The Southern exodus thus contributed to the vast urbanization of Italy that took place after World War II, although the major cause of urbanization was the movement from the countryside into cities within the same area. By 1966, one-third of the population lived in cities of 50,000 inhabitants or more. For Europe, the urbanization of Italy implied that Italy itself was beginning to offer to the Italian migrant the advantages of urban living and industrial wages that he had previously sought in the United States or Canada, and, more recently, in the factory cities of Germany or the mining towns of Belgium. Urban life in Italy was far more attractive to the migrant than that of the cold, rainy towns in northern Europe, where he was not accepted fully into the social life of the local community, the ways of which he rarely understood or liked. Most Italians were glad to remain in Italy for lower wages rather than face the unappealing way of life in the north of Europe.

9
The Problem of the South

The problems of unemployment and emigration were directly related to the economic difficulties of the South, and this poses a number of questions relevant to Italy's role in Europe. First, did the South act as a handicap to Italy in its economic competition with other western European countries? Second, to what extent had Italian government policies found a solution to the problem of the economic backwardness of the South? Third, could the South be regarded as an asset, either actual or potential? Finally, could the Southern problem be passed on to Europe as a whole, making it a common responsibility of all members of the Community? If it could, as Francesco Compagna has pointed out, Europe would be approaching one of the most crucial difficulties in integration, "the requirements that arise from integration between western Europe and southern Europe. The Mezzogiorno of Italy can and must be considered the 'pilot zone' of this integration."[1]

THE ORIGINS OF THE SOUTHERN PROBLEM

The division between the South and the rest of the country was already evident at the moment of political unification in 1861. Even then, the South was suffering from most of the ills that would plague it after World War II—a feudal structure, both of its society and of its economy; agriculture of very low productivity, concentrated on the production of grain, and cursed by the dual problem of latifondi and "pulverization" of peasant property; deforestation and erosion; small-scale industry, restricted markets, and shortage of capital; and a legacy of governmental exploitation, repression, or neglect.[2]

Italian economic writers in the early nineteenth century had advocated political unification as a stimulant to economic growth. Yet the immediate effects of unification were clearly harmful. Southern spokesmen like Francesco Nitti were already arguing by the end of the century that the South's share of public expenditure in public works or education was unjustly small in relation to the taxes paid, and that this tax burden was a primary cause of the South's poverty. Even more significant for its effects on the Southern economy was the tariff policy of united Italy. From 1861 to 1887, the tariffs were kept low, which meant that the South was left open to competition not only from the industry of Northern Italy but from the rest of the industrialized world as well. Both North and South, however, suffered from the low tariffs, and high tariffs were introduced in the 1880's, under the pressure of Northern businessmen who allied with large landowners seeking protection for their cereal production. This policy, sharply criticized by such Southerners as the eminent historian Gaetano Salvemini, raised the price of industrial goods in the South without stimulating the foundation of industry there, and further encouraged the concentration on wheat production. By 1900, the divergence between North and South was blatant. During the last two decades of the century, the North developed textile, metallurgical, and engineering industries; and the piercing of tunnels through the Alps linked it to the markets of northern Europe. The South, with a high birth rate, little industrialization, and negligible increase in agricultural productivity, saw emigration increase tenfold by 1900; the plots of land became even further subdivided among those remaining, and underemployment both of peasant proprietors and of day laborers grew.[3] During the Fascist period, while the North was undergoing the forced industrialization demanded by Mussolini's war goals, the South was plunging even deeper into agrarian stagnation.

The search for an explanation of the growing poverty of South Italy in the century following unification played an important part in the debate over Italy's participation in European integration. In the first place, the view of the Cavour liberals, that the union of South and North would stimulate the economic growth of both regions, had been decisively rejected, and it was universally held that the union of a weak with a strong economic region had led to the ruin of the former. When the lesson of this experience for Europe in the 1950's was sought, however, the critics and supporters of integration drew opposed conclusions from it. The critics held that the process of integration would be harmful to the Italian economy until the country was in a position of equality with its partners, and that Italy should not enter into an integrated Community but be satisfied rather with bilateral or multilateral trading agreements.[4] The supporters of integration argued, first, that the Italian example only illustrated the need to take measures to alleviate the temporary dislocations caused by the inherently healthy process of integration. If the advanced sector of the Community is large enough, they added, it can even accept the responsibility of beginning the process of development in whole regions where the economy is in a state of underdevelopment. Second, almost all agreed that Nitti and his followers were erroneous in speaking of the potential richness of the South at the moment of unification, although they were undoubtedly correct in their diagnosis of the social backwardness of the South as a factor in its poverty.[5] A far more realistic approach, it was felt, would be to accept the natural disadvantages of the South as the beginning of any program of improvement. Third, it was clear that the state could no longer restrict itself to provision of the infrastructure for Southern economic development, but must intervene directly in fostering industrialization and in compelling greater agricultural productivity. This posed a new question, whether Italy was rich enough to carry out the necessary program, both through provision of state funds and, in the more general sense, by provision of a consumer market for the absorption of the South's agricultural produce and the products of its coming industrialization.[6] In both the direct provision of funds and in the development a better economic environment for the South, European federation appeared in the mid 1950's to offer considerable advantages to the South.

APPLICATION OF DEVELOPMENT THEORY TO THE SOUTHERN PROBLEM

Between 1943 and 1950, a fresh diagnosis of the Southern problem was made. "The old literature on the Southern question is no longer of any help in solving the problems of the South," declared Professor Giuseppe Di Nardi. "Nowadays more complex tools are required if we are to get to the bottom of the problems and to work out a sound program of development."[7] What was new about this approach was its optimism, based on the dual belief that the disadvantage of the South in natural resources and location could be overcome by recent technological progress and that the shortcomings of the classical theorists of the South could be removed by treating the question "as part of the new international issue of underdeveloped countries."[8] Unfortunately, even within this new context, there was major disagreement as to the methods to be applied to start an underdeveloped region like the South on the road to economic progress.

The argument got off to a passionate start with the outraged reaction of many Italian economists to the suggestions of the eminent Swiss economist, Friedrich Vöchting, in his *Die italienische Südfrage*.[9] Not only did Vöchting deplore the break-up of the latifondi, he gave agricultural improvement low priority. Instead, he argued, the South should begin a program of carefully chosen industrial projects suited to the resources and market in the area and protect them by imposition of a regional tariff barrier against goods coming from the North.[10] This view, completely opposed to the ideals of integration, found little support in Italy, except among Sicilian separatists.[11] The case in favor of giving primacy to agricultural development accompanied by creation of the infrastructure for industrial development, rather than to immediate industrialization, was made by most of Italy's leading economists, among them Professors Giuseppe Di Nardi and Francesco Vito;[12] but probably the most influential supporter of this view was Professor Pasquale Saraceno, vice president and one of the principal promoters of the very effective Associazione per lo sviluppo dell' industria nel Mezzogiorno (SVIMEZ), a collaborator in the formulation of the Vanoni Plan, and vice chairman of the National Planning Commission. As Vera Lutz has pointed out, behind their views were three economic ideas that gained great popularity in Italy in the postwar years—external economies, capital-output ratio, and multiplier analysis.

According to Lutz, "it has become customary, in Italy as elsewhere, to use the term 'external economies' to describe the benefits which a firm setting up in any particular industry draws (in the form *either* of a reduction in the costs of the products it buys, *or* of an increase in the demand for the products it sells) from the simultaneous establishment of firms in a wide number of other industries."[13] During the first stage of its official policy toward the South, which lasted until 1957, the government assumed that its job was to create the industrial infrastructure, such as roads, bridges, schools, and communications, and that private industry, thus encouraged to invest in manufacturing plants in the South, would enjoy the benefits of "external economies." In short, given a favorable industrial environment created through state intervention, the establishment of one company would lead to the establishment of other, complementary companies. By 1957, it was clear that private industry had failed to profit from these putative benefits; and the government, without abandoning the theory of external economies, decided both to give greater financial encouragement to firms to invest in the South and to participate directly in the financing of industry in the South.

The "capital-output" ratio emphasizes that the growth of national income depends upon maintenance of a high relation of savings (that is, reinvestment) to income, in order to increase output by raising capitalization. This aim was, of course, basic to the whole economic policy after 1950, when the government, feeling that the period of reconstruction was over, became "convinced that it was possible to remedy, even if gradually, the distortions in our economic system, as a result of engaging the economic forces of the country in an organic policy for the increase of national income which would make possible the increase in the proportion of the income devoted to investments and to use those investments in a manner corresponding to the objectives to be reached."[14] The depressed condition of the South was one of the major structural distortions that the investment program was to remedy.[15]

"Multiplier analysis" was also used to justify greater investment in the South, especially in the early 1950's. It was held that investment has a multiplier effect in increasing income, which thereby creates greater demand for goods and hence greater employment for the production of those goods. In 1951 SVIMEZ made a highly influential analysis of the multiplier effects of investment in the South and concluded that, since much of the expenditure for public works projects in the South was for products of the North, the South was not enjoying the multiplier effects of the investment to the full. Not only should public works be carried through in the South but the products used in public works, such as cement and steel, should also be produced in the South. SVIMEZ's work encouraged a widespread belief that sufficiently large investment in the South could end unemployment there within a calculable period.[16]

THE FIRST PHASE OF POSTWAR DEVELOPMENT POLICY
IN THE SOUTH, 1950–1957

This optimism was at the basis of the program for the South elaborated in 1950–57. The program had three main elements: land reform; foundation of the Cassa per il Mezzogiorno; and fiscal and financial measures to encourage private investment in industrialization.

The land reform primarily affected the South. In the North-Center only 226,000 hectares were expropriated, compared with 493,000 in the South and the Islands. Yet land reform did not make a major contribution to solving the economic problems of the region. Only about 100,000 families received land; in most cases the parcels of land were too small, and thus failed to provide the income from agriculture which was regarded as a necessary stimulus to industrialization; many of the parcels were abandoned by their owners, who sought employment in the North or abroad; and the natural increase of the population was more than 2.5 million during the decade 1951–61, while there was an emigration of only 1.8 million Southerners, among them many of the most able of the farming population.[17]

Several months after the passage of the first land reform law in 1950, parliament approved the first over-all program for government intervention in the development of the South, to be carried out by a new agency called the "Cassa per opere straordinarie di pubblico interesse nell'Italia meridionale" (Fund for extraordinary works of public utility in South Italy), shortly afterward known simply as the Cassa per il Mezzogiorno. The original endowment of the Cassa was 1000 billion lire ($1.6 billion) to be spent over the decade 1950–60 in approximately equal amounts each year;

but this sum was increased as time went on. In all, a total of 2,107.5 billion lire were to be spent over fifteen years. The original law of 1950 was explicit in its requirement that 77 per cent of the funds be used for the improvement of agriculture. The rest of the money was to be for construction of aqueducts, roads, and tourist facilities. The novelty of the program was not only in the very great sums of money made available, but in the method of the program's execution. As the Cassa's president, Gabriele Pescatore, pointed out, "the Southern region was considered as a single area, in which the problems of economic development were to be treated . . . in a unified way, thereby making it possible to avoid sporadic and uncoordinated intervention."[18] Italian representatives in the European Community were later to claim that they had been the pioneers of regional programming, and that the experience of the Cassa should be taken as the only valid case in Europe on which future regional programs could be built.[19] The program was no longer tied to annual appropriations, but was to be secure in its financing for a whole decade. Execution of the program was not placed in the hands of the existing ministries, for whom most Italians had the greatest distrust, but given to a totally new body which would be free to act quickly without problems of conflict of jurisdiction among ministries. Institution of the Cassa, with its original emphasis on betterment of agriculture accompanied by the creation of an infrastructure for industry, was a great triumph for Saraceno and the theorists of SVIMEZ.

During the so-called "first cycle" of the Cassa's activity, from 1950 to 1957, its original tasks were broadened. In 1952, it was made responsible for forestation and water-control systems in entire mountain basins and for development of major railroad lines; in 1953, for special programs in the city of Naples; in 1955, for application of the Special Law for Calabria, which financed a twelve-year program of water-control, irrigation, and reclamation works. It was also given the right to contract loans abroad, and the duty to aid in financing industrial development. At the end of the seventh year of activity, projects valued at 884 billion lire had been approved; half of these were completed and 30 per cent were under way. Fifty per cent of the funds had been spent on reclamation and water-control systems in the mountain basins; 18 per cent on water mains and sewers; 18 per cent on roads; and the rest on railroads and tourist projects.[20]

At this point, the work of the Cassa came under sharp criticism for its lack of results and for its basic economic asumptions. The moment of the attack was particularly significant, as it coincided with, and influenced, the debate on the effects upon Italy of membership in the Common Market. If the critics were able to prove that little progress had been made in remedying the South's stagnation, then this disadvantage could be presented as a further reason why Italy should not join EEC. If, however, it could be shown that the difficulties of the South were on the way to solution, then supporters of EEC could argue that Italy needed only a transition period to allow completion of the development program for the South to prepare itself for the full competition within the Common Market and, moreover, that the cost of this program could be shared with Italy's new partners. This second view finally prevailed.

The first argument of the critics was that the expenditure in the South had failed to close the economic gap between North and South. Per capita income in the South had risen from 110,900 lire in 1951 to 164,300 in 1957, but per capita income in the North-Center had risen from 230,100 to 349,400. Total income of the South had risen from 1,958 billion lire in 1951 to 3,077 billion, but in the North-Center it had jumped from 6,878 billion to 10,651 billion. In spite of vast financial aid, no improvement in the South's relative position could be seen.[21] Moreover, the critics argued, the expenditures already made had often been used unwisely, on the wrong projects. Mountain roads were becoming worthless as the population left. Farm buildings were being abandoned. Larger public works were decaying for lack of maintenance. Funds had been spread too thinly and without proper regard for their most productive use. Above all, the critics attacked the theoretical assumptions behind the program. The administrators were accused of being dazed by "multiplier effects," and of creating consumption of any kind in the belief that this would multiply the increase of income of the region. They were criticized for overemphasizing the effects of their infrastructure investments and of the provision of "social overhead capital" as an inducement to private companies to move in to enjoy the profits from "external economies."[22]

The courses proposed by the critics varied enormously. Some Northern critics urged that the program be dropped, in order to relieve the financial burden on the North at the moment when

Italy's entry into the Common Market was going to make it necessary for the Northern industrial complex to invest its available capital in more directly productive enterprises. The Cassa's supporters replied that the shift in the South's share of public expenditure from 33 to 43 per cent of the national total was not large enough to cause any sudden change in the South's relative position; that many of the projects were still under construction, and that those already completed, such as dams, roads, and railroads, were long-term in their effects and were not intended to be directly productive; that there had been no alternative to spending 25 to 30 per cent of the funds in the North, since the South did not produce the tractors, bulldozers, and so on that were needed; and that "the increase in public expenditure has given the South new momentum."[23]

The upshot of the debate was the recognition that much of the activity of the Cassa within the directives of the law of 1950 had been effectively carried out. The Cassa had shown that a new administrative body, outside the framework of the old Italian bureaucracy, could be vigorous and efficient. The investments used to aid the peasant farmers in the land reform areas had increased productivity, absorbed labor in productive work, and brought marked social benefits to the more than 100,000 families who had been settled in new homes. The transportation system of the South, both roads and railroads, had been improved. Water had been brought to several million people through the construction of water mains. Marketing of agricultural produce had been aided by the improved road system and by the construction of processing plants. A small beginning had been made in private industrial investment aided by credit institutions in which the Cassa participated, since 223 billion lire had been invested in private industrial projects in 1950–56.[24] Where the critics had been right, the government admitted, was in their emphasis on the failure of the infrastructural improvements to encourage large-scale industrialization.

THE SECOND PHASE OF DEVELOPMENT POLICY, 1957–1965

The formation of the Common Market coincided with the "second cycle" of Southern development policy. This was laid down in the law of July 29, 1957, which extended the Cassa's activity until 1965, ended the priority given to agricultural improvement and infrastructural investment, and laid the emphasis of future investment on the creation of industrial production. Three methods of stimulating industrialization were to be coordinated. The activity of the Cassa was reoriented to the creation of carefully delimited "areas" and "nuclei" of industrial development; the state holding companies, especially IRI and ENI, were required to make 40 per cent of their investments in the South; and private industry, by further fiscal and financial benefits, was encouraged to found industrial plants in the South. It was assumed that EEC would support this program by direct financial aid and by provision of a wider market for the products of the new industries and of the improved agriculture.

The most important feature of the new law was the recognition that large-scale industrialization should be encouraged only in specific zones, where the prospects for successful development were good. In these so-called "areas of development," the local authorities were expected to form a Development Consortium (Consorzio di Sviluppo) to develop transportation, power, or water, or other needs of an industrial center, with the Cassa supplying up to 85 per cent of the funds required for these improvements. The "areas" had to possess a population of 200,000, some industrial activity, potential markets in their hinterland, flat land suitable for an industrial complex, banking services, and potential power sources. Smaller centers, called "nuclei of industrialization" (nuclei di sviluppo industriale), would receive Cassa aid, provided that they had a number of small and medium-sized industries working for a clearly delimited market, using raw materials locally available.[25] During the period of the second cycle, the proportion of the Cassa's expenditures devoted to infrastructure dropped from 42 per cent in 1956–57 to 13 per cent in 1965, while its aid to private investment, mostly in industrial projects, rose from 48 per cent to 82 per cent.[26]

The new emphasis on industrialization had not freed the Cassa of criticism, however. The growing exodus from the countryside during the second cycle gave support to those critics who had regarded much of the reclamation and land improvements and the land reform as economically unjustifiable. These criticisms, however, only echoed those of 1956–57. The more basic criticism was again of the theory behind the plan. The most vociferous criticism arose in 1962, when the census showed that, between 1951 and 1961, some 12 per cent of the population of the South had migrated from the region.[27] The critics argued that the Cassa's plans had failed to take account of this large-scale population movement, which would render the industrialization plans for the South unachievable. Without the great reservoir of manpower, which was the South's principal economic resource, private industry from North Italy and abroad would lose interest in starting new industrial plants in the region; and the expenditures in the new industrial zones would prove to be as wasteful as those spent in the first cycle on the roads into the abandoned mountain villages. Moreover, the huge influx of Southerners into the Northern cities was causing social problems of great difficulty, and necessitating the transference of funds to the North to pay for the housing, social services, transportation, roads, and so on needed there.

The old theme of the natural poverty of the South was again evoked to justify the idea that the South should concentrate almost exclusively on agriculture and food-processing.[28] The debate took a new turn with the publication of two articles by the penetrating British economist, Vera Lutz, who argued that "a quick solution to Italy's Southern problem would require that, for a certain period, the movement of Southern labor into Northern industry should assume proportions much larger than those which had prevailed during the 1950's."[29] Movement out of the South, Lutz argued, would exert a positive influence on Southern industrialization because, by raising the land-labor ratio, it would increase income per capita in Southern agriculture and thus increase the local market for industrial produce. At the very height of the debate, the Italian parliament abolished all restrictions on internal migration, and in that way dealt a final blow to the hopes of the few critics who had wanted to stem the movement of migration from the South by government intervention. What was needed was Southern planning to take more effective measure of the impact of migratory movements on investment plans. Thus, the argument over migration merged into the more general criticism of the industrialization projects of the Southern planners. Once again, it was argued that the Cassa was overextending itself in supporting small and medium-sized industry throughout the area and was neglecting the few promising regions as a consequence. In the industrial zones, however, the critics felt that the industrial projects had not been conceived to absorb unemployment or to supply the local markets, but were supporting instead large-scale automated factories intended to supply the North and foreign markets. And herein lay the failure of the areas of development to raise the average level of income and to create a self-propulsive growth process.

In the renewed debate in 1964–65 over the future of the Cassa per il Mezzogiorno, the administrators of the Southern program admitted that it was no longer necessary for the Cassa to share in most infrastructural improvements, and that these public works could be left to the normal government bodies in the future.[30] But they vigorously defended the achievements realized.

They noted that 11 million kilometers of water mains had been constructed to bring water to 7 million people; 16,000 kilometers of provincial roads had been paved and broadened; the railroad network had been modernized and the principal lines electrified; new hospitals had been built and old ones modernized; 1300 kilometers of irrigation canals, with 8000 kilometers of supplementary distribution canals, had been constructed, and 2500 kilometers of river valleys had been brought under flood-control systems; electricity had been brought to the homes of 1.6 million rural inhabitants. Subsidies had given incentive to large numbers of farmers to shift from wheat production to more productive activities, like cattle-raising for milk and beef, fruit and vegetables, and citrus fruits; and the construction of processing plants by cooperatives had been financed. Aid to the hotel industry would make 60,000 more beds available for tourists in an area notably lacking in tourist accommodations though rich in tourist interest. The construction of almost 150 professional schools for agricultural and industrial training had been financed, and 36 billion lire spent on professional and other forms of education. With the financial backing of the Cassa, local Consorzi di Sviluppo had presented plans for the creation of sixteen "areas" of industrial development and of 20 "nuclei." Financial aid had been given to the construction of 2382 new factories and to the enlarging of 2449 others. Demands for credit for industrial investment, which was regarded as the key factor in the industrialization of the South, had remained fairly low at 100 to 180 billion lire annually throughout the 1950's, but it had reached a high of 1262 billion lire in 1962, with the result that manufacturing in the South was being modernized, oriented away from the traditional mining industries and even from consumer goods, and directed toward investment goods and goods for immediate use in production.[31]

The Cassa's activities received parliamentary approval with the passage on June 26, 1965 of the law prolonging its work until 1980 and granting it 1700 billion lire for the period 1965–69. The emphasis on industrialization was made even more marked. The Cassa was to devote most of its funds to the areas and nuclei of industrial development and to the irrigated areas where major increases in agricultural productivity were being sought. The intervention in the South was to be coordinated with the national economic program for 1965–69, whose very existence owed much to the experience of the Cassa and to the demands of its administrators.

During the second cycle of the Cassa's activity, the requirement of 1957, that the state holding companies make 40 per cent of their investments in the South, had a major effect on Southern industrialization. In this period these companies accounted for more than half of the industrial investment in the South, their total investment reaching 1655 billion lire,[32] mostly in the basic industries of steel, petrochemicals, and cement. The most important investments were made in Taranto-Bari-Brindisi; Naples-Salerno-Caserta; Latina-Aprilia; Cagliari; and Siracusa-Catania-Gela.

At the heart of the Taranto industrial area was the integrated steel plant of Italsider, begun in 1960 and completed in 1965. With production of 1.5 million tons of steel in 1965, the plant already accounted for 12 per cent of Italian steel production, and this percentage was to grow with the planned expansion of production.[33] On the land adjoining the steel plant, the IRI cement division, Cementir, completed a new plant which, using the slag from the blast furnace, would be capable of producing 1.1 million tons of cement anually. By their coastal location, the new IRI plants ensured ease of supply of raw materials by sea and maritime transportation for their products both to other parts of Italy and for export. Taranto was to link up with the industrial complex of Bari and of Brindisi to form a highly industrialized triangle in Puglia, while the products would also serve the needs of the smaller industrial nucleus of Valle del Basento in near-by Basilicata.[34]

The oldest established area of industrial development in the South was the triangle of Naples-Salerno-Caserta. At the end of World War II, the triangle possessed one of the three major steel-producing complexes of Italy, IRI's plant at Bagnoli, which was transformed by 1964 to integrated-cycle production; several engineering plants, 70 per cent of them controlled by IRI; a large number of small and medium-sized companies engaged in food processing; shipbuilding yards controlled by IRI at Castellamare di Stabbia; and a number of textile companies. There was thus a fairly diversified base, a large number of industrial workers of widely varied training, a dense local market, and what economists called "agglomerative potential." During the first decade of the Cassa's activity, this area received the most important of its investments favoring industrialization, and as a result the area's growth rate was higher than that of any other Southern region. One of the first private companies to answer the appeal to move into the Mezzogiorno and to profit from the incentives offered was Olivetti, which founded a typewriter factory at Pozzuoli in 1951; but the major investments were made by IRI, notably the new steel factory and a cement plant at Bagnoli. The greatest change in the economy of the area, however, was the construction of Alfa-Sud, an automobile factory with an annual production of 300,000 Alfa Romeo cars of 1000 to 1500 cc., which was approved by the government after an enormous struggle with the Fiat company interests in 1967.

With the vast postwar growth of the city of Rome on its doorstep, the area of Latina-Aprilia was able to make rapid industrial process. The proximity of Rome provided a natural market as well as an urban center of attraction to migrants into the industrial complex that grew up around the city of Latina. Latina received over 7 per cent of the special investments for the South during the 1950's, and was thus able to develop light industries catering mostly to the Roman market.[35]

The industrial development of Sicily was dominated by the petrochemical industry, and hence by ENI.[36] Exploration began only in the summer of 1955, but it quickly led to the discovery of some small fields of natural gas near Catania and of one of Italy's largest oil fields on the southwest coast at Gela, whose reserves were estimated at 3 million tons a year.[37] By 1959, ENI had plans under way for the building of a large industrial complex at Gela, combining a power plant using petroleum coke, a petroleum refinery, and a petrochemical plant. By 1965, the complex was producing ammonia, plastics, and fertilizers, and was linked by pipeline to fields of natural gas discovered by ENI, at Gagliano Castelferrato.

On June 11, 1962, the Regional Government of the island of Sardinia was authorized to draw up a special thirteen-year Piano di Rinascita (Rebirth Plan) for the economic and social transformation of the island, for which 400 billion lire were to be provided in addition to the normal expenditures of the Cassa. The first efforts of the planners to further the island's industrialization were concentrated in the zone of Cagliari, which had only become a significant industrial center in 1960, but which was able to profit from the excellent water and power supplies of the Flumendosa dam, from a large labor reserve in Cagliari and the surrounding communes, and from its geographical location in the center of the western Mediterranean. Unlike earlier industrial projects in Sardinia, which had been based upon the mines of Sulcis and Iglesias, the new industrial plants were almost independent of the raw material resources of the island. A major oil refinery was constructed, and it was linked closely to petrochemical establishments, especially the huge Rumianca plant for production of soda, chlorine, ethylene, etc., and another plant for the manufacture of plastics.[38] In Sardinia, most of the industrial projects were carried out by private industry, with the aid of the infrastructural investments made by the national and regional governments and of the financial incentives offered by the Cassa and the Piano di Rinascita.[39]

In comparison with these large sums spent in the South by the Italian government and the state companies, the direct aid provided by the European Economic Community was small. Southern Italy had received a large share of the $269 million paid by the Orientation Section of FEOGA in 1962–68; and Southern workers had been the principal beneficiaries of the $27 million contributed by the European Social Fund. The EEC Commission financed a major study on the promotion of the industrial area of development in the Taranto-Bari-Brindisi region. The study was intended not only to single out the industries that could profitably be established in this region, but also to analyze the influence of the structure of Mediterranean commerce upon the character of Southern European industrialization in general.[40] The most effective of EEC's interventions in the South, however, was the loan program of the European Investment Bank. The Bank's president and many of its top officials were Italian; and no effort was made to disguise the fact that the Bank had been created by the negotiators of the Treaty of Rome as EEC's principal instrument for bringing the economy of the Italian South up toward the level of the rest of western Europe. By 1966, Italy had received 61 per cent of the loans made by the Bank, or $458 million, which had been spent mostly in aiding the industrialization of the areas of development in the South, in modernizing the South's railroad network and constructing its highways, and in financing agricultural improvements made by the Cassa per il Mezzogiorno. The Bank's resources were derived from loans it contracted and from direct contributions of $1 billion by EEC members, Italy's contribution being set at $240 million. The Bank's success was due to its refusal to disperse its funds on large numbers of small projects, but to concentrate on playing a supporting role to the Italian government's development policy, in supplying funds for certain marginal projects such as specific factories within the development areas.[41]

The existence of EEC did not provide the stimulus of vast new markets for Southern products that its supporters had hoped for. The common agricultural policy was a great disappointment and even a danger to the South. The high cereals price helped prevent the conversion from wheat to livestock; the expansion of Southern exports of fruit and vegetables was blocked by various forms of frontier controls and quality inspections by Italy's partners; and the association agreements with Greece and Turkey and commercial privileges granted to France's former African colonies weakened the Community preference that Italy had expected to receive for its Mediterranean products, such as citrus fruits. Very few of the products of the new industrial areas were sold within EEC. The geographical isolation of the South from the markets of northern Europe, combined with the expanding home market for the

South's new industrial products, prevented the establishment of close trade ties between the South and the rest of EEC in any way comparable with the ties that developed between the industrial triangle of the Po valley and its northern European customers.

EEC's most important effect on the South was rather to stimulate the rest of the country's economic growth, and thereby to produce beneficial results in the South itself. The increasing wealth of the North and Center made it feasible for the Italian government to finance the huge programs of the Cassa per il Mezzogiorno and the vast industrial projects of IRI and ENI, deliberately forcing the transfer to the South of investment capital accumulated in the North. Many Southern Italians left the farms, and that, combined with the increase of industrial employment in the development zones of the South, had the very healthy result of reducing the proportion of Southern labor engaged in agriculture—from 55 per cent in 1950 to only 36 per cent in 1967—and to increase the income per capita in the South from 40 to 48 per cent of that of Northwestern Italy during the same period.

By the end of the 1960's, for the first time, experts on the South were beginning to express a cautious optimism. "As far as the results of the Southern policy are concerned," Francesco Compagna declared in September 1969, "whatever the lacunae, the incoherency, the uncertainty, and the mistakes, we cannot consider it to have failed. . . . Thanks to the Southern policy, the foundations of industrialization have been laid, and thus one can demand, and we do demand, that the great industrial groups, public and private, orient their expansion programs in such a way as to reduce the emigration from the South and increase employment in the South."[42] According to Pasquale Saraceno, "for the first time in its history the South appears to be sharing in the general process of expansion of the country at a rhythm not less than the extremely intense pace from which the more advanced regions have profited." The reason, he concluded, was the combination of the government's development policy and the exceptional economic progress of the country since 1957. The continuation of these two elements for the next decade would, he predicted, eliminate unemployment and underemployment in the South by 1980, and end the economic inferiority of the South "in the not distant future."[43]

The problem of the South had not been sloughed off onto Italy's partners in EEC, nor had EEC contributed in any major way directly to the solution of its difficulties. But the Common Market had helped the Italian government and public and private industry in their vast efforts to promote the industrial development of the South, and those efforts were beginning to show signs of success by the end of the 1960's. Italy had thus shown that a large-scale effort, spearheaded by a national government, could prevent economic integration from increasing the disparity between the developed and underdeveloped sections of the country. And, by wise investment of the new wealth produced by the process of integration, it could bring about the profitable use of the material and human resources of its hitherto underdeveloped area.

10
The Industrial Decision-makers

A very small group of decision-makers determined Italy's role in European integration. According to the Swiss sociologist Jean Meynaud, the Italian "ruling class," those persons "capable of exercising a notable influence on the functioning of the society," comprised no more than four to five thousand persons. This class could be broken down into seven categories: 1000 to 1200 political and administrative leaders, including politicians, party and state bureaucrats, judges, and high military officers; 2000 to 2500 executives of the principal private companies and banks; 400 to 500 executives of the public companies; 250 to 300 leaders of the Church and of Catholic Action; 100 to 200 heads of the most important professional organizations, such as Confindustria; 50 to 100 trade union leaders; and about 100 of the most distinguished scientists and intellectuals.[1] This chapter will consider the influence of the executives of the public and private companies on Italian participation in European economic integration.

THE PUBLIC COMPANIES: IRI AND ENI

The public companies are the state holding companies known as "imprese a partecipazione statale," predominantly industrial companies in which the state owns a controlling interest. The more important of them are the wide variety of companies grouped under the Istituto per la Ricostruzione Industriale (IRI) and the oil, natural gas, and chemical companies grouped under the Ente

Nazionale Idrocarburi (ENI). These public companies are central to any consideration of Italy's role in Europe. By the 1950's, IRI controlled most of Italy's iron and steel production, shipbuilding, telephones, radio and television, civil aviation, and an important share of its engineering and cement industry. ENI had a monopoly on the exploitation of natural gas and oil in the Po valley and a large stake in these resources in the rest of the country. As a result of their combination of important economic and political functions, they wielded enormous power over decisions affecting the nation as a whole. Meynaud classified the heads of the public companies among the 400 to 500 persons who had "access to the inner circles of power and participated in the taking of the decisions that were most serious and influential." The peculiar relationship of the public companies to the state compelled them to consider the public well-being in addition to the normal objective of seeking a profit, and this dual character led many in Italy to question whether the public companies might not constitute a disadvantage when Italy entered the European Community. The critics attacked from opposite ends of the spectrum. The Communists and Socialists criticized the public companies for operating as private companies in a capitalist society, and hence for ignoring their duties toward the state, especially that of preparing the backward sections of the country and the unskilled classes of society for a full share in the economic development of Italy within the integrated economy of western Europe. The conservative groups claimed that the public companies, far from running at a profit like private companies, were unfairly favored by the state in order to carry out political objectives that lacked economic rationale. Both Left and Right therefore felt, for different reasons, that the public companies were a liability. Yet the public companies themselves claimed that they were able to operate according to the same principles of profit as the private companies and, at the same time, to fulfill the tasks imposed upon them by the government. They believed that they were able to meet the competition from the other countries of EEC, and were unreservedly in favor of European integration throughout the postwar period. We must therefore ask whether the public companies were correct in asserting that they were no longer akin to the artificially supported, economically nonviable companies Mussolini had created, but rather that they were efficient, rational, productive units, comparable to the most dynamic private companies in western Europe.

ISTITUTO PER LA RICOSTRUZIONE INDUSTRIALE

Mussolini had created the Istituto per la Ricostruzione Industriale in 1933 to prevent the collapse of the leading Italian banks that had become too heavily involved in industrial financing. IRI took over three leading banks and a number of companies they owned, including steel companies, shipyards, several engineering companies, and many smaller firms. As war approached, the Fascist government used the Institute more and more as an instrument of its autarkic policies. IRI grew in the number of companies it controlled, and its direct involvement in the state's economic planning increased.[2] By the end of the war, IRI was in control of several of the sectors of the economy that were to face the greatest difficulties in the postwar period. Its efficiency, in Professor LaPalombara's words, was hampered by the tendency developed in the 1930's "to do whatever possible to keep the marginal producer in the field, even at a cost of continuous deficits to be covered by the public budget."[3]

One of the most remarkable features of Italy's postwar economic miracle was the manner in which IRI, while under constant attack from its critics in parliament and industry, was able to transform itself into one of the most efficient instruments of the country's industrial progress. Between 1945 and 1948, the group converted from wartime to peacetime production, and carried out reconstruction of its devastated plants, which had suffered far more than other sectors of the economy. Most of IRI's investments were poured into the engineering sector for conversion to production of tractors, railroad machinery, and electrical equipment. But only a small reduction of the labor force was permitted, so large funds had to be used to pay unneeded workers; few plants were closed, whether their conversion was economically feasible or not; and constant turnover of leading administrators hurt efficiency. From 1948 on, however, the group was able to apply the so-called "IRI formula," a pragmatic method, developed during its years of operating experience, by which the state could take an important role in the economic life of the country without embarking on a program of nationalization.

The features of the IRI formula were as follows: The state bought all, or a majority, of shares in private companies, and set up public agencies (enti pubblici) for those companies. These public agencies ran the companies on the same principles as private companies, i.e. they were financed on the open market without receiving state subsidies, and they showed a profit in fair competition with private companies. The companies responded to modern conditions of productivity by their size and their "polysectoral" character, which, according to IRI's president, Giuseppe Petrilli, provided "functional integration between the different activities directed by it and made it as a result a precise instrument for the implementation of a policy of planning."[4] Unlike private companies, they directed their activities to those spheres that the state considered to be significant for over-all national development, such as the basic public services of banking, sea transport and highways, or to "propulsive" industrial sectors, such as steel and power, and they took a major role in gigantic projects of national importance, such as the industrialization of the South. IRI retained its original role as a "hospital for sick companies," taking over the ownership and management of companies that the state felt should, in the national interest, be restored to economic health.[5] The task posed by the IRI formula's conditions was enormous; and many of IRI's difficulties were due to the burden of carrying whole economic sectors that could not be effectively reorganized.

From 1959 on, faced with increased competition inside the Common Market and aided by the beginning of the Italian economic boom, IRI gave greater emphasis to increasing the efficiency of its weaker sectors, which greatly reduced those companies' losses. Its role in determining the direction of the country's economic development was also enhanced by the adoption of national economic planning in the 1960's.

From the economic point of view, IRI's part in preparing the Italian economy for European integration was largely positive. The most important sectors it controlled, especially steel, light engineering, and cement, were run with the highest efficiency and obtained results equal to those of any of the private companies. A second group of companies, providing public services such as telephones, radio and television, and airlines, was run effectively and without significant public criticism, even though these companies operated as public monopolies. A third group, however, consisting mainly of heavy engineering, shipbuilding, and shipping companies, was run at a heavy loss, partly to avoid unemployment and partly because these operations were considered to be in the national interest. Nevertheless, especially in the 1960's, the application of IRI's management techniques, the availability of its financial backing, and the determination to apply the criterion of "economicità" within the government-imposed limits of labor redundancy, raised even the weak companies to higher levels of productivity. The fact that these results were achieved within the IRI formula also served Italy well. During the years of the Cold War, when Italy's internal divisions were being sharpened by the opposition of the Atlantic and Soviet blocs, IRI provided a method for state control of industry that lay midway between the liberalism of the right-wing parties and the nationalization demanded by the left-wing parties. The formula of the "mixed economy" was made workable, so that the significant share of Italy's industry that was under state control was able to compete successfully with private industry in the Common Market. Hence, IRI's leaders throughout the postwar period were in the vanguard in persuading men in political circles and the public in general that Italy was prepared for the economic integration, and needed the political integration, of western Europe.

The most outstanding of the spokesmen for IRI were Oscar Sinigaglia of Finsider (the single person most responsible for making Italy's steel industry confident of its ability to prosper in the European Coal and Steel Community); Professor Pasquale Saraceno, director of the Ufficio Studi of IRI; and especially Giuseppe Petrilli, chairman of IRI, president of the Italian Council of the European Movement, and former head of the European Investment Bank. Petrilli became the exponent of a clearly reasoned philosophy of Europeanism and of IRI's role in it.

For Petrilli, Italy had made its "basic choice" in the immediate postwar years by throwing over protectionism in favor of "a structure open to the outside, participating broadly in international trade." This development policy, based upon the progressive alignment of Italian productive conditions with those of the other countries of western Europe, arose in the same way as the policy of Europeanism, "which, far from constituting an alternative to the policy of economic development, constituted the greatest stimulus to such a policy that can come within a market economy." But merely to establish free trade, as OEEC did, was not enough to bring about the coordination of economic policies and of development programs and thus the renunciation of part of national sovereignty; the real integrative character of ECSC and EEC, Petrilli felt, was needed for that purpose.[6] The European Community provided the vast geographical area within which the individual countries of Europe could develop companies of a size sufficient to meet the technological demands of the "new industrialization," characterized by such technological achievements as atomic physics, synthetic chemistry, and electronics. The result of the new industrialization was to give the manufacturing company a far greater impact upon the character of society, and thus to make its activities a political and social responsibility to be planned in alliance with the organs of state. Europe's technological backwardness, however, made the problem of the state's relation to the new industrialization a common one for all European states, and provided a justification for political coordination that had been lacking even during the early successes of economic integration within the European Community. European integration, Petrilli stated, must thus create a "new dimension for European industry, given the undeniable connection existing between the achievement of a larger company size on the one hand, and the capacity to achieve that technological 'leap-forward which is the necessary condition for the new industrial revolution.' . . . Only the largest companies are in a position to achieve the necessary effort."[7]

In Petrilli's opinion, there was a direct tie between a state-controlled company like IRI, economic planning by the national state, and Community-wide planning of the EEC Commission. The vast modern company, he held, exercises enormous influence on society, while planning in terms of its own economic progress; IRI, because of its size, its concern with the basic or propulsive sectors of the economy, and its responsiveness to the social goals of the state, was able to orient the direction of economic development, as, for example, in greater capital accumulation, or in the industrialization of the South. IRI could take a major role in the activation of a state program of economic development, without state interference in the running of the private sector of industry.[8] But this economic planning would be insufficient if it were conceived solely in national terms. Only a Community program, such as the medium-term economic policy proposed in 1966, could provide the wider framework in which Italian development could be harmonized with the rest of western Europe. IRI, and the public companies of the other EEC members, would thus become important instruments for the "rationalization of the functioning conditions of the Community economy."[9] There was, therefore, no conflict between Petrilli's goals as president of IRI and his aims as president of the Italian Council of the European Movement. IRI, like the European Movement, was devoted to "militant Europeanism."[10]

ENTE NAZIONALE IDROCARBURI

The executives of ENI (the National Hydrocarbons Agency) never gave more than token support for European integration, and they never showed either enthusiasm for its benefits or fear of its consequences. Italy's main European markets for petroleum products were in Switzerland and Austria, rather than in EEC; and ENI's major incursion into EEC, the central European pipeline to Bavaria, was an expensive failure. But ENI's activities were vital to the Italian economic miracle and hence to Italy's success in the Common Market, owing to its achievements in supplying ample and reasonably priced sources of energy for Italy's expanding industry. Between 1950 and 1965, Italy's consumption of energy increased fivefold; and ENI deserves much of the credit for satisfying that need.[11]

ENI was founded in February 1953 as a state holding company for the various public companies already operating in the field of natural gas and petroleum production. The most important of these public companies was Azienda Generale Italiana Petroli (AGIP), which, from its foundation in 1926, had taken a large role in the search for petroleum deposits, in refining, and in distribution inside Italy.[12] In the first eight years after the war, AGIP scientists discovered rich fields of natural gas in the Po valley. The discoveries led to great demand, both from foreign companies and from large Italian companies operating in other gas fields, for a share in the search for and exploitation of these fields. After a two-year debate, in which AGIP's critics argued that a state monopoly would be inefficient, unimaginative in its research, and too expensive, the Chamber of Deputies established ENI as a holding company on the lines of IRI. Under it were grouped all the oil and natural gas companies in which the Italian state participated. ENI was given a monopoly in the exploitation and distribution of the natural gas and oil of the Po valley. General policy for the company was to be laid down by three of the Cabinet ministers, but administration was to be the company's responsibility. Until his death in a plane crash in 1962, ENI was identified with the frenetic genius of Enrico Mattei, its first president. Far more than any head of IRI, Mattei left his own personal imprint on a major section of the Italian economy; and he also used the power of his economic position to influence the direction of Italian foreign policy.[13]

After creating a coherent structure for the operation of its component companies, ENI set out to develop and distribute Italy's own resources of natural gas and oil. More than a thousand wells were sunk in the Po valley alone; and ENI's total production was raised from 2.7 billion cubic meters of natural gas in 1954 to 9.7 billion in 1968. Minor oil fields were discovered in Central and Southern Italy and a somewhat larger oil field at Gela in Sicily. The pipeline network for the distribution of natural gas was increased to 3280 miles, and this made available to Italian industry in large parts of the peninsula the cheapest fuel in all Europe. Major progress was made in refining, through the building of a refinery at Cortemaggiore and the improvement of the quality of refining at several other plants. But ENI found itself involved deeply in international politics when Mattei decided to satisfy Italy's need for imported crude oil without bowing to the "seven sisters," the seven great Anglo-American petroleum companies that controlled most of the oil production of the Middle East.

Mattei's crusade against the international oil companies arose partly from his own character and past and partly from economic necessity. Mattei was a self-made businessman, who had been the supreme financial organizer of the partisan movement in North Italy, and he was one of the principal Christian Democratic representatives in a predominantly left-wing movement. He was rewarded at the end of the war with the position of Northern Commissioner for AGIP, at the time when the company was making its important discoveries of natural gas in the Po valley. He at once became the spokesman of several highly emotional causes. He proclaimed Italy's right to equality with the great powers at a time when the imposition of the peace treaty had roused great resentment; and he focused this resentment against the "seven sisters." He posed as the defender of the Italian people from the power of the big monopolies at home, declaring that state enterprise was the weapon by which these companies could be kept in check. And he appealed to all groups, at home or abroad, who felt themselves exploited, whether they were the Arabian oil producers or those of the less developed regions of Switzerland and Germany. The economic justification of this attitude lay in the position of the great international oil companies, particularly the British and American seven—Esso, Socony-Mobil, Standard Oil of California, Texaco, Gulf Oil, Shell, and Anglo-Iranian—who sold Middle East oil at very large profit margins, which they shared equally with the governments of the producing countries. Faced with Italy's rapidly growing need for petroleum and by the failure of AGIP and then ENI to find any really large oil deposits in Italy, Mattei was forced to buy the oil his companies needed from the international oil companies. Following the nationalization of the Anglo-Iranian company in 1951–52, Mattei demanded a share in the new National Iranian Oil Company that replaced it; but the American, British, Dutch, and French participants refused him.[14] Mattei retorted that the freedom left to the great oil producers to determine production, export quantities, and prices gave them too great a power over the economy of the producing countries. He proposed instead that each producing country should become a partner with the oil company, paying a share of the exploration cost once oil had been located and receiving the equivalent of 75 per cent of the profits, rather than 50 per cent. He thereby disturbed the whole royalty system and compelled the international companies to renegotiate their agreements with the Arab governments. But the concessions granted to ENI in Egypt and in Iran under the new formula proved to be of little value, since the Italians failed to find any major oil field, and his policy failed. Mattei then carried out another coup in 1960: he concluded an agreement with the Soviet Union for a massive barter of Italian products, largely from ENI and IRI, in return for Russian oil.[15]

Mattei thus attempted to divert Italian foreign policy away from its concentration on western Europe and the Atlantic Alliance. His goal was to make Italy a welcome ally of the underdeveloped countries in Africa and the Middle East. As the colonial powers withdrew from Egypt and Morocco, he moved in. He earned France's distrust by refusing to join in the exploitation of Sahara oil during the Algerian war. And he saw his dealings with the Soviet Union as a blow to the worldwide power of the oligopoly of British, American, and Dutch oil companies. In this way he was able to implement several of the tenets of the left-wing Christian Democrats, especially those around President Giovanni Gronchi. This policy, known as neo-Atlanticism, was a reassertion of the neutralism expressed during the earlier debates on the Marshall Plan and the Atlantic Pact—the desire for Europe to detach itself from its dependence upon the United States and to take an independent stand in world affairs, particularly by appealing to the emerging Arab and African countries. This policy, as Dow Votaw has pointed out, originated in Mattei's own brand of nationalism, which made it impossible for him to understand or support the Common Market. "Mattei always seemed to see even his own markets abroad through nationalistic eyes. He probably also saw the Common Market as a weakening influence on his nationalistic approach to trade and a threat to some of the barriers that protected his flanks in Italy, not only with regard to petroleum but in many of the other fields in which ENI was active."[16]

At the time of Mattei's death, the economic results of his presidency were still mixed. He had succeeded in giving ENI the size that made it able to bargain successfully on a par with the "seven sisters," and to achieve the economies of scale essential in the oil industry. Production of natural gas had reached almost 7 billion cubic meters, and crude oil production in Italy and abroad exceeded 4 million tons. A major petrochemical subsidiary had been created. And ENI's pricing policy inside Italy had forced its foreign competitors to cut their prices to the consumer. ENI claimed that in 1966 alone its policy of low prices had saved the Italian consumer 75 billion lire.[17] Many of his more flamboyant ventures, however, were criticized as unnecessary drains on Italy's resources. Mattei's critics claimed that money spent on unsuccessful exploration for oil abroad could have been better spent on Italian wells; that Italian oil cost more than oil that could have been obtained by buying directly from the big companies; that diversification at home, often in elaborate plants like the petrochemical complex at Ravenna, served more to impress the representatives of underdeveloped countries than to meet Italy's economic needs; and that ENI's accounting methods hid its more glaring errors.[18]

Mattei's successors, Marcello Boldrini and Eugenio Cefis, while carrying on the expansion of ENI on the technical lines laid down by Mattei, were careful to avoid continuing his more questionable ventures into foreign policy; and the economic results were immediately evident. Sales almost tripled between 1962 and 1968, as did crude oil production in Italy. Natural gas production was boosted from 6.9 billion to 9.7 billion cubic meters, and the gas pipelines were extended from 4434 to 6840 kilometers.[19]

After 1962, ENI also took a larger interest in the European market. Mattei himself had hit upon the idea of breaking into the central European market with pipelines from Italian ports across the Alps into Switzerland and South Germany. By constructing a pipeline from Genoa to a new ENI refinery at Ingolstadt, he had hoped to bring Bavaria into the Italian orbit. This grandiose project was completed in 1966, and 6 million tons of crude oil were pumped through it, about one-quarter going to the refinery at Ingolstadt.[20] Nevertheless, the project lost money; construction and operation would have been less expensive from an Adriatic port than from Genoa, and competition with the big oil companies in Germany and with subsidized coal production greatly reduced the profit margin on sales. ENI, however, continued to penetrate carefully chosen markets, through its German subsidiary and through a new French subsidiary that opened in 1968. In 1966, AGIP exported almost 1 million tons of petroleum products to Europe, and its subsidiaries in Austria, Germany, and Switzerland sold another 2.6 million tons. ENI proposed to expand these operations in the future. It therefore worked with the other petroleum and natural gas companies in the Community in pressing for establishment of a common energy policy that would not discriminate against petroleum or natural gas in favor of coal and that would enable the companies within the Community, by such means as a Community-wide depletion allowance, to compete on equal terms with nonmember countries.[21]

ENI's interest in European integration thus grew with the expansion of its marketing operations and the need to take account of the Community administration as a policy-making body that could offer substantial benefits to ENI itself. But just as with the Italian steel industry, ENI's main concern was to supply Italy's own needs. It regarded integration favorably only as a stimulus to the increased demand for energy; and its collaboration with the Community was directed toward satisfaction of that demand.

THE LEADING PRIVATE COMPANIES

More than in any other country of EEC, the Italian economy has been characterized by the dominance of most branches of private industry by one giant company. Although in the 1960's there were signs of the incipient erosion of this system, in the two decades following the war an "establishment," comprised of the leading officials of the major companies, spoke for private Italian industry on most political issues and found ready acceptance of its views in the parties of the Right and in all sections of the predominant Christian Democratic party except that of its left-wing members.

The dominant position of a few great companies was due in the first instance to the small size of the Italian market in the century following unification, and then to government support through high tariff policy from the 1880's on and to direct governmental assistance under the Fascists. Once dominant, these companies restrained their production when necessary to maintain a stable market with high prices. No attempt was made in the immediate postwar years to restrict their position by governmental action; the first challenge to their hegemony of the Italian market came from outside, with the first moves to trade liberalization in the 1940's and to economic integration through ECSC and EEC in the 1950's. This challenge forced the big Italian companies to ask themselves whether their own prosperity lay in the maintenance, if possible, of their own privileged position in Italy, or whether the century of isolation had given them the size and efficiency they needed to profit from trade on a continent-wide scale. After initial misgivings, the largest companies all chose the wider market.

The most important private companies were Montecatini-Edison in chemicals, Fiat in automotive production, Pirelli in tires and rubber, Olivetti in typewriter and calculating-machine manufacturing, and Snia-Viscosa in artificial fibers. Their relative strength is shown in table 4, taken from *Fortune* magazine's survey of the largest industrial companies outside the United States.[22]

Table 4. Largest Italian Industrial Companies in 1969
(Ranked by sales in millions of dollars)

Rank Outside U.S.A.	Company	Sales	Assets	Net profit	Invested capital	Employees
8	Montecatini-Edison	2315.7	4561.3	66.2	1873.9	142,326
13	Fiat	2135.7	1628.2	55.1	516.9	158,445
28	ENI	1444.0	4026.0	6.2	1295.2	59,960
54	Pirelli	949.9	993.3	25.0	213.5	69,289
64	Italsider	886.7	2649.2	22.0	478.7	37,427
101	Olivetti	592.8	332.4	11.6	111.6	60,681
135	Snia-Viscosa	441.6	432.0	13.6	145.1	29,500
185	Alfa-Romeo	316.5	286.4	9.6	117.8	17,858

Adapted from the 1969 Fortune Directory by special permission; © 1969 Time Inc.

Montecatini-Edison: The Montecatini-Edison company was formed in 1966 through the fusion of the two largest chemical companies in Italy, the Montecatini and Edison companies. Together they controlled 72 per cent of the assets of the Italian chemical industry, and they had absolute dominance in almost every branch of chemical production, from sulphuric acid to plastics. The new company was the sixth largest chemical company in the world, exceeded in the Common Market only by Bayer and in the European Free Trade Association by Imperial Chemical Industries of Great Britain.

The Edison company was founded in 1882 to set up the first electrical energy plant in Europe, which was built in Milan. At the end of World War II, Edison was the principal supplier of electricity to the Northern industrial triangle, but it had also spread into other fields of industry. It supplied gas to Milan, and would dearly have loved a share in the natural gas exploitation of the Po valley that was finally granted exclusively to ENI. It produced steel, electronic equipment, domestic appliances, machine tools, and, especially after 1950, a vast array of chemical products. In 1956, with assets of 337 billion lire and profits of 10.9 billion, Edison was a major force in the Italian economy. It felt itself capable of plunging into wider markets outside Italy to sell its chemical and other manufactured products, while it saw great opportunity for expansion of its principal activity of electricity production in the development of the Northern industrial companies. It welcomed the Common Market on the ground that "many of our problems, above all that of unemployment, can find a more satisfactory solution with the insertion of our economy into a vaster European sphere, and . . . a more rational development of the national economies that are limited at the moment."[23] But Edison's welcome in principle was dimmed by practical recurrent worries about the inability, or unwillingness, of the Italian government to make the necessary provisions for meeting the problems deriving from the Common Market. In particular, it reacted to the institution of the Common Market by attempting to satisfy two of the company's greatest demands—restraint on the intrusion of the government into productive activity and reform of the legislative and administrative structure of Italy. The company's conception of the new Community thus was identical with that of the conservative political groups, especially the Liberals.[24] While the Common Market was unsympathetic to Edison's complaints against the public companies, the Center-Left government of Amintore Fanfani made its most notable concession to Socialist demands by nationalizing the electrical division of the Edison company along with the rest of the Italian electrical industry in 1962. The justification given for the move was that the great electrical companies made huge, undisclosed profits by supplying a public utility; that they were able to avoid public regulation of their rates by exercising political pressure; and that their financial exploitation of the public was supported by all the other monopoly companies. Moreover, nationalization of the electric industry seemed necessary to keep Italian industry competitive within

EEC. Expensive and inadequate electricity had been hampering industrial development. The multitude of private companies had adopted no rational structure of production and service, and had little interest in bringing electricity to the poorer areas of the country. Nationalization also proved a further, and somewhat unexpected, boon to the restructuring of the Italian chemical industry. Edison, seeking a suitable investment for the vast capital it had received in payment for its nationalized assets, proved a natural partner for the Montecatini company, which, to compete successfully with the great chemical companies of Germany, was looking for new capital. Both companies wanted just such a merger.

The Montecatini company, founded in 1888 to mine copper, moved into chemical production in the early twentieth century. Between the wars it became a major producer of sulphuric acid, sodium products, ammonia, fertilizers, and dyestuffs. By the mid 1950's, it accounted for half of Italy's production of fertilizers, synthetic fibers, and dyestuffs, and was in the process of extending its interests into electrical energy needed by the company's factories, into banking, and into commercial outlets for its products. Montecatini's size and its dynamic progress in the development of the newer chemical products like synthetics did not, however, make the company look without apprehension upon closer ties with the other countries of western Europe. Beyond the Alps stood Montecatini's most powerful competitors, the vast chemical companies of Germany—Bayer, Hoechst, and the Badische Anilin- und Soda-Fabrik (BASF), the descendants of the prewar colossus I.G. Farbenindustrie, while across the Channel was the largest chemical company in Europe, the redoubtable ICI. But Montecatini's judgment of its own prospects was essentially positive, if not ecstatic. "We have . . . re-examined our factories and our cycles of production; we have gone over the whole range of our products and the height of our costs; and we have reached the firm conclusion that the company—after overcoming, if necessary, a brief period of initial readaptation—will be able to obtain in the European framework definitely better prospects than those it always had and profited from, operating principally within the Italian economy."[25]

During the first decade of the Common Market, the whole Italian chemical industry, and Montecatini in particular, made spectacular advances in production and sales; and in this it showed greater progress than any other member country. But it is hard to ascertain whether the existence of the Common Market was responsible. Only in plastics were important markets for Italian chemical exports established in EEC. The greatest part of inorganic and organic chemical products and chemical fertilizers was sold to third countries, the most important being Egypt, Communist China, Taiwan, Greece, Yugoslavia, and Spain. A large increase in imports into Italy of chemical products from EEC followed the establishment of the Common Market, between 50 and 70 per cent of Italy's chemical imports coming from EEC countries. This increased pressure, upon a company that had enjoyed virtual freedom from competition, was a major factor in persuading Montecatini to continue its diversification, to seek closer ties with Italian companies in fields other than chemical production, and to conclude production and patent agreements with chemical companies both inside and outside EEC. But the greatest change in the company's history was precipitated by the great merger movent in the world chemical industry, and especially within EEC, in the 1960's, which made Montecatini fear that it was about to fall behind its competitors in research potential, economy of operation, and capital. Faced with fifteen mergers of chemical companies in Germany alone, and five large mergers and cooperation agreements in France, Montecatini sought a way to strengthen its own position. The result was the merger of the Montecatini and Edison companies in 1966. The new company had assets in 1967 of 2677 billion lire and profits of 41,344 million lire. In the fields of basic chemicals, fertilizers, plastics, and synthetic fibers, it was of a size and capacity to meet the growing challenge of both the European and American companies.[26] This merger was perhaps the most dramatic result in Italy of the Common Market's pressure on European companies to attain the scale demanded by modern technology.[27]

Fiat: Except for a brief period of apprehension in 1956–57, the Fiat company was one of the most enthusiastic supporters of integration in Italy. Its confidence was shown to be justified in 1967, when it achieved the largest sales of any automobile manufacturer in EEC, exceeding even Volkswagen.[28]

The Fabbrica Italiana Automobili Torino (Fiat) was founded in 1899 in Turin by Giovanni Agnelli. Although it was only one of forty automobile companies started in Italy around the turn of the century, Fiat quickly established its dominance of the industry through the engineering and sales skills of the Agnelli family. By World War II, Fiat was already a vertically integrated company, controlling the whole gamut of production from iron ore mining to final sales; and after the war it continued to broaden its interests in activities related to automobiles, such as highway construction.

From 1945 to 1949, Fiat concentrated almost exclusively on the home market, engaging in reconstruction, with strong financial aid from the Marshall Plan for the acquisition of machinery. From 1949 to the mid 1950's, enjoying an almost impenetrable defense against foreign competition through high tariffs, it saturated the home market. Then it began to seek outlets for its expanding production abroad, not in Europe, but in the United States and in the developing countries.[29] From the mid 1950's on, however, after first voicing suspicions of EEC and requesting continued protection in different forms, it sought to profit from the vastly expanding markets of western Europe, and especially of Germany and France.[30]

To meet the challenges of the Common Market, Fiat carried out a vast investment program. It reached an average of $100 million from 1959 on, with most of the investments being made in enlargement and improvement of its Mirafiori plant in Turin.[31] With extensive use of new machine tools and the introduction of automation, Fiat boosted its production from 269,000 cars and trucks in 1958 to 1.4 million in 1968. It introduced many new models, fifteen of them between 1964 and 1968. To streamline operations at home, many of its subsidiaries, such as its battery-making division, were consolidated within the parent company. Throughout the Common Market it opened efficient sales and servicing facilities; and, during the first decade of EEC, it almost tripled its sales to the Common Market countries. Recognizing the value of mergers within the Community, the company moved to take over the French Citroen company; and in 1970, the French government permitted Fiat to take a 49 per cent holding in Citroen. In Italy, Fiat purchased the small Auto-Bianchi company and established closer financial and technical ties with the other major Italian companies.[32] It collaborated with Ansaldo in work on a nuclear-engined tanker that was partly financed by Euratom, and with Montecatini for construction of nuclear reactors.[33]

While Fiat president Vittorio Valletta had cautiously supported the Treaty of Rome, his successor, Giovanni Agnelli, grandson of the company's founder, became one of the most persuasive advocates of the need for more rapid progress in both economic and political integration. Agnelli was only forty-five years old in 1966, when he took over the presidency of the company. He claimed to speak for the younger generation in placing Europe's primary goal in the "need for achieving its political unity." Like Petrilli of IRI, Agnelli saw the great industrial companies playing a vital part in the abolition of national frontiers.[34] European industry, he felt, had to combine to develop highly advanced technology in order to avoid becoming a mere adjunct to more advanced industrial systems. To achieve this position, industry should press the EEC administration to move beyond the customs union to economic union, work to aid the industrial companies by passing legislation to create "European companies," establish a European capital market, and support common scientific research, as well as develop European economic planning. Agnelli had taken upon himself the role of needling the governments and even the Community itself toward greater supranationalism, for he was convinced that such progress was essential to the progress of companies like Fiat. And Fiat's own achievements during the initial decade of integration seemed to prove him correct.[35]

Pirelli: Pirelli, almost more than any other Italian company, had a long record of involvement in foreign production and sales. By 1968, it had plants operating in sixteen countries, and made half of its $700 million in total sales abroad. Above all, the company's great success was due to its position in the vanguard of technical progress. When it was founded in Milan in 1872 by Giovanni Battista Pirelli, it was Italy's first rubber factory. The company first produced technical and household rubber goods, then insulated electric cables, tires for bicycles, and finally, at the turn of the century, automobile tires. It set up a factory in Spain in 1902, and another in England in 1914. By 1921 its international investments had become so large that it established an international holding company, the Société Internationale Pirelli; and before World War II it had started factories in Argentina, Brazil, and Belgium. After the war, Pirelli looked with renewed interest to foreign markets. The company already controlled about 45 per cent of the Italian market, and could see good prospects of expansion with the growing motorization of the Italian population and with the use of its electric cables in Italian industry. But the leaders of the company, especially the Pirelli family, who maintained their control over the company from its foundation, felt that foreign expansion offered major benefits. As President Leopoldo Pirelli pointed out in 1968, the rotation of Pirelli's personnel between the national and international branches had given them broad knowledge of various forms of international business, while the products of the company had been diversified to meet the variety of demand abroad and to challenge the competition of foreign producers. Research costs were divided among all the company's branches, while products such as the radial "cinturato" tire, which required vast research expenses, could be financed by sales over a world market. Worldwide operation spread the risks and reduced the effects of any local recessions on over-all operation. Pirelli thus felt, from its own practical experience over half a century, that it had the technological and financial capacity to operate abroad with great success.[36]

Pirelli approached integration with long experience, and with an optimism which was quickly justified. New companies were founded in the Common Market countries—at Saleux (Somme) in France, at Sandbach in Germany, and at Baudour in Belgium; and all company operations within EEC were brought under direct control of the Pirelli headquarters in Milan, and thus were separated from the operations of the Société Internationale Pirelli. While company reports do not identify exactly the contribution to Pirelli's progress made by exports to Common Market countries and by subsidiaries in EEC, profits of Pirelli S.p.A. rose from 3.6

billion lire in 1957 to 7.8 billion lire in 1967, while sales volume doubled, to reach 198 billion lire.[37]

Olivetti: Olivetti hardly ranks with Montecatini-Edison and Fiat in size and influence.[38] But it has exercised a virtual monopoly in one industrial sector in Italy, the production of typewriters and office machines; and it has been in the vanguard of Italy's industrial progress. It serves as an excellent bridge between the vast monopoly companies and the wide range of dynamic medium-sized companies that contributed to the Italian economic miracle.

The company was founded in 1908 by Camillo Olivetti, a Jew born in the ghetto of Ivrea, in the Alpine foothills near Turin, who was married to a Waldensian Protestant.[39] Both by background and geography, the Olivetti family were thus set apart from the mainstream of Italian development; and, like other inhabitants of Europe's border regions, it was natural for them to look beyond the national confines. Camillo had studied electrical engineering in the United States at Stanford University, had met Thomas Edison, and on his return to Italy had founded an electrical precision instruments factory at Ivrea, in 1896. In 1908, however, he had turned to the manufacture of typewriters; and two years later he brought out the M-1, the first typewriter manufactured in Italy. By 1939, the company was making 23,000 office machines and 19,000 typewriters a year. It had already established itself as a leader in the provision of social services to its employees, in the attempt to humanize factory employment, and especially as a pioneer in the idea that industrial products be elegant as well as functional. Adriano Olivetti, Camillo's eldest son, who became director general of the company in 1933 and retained control until his death in 1960, inherited his father's interest in the wider aspects of industrialism, from product design to city planning, his intense feeling for the well-being of his workers, and his concern with political and social philosophy.

Under Adriano, both the company and its philosophy were expanded and diversified. Before the war Olivetti made a start in the production of adding and calculating machines. After the war, in the 1950's, Olivetti's Research and Development group developed a computer, the Elea 9003, with which the company hoped to challenge the incursion into Europe of IBM machines, especially within the Common Market. It also expanded its production of office furniture. Adriano laid great emphasis on establishing foreign factories, in Barcelona, Glasgow, Buenos Aires, São Paolo, and Johannesburg, and had bought a controlling interest in the American Underwood Corporation, which had once been the giant among typewriter producers. Almost two-thirds of the production from the five factories in Italy went to export. Adriano Olivetti could only welcome the reduction of customs barriers within Europe, since, he told the shareholders in 1957, "it would have over-all a beneficial and stimulating effect on the Italian economy and, in particular, will bring advantages to our company."[40]

Adriano Olivetti wanted to be far more than a company president, however. He had escaped the Germans when they had occupied Rome in 1943, and, during his wartime exile in Switzerland, he had turned to political philosophy. To find the solution to the problem tormenting him, "the reconciliation of political freedom with the specific tasks of the class in power," he had studied the theorists of the past, and finally embodied his own views in a book which he had printed in Switzerland, *L'ordine politico della comunità*. He followed up this first manifesto with two later works, *Società stato comunità* and *Città dell'uomo*.[41] In these three books he attempted to lay out a plan for the total reorganization of society. The average citizen had lost touch with the political institutions of his own society, he felt, and the solution was a new size of territorial unit in which the citizen would be able to exercise a form of direct democracy. This unit, 100 thousand to 150 thousand people, Olivetti called the "Comunità." In the valley of the Canavese, where the Olivettis had created such a community in the factories and housing of Ivrea, he saw a demonstration of this new form of society.[42] The link of all these ideal units would be federal, with a Regional Council linking the communities. The nations of each area, such as Europe or Latin America, were to be joined in vaster federations, and all were to unite in a supreme world body. Yet at the basis of this world society would be the Comunità—the electoral and administrative unit, the new organ of a decentralized industry that would replace the dehumanized metropolitan centers.

Olivetti was one of the most passionate federalists in the postwar period, but the emphasis of his federalism was on the decentralizing of power. His supreme effort to win acceptance for his ideas ocurred in the elections of 1958, when he spent $500,000 to run candidates for a new Comunità movement throughout the country, but succeeded only in getting himself elected. Even so, in many other way, he attempted to support the federalist groups in Italy through his publishing house, Comunità, and with financial support.

Adriano Olivetti died in 1960, but the company's spectacular progress continued. While the Olivetti company still sold its traditional products, it decided to meet the increasingly dangerous problem of Italy's technological backwardness, especially in the electronics field. In 1964 it collaborated with the American General Electric Corporation to form the Olivetti–General Electric Company, which produced computers especially for the European market. The new company appointed one of Italy's most experienced Europeanists, Ambassador Attilio Cattani, as its president. By 1968, Olivetti was the undisputed leader in Europe in the production of typewriters and calculating machines, and was winning a sound reputation as a leader in electronics, particularly computers. Seventeen per cent of its total sales were made within the Common Market, for a value of 53 billion lire. It is not true that Olivetti's sales to the Common Market countries increased more rapidly than those to other regions, however; there was an over-all expansion of the company's sales, with an increase of 318 per cent during the first decade of the Common Market's existence.[43]

SNIA-VISCOSA: The Società Nazionale Industria Applicazioni Viscosa, or Snia-Viscosa, had originally been a shipping company founded by Giovanni Agnelli of Fiat; but it had moved into the production of rayon, a product of cellulose, using the viscose process. It prospered greatly during the Fascist period, and by 1945, it produced almost two-thirds of all the man-made fibers in Italy (one-quarter was produced by the Montecatini and Edison companies). This dynamic sector of the economy, which, through its technological and capital requirements, could only be successfully developed by very large companies, was thus dominated by three of Italy's largest companies; and the successful exploitation of the openings presented by European integration depended upon these three companies alone.

Snia-Viscosa made great progress in rationalization of production after the war. It extended its vertical organization from agriculture (for the production of cellulose), to electricity for its own power requirements, to textiles and clothing, to department stores for sale of its goods. It moved rapidly into plastics production and into all new forms of synthetic fibers, and was thus able to profit from the expansion of the smaller manufacturing companies in textiles, household appliances, toys, and so on, in the late 1950's. At the time of the negotiation of the Treaty of Rome, the company felt itself highly competitive, even with the major German and French companies, and it also felt the need of a wider market. In Italy, the consumption of textiles and plastics per capita was relatively low. Italy's exports of synthetic fibers and plastics to the Common Market far exceeded its imports, and Snia-Viscosa was one of the major gainers from this evolution. The company's interest, however, extended far beyond the Common Market: it was interested in British membership in EEC as a result of its financial and technological ties with Courtaulds and in easier trade with the United States through a successful conclusion to the Kennedy Round of tariff negotiations.

The attitude of the largest Italian private companies toward European economic integration was enthusiastic. There was a general recognition that the period of protection and autarky, during which they had employed their semimonopolistic position to reach their present size, had prepared them for meeting competition from companies outside Italy. The Italian market, even if controlled monopolistically, was no longer adequate to support industries of the scale required by the advances of modern technology, and most of the major companies were ready to enter a Community where wider markets and stimulus to greater efficiency would be the reward for acceptance of increased competition. These major companies, however, did not increase their trade within the Common Market countries more than they did with the developing countries of Asia and Africa or with the Communist bloc; the greatest fear of these companies was not of competition from outside, but of lack of governmental action at home to force the necessary changes in the legal, fiscal, and economic structure that would enable them to operate competitively with companies in other member countries. Some even regarded the Common Market as an instrument for the preservation of liberalism in economic life and for the prevention of future interference—and reduction of the existing interference—by the national state in economic activity. While company leaders often voiced acquiescence in the goals of European political unity, they felt secure in doing so because they knew their support was based upon a realistic appraisal of Italy's economic situation.

11
Pressure Groups in Industry and Agriculture

Few issues in the postwar period roused Italy's industrial and agricultural leaders more than that of participation in European integration. The pressures exerted and the goals sought by the industrial, commercial, and agricultural leaders lie in the difficult realm of the operation of interest groups in Italy.[1] Fortunately, research over the past decade, especially the work of the Centro Italiano di Ricerche e Documentazione, and that of Professor Joseph LaPalombara and his collaborators, has enabled us to identify with some accuracy the normal methods of operation of Italian interest groups.

From the first, the industrial and agricultural leaders set out to make their views widely known, in as persuasive a form as possible, both to the members of their own groups and to the general public. Newspapers were regarded, as LaPalombara points out, as "a critical means of providing information and disseminating propaganda." Both public and private companies controlled major newspapers. Fiat, for example, dominated *La Stampa* of Turin, and ENI spoke through *Il Giorno* of Milan.[2] There were also vast numbers of reviews, specialized journals, and group publications that expressed the views of special groups, such as *Rivista di Politica Economica* of Confindustria and *Mondo Agricolo* of Confagricoltura.

One of Italy's favorite institutions is the convegno, a conference where a series of papers presented by experts are discussed by an influential group of highly placed government officials, politicians, and scholars, the proceedings usually being published in book form. Whenever decisions concerning European integration arose, industrial and agricultural leaders were more than usually willing to take part in such a conference. Of the hundreds of such meetings held to discuss integration, those that attracted the most attention were two sponsored by Confindustria, one in 1952, on the Schuman Plan, and another in 1958, on EEC's relations with nonmembers; the convegno on the Common Market organized by the Centro Informazioni e Studi sul MEC in Milan, in 1960; and the Coltivatori Diretti's convegno, held in 1958, devoted to "Agriculture and the European Common Market." Provincial Chambers of Commerce held scores of these meetings: there was one in Sardinia on the "European Community and the Rebirth Plan," in 1963.[3] The public companies were prominent in these activities also. Petrilli and Visentini spoke at convegni all over Italy, while IRI itself organized an important meeting in Rome in 1962 on the function of the public company in the economy of the Common Market.[4] All these meetings enabled politicians and businessmen to argue out their differences under the mediating supervision of the country's leading economists, thereby making most of the economic and political leaders of the country aware of the complex issues involved in integration.[5]

The interest groups also exerted pressure on the legislative process. Both industry and agriculture had spokesmen in parliament on whom they relied for presentation of their opinions on issues concerning integration, and frequently they had advocates within the Cabinet itself. A few of these men were industrialists themselves, like Giuseppe Pella. Others, like Giulio Andreotti, were felt to be sympathetic toward conservative business groups. One of the politicians interviewed by LaPalombara's research group reported that "all major industries have their hand-picked deputies," who are rewarded by fees for consulting work done for the firm, or by provision of jobs in the industry for the politician's election staff.[6] Several of the more powerful groups had deputies in parliament who were openly identified with them. The Coltivatori Diretti was the most outstanding example: thirty-seven deputies were employed in the local offices of the confederation and another thirty-five were regarded as habitual members of their parliamentary group.[7]

The views of these interest groups were presented directly to the bureaucracy through personal contacts maintained with the government ministries. Confindustria, for example, had entrée to the Ministry of Industry and Commerce. The Ministry of Agriculture paid close attention to Fiat's interests in tractor production and to Montecatini's in fertilizer manufacture. Decisions affecting the major industries were always taken after consultation with the companies concerned; and, indeed, as LaPalombara's study has shown, the ministries were often compelled to rely on the companies and the trade associations for technical information that the anachronistic and poorly financed bureaucracy was not in a position to collect.[8] Of course, when any company or confederation that has a vital concern in the effect of national or Community decisions provides such information, that in itself is a form of pressure.

The official spokesmen for industry and agriculture, and their normal instruments for pressuring both legislature and bureaucracy, were the major professional associations. Industry was represented by the Confederazione Generale dell'Industria Italiana (Confindustria); commerce by the Confederazione Generale del Commercio e del Turismo (Confcommercio); the large agricultural proprietors by the Confederazione Generale dell'Agricoltura Italiana (Confagricoltura) and the smallholders by the Confederazione Nazionale Coltivatori Diretti (Coltivatori Diretti). By studying the goals of these instruments of organized business, commerce, and agriculture with regard to European integration, we shall be able to establish to what extent they were successful in shaping the decisions reached at the political level.

THE CONFEDERAZIONE GENERALE DELL'INDUSTRIA ITALIANA

Confindustria was founded in 1910 as an outgrowth of the local Turin Industrial League. It flourished during the Fascist era as one of the instruments of the corporate state, and it was reorganized in 1944 without significant changes. It was still dominated by the more conservative companies, like Edison, but was generally supported by all the larger private companies.

Under its first postwar president, Dr. Angelo Costa (1944-55), the confederation was careful not to take an active political role, because of its former identification with the Fascist state. Costa was satisfied to maintain close and fruitful ties with the center and right-wing groups in the Christian Democratic party, with the more conservative parties, and with the bureaucracy. Largely through De Gasperi's complaisance, Confindustria achieved its principal goal: acceptance by the government of the principle that industry should be left free to carry through economic reconstruction "in its own way and according to the dictates of the changing economic situation."[9] It naturally followed from this principle that direct state participation in the productive sector was anathema. The creation of IRI, ENI, and the state electricity agency, ENEL, was a direct affront to Confindustria's principles. After 1956, the government forbade the membership of the public companies in Confindustria, and thus ended the confederation's powerful influence over their policies. At that point, the confederation began to attack the companies—first their methods of operation, then their very existence. Confindustria held that the public companies did not operate on a profit-loss basis, but were frequently operated at a loss and subsidized by the state; that they enjoyed privileged methods of financing from the state; and that they weakened the country's economy by engaging in unfair competition with private companies that did not enjoy these privileges and by maintaining non-viable companies that ought to have been allowed to go out of business. Confindustria concluded that the public companies unjustly and unnecessarily hampered private industry in its efforts to adjust Italian production both to the openings in foreign markets and to competition from abroad in the home market. It used this last argument especially when the effects of the liberalization of foreign trade and later of economic integration through the European Communities were being felt. The confederation's attitude to integration, as established under Costa and carried on under his successors, was an outgrowth of its conception of the economic system at home. Liberty of the individual company to act in its own best interests within the fair competition of a free economic system was regarded as the only sound way to general economic progress; and the leaders of Confindustria welcomed any measure of integration that could be regarded as furthering that goal.[10]

Confindustria's views on integration emerged piecemeal, as

every new proposal for the closer unification of the European economies forced it to take a stand. The liberalization of trade in 1949–51, Confindustria felt, was a disagreeable necessity, "the only concrete way, in conjunction with monetary convertibility, . . . toward the achievement of the integration of the countries of western Europe." But its concept of integration at that time was so demanding that it was not likely to be achieved: "Would it not have been better," the president's report of 1950 concluded, "to consider the conditions of production, attempting to create almost identical environmental conditions" among the European countries, so that "liberalization, instead of being the first act in the economic unification of Europe, should be the result of many other actions instead?" Support of this kind would have postponed integration indefinitely.[11]

The Schuman Plan compelled Confindustria to ask whether it really wanted European unification, through liberalization or any other means.[12] The most dramatic presentation of its views came in 1952, during its Sixth Convegno di Studi di Economia e Politica Industriale, when President Costa found himself at grips with one of the most tenacious and talented of Confindustria's critics, Professor Ernesto Rossi. Rossi dismissed as so much poetry the introductory report, in which Professor Amoroso waxed lyrical over the spiritual unity of Europe but condemned the Schuman Plan as "economic oppression." Rossi demanded immediate action for the creation of a supranational federal government with real powers. Costa retorted that such a government would result in oppression of the minority by the majority so long as economic interests of the members were opposed, and that a federation could only be created after differences of interest had been resolved.[13]

Costa's bitterness was a good indication of the growing friction between the confederation and the federalist movement. Professor Rossi always "sees evil on every side," he said. "If we persist in scattering poison to right and to left, in casting gibes wherever possible, bundling together decent people and rascals in order to uphold predetermined theses, we shall only create divisions and hatreds beginning here at home." Costa then justified his conception of union in words that would be echoed a decade later by French President Charles de Gaulle. "No government leader can accept any undertaking of an international nature by which his nation's conditions of life and death could be decided by a majority of the representatives of other nations. . . . Only madmen could agree . . . to create the European federalist constituent assembly and to delegate to its majority every power of decision." Costa then went on to spell out his own ideas on economic integration. Larger economic areas were necessary to reduce the costs of industrial products through greater specialization, to increase the size of the market, and to make possible greater volume of production. But, Costa insisted, customs duties are an essential protection to industry while the other barriers to free trade, such as quotas and fiscal restrictions, are being removed.[14] A complete customs union, especially one including agriculture, could not be achieved. The Schuman Plan in no way corresponded to the confederation's conceptions. The confederation regarded it as a political measure that ignored economic realities. Sector integration, for coal and steel, agriculture, or any other economic area, was totally unsuitable for achievement of general unification. The Schuman Plan favored the countries with ample raw materials and large-scale industry. Above all, the Plan was interventionist (dirigistico), especially in its attitude toward industrial concentrations and in the excessive powers given to the High Authority. This antiliberal character, rather than the possible economic danger to Italy, lay at the basis of Confindustria's opposition to ECSC.[15]

Under Costa, Confindustria's attitude toward European integration was approval in principle, both political and economic; determination that progress should be slow and should begin with increased circulation of goods within clearly established customs barriers; opposition to any form of interventionism, especially through the creation of supranational authorities with powers over the economy; and demand for state protection from, or compensation for, the effects of wider international competition.

These principles remained unchanged under Costa's successor, Alighiero De Micheli (1955–62). De Micheli, the president of Assolombardo, the regional industrial federation centered on Milan, was a younger and more dynamic man than Costa, and was chosen especially for the purpose of bringing Confindustria more actively into politics. The period of the negotiation and ratification of the Treaty of Rome coincided with De Micheli's all-out effort to make Confindustria a major political force. The political drive had two main facets. Industrialists were encouraged to seek election themselves, at every level of government from the commune to the Chamber, and as representatives of any party, from the Christian Democrats through the right-wing parties. The confederation itself was to intervene financially on a large scale in support of those parties friendly to business, especially the Liberal party under its new chairman Giovanni Malagodi, in the local elections of 1956 and the national elections of 1958. Although this program failed, from the electoral point of view, and was unable to stop the erosion of the parties of the Right, the failure was not evident until the results of the 1958 elections were known. During the crucial period of EEC negotiations in 1955–57, Confindustria was able to engage in open political pressure for its concept of integration as well as in its more normal informal contacts with the bureaucracy. Partly as a result of this pressure, the Treaty of Rome, unlike the Treaty of Paris, was quite satisfactory to the confederation.[16]

After the Messina conference, the confederation came out in favor of a union of western Europe on political grounds, to meet the menace of the Soviet world to "the attractive force of our economic and productive system, based on property and private initiative, and to our political system, based on liberty."[17] The work of the Spaak Committee (July 1955–April 1956) was followed closely by the confederation's technical experts, copies of the committee's report were mailed to all member associations for their comments, and a general meeting of all the associations, held in October 1956, in Rome, was devoted to the report. The findings of these meetings were presented to the responsible government ministers and to the Interministerial Committee set up by the Ministry of Foreign Affairs. Confindustria felt that the necessary harmonizing measures were lacking in the report, whereas the suppression of tariffs was dealt with fully. The confederation pressed the Italian negotiators of the treaty to demand the end of all quantitative limitations on trade; free movement of capital, services, and labor; the creation of an agricultural policy that would take into account the effect of the prices of many agricultural products on industrial prices and the effect of the level of agricultural income on industrial sales; and the inclusion within the Common Market, under special conditions, of the overseas territories of France and Belgium, since their raw materials were important to Italian industry. Finally, the confederation felt that industrialists should be given a specific role within the new Community, both through their associations and in a Consultative Commitee for the Community.

Unlike the Schuman Plan, the Treaty of Rome, as it finally emerged from the Brussels negotiations, was welcomed by Confindustria "not only for the possibility of working within a vaster and, naturally, more dynamic market, but for the affirmation of liberal principles made by the treaty." The Common Market, in short, was regarded by the confederation as a major instrument for the maintenance of liberal economics against the supporters of state intervention. Yet they demanded, somewhat illogically, that the conditions of competition within the new Community should be tempered by many forms of intervention, both by the state and Community governments. The lack of these safeguards within a Free Trade Area, as proposed by the British, was the main reason for the outright rejection of such a proposal by Confindustria.[18]

Confindustria argued that the existence of a Community governed by liberal economic principles would make more urgent than ever the solution of several problems that were peculiar to Italy, problems which it had been raising for years. Among these were technical education; territorial location of industry; industrialization of the South; sources of financing; and especially the unfair governmental support of state-controlled industries, which distorted competitive conditions within Italy itself. Italian industry would meet the problems of the Common Market successfully only if supported by major reform efforts of the Italian government. European integration thus became another argument that could be used by Italian business in its demands on the government at home.[19]

This attitude to EEC did not vary during its first decade of operation (1958–68). From the very beginning, even before the tariff reductions had caused any direct effects, Confindustria joined the industrialists in all the other member countries in recognizing the stimulating psychological effects of the prospects of the wider market.[20] This optimism was due in large part to Confindustria's belief that its hopes in the liberal character of the Common Market were being realized. In 1962, Dr. Furio Cicogna, De Micheli's successor as president, noted that the "courageous initiatives of the six countries of western Europe are beginning to bear the expected fruits, proving the liberal and non-protectionist character of the European Economic Community." Given the basis of the Community in the "market economy," Confindustria was in favor of the rapid conclusion of a political basis to the union, because "it is the political commitment that offers the indispensable guarantees for continuity and irreversibility." How else could the industrialists justify "the profound and costly adaptation that the economic union is demanding in every form of activity"? Cicogna seemed to see, in the submersion of Italy within a wider European union, the possibility of slowing the state's intervention in the economy that the movement to the Left within Italy was encouraging.[21] Confindustria directed its activity within EEC toward ensuring that the Community's development followed the desired principles of economic liberalism, while, at the same time, it used the existence of a Community based upon these principles as a means of pressuring the Italian government to adopt policies in keeping with this economic and political philosophy.

Within the Common Market, Confindustria rapidly developed methods of making its opinions respected. Several of its most able representatives took part in the meetings of the Social and Economic Council; in 1961, for example, its representatives included Vice President Quinto Quintieri and its former president, Angelo Costa. The organization took an active role in the Union des Industries de la Communauté Européenne, and encouraged its member organizations to take part in the many Community associations of sectoral groups within the six.[22]

Having achieved a treaty with which it was satisfied, Confindustria acted, from the creation of the Communities in 1958, as if it were the guardian of the treaty. Although it recognized the stimulating effects of EEC, it firmly opposed the French employers' association's proposals for acceleration of the timetable of customs reduction; and when the EEC Commission proposed the imposition of an additional 20 per cent tariff cut and a more rapid establishment of the common external tariff, both to start in February 1960, Confindustria was vehemently opposed.[23] It was slightly appeased when the Council of Ministers, in November 1959, reduced the acceleration planned for 1960 to 10 per cent and called for more rapid realization of the economic union in areas other than tariff reduction.[24]

Another problem that worried the confederation during the early years of EEC was the formulation of the Community's policy toward concentrations and ententes. Italian industry was the weakest in EEC in its structure and the size of its productive units, Confindustria held, and it must be free to carry through the reorganization and fusions necessary to meet the competition of the colossi of Europe and the rest of the world. The confederation felt that Italian industry had been struck a dangerous blow by the national law for the maintenance of free competition, passed in 1959 as a result of the report of the parliamentary commission of inquiry on competitive conditions in Italy. Confindustria believed that this law was hamstringing the Italian companies at a time when they were facing competition from other EEC companies within their formerly protected home market. Ententes, the confederation said, "instead of constituting a drag on economic development, are the necessary instrument for avoiding the inconveniences that could arise on the practical level from a competitive struggle pushed to the extreme."[25] The Community policy, Confindustria concluded, "should not be an a priori and demagogic criterion of condemnation and indiscriminate persecution of all ententes." The Commission's proposals of October 1960 were more moderate than Confindustria had feared they would be. Far from banning concentrations and ententes, the proposals assumed that many were desirable because they promoted efficiency and specialization. But Confindustria objected to the decision that all new ententes had to be presented to the Commission for sanction, especially as the Commission would enjoy the theoretical right of inspecting the books and records of the companies concerned.[26]

Confindustria was also interested in having the other aspects of the economic union achieved in parallel with the customs union. In particular, the confederation was concerned with development of Community rules for the free movement of labor; for the free establishment of businesses in other countries of EEC and for the Community-wide offering of such services as insurance;[27] and for the harmonization of commercial and especially fiscal policy, which Confindustria considered to be one of Italy's greatest handicaps. The Commission's formulation in October 1962 of the Action Program for the Second Stage was welcomed by Confindustria, in spite of the Commission's evident intent to seek economic planning on an international scale. And, perhaps even more surprisingly, the confederation pressed continually for the conversion of the Community into a true political union.[28]

This demand, expressed as early as the president's report of 1959, which regretted the "partial integration" characterized by retention by the nation-states of "several delicate levers of economic policy," was continually reaffirmed by Confindustria's leaders.[29] Undoubtedly, the anti-Communist position of most Italian industrial leaders led them to regard EEC as a bulwark against Soviet pressure. De Micheli and Cicogna did not conceal their view that the "immanent dangers" of the Soviet world could only be met with "the realization of a substantial union of the countries of western Europe and with the closest agreements with all the other countries of the world of a similar ideological orientation." But the growing worry about the character of the movement toward the Left inside Italy also persuaded Confindustria of the value of a political union that would relieve the Italian government of its powers of interference with Italian industry. Assuming that the Community would retain the liberal character Confindustria saw in the Treaty of Rome, particularly with the influence of West German free enterprise, the confederation believed that a supranational government of the six would be less inclined toward direct intervention in the economy than its own government would. Indeed, Confindustria's opponents believed that its support for political union of the six was due primarily to the confederation's belief that the industrialists' power within the new union would be so great as to condition not only the functioning of the market but "the very conception of the public interest."[30]

Confindustria's attitude toward integration went through two clearly marked stages. Between 1945 and 1955, it expressed vague support for the idea but felt that overwhelming material difficulties stood in the way of its realization. During this period, the measures it opposed—such as liberalization of trade, currency controls, and the Schuman Plan—were implemented in spite of the confederation's attitude; and it was clear that, in spite of the confederation's reputation of exercising political power, it was unable to prevent the adoption of foreign policy measures that the governmental coalition felt were politically justified. After 1955, however, the confederation supported the broad plans for integration, and it found that its detailed criticisms were in many cases accepted. With the creation of the Common Market, Confindustria discovered that the economic philosophy of the Community was in fact more to its liking than were the policies being implemented within Italy by the governments of the Center-Left, with the result that Confindustria found itself on the point of seeking an "escape into Europe" as a guarantee of its own position inside Italy.

THE CONFEDERAZIONE GENERALE DEL COMMERCIO E DEL TURISMO

Confcommercio was the weakest of the three big federations— Confindustria, Confagricoltura, and Confcommercio—that the left-wing groups often accused of dominating Italian economic life. It did, however, represent that sector of the economy generally recognized, even by its own members, to be one of the most backward in Europe. Were no reforms instituted in the sector, it would act as a drag on the rest of the economy, for European economic integration obviously would result in highly competitive conditions. If the coming of integration forced the sector to reform itself, or to be reformed from outside, then a large number of its inefficient or redundant members would suffer financially. Confcommercio's attitude to integration was mixed; it desired reform and feared its consequences.

The weakness of the Italian distribution system extended from the sale by the original producer through the sale to the final consumer. In agriculture, the multitude of small producers and the rare use of cooperatives made large-scale purchasing almost impossible, except in the larger farms of the Po valley; and a vast number of middlemen enjoyed traditional rights of handling the various stages of sale. A similar situation existed in industry, especially in the marketing of the products of the many tiny factories in such fields as textiles and artisan products. The census of 1951 showed that there were 66,974 wholesale companies. Two-thirds of the companies dealing in wholesale commerce in agricultural goods and more than half of those dealing in industrial products had no more than two employees.[31] Retail outlets, typified by the small shops specializing in bread and pasta, or clothing, numbered 558,685 in 1953, but this number rose steadily every year to reach 913,252 by 1962, one shop for every 74 inhabitants.[32] The distribution cost represented at least half of the final retail price of goods, and, in many cases, particularly in foodstuffs, it represented 70 to 80 per cent of the retail price.

Several attempts were made to renovate Italy's distribution system. By 1963, there were 276 department stores. Most of them were in the big cities of North and Central Italy, and most were branches of the vast chains of Rinascente, Standa, or Upim. There were also many supermarkets; almost every Italian city of 100,000 inhabitants had one. And as these department stores and supermarkets began to take over sales, the smaller merchants reacted by forming their own associations so that they could offer the same economies to their customers that the large distribution outlets did. The number of big stores could only grow, however. In 1963, they controlled less than 2.5 per cent of retail sales in Italy, yet it was projected they could easily control 17 per cent. The large industrial companies were showing increasing awareness that investments in wholesale and retail distribution were not only a source of high returns on capital invested, but also aided the productive process itself by removing one of the major bottlenecks in the country's economy.[33]

Confcommercio naturally found itself in the middle of the struggle between the thousands of small wholesale and retail merchants and the vast new distribution companies. The confederation represented all the sectoral groups engaged in wholesale or retail trade, either in internal or foreign commerce;[34] but it clearly sided with the larger commercial groups when their interests conflicted with those of the small or medium-sized groups, in much the same way that Confindustria sided with the large industrial companies when their interests went against those of the small and medium-sized companies.[35] The crucial moment in the internal history of the confederation came when the Associazione Italiana delle Grandi Imprese di Distribuzione al Dettaglio, which represented the department stores and supermarkets, sought membership in Confcommercio. Since these companies were controlled in large part by the major industrial companies, this was equivalent to allowing the controlling forces in Confindustria a major role in Confcommercio. The Association was admitted, against the wishes of the majority of the small and medium-sized commercial firms. The confederation had accepted the inevitability of the change in

Italian merchandising to large-scale operations, with the resultant lessening in number of the small merchants. The coming of the Common Market played an important part in convincing the confederation of the need for this evolution.

When the Treaty of Rome was signed, Confcommercio's president, Sergio Casaltoli, claimed that the confederation's "doubts and uncertainties about the Common Market had been overcome," and that the confederation had concluded that the "Common Market was a goal now immutably located on the world's present trajectory." In this unavoidable change, Casaltoli felt, there were great opportunities for a "hard-working, passionate, brilliant people like the Italian."[36] In 1958, however, Casaltoli was extremely concerned that the rationalization of distribution might destroy the family character of the retail shops in Italy; and, adopting much the same tactics as the leaders of Confindustria, he claimed that, because of the coming of the Common Market, immediate government action was required to aid the small shopkeepers. A large-scale plan, financed by the government, was needed to help the professional training of the small merchant, to give him social security benefits, to protect him from unlicensed retailers, to cut his taxes, and to extend him medium-term credit. The confederation itself was running special courses in modern distribution techniques and was setting up a "center for the development of exports"; but it was especially concerned with the successful development of Confintesa, the agreement on common political activity among the Confindustria, Confagricoltura, and Confcommercio, which was concluded in February 1956. Confintesa, Casaltoli felt, was essential as "an organ for coordination of the three great Confederations for dealing with problems arising from the Common Market, problems whose basis is the collaboration of businessmen in order to accelerate progress." Confcommercio was encouraging businesmen to enter political life at this time because it felt that "the legislative and administrative action of the state should take account also of their demands and their possibilities." The Common Market was thus a justification for the entry of the businessman into politics.[37]

Speaking to the International Chamber of Commerce in March 1957, Casaltoli spelled out the meaning of the Common Market for Italian commerce. Effects would be twofold. The lowering of barriers would cause great changes in various manufacturing sectors, and these changes would have great repercussions upon the sales of wholesale and retail merchants, who would be compelled to break long-established business relationships, restructure their companies, perhaps relocate in more favorable areas, and often dismiss some of their workers. Retail merchants would find themselves compelled to meet the highest standards within the Community, even though they were not directly affected by competition from outside Italy, since these standards would be demanded by the consumers, the manufacturing sectors, and the state. What was needed was nothing less than a total renovation of the distribution system—reduction of distribution costs by "company reorganization, modernization of equipment, change in traditional systems of sales, transformation (in many cases) of mentality." Yet this was demanded of a million people whose training and financial resources were well below those of the average European industrial worker and whose income was higher only than that of the Italian agricultural laborer.[38] It was hardly surprising that Confcommercio demanded a plan for the renovation of commerce of the same character and scale as the plan adopted for the South.[39]

The opening of the Common Market brought Confcommercio gradually closer to the position of Confindustria, and more perceptive of the benefits of large-scale operations, even in the distribution trade. By the end of the 1950's, Confcommercio, like Confindustria, had become a defender of the Treaty of Rome. De Gaulle's attitude toward the Common Market roused Confcommercio's fury, for it combined those very attitudes of protectionism and national self-interest that the confederation feared most. British entry to the Common Market was vigorously supported by Confcommercio; and de Gaulle's veto provoked an outraged condemnation from Casaltoli at the annual assembly of the confederation in 1964. Those who conceive the EEC as a purely "regional organization, almost as a new instrument of protectionism, to be substituted for the old arms of economic nationalism," he charged, were leading Europe not to political unification but to political division, of Europe itself and of the six from the rest of the world. The Common Market had been conceived as exercising an "irresistible force of attraction," and, since it demanded harmonization of legislation as well as a customs union, it could only result in a perfect political vision. "Was this only a Utopia, when no alternative can reasonably be suggested?"[40]

COLTIVATORI DIRETTI AND CONFAGRICOLTURA

The attitude of Italian agrarian groups to specific issues of EEC agricultural policy has been described earlier, but mention must be made of their organization within Italy, since these interest groups exerted more direct power within the legislature and bureaucracy than any others. Before the war the most influential of the agricultural organizations was the Confederazione Generale dell'Agricoltura Italiana (Confagricoltura). However, it lost its broad base with the foundation in 1944 of the smallholders confederation, the Confederazione Nazionale Coltivatori Diretti. Confagricoltura remained significant as the voice of the larger landowners, controlled a small group of deputies in parliament, and received firm support from the right-wing members of the Christian Democratic party and all the right-wing parties.

Coltivatori Diretti was largely the creation, and became the personal fief, of Paolo Bonomi, a brilliant Christian Democratic organizer who was able to convert the Fascist syndicates of smallholders into a huge interest group responsive to, but also an influence on, the Christian Democratic party. Backed by Catholic Action and by many members of the Vatican hierarchy, and able to offer direct financial and technical aid to the small farmers, Coltivatori Diretti increased the number of workers enrolled from 221,000 in 1944 to 3.5 million in 1968. While the confederation itself offered a vast range of services to its members, including education, help with tax or insurance problems, and technical advice, its financial power lay in its control of the Federconsorzi, the semipublic agrarian cooperatives entrusted by the government with many tasks of vital concern to the smallholders—the stockpiling of wheat, rural credit, and the distribution of gasoline and fertilizer at reduced prices. The Federconsorzi, through use of the large financial resources made available to it by the government, was able to buy controlling interests in several large agricultural processing companies and other industries related to farming. In the first elections after Coltivatori Diretti was formed, the candidates named by the confederation took almost complete control throughout the country, and in 1955, Bonomi's power was further strengthened by the institution of Casse Mutue (Insurance Funds), which extended compulsory insurance for sickness to smallholders. With a huge, faithful electoral base, secure financing, and leverage in both parliament and the bureaucracy, the Bonomiana, as Coltivatori Diretti was frequently called, was in a position to make its wishes in matters of Community agrarian policy respected at the national level, especially as Confagricoltura took a similar stand on most issues of European concern.[41]

The general objectives of Coltivatori Diretti were to preserve the family character of most Italian farming and to reduce the gap between industrial and agricultural incomes, particularly by increasing the efficiency of the family farm. The confederation demanded both national and Community measures that would further these goals. It had no illusions about the antiquated character of most Italian farming, the overpopulation of the countryside, the fragmentation of property, and the unwise choice of crops; and it was urgently aware of the necessity of raising productivity. The coming of the Common Market, Bonomi pointed out at the conclusion of his annual report of April 1957, was a "revolutionary event" that forced immediate consideration of these age-old problems of Italian agriculture. The confederation, he claimed, had always been in favor of "any effort at economic understanding in the European sphere," provided it met two fundamental requirements: to "give wider scope to the most typically [Italian] products, and [to] reduce the demographic pressure on the land." Liberalization had failed because unfair protection had persisted. Within EEC, a genuine common market for agricultural products had to be created, with a common price as the prime factor; free movement of people, as a prerequisite to lessen the pressure on the land; and financial aid from the state, as a necessary stimulus to more effective production.[42]

In 1957–58, both Coltivatori Diretti and Confagricoltura made great efforts to predict the effects of EEC upon Italian agriculture. In 1958, the former called on the economists Francesco Vito, Pasquale Saraceno, Corrado Bonato, and Mario Bandini to present reports to its convegno on the Common Market.[43] Both confederations were represented at the EEC agricultural conference at

Stresa, in 1958, where the lack of clarity, both in the Treaty of Rome and among the governments, as to the method to be adopted for inclusion of agriculture in the Community finally became evident. In spite of their disillusionment with the Stresa conference, there is not much evidence that either confederation became aware until too late that the common agricultural policy, as it was formed in 1960–64, was oriented toward northern European products, especially cereals and livestock, rather than to the products that particularly interested Italy, especially fruit and vegetables. The cost to Italy of the early years of operation of FEOGA came as a surprise to those in Italian agricultural circles. They blamed governmental incompetence in choice of negotiators, in spite of Bonomi's earlier promise that his confederation would step up the pressure on the government to ensure acceptance of its demands.[44]

In 1967, reviewing the progress of the common agricultural policy at its convegno, the "Economic Development Program and the European Community," Coltivatori Diretti indicated its partial satisfaction. The market regulations and common prices had "both light and shade." Certain products had been encouraged, such as cereals, especially rice, and eggs and poultry, although others, such as milk, had suffered. But the complaint of Coltivatori Diretti was less against the Community than it was against the national government. "The difficulties of the Italian farmers are undoubtedly worse than those arising naturally from the EEC regulations, for internal and not Community reasons." Not only was the national government remiss in making use of Community decisions—delaying the payment of Community subsidies, for example, or failing to apply Community norms for associations of fruit and vegetable producers—it was still unwilling to make the financial investment necessary to carry through the required structural reforms, or to use social insurance as part of an income policy that would transfer part of the country's income from industry to the agricultural worker. Coltivatori Diretti had accepted the Community system, in spite of its shortcomings, and used the pressure of EEC to renew the struggle at the national level for specific governmental measures to aid agriculture. Confagricoltura, on the other hand, was more critical of EEC itself. It laid greater emphasis upon the power over Italian agriculture wielded by the

Community, and found that the first decade had been far from satisfactory. On the tenth anniversary of the signature of the Treaty of Rome, *Mondo Agricolo* noted that EEC "has imposed and is imposing on Italian agriculture noteworthy sacrifices that will become heavier." But, like Coltivatori Diretti, Confagricoltura also blamed the national government. "The weight of these burdens, which Italian farmers accept on the altar of the political and economic integration of Europe, has been and is made worse . . . by an internal agrarian policy that has not always been up to the requirements of the situation."[45] Both agricultural federations, therefore, believed that the future of Italian agriculture, in spite of the institution of EEC, was primarily dependent upon national decisions; and at the end of the 1960's they still felt that little had been done.[46]

12
The European Policy of Italian Labor

The divisions of opinion within the business classes toward European integration were minimal compared with those within the Italian labor movement. Labor represented, in a way that business obviously did not, the vast spectrum of Italian politics. As Professor LaPalombara pointed out in 1957, "the critical Italian encounters between the ideologies of East and West unfold primarily on the labor scene. The major trends and episodes of Italian politics tend in large measure to reflect the skirmishes and major campaigns that are fought among the trade unions for the allegiance of the workers and peasants."[1] Yet even the most ideologically inclined of labor's leaders placed the interests of labor ahead of, or at least beside, his ideological aims. To discover labor's influence on the formulation of Italy's role in Europe, one must therefore ask, first, how did the labor unions assess the effect of European integration on the interests of the Italian worker? And, second, to what extent was this assessment influenced by ideological motives?

THE CONFEDERAZIONE GENERALE ITALIANA DEL LAVORO (CGIL)

The CGIL was created in the spring of 1944 as a union of Communist, Socialist, and Christian Democratic labor groups.[2] In the Pact of Rome it was agreed that the three should have equal representation in all executive bodies, while the confederation was to be headed by three secretaries—Giuseppe Di Vittorio for the

Communists, Oreste Lizzadri for the Socialists, and Achille Grandi for the Christian Democrats.[3] In the following year, the Communists came to dominate the CGIL and much of the labor movement. The Socialist Bruno Buozzi, probably the only labor leader with the prestige and ability to stand against the towering personality of Di Vittorio, was captured by the Germans and shot; Grandi was old and weakened by cancer; and Lizzadri, a young Resistance fighter, honestly sought to collaborate with the Communists. In the North, the work of the Communists in the Resistance won them popularity and a key position in the labor unions; in the South, their well-trained cadres were able to seize control of many local chambers of labor.

Di Vittorio himself played a major role. The son of a day-laborer in Puglia, he became a labor organizer at thirteen and secretary of his chamber of labor at fifteen. After 1918, he took a leading role in the general strikes, was arrested several times by the Fascists, and finally went into exile in France. At the outbreak of the Spanish Civil War, he joined the First International Brigade; in 1941, he was arrested in France and turned over to the Italian government, which imprisoned him on the island of Ventotene. Freed in 1943, he at once became the dominant force in the trade union movement, as a man whose ability and integrity were admired even by his most vigorous opponents.

The history of the Italian labor movement did not encourage a productive role for the new union in any moves to unify Europe. Emphasis on the ideology of class war had been strengthened by a century of conflict with the industrial interests and exacerbated by the rigid controls of labor-management relations imposed by the Fascist state. The rise of the Communist party in the labor movement ensured that European unity, conceived as part of an Atlantic grouping, would be opposed by the most powerful of the labor groups, while it would be supported by management. The issue of West European unity would therefore become a further irritant in the relations between Italian industrial owners and labor. Yet in 1944 the unification of all labor groups into one confederation, with labor leaders of different ideologies, seemed to many to be a move toward the kind of European federation that the Resistance had dreamed of, one embracing both western and eastern Europe. The next four years saw the rapid extinction of that hope.

THE PERIOD OF THE UNIFIED CGIL, 1944-1948

Almost from the start, the leaders of the different groups within the CGIL gave up the attempt to harmonize their ideological positions. Instead, they concentrated on material issues, in order to avoid breaking the infant organization apart. The CGIL negotiated a series of nationwide agreements with Confindustria, called interconfederal agreements, which established a wage-structure according to classifications of skills, zonal differentiation, and cost-of-living allowances, and laid down industry-wide policy on vacations, grievances, and end-of-year bonuses.[4] This policy did safeguard the interests of workers employed in large-scale industry. They became a privileged class, enjoying higher pay, greater social benefits, and more secure jobs than those who were unable to break into the group. But because the policy created classes of workers, it contributed directly to the formation of that "dual labor system" which helped prolong underemployment and unemployment and hampered the country's general economic progress. The benefits enjoyed by the sector of the labor force represented by the large unions led many Italian union members to experience the same fear of entry into a European Community that a similarly protected British laboring class felt.[5]

Tensions between the three political groups of the CGIL became evident as early as 1946. The Christian Democrats, as well as some Socialist leaders, were worried by the Communists' success in placing their members in key positions in national federations, such as the metal workers' union, and in capturing a majority of the rank-and-file members in most factories. The national CGIL Congress, held in Florence in June 1947, one month after the Communists had been forced out of De Gasperi's government, was bitterly divided, especially over the Communist demand that power in the confederation be apportioned according to voting strength.[6] Although the tripartite arrangement was maintained, the dominance of the Communists was recognized by the appointment of Di Vittorio as secretary general and by the confederation's resolution, passed against the Christian Democrats' wishes, that it would take a political stand on issues of interest to all workers. Just such an issue was provided while the CGIL Congress was still in session, for on June 5, Secretary of State Marshall gave the commencement address at Harvard in which he proposed the Marshall Plan.[7] Following the Soviet rejection of Marshall aid, the Communist and left-wing Socialist political leaders announced their opposition, and the Communist leaders of the CGIL quickly followed suit. Obedient to the instructions given at the founding session of the Cominform in September, they called a large number of strikes. They planned to paralyze the country by gradually increasing the geographical area and the intensity of these strikes, in order to compel the government to reject the Marshall Plan. These political strikes began the final showdown in the CGIL. The Christian Democratic and right-wing Socialist leaders voted against the strikes, and in December 1947 the Christian Democrats ordered their members not to take part in a general strike in Rome. Di Vittorio thereupon accused them of strikebreaking, while the more extreme Communist leader Renato Bitossi hinted that such a "fifth column" could not be tolerated much longer in the CGIL.[8]

On July 4, 1948, a right-wing student attempted to assassinate the Communist party leader Palmiro Togliatti. Spontaneous strikes then occurred throughout Italy, and were sanctioned by the CGIL leaders, who called for a general strike. The Christian Democratic leaders, fearing an insurrection under Communist leadership, demanded that the strike be limited to twenty-four hours; and when it continued, they pulled their members out of the CGIL organization at all levels. Shortly afterward, they declared that the Pact of Rome had been broken by the strikes and that they would form a new, nonpolitical, democratic trade union. The CGIL Executive Committee then expelled all those who had supported that move.

The new Christian Democratic union, the Libera Confederazione Generale Italiana del Lavoro (LCGIL), was established on October 16–18, 1948. Only in May 1949, however, did the Republicans and Social Democrats leave the CGIL, when it became clear to them that the withdrawal of the Christian Democrats had left the Communist-Socialist leadership of the CGIL with little further reason to respect minority opinions and with no hindrance to its violent obstruction of the Marshall Plan and the Atlantic Pact. The Social Democrats and the Republicans formed their own union, the Federazione Italiana del Lavoro (FIL) on June 4, but almost immediately negotiated a fusion with LCGIL under pressure from the Christian Democratic party and from American labor officials and diplomats. The fusion, by which the Confederazione Italiana Sindacati Lavoratori (CISL) was formed in April 1950, was forced through against the opposition of the rank-and-file members of the FIL and of the Republican party, who feared the clerical character of the LCGIL; and in March 1950, these dissident groups, joining with yet another group of dissident Socialists, formed a third labor union, the Unione Italiana del Lavoro (UIL). Finally, in the same month, a fourth small labor union, of right-wing persuasion, the Confederazione Italiana Sindacati Nazionali Lavoratori (CISNAL), was formed. It was made up of monarchists and neo-Fascists and acted as the labor union counterpart of the Movimento Sociale Italiano, the neo-Fascist political party.

Thus, the issue of Italian participation in the Marshall Plan and in the Atlantic Alliance provoked the fission of the CGIL, with important effects on the political influence of the Italian labor movement. Although the CGIL was still the most important labor organization in Italy after it broke up, it was generally ignored when decisions were made on the country's international role, even in economic matters. The unions that were consulted by the government were either Christian Democratic or Social Democratic in orientation, and they were committed in advance to the ideal of the unity of "free Europe." The role of the leaders of these unions, which were small in membership compared with the CGIL, was correspondingly magnified because of the obstructionist attitude of the CGIL leadership and because of the Christian Democratic governments' refusal to permit the CGIL a role in decision-making on foreign issues. Finally, the success of European integration caused a corresponding increase in the popularity of those unions that had supported it, and forced CGIL to take a more positive attitude toward integration.

THE ECONOMIC GOALS OF THE CGIL

The CGIL remained by far the most powerful of the labor unions, in spite of its losses in membership through the foundation of three rival unions. Probably about 6 million workers, or 30 per cent of the Italian labor force, were union members, and about

3.5 million were in the CGIL. Most of those in the CGIL were recruited from the braccianti and mezzadri in agriculture and the workers in the engineering industry, the ports and the railroads, and the government bureaucracy.[9] The union was closely tied to the Socialist and Communist parties.[10] Many officials of the CGIL were chosen simply because they were supported by these parties.[11] Fifty CGIL officials were members of the Chamber of Deputies, 35 of them Communists and 15 Socialists, while in the Senate the CGIL had 12 representatives, 9 of them Communists and 3 Socialists. The CGIL thus had a bloc of nearly one-tenth of the members of the Chamber, which alone would have made it a major political force. At the same time, many national officials of the CGIL held important positions in the top ranks of the Communist and Socialist party organizations. The most revealing of these interlocking positions, however, were those in which Communist officials with no labor union experience held positions in CGIL. According to LaPalombara, "these men must be considered political commissars who function primarily to guarantee that the confederation will not deviate from doctrinal, strategic, and tactical lines laid down by the party." The most important among them was the future secretary general, Agostino Novella. Within the union administration, the Socialists played only a minor role. Daniel Horowitz concludes that "the Communists attempted to keep Socialist officials in their cooperating positions, but, except for the most trusted pro-Communists, gradually succeeded in isolating them from the memembership and removing any genuine organizational responsibility from among their duties."[12] The Communists within the CGIL were thus able to lay down the union's policy to the smallest detail.

The CGIL had the dual function of voicing the official policy of the Communist party on issues of immediate interest to the workers and of taking direct action to pressure the Italian government to adopt policies of ideological interest to the Communist party. The goals it sought were of three kinds—immediate benefits for unionized workers; long-term policies for the development of Italy's economy and society; and changes in Italian foreign policy. Each of these goals was of direct relevance to Italian participation in an integrated Europe.

After 1950, CGIL's most obvious activity was that of forcing immediate economic gains for the industrial workers. At first it pressured the other unions into continuing the nationwide interconfederal agreements on wages and social security benefits that had been carried on from the Fascist period, a fantastically complicated system that was a great hindrance to economic progress. In 1954, however, the other unions signed a nationwide salary agreement (conglobamento) with Confindustria, without CGIL's backing. The agreement established a regular, higher rate of pay; set up new geographical zones for pay differentiation; and provided greater compensation for skill. It was modified in 1957 to link wage increases with any rise in living costs. This new system, which CGIL was forced unwillingly to accept, proved far more efficient and more satisfactory to the workers than the interconfederal agreements had been. CGIL's opposition was undoubtedly linked to its determination to use the syndical agitation of 1953–54 as part of its campaign against the European Defense Community and the Western European Union. But its opposition to the new wage system helped lessen its popularity, and played a part in the CGIL's defeat in the internal committee elections in the Fiat factory in 1955. This defeat was hailed by CGIL's opponents as a symbol of the end of its position of supremacy in the labor movement.[13]

In 1959, the new secretary general of the CGIL, Agostino Novella, declared that "the industrial revival, with its reduction of pressure on the level of employment . . . opens new possibilities in the struggle to demand better living and working conditions and to achieve in more favorable conditions an economic policy of structural reforms and full employment."[14] Working in fairly close harmony with the CISL and the UIL, the CGIL pushed hard for substantial wage concessions in the spring and summer of 1959; and joint strikes by the three unions forced management to agree to new pay raises of about 8 to 9 per cent.[15] The pressure continued into the 1960's, when growing evidence of the Italian industrial boom seemed to justify a demand for a long-overdue adjustment of the workers' share of the national income. For the first time since 1951, salaries in industry rose faster than productivity, especially in the great pay raises of 1960–64. These pay raises were, ironically, an important factor in causing the Italian recession of 1963, with its increase in unemployment.[16]

Far from accepting the blame, however, the CGIL charged that the employers were trying to slough off the effects of the recession onto the workers by freezing salaries, reducing employment, raising productivity without giving corresponding compensation to the workers, and tightening factory controls over workers. The CGIL, Novella concluded, saw no reason not to continue the struggle for higher wages, "knowing that the increase in the purchasing ability of the workers constitutes realistically another impulse to the increase in production and the reduction of costs." But the ultimate lesson of the recession was the need for the CGIL to continue its battle for structural reforms in Italian society, reforms that the capitalistic development within the Common Market were rendering more urgent than ever.[17]

The recession thus brought out the opposition of CGIL and the employers over the interpretation of EEC's effects upon the Italian economy. As Novella rightly pointed out, the employers looked on the economic miracle, which they attributed in part at least to the effects of the Common Market, as making unnecessary the structural reforms in Italian society demanded by the trade unions; and, indeed, the employers did regard the economic miracle as proof that these reforms would have destroyed the effectiveness of the existing economic system. Far from making the reforms unnecessary, however, the CGIL felt the economic miracle had made them more than ever possible.

CGIL's first proposal for long-term reforms, the Piano del Lavoro, presented to its Congress of Genoa in October 1949, was Keynesian in its approach to the problems of full employment. It called for construction of new hydroelectric plants, irrigation and land reform, and a vast program of public works. In 1952, the CGIL's demands were expanded to include the nationalization of the electricity industry, of the engineering companies in IRI, and of the Montecatini company.[18] CGIL believed that in this way the problem of unemployment would be met—by secure provision of electrical energy at a low cost, expanded production of industrial and agricultural machinery, and increased consumption by the better-paid workers. These proposals led to a conflict between CGIL and Confindustria over the principles by which Italy could achieve more rapid economic progress. Confindustria accused CGIL of weakening the competitive position of Italian production through its wage demands and attempting to destroy the very system of free enterprise which alone could raise living standards for the workers. CGIL, on the other hand, declared that the free enterprise system could only work successfully by restricting wages; reducing employment, by allowing competition to wipe out less efficient companies; and encouraging emigration. It attributed the battles with the employers in 1950–55 to the determination of Confindustria, backed by the government, to make the workers accept the tenets of the free enterprise system, and, indeed, to make them agree to the dominance of the great monopoly companies—this at the time when Italy was entering the various European economic unions which, CGIL felt, would strengthen the monopolies at the expense both of the small and medium-sized industries and of the workers.[19]

In the aftermath of the Soviet repression in Hungary, which greatly lessened its popularity, CGIL tried to restore its appeal by seeking collaboration with the other unions in gaining concessions from the employers. By the 1960's, the undeniable progress made by the Italian economy, both in increase of the national product and in reduction of unemployment, were making CGIL's former demands less appealing to the mass of the workers; and so, in the Congresses of 1960 and 1965, CGIL's leaders expressed their goals in terms that were in harmony with the planning methods of the Center-Left government. This new union policy took the fashionable form of support of a governmental policy of "economic development" through national economic planning. In 1960, to the CGIL's usual demands for nationalization of sources of power and for agrarian reform, Novella added the "struggle for a national program of industrialization and of agricultural transformation, and for strengthening of the transport and distribution sectors."[20] In practical terms, these goals implied full employment; reform of the state's instruments for intervention, such as taxation and the bureaucracy; direct intervention in industry, from orientation of investment and location through nationalization; agrarian reform; a new distribution network; the end of real-estate speculation; renovated public transport; and educational reform.

In the debate over national economic planning, CGIL came out strongly in favor of the general concept and the long-term goals of the plan, which was developed by the Center-Left government in 1962–65. The union, however, criticized the project for assuming the maintenance of the then existing distribution of the national income, rather than planning for a readjustment in favor of the workers, and for supporting the reorganization of industry on monopolistic lines.[21] This conflict over the content of national economic planning was linked to the debate over Italy's position within EEC. According to Novella, Confindustria was claiming that a rise in salaries would weaken Italy's already poor competitive position, and was therefore using national economic planning as a means of "permanently opposing the development of a policy of union demands that would advance labor's income in relation to national income."[22] To CGIL, the growth of ever vaster companies under the justification of meeting the conditions of the expanded European market meant that the weakest sectors of the Italian economy—small and medium-sized industry, agriculture, public housing, and retail commerce—would be ignored. The final acceptance by the government of economic planning, influenced by the great capitalistic development within EEC, thus had the effect of forcing CGIL to transfer its pressure against the economic trends reinforced by EEC to the battle over the content of that planning.[23]

THE INTERNATIONAL POLICY OF THE CGIL

The debate over economic planning was a further illustration of how, for the CGIL, international and national issues coincided to a far greater extent than they did for the other trade unions, thus affecting CGIL's attitudes toward Italy's basic choices in foreign policy, and especially toward those concerning European integration. In the early debates over the Cold War, the CGIL espoused the Socialist position, proclaiming that Italy should remain neutral in the struggle between the two great powers. But with the ouster of the Communists and Socialists from the government in May 1947, and the Russian rejection of the Marshall Plan in July 1947, the Communist and Socialist leaders of CGIL adopted a firmly anti-American stand. The reasoning of the Communist and Socialist leaders of CGIL was advanced at length at the Congress of Genoa in 1949. Its origin lay in the adoption in late 1947, by the Central Committee of the Communist party of the Soviet Union, of the theory of Zhdanov and planning chief Voznessensky —that a vast economic crisis was about to overwhelm the United States' economy, and hence the economy of the whole capitalistic world.[24] According to Di Vittorio, the "peculiar symptoms of a great general crisis which is hammering at the doors of the capitalist system" were a fall in prices, a major rise in unemployment, and decreasing production, and "imperialism" was applying the usual ways of overcoming this crisis—exploitation of workers and middle classes and preparation for a war of conquest to gain new raw materials, new outlets of trade, and new peoples to exploit. Italy, as one of the weakest of capitalist countries, was feeling this crisis in its most acute form, especially since the Italian capitalist classes, unable to deal with the crisis themselves, were placing themselves at the service of American imperialism. According to Renato Bitossi, the Americans had accumulated vast profits from war production and from the Marshall Plan itself. Bitossi argued that American companies were making investments in Italy because American capitalists were unable to find new profitable outlets in the United States, and that these investments would lead to the permanent conquest of the Italian economic system.[25] The CGIL's rejection of the Marshall Plan, and its ideological justification for the rejection, were harmful to the organization itself. The beneficial results of the Marshall Plan were soon evident to almost everyone, making nonsense of Di Vittorio's claim that the consequences had been "aggravation of unemployment, aggravation of poverty, and lowering of the workers' standard of living." The political character of the opposition to the Plan, with its resultant weakening of the ability of the CGIL to win direct economic benefits for its members, made many leave the union in disgust. The CGIL's reaction to the Marshall Plan marked the beginning of a major decline in the union's popularity and power.[26]

The CGIL's attitude toward the various measures of European integration must be seen against the background of its rejection of membership in the Western bloc in the Cold War.[27] Fully believing in the coming collapse of capitalism in the West, the CGIL and its associated unions in the different industrial sectors found themselves in an ideological quandary when they approached any scheme whose purpose was to make the economic structure of the West more productive. They did not want to postpone the capitalistic collapse, but they did want to raise the living standard of the Italian worker. This difficulty underlay the attitude of the CGIL from the first proposal for the foundation of a coal and steel pool.

CGIL first reacted to the Schuman Plan by declaring that it was yet another aspect of the American attempt "to transfer to a wider, international plane its own crisis and its own internal contradictions." According to Bruno Trentin, one of CGIL's economic theorists, the Schuman Plan was part of a broadly conceived policy for "absorbing all the economic life of the satellite nations and controlling their political and social structure as well." Trentin claimed that "the Italian governing classes, both political and economic, fell directly into this American plan, partly because of their own complete incompetence to run an independent policy" and partly because of their "idyllic trust in the birth of a European federation." Membership in this new cartel, Trentin argued, would end any possibility of reforming the economic and social structure of Italy on the lines proposed by the CGIL, since the Italian state would have given up to an international or supranational authority dominated by monopoly capitalists those powers of intervention in the national economy needed for carrying out these reforms. Trentin and the other theorists of the CGIL felt compelled to become nationalists. Those industrialists who had seen the inability of modern industry to function within the restricted boundaries of the Italian economy were accused of incompetence; and the Italian Left inherited the position held for a century by Italy's industrialists, that of demanding protection and rejecting competition. Patriotism was interpreted as the ability to carry through a policy of economic growth and social reform within the nation's boundaries.[28] CGIL was true to its ideology in rejecting the Schuman Plan; however, it had failed to understand the economic effects of integration. The formation of the Common Market compelled it to rethink its position.

CGIL's attitude toward the Common Market went through three clearly marked stages. During the negotiation of the Common Market treaty in 1956–57, the CGIL leadership was split between the hard line followed by the Communist members, who opposed the idea of Europeanism *in toto*, and the much softer approach followed by the Socialist members, who found Euratom easy to support and avoided raising objections to the principle of the Common Market.[29] Di Vittorio finally decided to accept the Socialist position; and on July 19, 1957, CGIL's Executive Committee issued a position paper on the European Common Market that showed a remarkable appreciation of its goals:

> The Executive Committee of CGIL notes that there exists a tendency toward forms of international economic understanding and of integration of the European markets. This tendency—although it is favored by the conservative forces in Europe for the purpose of Atlantic collaboration—is also based on objective necessities, such as the need to guarantee wider markets for the progress being made in productive technology, to coordinate the efforts for a more rational exploitation of technical, energy, and human resources, and to guarantee a more rapid development in the economically backward regions which constitute a drag on the economic stability of all the European nations. In spite of inconveniences of a transitory nature that might arise for some sectors of production from the development of such a tendency, the Executive Committee holds that it should be supported and encouraged because it could contribute in the future in a fundamental and—to some extent—irreplaceable way to the general development of the European economies and to the improvement of the living conditions of the workers. The CGIL therefore favors supporting every national and international initiative, even if limited to a few countries, which aims, within a policy of peace, to bring to effective solution the economic and social problems connected with an economic integration of Europe.[30]

In taking a favorable attitude toward EEC, CGIL had for the first time taken a stand at variance with that of the Communist party.[31] Had CGIL followed the line sketched out in this document, offering full and positive collaboration in the work of EEC, it might have been able to win a role for itself in the formative work of the Community. Since it did not, a majority of Italian workers found themselves unrepresented at the trade union level in the Community organization.

Di Vittorio died on November 3, 1957, and control of CGIL

passed to Agostino Novella, who espoused far more rigidly than had Di Vittorio the ideological directives of the Communist party. That line had been spelled out by the Executive Committee of the World Federation of Trade Unions (WFTU) at its meeting in Moscow in July, only a few days after CGIL's cautious endorsement. With the Common Market, the WFTU declared, "the European monopolies, with the active intervention of the monopolies of the United States, are trying to overcome the contradictions that bring them into conflict with each other, in order to exploit through common agreement the resources of Europe and Africa. The alignment of the economic and social policies of the six countries of Europe that are interested in the European Common Market can only in these circumstances cause a leveling down toward the lowest standards of the living conditions of the working masses."[32] This determined opposition lasted for the next four years, and the Italian government profited from this attitude. It excluded CGIL's representatives, as would-be saboteurs, from all representative organs in EEC and from the national delegations to all policy-making conferences of the EEC countries. CGIL therefore made common cause with the Communist-dominated union in France, the Confédération Générale du Travail (CGT) in their opposition to EEC from within, in spite of a real lack of sympathy with the French union's dogmatism. Meeting in Prague in February 1958, the two unions sketched out their future policy. They agreed that the Common Market would be used by the capitalist groups as a means of refusing the salary demands of the unions, and that therefore the two unions should "coordinate their action" with regard to salaries, working hours, full employment, rights of emigrants, and union representation within EEC; and they urged unity of action with the other unions in EEC, whether or not they were members of the WFTU.[33] A first attempt to achieve common action with the other trade unions in EEC was made on January 22, 1959, when the secretariats of CGT and CGIL sent a letter to all the national trade unions in EEC, of whatever political complexion, spelling out again their theory that the Common Market was being used by the monopolies against the workers and calling for a conference to discuss the necessary measures to take within the Common Market.[34] Although only the trade unions of Communist or left-wing Socialist character agreed to collaborate, the conference decided to form a Trade Union Coordination and Action Committee of the Countries of EEC. The committee, however, merely continued to repeat the propaganda line laid down by the WFTU.[35]

The first sign of a break in the CGIL's negative attitude came at the Fifth Congress of the World Federation of Trade Unions in Moscow, in December 1961, when the representatives of CGIL publicly dissented from the final report;[36] and Fernando Santi declared that the capitalistic expansion within EEC was producing "an increase of investments and an increase in employment, at least in Italy," and thereby compelling the unions to adopt a new, more ambitious form of struggle within an expanding economic system.[37] The next year, speaking at the Executive Committee of the WFTU in Budapest, Santi returned to the language of CGIL's first pronouncement on EEC: "The CGIL, always against any form of economic nationalism and of autarky, considers that an enlargement of markets on an international scale is an objective tendency of our time. . . . Today, EEC is a reality which one can only recognize in order to better organize the unified action of the workers for the defense of their common interests that are harmed by the action of big capital." CGIL's conclusion was that participation in the EEC organizations was essential.[38] Shortly thereafter, the CGIL leaders came into direct conflict with the WFTU over the attitude to adopt toward the Common Market. On December 14–16, 1962, the WFTU held a conference at Leipzig to discuss the social and economic effects of the Common Market, at which the Italian delegation took the unpopular position of upholding the inevitability of economic integration, given the scale of modern industrial production. The correct attitude was to work within the development process, through unity of action among the workers and in collaboration "with those social classes favorable to integration but opposed to its monopolistic utilization," in order to convert EEC into an instrument for the betterment of the workers.[39] For a start, the WFTU should open an office in Brussels to coordinate this common action. The World Federation's Executive Committee was scandalized by this maverick position of the CGIL, and its meeting on January 29–31, 1963, saw a vigorous clash of opinions, which ended with the CGIL refusing to accept the majority resolution. The CGIL declared that it did not share the attitude of the WFTU toward the Common Market; and it pressed its attack by demanding a revision of the organization and leadership of the World Federation.[40] CGIL received so little support for the opening of a Brussels office that it decided the next month to start the office itself, with the blessing but without the active participation of the unions in France and Luxembourg which belonged to the World Federation.[41]

For the next five years, the CGIL pursued a double goal—to persuade the WFTU to take a more conciliatory policy toward non-Communist unions and to persuade those unions to collaborate with it inside EEC. Among the four documents approved unanimously at the Sixth National Congress of the CGIL was a long analysis of "International Trade Union Policy," which claimed that the time had come to leave behind the "schematic contrapositions between the various central trade unions inherited from the Cold War." The high level of economic integration being achieved in EEC, marked by "the intensified penetration of American capital in all the countries of western Europe, the liberalization of markets, the supranational dimension of the monopolistic groups," had not been met by a similar unified action on the part of the trade unions. The CGIL proposed to carry the battle for structural reform and control of monopolies to the Community level, beginning by pressuring the Italian government to obtain satisfactory conditions in EEC for emigration of workers and to establish more uniform social policies.[42] In certain practical ways, the CGIL did become involved in the work of EEC. It participated in the placement of Italian workers in the jobs offered by EEC members through the Italian government; it established many offices throughout EEC to aid Italian emigrants; and it took part in the negotiations with the foreign labor unions, by which Italian emigrant workers were given the right to membership and the right to run for office in the foreign unions. And two Socialists from CGIL (Piero Boni and Fernando Montagnani) sat as members of the Social and Economic Committee. Relations with the French CGT became closer, and a common committee was formed to discuss problems of wages, contracts, and maintenance of employment at the EEC level and the possibility of common action. In May 1967, the committee set up an office in Brussels which replaced the CGIL's office, but it had no more success in opening official relations with the EEC administration or with the other trade union representatives than the CGIL's committee.

Thus, the CGIL's attitude toward EEC between 1961 and 1968 was one of recognition of its productive achievements and of its effects in reducing unemployment. Many specific features came under criticism;[43] but the decisive change to a favorable and even cooperative attitude to EEC remained constant. No greater proof of the success of integration in Italy could have been found.

THE CONFEDERAZIONE ITALIANA SINDACATI LAVORATORI (CISL)

Although the CGIL remained the largest union in membership, the most influential Italian union, both in internal and international matters, was the Confederazione Italiana Sindacati Lavoratori. At its formation in 1950, CISL claimed a membership of about 1.5 million. This rose to 2 million by 1953 and 2.3 million in 1958.[44] Even at its most ambitious, however, CISL never claimed to have achieved a membership of more than two-thirds that of the CGIL. CISL's influence was due to its favored position within the Italian political system and, at the international level, in the non-Communist labor movement.

CISL always enjoyed close ties with the ruling Christian Democratic party. Many CISL leaders ran for election to parliament as Christian Democrats—in 1953, 22 were elected to the Chamber; in 1958, more than 30 were. As a result, about one-tenth of the Christian Democratic group in parliament was from CISL. The CISL members within the DC were usually active within the left wing of the party, and thus played an important role in pressuring the party to maintain a program of social reforms and later to form the Center-Left government.[45] The CISL deputies also sponsored the successful moves to form a committee to investigate the conditions of labor and to force the withdrawal of the state companies from Confindustria.[46] In most matters, however, the CISL deputies followed the party line within parliament; and as a result the more activist members of the union often accused them of subordinating union interests to party interests. As early as the first National Congress in 1951, delegates suggested that trade union leaders should not sit in parliament. This criticism became more violent in the 1960's, when younger union leaders charged that the double loyalty to union and party of the older leaders was preventing them from adopting progressive social and economic policies.[47]

CISL's role within the Christian Democratic party gave it special privileges in making its wishes known, and to some degree respected, within the bureaucracy and in the various consultative committees established by the government. LaPalombara's study of interest groups in Italy revealed that CISL received far more favorable treatment from the Ministry of the Treasury and the Ministry of Labor and Social Security than either CGIL or UIL. In the Consiglio Nazionale dell'Economia e del Lavoro (CNEL), an extremely important body consulted by the government on major economic decisions, CISL was originally given larger representation than the CGIL; and when CGIL protested, it was given only the same representation as CISL.[48] When representatives for international bodies were named, the Italian government usually ignored the CGIL completely. Moreover, at the international level, CISL's position was strengthened by its membership in the International Confederation of Free Trade Unions, which was by far the more important of the two international trade union groups (the International Confederation of Free Trade Unions, ICFTU, and the International Confederation of Christian Trade Unions, CISC) with which the administrators of EEC and ECSC maintained official contacts. In discussing CISL in its attitudes toward integration and related economic and social issues, we are considering an organization whose influence was directly felt at both the national and international levels.

CISL was strongly anti-Communist. "Two opposed principles of life are in conflict," CISL declared in 1951. "One is based on the right of self-determination and on free expression of conscience; the other is founded on the prohibition of the freedom of opinion and on the imposition of forms of thought and of action conceived and ordered by a dictatorial authority."[49] However, according to CISL's first secretary general, Giulio Pastore, the break with CGIL forced his union to "clarify" its program and its ideology; and, in the course of the next few years, CISL was able to go beyond a merely anti-Communist policy.

To establish CISL's unique position in the history of Italian trade unionism, CISL's leaders attempted to prove that they were "a unitary workers' movement freely associated and independent of any subjection to ties with external political and religious forces." In short, they claimed to have no ties with Christian Democracy or with the Catholic Church.[50] To many, this claim seemed as specious as the CGIL's claim that it was independent of the Communist party; but for both practical and ideological reasons, Pastore and the other leaders of CISL never ceased to assert it. They felt that CISL's total identification with the Christian Democratic party would reduce their influence within the party, giving them less opportunity to press for reformist programs. At the international level, they felt their influence would be greater within the ICFTU rather than within the much weaker federation of Catholic unions, CISC.

The significance of this whole argument lies in CISL's claim that its alignment with the Western bloc in the Cold War, including its rejection of both Communism and neutralism, was not due to subordination to the wishes of the DC or the Catholic Church, but due to its own unique ideology. Christian Democracy, it was argued, had failed to include matters of trade union concern in its ideology; and thus it had been necessary for some members of CISL, through the group of DC deputies called Forze Sociali, to present this ideology within the party, and, by maintaining the independence of the union, to enable it to fight for that ideology in the country at large. As Bruno Manghi points out, rather than turning to the Christian syndicalism of the great Catholic union leader Achille Grandi, CISL found the basis for this new approach in the practice of the American trade unions, in "the serious effort to study how it might be possible to apply in Italy the model of trade unionism in the United States, that is, of a trade unionism which combines loyalty to the institutional system with a noteworthy drive toward industrial conflict and with great organizational efficiency."[51]

This conception of the role of a trade union within a capitalist society, combined with CISL's fundamental belief in the incompatibility of political democracy and Communism, dictated CISL's policy on both internal and foreign questions. During the 1950's the increasingly professional and technically competent leaders of the union sought to develop more effective ways for a moderate trade union to further the well-being of the working classes within the structure of the capitalist system. In effect, having made its first ideological choice in the commitment to the Western bloc and to that bloc's political and economic structure, CISL turned to the necessary corollary to that first decision—to make the system they had accepted more efficient and more just.

For Italy to function effectively within an integrated European economic system, it was essential that CISL should make rapid progress toward viable worker-employer relations within Italy, especially in view of the damage they believed had been done by CGIL's negative attitude toward the economic system and toward attempts to increase the system's effectiveness, such as Marshall aid. In this sphere CISL made notable progress. Even though CISL recognized that grave inequities existed in Italy, it insisted that its goals served the national well-being through "cooperation of owners, managers, technical experts, and workers," first through a National Productivity Committee and then through productivity committees at the factory level.[52] Its intention in the short run was to achieve full employment, fairer distribution of income between workers and owners, better social security benefits, and wider professional training, and in the long run to achieve the participation of the workers in decisions at the plant level as well as in national economic planning, and the increase of controls over the industrial monopolies. But its chosen methods were extremely moderate—linking increases in productivity to increases in salary, using taxation to distribute income more justly, and pushing for government action to set priorities for investment and for use of raw materials and to control prices. In its relations with management, it claimed to resort to strikes only in the last instance, and never for political purposes. It also demanded that the national wage level agreements should be supplemented by bargaining in the individual plants, thereby introducing much greater flexibility into the process of establishing wages and into control over working conditions.[53] This moderation in pressing wage demands during the 1950's, combined with an overcentralized bargaining system which was accepted by all three unions up to 1957, was of considerable significance in making possible the Italian economic miracle. Low wages gave Italian goods competitive prices and made possible the process of reinvestment that accelerated the "take-off" of the Italian economy in the late 1950's.

CISL was not content, however, to leave to the entrepreneurial classes complete control over the direction of Italian economic development. As early as 1951, CISL began pressing for the modification of the existing capitalist system through a national program of economic development. The union demanded government action to orient investment and credit; immediate land reform and changes in the mezzadria contracts; and the strengthening of the public companies, especially IRI and ENI, to make them effective instruments for the realization of the state-sponsored development programs.[54]

In the late 1950's, CISL began to demand much broader national economic planning.[55] The appointment of Giulio Pastore as minister for the Cassa per il Mezzogiorno in 1958 was felt by the union to be a significant chance for the representative of labor to work directly in the economic development of the South and the depressed areas. Pastore's successor as secretary general, Bruno Storti, continued to press for a wider role for labor in drawing up a national economic program. The long negotiations of 1958–62 for the formation of a Center-Left government were of particular interest to CISL, because one of the fundamental goals of the new coalition was to be national economic planning; and, within the Christian Democratic party, CISL's representatives worked for agreement with the Nenni Socialists.[56] CISL played a significant part in the long struggle for the national economic program that was finally adopted by the Chamber in 1967. A similarly positive position was taken by CISL's leaders toward the development of the capitalist system at the international level, particularly through West European integration.

The Christian Democratic union leaders saw no alternative to the division of Europe into two ideological blocs.[57] Pastore attended the trade union conference in Geneva, in June 1949, where delegates from thirty-five countries decided to set up a new International of "free trade unions," and he was elected to the Preparatory Committee that was to draw up a constitution for the new International. This organization, the International Confederation of Free Trade Unions, was founded at London on November 28–December 9, 1949. It was distinctively anti-Communist, and was intended to be "a powerful and effective international organization, composed of free and democratic trade unions, independent of any external domination."[58] The ICFTU subsequently endorsed such major American initiatives as the Marshall Plan and the Atlantic Pact. This pro-American orientation of ICFTU was entirely satisfying to Pastore's union, which was deliberately taking American unionism as its model.

From the early 1950's, CISL welcomed economic integration of western Europe as a necessary step toward the improved working of the capitalist system. In this decision, the International Confederation of Free Trade Unions played an important role. It had already stated, in its constitution, its aim of "increased and properly planned economic cooperation among the nations in such a way as will encourage the development of wider economic units and freer exchange of commodities"; and in November 1950 it set up a European Regional Organization with a small office in Brussels. This Organization, which originally represented sixteen non-Communist countries, took a consistently favorable attitude toward European integration. It had direct relations with the Organization for European Economic Cooperation, established a special committee to push for the integration of agriculture, and supported the formation of the Coal and Steel Community.[59] While favorable to the Common Market and Euratom, its members split over the Free Trade Area plan, the representatives from the six opposing the British conception of liberalization without economic and political integration; and it was probably through suspicion of Britain that the trade unions of the six decided, in January 1958, that the European Regional Organization should not be given an important position in their dealings with the Common Market authorities.[60] Instead, as they had done for the Coal and Steel Community, the ICFTU members from the six set up their own "Organization of ICFTU for the Six Countries of the European Communities."[61]

Thus, at the European level, CISL shared in the expression of views, and in the direct contacts with the European Communities, of ICFTU, of its European Regional Organization, and of the ICFTU organization of the six. In general, these views were favorable to the process of integration, to the broadening of the Communities by admission of new members such as Britain and the Scandinavian countries, and to conclusion of association agreements, as, for example, with Israel. The specifically syndical goals were sought by pressure for Community-level economic planning and for more rapid movement from a customs union to an economic union through institution of a Planning Commissariat and development of Community policies for agriculture, transport, energy, price competition, and social development. This evolution would only be feasible, the ICFTU organization of the six felt, if a supranational political authority were instituted.[62] The European trade union organizations were determined to press for a particular conception of European unification, "economic and social integration by way of planning."[63] At the European level, this pressure took many forms—direct contacts with members of the High Authority and of the Commissions of EEC and Euratom and with the Community officials; special meetings with officials on topics of trade union interest, such as acceleration of customs reduction; consultation of trade union experts by Community officials; direct participation of union representatives in the work of the Communities, as in the European Social Fund; representation on the Social and Economic Committee; and especially collaboration in drawing up EEC's plan for a medium-term economic policy.[64] Yet most union leaders admitted that their most significant activity in European matters was exercised at the national level.

In one of its first pronouncements, made in June 1950, CISL's General Council had stated its belief in integration on the widest possible scale, including "economic unification of markets, political unification of the states, and liberalization of world commerce." CISL's representatives welcomed the Schuman Plan and voted for it in the Chamber of Deputies, in spite of fears of unployment in the non-competitive Italian mines and steel factories.[65] After the Messina conference in June 1955, and the European Regional Organization's conference on the Common Market in August, CISL endorsed the idea of extending the common market in coal and steel products to other sectors like transport and atomic energy, and it particularly welcomed the institution of a European investment fund for the aid of underdeveloped regions. CISL's General Council declared that it would put every level of its organization to work "to win the great working masses over to the European idea, in order to make them a dynamic element in the realization of a United Europe."[66] Following the acceptance by CISL of membership in Jean Monnet's Action Committee for the United States of Europe, the union called for immediate support in parliament of Monnet's draft motion in favor of Euratom, seeing the "new Community as a particularly suitable instrument for meeting the great problems of economic development that concern the countries of the Community, and Italy in particular."[67] In recommending ratification of the EEC and Euratom treaties on July 27, 1957, the executive committee demanded that the government, to prepare the country, immediately realize internal economic reforms CISL had been suggesting for the preceding seven years, and that it ensure trade union representation in the Community parliament, in choice of Commission members, in the Social and Economic Committee, in the Social Fund, and in the European Investment Bank.[68]

Once EEC and Euratom had been founded, CISL supported the rapid achievement of the customs union through the acceleration decisions of 1960; it shared in the formulation of the common agricultural policy; and its representatives helped force the Italian government to demand the improved regulations on migration of workers within the Community. But the confederation's main concerns were to prevent the Community from becoming a closed, protective unit; to combat the "liberal" conception of the economic union, in favor of a more interventionist view; and to ensure greater democratic controls and strengthened political powers for the Community authorities.[69] It welcomed Britain's application in 1961 and again in 1966, and strongly condemned de Gaulle's vetoes on both applications.[70] More important, however, was CISL's fear that the Community, because the Treaty of Rome was "inspired by the most traditional liberalism, tends to regard social policy essentially as a sub-product of the liberalization of the exchange of goods and of productive factors."[71] Ten years after the signature of the treaty, CISL felt social policy was in a state of "progressive paralysis" in such matters as harmonization of social security, wage levels, pension rights, and so on. This liberal conception extended beyond social policy, however, as CISL President Bruno Storti pointed out, making Community action on "necessary common policies which aim to establish common basic conditions for productive activities, in commerce, transport, fiscal action, and social policy . . . irrelevant and contradictory."[72] In spite of its good relations with the Community authorities, CISL felt that the unions were insufficiently represented; and, at the time of the fusion of the executives of the three Communities in 1967, it joined in the common memorandum of the ICFTU and CISC which demanded that the new, broadened Commission be more responsive to the trade union movement.

From the start, CISL supported the Western bloc and all movements of integration within that bloc. In Italy, it contributed to the improvement of the working of the capitalist system by emphasizing the need for planning for a process of economic development, rationalization of the process of wage demands, structural reforms in agriculture, and a broader program of welfare benefits. CISL's responsible attitude in labor-management relations, its presence as a strong left-wing group within the ruling Christian Democratic party, and its role in pressuring for national economic planning all helped make possible the Italian economic miracle and Italy's successful entrance into the European Community.

THE ASSOCIAZIONI CRISTIANE LAVORATORI ITALIANI (ACLI)

While CISL was attempting to refute the charge of being a purely Catholic trade union, the Associazioni Cristiane Lavoratori Italiani claimed from its foundation that it existed for the general well-being of Catholic workers. Although its activities were supposedly educational, cultural, and social, it exercised great influence in determining the attitude of its very large membership toward Italy's foreign policy choices.

ACLI was founded in August 1944, in direct reaction to the unification of the trade union movement in June of that year. It was established to give Catholic training to workers outside of the CGIL. The association was set up parallel to the regular trade unions, but it differed in that Churchmen were present as advisers at every level and in that its direct program was limited to professional education, cultural activities, economic assistance, and recreation. These activities remained the basis of its influence on the workers, which was the justification for its self-proclaimed role as a pressure group at the national level. By the 1960's, ACLI was running a huge program for one million members through 7800 local clubs and 1000 factory groups.[73] Its educational role was conceived directly in religious terms: "The basis and ultimate goal of this educational work, of work that does not intend to be ephemeral but lasting and eternal, is the religious education of the worker. ACLI wants to bring back the fullness of Christian thought and life into the thought and life of the workers."[74] ACLI proposed to train the worker in an understanding of the Catholic conception of society, in which the interests of the workers must, through specific reforms, be harmonized with those of the national community.[75]

At the national level, ACLI also had a clear ideological basis for its action, in Papal doctrine from *Quadragesimo Anno* of Pius XI to *Mater et Magister* of John XXIII. The First National Congress of ACLI, held in September 1946, proclaimed the "primacy of Christian Social Doctrine," which, "confirmed in recent Papal messages, proposes a fitting solution to all the problems of the workers . . . overcoming the positions of class antagonism and of the pre-eminence of the rights of property and of the industrial company (whether public or private)."[76] Since Italian society clearly did not correspond to the ideal society envisaged by this doctrine, ACLI saw its role as the constructor of "a new society founded in a Christian way upon labor."[77] It therefore supported most of the reforms that CISL had demanded, and it took credit for many of the ideas in the Vanoni Plan, for the parliamentary inquiry into the conditions of the Italian worker and the social reforms that followed the inquiry, and for the reform program of the Center-Left government. By its warning to the workers "no longer to orient their action predominantly toward wage demands and toward the conquest of one-sided and sectoral benefits, but rather to contribute to and support the organic development of the whole community," it felt that it had brought a more responsible approach to worker-management relations and thus contributed to the economic progress of the country.[78]

At the international level, Christian Social Doctrine required an enthusiastic participation in the Western bloc and in all movements toward the integration of western Europe. This orientation implied a constant policy of anti-Communism. During the period of the unified CGIL, 1944–48, ACLI increasingly took the position of being "the expression of the Christian current in the trade union field," even though that current was also represented within the CGIL. In this position, they were directly backed by the Vatican. Pope Pius XII, in giving his blessing to ACLI on March 11, 1945, had warned that the Catholics could not continue to cooperate with CGIL if it overstepped its purpose of representing the workers in labor contracts; and in June 1948 he indirectly invited ACLI to lead the Catholic workers out of CGIL.

> What should one think of the exclusion of a worker from work because he is not a person pleasing to the trade union, of forced work stoppages for achieving political aims, of straying into many other erroneous byways, which lead far from the true welfare and the much invoked unity of the working class? . . .
>
> If the present form of the trade union should come to endanger the true scope of the movement of the workers, then the ACLI would certainly have the vigilance and action which the gravity of the case would require. Truly there are involved today important decisions and reforms in the national economy, in the face of which a class struggle based upon distrust and hatred would succeed in compromising the trade union idea, if not in leading it directly to ruin. Therefore, you must make Christian principles definitely prevail in the trade union; then it will prosper to the advantage of the workers and of all the Italian people.[79]

Two weeks later, the Catholic members withdrew from the CGIL, and at a special congress of ACLI in September 15–18, they formed a new, democratic trade union, the LCGIL, which was, theoretically, free of ties to any church.[80] ACLI thereupon resumed its role as a social movement; and, indeed, those critics who wished to see CISL linked to the Catholic Church, like ACLI founder Giuseppe Rapelli, were disturbed at its reduced political role.[81]

Nevertheless, ACLI continued to speak out on the major issues affecting the workers, and was especially firm in its support of European integration. More openly than CISL, ACLI based its attitude toward integration upon Papal teachings, finding their highest embodiment in John XXIII's Encyclical, *Pacem in Terris*. "ACLI workers," according to the association, "have seen the fundamental aspiration of humanity for a peace founded on security and freedom condensed in this document. In this spirit they see in a rapid process of European integration and Atlantic partnership two factors which are leading to success for the cause of peace and which are necessary premises for a general and controlled disarmament."[82] In ACLI's view, the Europe that should unite would be one of "peoples who through a common cultural heritage, of traditions and of civilization, believe in a community of destiny and freely associate across their frontiers."[83] ACLI thus carefully excluded the Communist countries, and, by emphasizing the cultural rather than the religious ties of the West, avoided the problem of Catholic-Protestant relations within a unified Europe. The gradual process of economic, social, and political unification through the European Communities was held to correspond to the deepest ideals of ACLI's members, both as Christians and as workers; and it was "the interest of workers in general, and the duty of Catholic workers in particular, to understand and to support—participating actively and responsibly—this irreversible process of unification."[84] In economic terms, ACLI recognized that Europe must create a large economic area to develop technologically and to meet the challenge of the American and Russian economies; and on these grounds the National Council declared its approval of the institution of the Common Market, on March 17, 1957.[85] But it did not lose sight of its ultimate goal, "the construction of the United States of Europe, a supranational economic and political Community." It continued to press for the admission into the Community of the other western European nations that shared democratic ideals; and it sharply criticized de Gaulle for his veto on British entry in 1963. It called for the strengthening and broadening of the powers of the Community institutions, and especially for the election of the European Parliament by universal suffrage.

ACLI was one of the strongest supporters of European integration within Italy. In its educational work it taught the ideal of a united, if anti-Communist, Europe. Its members in the Chamber, usually about twenty in number, worked within the DC to ensure respect for ACLI's demands for legislation concerning integration. Perhaps the most significant example of this was Giovanni Bersani's work for the election of the European Parliament by universal suffrage. The association was one of the founding members of the Italian Council of the European Movement; and it later popularized the work of the European Organization of the International Confederation of Christian Trade Unions. ACLI's strong support of the integration movement inside Italy is a clear and important example of an organization whose primary purpose in seeking to unify Europe was ideological rather than economic; it is also an obvious illustration of the Papacy's specific goals for Europe.[86]

THE UNIONE ITALIANA DEL LAVORO (UIL)

The Unione Italiana del Lavoro was a union made up of Republicans, Social Democrats, and ex-Fascists, united by their anti-clericalism and anti-Communism. In spite of the protestations of its leaders, it quickly became identified with the Social Democratic party and, to a lesser degree, with the Republicans. At its founding, it claimed a membership of about 250,000, rising by the mid 1950's to 750,000. Most observers consider that its true strength remained at about 300,000.[87]

The UIL was determined to offer a middle course between what it regarded as the Communist-dominated CGIL on the Left and the Church-dominated CISL on the Right. While constantly affirming its opposition to Communism, it was willing to be flexible in its relations with the CGIL, especially in keeping contact with the Socialist members of that union. In 1950 it offered to work with both CGIL and CISL on specific trade union isues, an offer that was accepted by the CGIL and denounced by CISL, and it attempted to match the militancy of the CGIL in demanding immediate improvements in the workers' standard of living, saying that they must be won by strikes if necessary.[88] To the CISL, the UIL's willingness to cooperate with the CGIL was intolerable; and UIL's leaders constantly found a more hostile reception from CISL than they did from CGIL. Its membership in the ICFTU was blocked for a year by CISL, which received strong backing from the American Federation of Labor,[89] and CISL was able to ensure that it received little or no financial aid from American unions. The turning point in the relations between the two unions came in 1953, when CISL agreed to consultation and cooperation on specific issues. A major result of this cooperation was seen in the conglobamento wage agreements of 1954, from which the CGIL was excluded. UIL, in short, had found its place: it offered a Social Democratic alternative to those workers who found they could no longer accept Communist dominance of the CGIL. It is not surprising that its largest jump in membership occurred at the time of the Soviet suppression of the Hungarian uprising in 1956.[90]

From 1953 on, UIL demonstrated that it shared with CISL not only immediate labor demands, but also long-term policies for Italian economic development and a commitment to the Western bloc and to European integration. It welcomed the Vanoni Plan, and took an active if critical part in the National Productivity Committee. It strongly supported the Center-Left experiment, and regarded both national economic planning and the Green Plans as essential preparations for the entry of Italian industry and agriculture into a unified Europe.[91] It urged the reunification of the Socialist party, both as a necessary corollary to the Center-Left experiment and as a means of bringing greater Socialist influence in the development of an integrated Europe.[92] It obviously hoped that a similar reunification of Socialists would take place within UIL, if the Socialists were to leave the CGIL. Thus, at the national level, UIL proclaimed the Social Democratic doctrine that in an economy based upon class antagonism a peaceful democratic method for improvement of the conditions of the working classes lay in increasing the powers and the area of intervention of the state.

At the international level, UIL also adopted a similar policy to that of CISL, although in the first two years after its founding some of its members leaned toward neutralism in the Cold War. It sought membership in the Italian Council of the European Movement and gave its support to most of the initiatives of the Italian federalists; it approved the creation of the Coal and Steel Community as a contribution to the ending of the rivalry between France and Germany and as an impulse to the creation of a supranational power in Europe. Above all, UIL regarded the Common Market as a major achievement: it encompassed all sectors of economic life and it was something more than a free trade area; its founders "had created a single economic policy, a single financial policy, a single social policy. It was not political Europe, certainly, but it had opened the way to an irreversible process of integration."[93]

Looking back on the tenth anniversary of the signature of the Treaty of Rome, UIL's newspaper, *Il Lavoro Italiano,* felt that much had been done, but it lamented certain shortcomings. It regretted above all the failure of European Socialists to unite in the late 1940's, and stated that "it would have been possible to block the Stalinist advance, to make ourselves independent of American protection, to reconstruct all Europe—from the North Sea to Moravia—on democratic and socially advanced bases, making it become a democratic, anti-colonialist, anti-imperialist third force, a mediator between the two greatest powers in the world." The scission of the unified CGIL, UIL claimed, was another result of Europeanism, "the way of a third force between the two titanic powers, the hope of an autonomous renaissance, of a policy of progress and peace in liberty, the right way to overcome the tensions of postwar imperialism." (Obviously, the neutralists' hopes died hard.) The paper then noted that the lessons of the early 1950's were that European unity had to go beyond simple cooperation, as in the Marshall Plan; that it could not be created through constitutional schemes proposed by the federalists; and that the one solution had been found in ECSC and EEC—"to create a situation in which, beginning with the indisputable fragility of each one of the member states and from their reciprocal interest in integrating their respective economies, it would become absolutely necessary for practical reasons to create political institutions for the economic Community at the end of the transitional period."[94]

UIL had originally approved of European integration in the hope that it would create a third force in the world, between the Soviet Union and the United States, much as it saw itself a third force in Italy, between CGIL and CISL; and it never budged from its original attitude to the Treaty of Rome, which summed up its whole attitude toward integration: "We are aware that European unity does not yet exist. Real unity exists only in the sector of cartels and private monopolies. It is up to the workers and to the democratic Left . . . to move resolutely for the conquest of the main responsibility within the new Communities."[95]

13

Christian Democracy and Its "Currents"

The semimonopoly of political power held by the Christian Democratic party in the postwar period did not lead to the imposition of a monolithic rule in accordance with any fixed ideology. The Christian Democrats were divided into a number of "currents," organized groups which competed for control of the party and of policy formulation. The other political parties worked to change the direction of Italian governmental policy by joining in the internal struggles within the Christian Democratic party. This produced a unique political system, totally different in character from the two-party system of the Anglo-Saxon democracies and from the genuine coalition government of the French Fourth Republic. As Giorgio Galli pointed out in his study of the left-wing currents in the DC:

> They were not simply opposition currents within the party. Since the Christian Democratic party held power in a stable manner, the currents ended up assuming the function of true and proper national oppositions. To them was reserved the privilege which the other oppositions did not have, that is, the possibility of attaining power in the country through control of the party. . . . The opposition parties can increase or diminish their power by participating in the struggle that develops for control of the Christian Democratic party itself. The struggle among the Christian Democratic currents thus has national significance. In it participate all the groups that are struggling for political power in Italy,

whether they are political parties, interest groups, or religious organisms like the Church.[1]

Italy's role in Europe was therefore defined at the political level by the dominant currents within the Christian Democratic party.

CONSTITUENT CURRENTS OF THE CHRISTIAN DEMOCRATS

From its foundation in 1943, the Christian Democratic party combined several diverse groups. In 1928, a Movimento Guelfo had been founded in Milan by Piero Malvestiti to combat Fascist ideas through propaganda and educational activity. In 1941 the movement produced a Programma Guelfo, with a strongly left-wing orientation, which it presented to De Gasperi as a program for the new Catholic party.[2] Malvestiti himself was already a spokesman for Christan internationalism, and in fact he had been tried in 1933 for conspiring "to weaken or destroy national feeling."[3] He was one of the earliest proponents of European unification and of national economic planning in the DC, and later he became president of the High Authority of ECSC.

Another group was the Italian Catholic University Federation (FUCI), a very lively branch of Catholic Action, which aimed at creating a Catholic movement untainted by Fascism. Its leaders were a young layman, Igino Righetti, and his ecclesiastical assistant, Giuseppe Montini, the future Pope Paul VI. Within this group were some of the most important leaders of the DC—Guido Gonella, who became the political editor for *L'Osservatore Romano* and the first editor of the DC's *Il Popolo;* Aldo Moro of Bari, who rose to be party secretary and premier; and Giulio Andreotti, a leader of the Christian Democratic Right and a perennial minister. FUCI's leadership was characterized by an almost excessive religious fervor, by a strict adherence to the Vatican's foreign policy line, and by a moderate nationalism. They were only mildly interested in European integration and opposed widespread economic intervention by the state.[4]

A third group, which operated in the Catholic Action of Florence, was led by Giorgio La Pira, a professor of Roman Law who preached the dominance of spiritual over political and economic values and the consequent dominance of the Church over the State. By 1943 La Pira had already developed that body of ideas that was to make him, "as far as ideology is concerned, the most representative personality of the Christian Democratic Left, . . . the only person who succeeded in making his own ideas circulate among all the groups of the Christian Democratic Left."[5] From La Pira were to come the neutralism, the concept of Europe as a third force, the opposition to the capitalistic organization of the Italian economy, and the nostalgic conception of the Middle Ages as an ideal, all of which characterized much of the thinking of the DC's Left.[6]

A fourth group, connected with the Catholic University of Milan, broke with the Fascist regime after the outbreak of World War II.[7] Its leaders, Amintore Fanfani and Paolo Emilio Taviani, both followed the economic ideas of Professor Francesco Vito, the Catholic University's distinguished professor of economics and one of the most influential economists of the postwar period. The economic doctrine taught by Fanfani and Taviani, called "neovoluntarism," held that economics must be subordinated to morality, and that at a certain point either the state or even the capitalists themselves must intervene in the working of the system to ensure its respect for ethical values, such as the payment of a just wage. After first believing that Fascist corporatism had applied this doctrine, Fanfani turned to the democratic state as the new instrument of neovoluntarism, because the state had the capacity to intervene in the economy. By 1946 he was already well on the way to the reformist position that was to make him the leader of those left-wing Christian Democrats who sought an intermediate position between the uncontrolled capitalism espoused by the right-wing Christian Democrats and the socialism of the left-wing parties.

Finally, there were the former members of the Partito Popolare Italiano, the Catholic political party that, in the brief period between its foundation by the reform-minded priest Don Luigi Sturzo in 1919 and its suppression by Mussolini in 1926, had tried successfully to become a widely based center party whose Catholicism would enable it to act as conciliator between the antagonistic social classes of Italy. The ideology accepted by most of the Popolari consisted of a broad and rather vague set of principles, including political democracy and civil rights; local power and decentralization of government; the aconfessional character of the party, established through its freedom from ecclesiastical controls; agrarian reform, by redistribution of uncultivated estates and better contracts for sharecroppers; economic and social reform, through social security and national investment programs; and a foreign policy of benevolent internationalism, based on cooperation of independent nation-states. The strength of the ex-Popolari lay in the character of their leaders, especially of Alcide De Gasperi, who had taken over the party secretaryship from Don Sturzo in 1923.[8]

All these groups were represented in the new party called Democrazia Cristiana. In 1942–43 two programs were drawn up, one largely the work of De Gasperi and his collaborators in Rome, called *Idee ricostruttive della Democrazia Cristiana,* and the other the work of a sixteen-man committee appointed by the party but written largely by Malvestiti, called the Manifesto of Milan. The contrast between the two is instructive. De Gasperi's document was filled with devotion for the Church and its doctrines: "Representative democracy . . . [must be] animated with the spirit of fraternity, which is the vital ferment of Christian civilization. . . . It is the particular interest of democracy that such Christian leaven should ferment in all social life, and that the spiritual mission of the Catholic Church should develop in complete liberty, and that the voice of the Roman Pontiff . . . should sound freely in Italy and in the world." The reforms suggested were moderate— the creation of autonomous regions, participation of the workers in the administration and ownership of the companies where they worked, the destruction of monopolies "that are not by the nature of things or for technical reasons truly inevitable," and agrarian and tax reform. Internationally, De Gasperi proposed "vaster solidarity between free peoples . . . confederal organisms with continental and intercontinental ties," equal access to raw materials, freedom of emigration, and "ever broader achievement of freedom of trade."[9] In 1943 De Gasperi had not yet come to the idea of uniting Europe into a political unit, and his views on economic integration had not advanced beyond the freeing of trade. Malvestiti, on the other hand, began his manifesto with an outright demand for European federation. The very first point read:

> Within the framework of a renewed society of Nations—the expression of the solidarity of all Peoples—a Federation of the European States governed by a system of liberty. Direct representation of the Peoples—beside that of the Governments—in the one as in the other. General and simultaneous disarmament, armed forces and voluntary recruitment at the exclusive disposition of the international community. Voluntary law and European citizenship beside that of national citizenship. Juridical equality between citizens of all States. Application of these principles to the national and international economy.[10]

Thus, in one paragraph, Malvestiti raised the questions of political integration of the non-Communist European states, of a directly elected European parliament with real powers, of an integrated European army, and of economic integration. Seven years went by before De Gasperi accepted these ideas. When he did, however, he took them in their entirety; and he fought for them so strongly that he himself came to be regarded as their original sponsor in Italy.

In the period between the armistice of September 1943 and the end of the war the party won the largest following of any political group. The moderate reform program espoused by Gronchi and Malvestiti attracted those segments of the working classes who did not wish to embark upon revolutionary change. The emphasis upon the family farm and upon the small property-holder appealed to the peasantry. Yet the conservative classes, both well-to-do industrialists and landowners and groups such as the bureaucrats and the white-collar workers, who had a vested interest in the status quo, also turned to the Christian Democratic party. It was the only mass party with an openly bourgeois ideology of acceptance of the existing character of Italy's economy and society. The immediate effect of this conservative support was to minimize the strength of the party's reforming wing and to make of the DC, even before the war was over, a restoring rather than a reforming party.[11] The dominance of De Gasperi within the DC became complete because he alone was able to harmonize the personal and ideological conflicts within the party. His towering moral stature, his superb sense of politics and of the state, his position of esteemed mediator between the Church and the party, combined to make the DC his own instrument, at least during the early years of social and economic upheaval.

Christian Democratic policy through the first four ministries of De Gasperi, from December 1945 to May 1948, had one consistent theme: the development and application of a policy of anti-Communism, both nationally and internationally. The extreme difficulty of enabling the DC and the Communist party to work together in a coalition government was evident long before the end of the Parri government;[12] but it was only at the end of 1946 that the majority of the members of the DC were ready for the break. By then, the Christian Democrats felt they had good reason to be discontented with the Communist-Socialist alliance. They found themselves fighting continually to maintain their own economic policy against the radical demands of the left-wing parties, who seemed to have scored a signal success by ousting Treasury Minister Corbino.[13] They saw in the struggle for local power, especially within the local administrations and the police, one aspect of a Communist attempt to lay the groundwork for an eventual takeover of the state; and in the hidden caches of military equipment discovered in Emilia they saw more direct evidence of the proximity of a Communist *coup d'état*. In foreign policy, they were disillusioned with the policy of neutralism espoused by Foreign Minister Nenni and ostensibly supported by the Communists, and were demanding a closer alignment with the Western powers, and particularly with the United States. Above all, the Papacy was using its influence more and more strongly to urge the end of temporizing with the supporters of "the impossible omnipotence of a material state without spiritual ideals, without religion, and without God."[14]

Pope Pius XI had already forbidden Catholics to work with Communists in his Encyclical of 1937, *Divini Redemptoris*: "Communism is intrinsically wrong and no one who would save Christian civilization may collaborate with it."[15] After the war, faced with the direct challenge to Church influence inside Italy from the Italian Communist party, Pius XII decided to involve the Church fully in the ideological struggle to block the advance of Communism both internationally and nationally.[16] Within the Vatican, he allied with the more conservative forces, led in the immediate postwar years by Cardinal Domenico Tardini and by the small group whom Carlo Falconi called the "Vatican Pentagon," who espoused an uncompromising defense of the capitalist system and of Western democracy, if necessary through a Cold War with the Communist powers. The culmination of this policy came in July 1949 with the Holy Office's decree of excommunication for all Catholics who collaborated with or joined the Communist party. Pius XII had given up the "Church's traditional neutrality" in international politics,[17] and he logically went on to disavow the neutralism being preached by the left-wing current of the DC. At the time of the elections of June 1946, he had told Catholics that they must choose between "the champions or the destroyers of Christian civilization;"[18] and, in a speech to a huge crowd in Saint Peter's Square, on December 22, 1946, he had called Catholics to militancy:

> On Roman soil the first Peter, surrounded by the threats of a perverted imperial power, raised the proud cry of alarm: Resist strong in the faith. On this same ground we repeat that cry today with redoubled energy to you whose native City is now the theater for unceasing attempts to inflame the struggle between two opposed camps: for Christ or against Christ, for his Church or against his Church.[19]

Thus, months before the break, the polemic between the Catholic hierarchy and the left-wing parties had come into the open. During his third ministry, De Gasperi found himself in the anomalous position of supporting the coalition with the Communists, in order to strengthen the Church's position under the Constitution, while the Church itself was opposing that coalition.

The necessity for a renewed effort to deal with the worsening economic situation became the final cause for the break. While De Gasperi had been concerned with establishment of the international position of the Italian state through negotiation of the peace treaty and the restoration of internal stability through passage of a moderate Constitution, his economic policy had been largely passive. To maintain the Communist-Socialist alliance, he had merely avoided altering the economic structure of the country. But by 1947, he had to make a choice between the radical social reforms proposed by the left-wing groups, including those within his own party, and the harsh program of fiscal austerity proposed by Luigi Einaudi, governor of the Bank of Italy, and supported by the business classes.[20] In this instance, the choice of an internal economic policy was clearly a political choice, with both national and international consequences. On May 12 the minister of industry and commerce, a Socialist, criticized De Gasperi's economic proposals, which were to be presented to the Constituent Assembly, and the Premier decided to make this lack of agreement a reason for resignation the next day. The crisis lasted for seventeen days, at the end of which De Gasperi formed a government composed exclusively of Christian Democrats and politicians without party affiliation.[21] In his fourth cabinet, De Gasperi created the governmental formula that was to take Italy into Europe—the Foreign Ministry in the hands of a convinced European, Sforza; economic policy in the hands of liberal economists, Einaudi and Del Vecchio; education in the hands of a Catholic Action member, Gonella; and social reform in the hands of the left-wing currents. The makers of internal policy could accept the policy of Europeanism because the economic Right (Pella, Merzagora) saw the liberal character of the Italian economic system preserved by their own policy at home and strengthened by the emphasis on increased competition implied by European integration, while the reformers saw the process of integration providing the economic prosperity essential to their own reforms at home.

The Christian Democrats made the campaign for the election of the First Legislature of the new Republic, on April 18, 1948, a plebiscite on the government's policy of anti-Communism and alignment with the West, and they won by an even greater margin than they had hoped. Their total vote increased by 5 million over the results of 1946, to 13 million, or 48.4 per cent of the total vote. Through the system of proportional representation, the party enjoyed an absolute majority in the Chamber of Deputies, 304 seats out of 568. De Gasperi was thus assured of the premiership for five years—years in which the party could move on to spell out the more detailed choices of policy consequent upon the general commitment to anti-Communism.

DE GASPERI'S HEGEMONY, 1948–1953

After the elections, the Christian Democratic party found itself compelled to formulate a new role for Italy, and for its neighbors in western Europe, within the American bloc. In making these choices, the currents within the party divided more sharply than they had during the period of breakdown of the anti-Fascist coalition, because the decisions within the party were no longer choices to be supported with ranks closed against opposition in a coalition government, but decisions of national policy, enforced by an absolute majority in parliament.

The Currents of the Left: The development of well-organized currents within the DC took place only after the 1948 elections. As Thierry Godechot has shown, the process, although forbidden by the statutes of the party, was quite natural. Each current began with one leader, around whom a group of deputies and party members gathered. They would publish a review expressing their policies, and sometimes they would found a press agency and choose a regular meeting-place. After 1953, a more elaborate organization was created. The current would form a nationwide organization, with control of the province from which its leader was elected as the base of its power. The leader, using his position in the party administration, would place his own followers at all levels of the party structure. The final stage was reached when each Christian Democrat within the party or government administration had given his allegiance to a particular, identifiable current. "One thus observed the birth of genuine minor parties within the Christian Democratic Party."[22]

Giovanni Gronchi had already marked out a distinctive line of policy, at variance with De Gasperi's on many points, in the period 1945–48. Gronchi, as a founding member of the Popular party and a leader of the pre-Fascist Christian trade unions, was second only to De Gasperi in influence within the Christian Democratic party. Around this passionate, crusading, ambitious leader, the first left-wing current was bound to form. His current's review, *Politica Sociale*, first appeared in March 1946, with a demand for a radical reform of capitalistic society as recommended in Papal teaching, and for the "pre-eminence of labor," rather than of the industrial classes, within the party. In 1948, Gronchi argued that the government's foreign policy, influenced by the same conservative groups that guided its economic policy, was taking the wrong direction. He felt that Italy should remain neutral in the Cold War, and should not become tied to such military alliances as the Brussels Pact and especially not to a military alliance with the United States. But Gronchi, far from supporting the concept of a unified Europe as a third force, turned to a form of nationalism. He denounced the government for having lost Italy's colonial empire and for failing to use its participation in the Atlantic Alliance as a bargaining counter in getting Trieste. (One cannot be both European and Italian, he wrote in 1951.) Immediately after this attack on the government's foreign policy, Gronchi and his followers were removed from important positions in the government and the party, and they were kept out of these positions for the whole period of De Gasperi's dominance, from 1948 through 1953. They became an active opposition within the DC, stimulating the party's willingness to proceed with internal reform and preparing the way for the eventual "opening to the Left." But they were dangerously shortsighted in their suspicion of Italy's participation in European integration.[23]

The second left-wing current of the DC was the syndicalist group that, under Pastore's leadership, broke away from the Gronchiani. Their political ideology, expressed in CISL, was discussed in Chapter Twelve.

The third current, grouped around the review *Cronache Sociali*, consisted of the followers of Giuseppe Dossetti, a professor of law at the Catholic University of Milan. Most of its members were young professors and writers who had worked together in the Resistance. The Resistance, they believed, was the experience that had converted their advanced Catholic ideology of social change into a mass movement responsive to those forces that had been excluded from participation in the pre-Fascist state. Their roots in the Resistance gave the Dossettiani their wish to work with the parties of the extreme Left, their determination to bring about social reforms, and their opposition to Italian participation in a Western Alliance engaged in a Cold War with Russia and the Eastern bloc.[24]

In the year between the elections of April 1948 and the Third National Congress of the DC in Venice on June 2–5, 1949, the Dossettiani, through Fanfani as minister of labor, were responsible for the DC's only significant piece of social legislation, the creation of a state housing program for workers. But the failure of the government to present the promised land reform, or to push through the reform of the mezzadria contracts, drove Dossetti to demand a new approach to economic policy, to reject a laissez-faire policy influenced by vested interests for one favoring the workers, and to place considerations of social justice ahead of productivity.[25] The Dossettiani's plans—if they had ever reached practical formulation—would have resulted in a far-reaching redistribution of national wealth through taxation, changes of landownership, and an increase of state participation in industrial production. De Gasperi fought against the Dossettiani's influence almost too successfully; with the growing emphasis on productivity, the ideal of social reform became subordinate. The Dossettiani were also opposed to the participation of Italy in the Atlantic Pact. In Dossetti's view, Italy was becoming involved in the strategic interests of the American bloc, whereas its interest should be to preserve the autonomy of Europe. This autonomy could be achieved under "the banner of federalism," but would not be advanced, as some argued, by linking the European nations within the Atlantic Pact. Through federalism, he argued, the impulse to unity of the European peoples would force the governments to accept a limitation of their sovereignty, while membership in NATO, on the other hand, would be a serious obstacle to an "autonomous attempt at unification."[26] Thus, *Cronache Sociali* kept alive the concept of a neutral Europe through the debate on the Atlantic Pact, rejecting the basic assumption of the DC majority that European unification meant the integration of western Europe within a larger Atlantic Community.

At the Third National Congress the Dossettiani attacked vigorously. La Pira demanded a "crusade on poverty"; Dossetti demanded reform of the organs of the State, especially of the state bureaucracy. Dossetti's criticism apparently stung De Gasperi, because he devoted one-third of his closing speech to saying "a few words to our friend Dossetti." Fortunately, he remarked, experience had prevailed over culture in the decision to break with the

Communists and Socialists; the whole attitude of the young, of criticizing the government for errors without seeing its good side, was "uneducational." Nevertheless, the proposals of the Dossettiani for a coordinated attack on the problem of unemployment and for state reform were embodied in the final motion of the Congress.[27] The following two years, however, were a complete disappointment to the Dossettiani, and they devoted their energy to attacking the economic policy of Budget Minister Giuseppe Pella, one of the foremost representatives of the right wing of the party. This pressure from the Dossettiani, combined with peasant seizures of unoccupied land in the South, persuaded De Gasperi to push through parliament the first "slice" (stralcio) of a national agrarian reform, beginning in the Sila, and the foundation of the Cassa per il Mezzogiorno. De Gasperi had made a vital change of direction in seeking the support of the left wing of the party for an open challenge to the right wing on land reform, the Cassa, and state control of the natural gas deposits of the Po valley. As Giorgio Galli has pointed out, this new alliance had profound effects upon both De Gasperi's Center current and on the Dossettiani. By attacking the landowners of the South, De Gasperi thrust them into the hands of the monarchists, who, in the political crisis of 1953, were able to unseat him, and this opened a new phase in the political development of the DC. The Dossettiani won for themselves the enmity of the industrial classes, who saw in them aspirants for a new distribution of economic power in Italy. These classes finally succeeded in destroying the current. However, the Enti di Riforma, the Cassa, and ENI, created under pressure of the Dossetti current, became the training ground of a new political group that influenced the character of the DC after 1954, taking up in new ways the struggle of the Dossettiani.[28]

The Dossettiani disappeared as a separate current in 1951–52. Both La Pira and Dossetti retired from national politics; and Fanfani established himself clearly as the leader of a new, influential current on the Left, which took its name from its review, *Iniziativa Democratica*. Around Fanfani gathered the less doctrinaire followers of Dossetti, especially Aldo Moro and Luigi Gui, and the more progressive members of De Gasperi's Center, such as Mariano Rumor and Paolo Emilio Taviani. This new group used the last years of De Gasperi's hegemony to prepare for the seizure of control of the party from the ex-Popolari of the Center, by moving into as many crucial positions as possible within the party, into the Ministry of Agriculture, and into IRI and ENI.[29] At the same time, the syndical wing of Pastore also began to press for a greater role within the party, and to achieve it they sought better organization. The result was the foundation in June 1953 of a new review, *Forze Sociali*, from which the syndicalist current took its name. Only Gronchi continued during 1951–53 to campaign for major changes in governmental policy—a return to neutralism, an end to rearmament, and an increase in employment by governmental intervention in the economy. But during the years when the Schuman Plan was being passed by parliament and the Pleven Plan and the European Political Community were being negotiated, most of the forces within the left wing of the DC made little effort to influence foreign policy.

The Christian Democratic Right: The right wing of the DC was an alliance of the industrial interests of the North and the great landowners of the South, which had support of an important section of the Vatican hierarchy and of Catholic Action. The Right gave solid support to membership in the Western bloc and to a European economic union, but on specific conditions. They supported the Marshall Plan, on condition that it would not strengthen the role of the state in industry. They welcomed the Atlantic Pact as a bulwark against Communism, internal and external, but objected to the expenses of rearmament as a harmful diversion of funds from more productive uses. They were in favor of a liberalization of trade, but in terms of mutual concession. They acquiesced in the Schuman Plan, but fought for a long transition period in its implementation. Their conception of a unified Europe was a grander version of their conception of an ideal Italy —a liberal economic unit in which economies of scale could be made, but without the necessity of paying the price of increased governmental controls, at either the national or supranational level. De Gasperi found himself in the position of turning to the party's left wing for support in making internal social and economic reforms, but to its right wing for support in getting Italy into the Atlantic Pact and the European Coal and Steel Community, and for freeing of trade.[30]

De Gasperi probably strengthened the Right by driving many Southern landowners from the party by his land reform program and many Northern industrialists by creating ENI, two actions that the Right had opposed. By losing its more extreme elements to the monarchists and the neo-Fascists, the Right became a moderate conservative group, with a dual program of economic liberalism and increased Church influence; and it effectively represented Confindustria and the Vatican within the party. Since both Confindustria and the Church accepted the goals of European integration, the influence of the right wing was positive at least in the sense that it supported Italian entry into the European Communities.

The Center and De Gasperi: The Christian Democratic Center was dominated by the older generation of ex-Popolari. After De Gasperi in importance came Attilio Piccioni, a Tuscan lawyer, who became political secretary of the party in 1946-48 and was responsible for its organization during the preparation for the election of 1948;[31] Mario Scelba, a younger, strong-minded lawyer from Sicily, who had been the private secretary of Don Sturzo when he led the Popular party; Antonio Segni, a Sardinian professor of agrarian law, who, as minister of agriculture in 1946-51, was responsible for the planning of the agrarian reform laws; and Pietro Campilli, a banker and industrialist from Rome, to whom De Gasperi entrusted major economic missions, including the leadership of the Italian delegation to OEEC in 1947-49 and the presidency of the interministerial committee that planned the Cassa per il Mezzogiorno. De Gasperi had around him a circle of men he had known for more than twenty years, men who brought to the Christian Democratic party the ideals they had elaborated in the Popular party and who saw little reason to change.

The basis of the ideology of the Center was recognition of the pre-eminence of Catholic teaching. As De Gasperi wrote during the war, the party member "continues to derive from the Christian patrimony the vital inspiration which will guide him in his public activities."[32] But this did not mean that his government should become an instrument of the Vatican. "Governing a state," he said in 1946, "creates an intimate bond with God, our Father. . . . There, friends, is my tie with the Vatican. It is not a tie of political directives. It is a bond of intimate understanding." But De Gasperi never created an electoral machine that could make the party independent of the parishes and of the civic committees of Catholic Action, and he himself at times called upon the Papacy for direct support in specific policy matters, such as ratification of the Atlantic Pact. The influence of the Catholic Church became greater at every level—in the choice of public administrators, officials of public companies, the land reform agencies, CISL, and the Coltivatori Diretti. As a result, a majority of Italians felt that the Christian Democrats had permitted Italy to become a theocracy.[33] Togliatti, in one of his most significant books, *L'Opera di De Gasperi: Rapporti tra stato e chiesa*, argued that De Gasperi had allowed the Catholics' political party to become the Church's primary instrument in its new strategy for achieving its traditional goals, "to become the undisputed civil power, the dominant political power, and thus to dominate the State."[34] By 1953, there was a widespread feeling that De Gasperi had failed in his primary goal of keeping the DC autonomous from the Church, and this helped bring about his political ouster.

De Gasperi felt it was his duty to embark upon a program of anti-Communism. Communism was the enemy for several reasons. It was based on materialism, and thus must be opposed by those who accept the primacy of spiritual values. It did not respect the rights of the individual, but subordinated them to the supposed well-being of the collectivity. It rejected Christian idealism, which was the essential element in the formation of Italian civilization, and therefore its victory would not only defeat the Church, it would also destroy the character of Italy itself. For De Gasperi, this theme, linking the defense of Christian values with those of Italian civilization, was central. He told the first National Congress of the DC in April 1946, "I feel in my deepest conscience that, if we were no longer to believe in the spirit that created and made fertile the life and history of Italy, but only in the determinism of positive economic facts, we should not have lost an electoral battle but we should have lost the battle of civilization and of culture."[35]

The economic policy that De Gasperi derived from Catholic theory was that private enterprise should be defended, but that it should be aware of its duty to ensure social justice. The state's function would be to help create those conditions in which private enterprise could most successfully further the country's economic development, by such actions as currency stabilization, tax policy favoring capital accumulation, or direct financial aid. This policy was entrusted to Einaudi and later to Pella, so Togliatti was probably correct in asserting that in 1948–50 economic reconstruction became capitalistic restoration.[36] Togliatti was also correct in asserting that De Gasperi's lack of interest in economic problems, especially in long-term goals, was a major factor in persuading him to leave economic policy in the hands of the conservatives, both in his own party and outside. But De Gasperi and the Popolari still felt it their duty to intervene on behalf of those whom the economic system ignored. In one form, this can be seen in the government's refusal to allow companies to fire their unneeded workers. In more constructive forms, the intervention can be seen in the housing program, in the land reform, and in the attempt to build the economy of the South through the Cassa per il Mezzogiorno. Under De Gasperi, these measures remained peripheral to the main task—that of aiding the economic revival carried out by the entrepreneurial classes. However, as Fabrizio Cicchitto points out, the reforms adopted by the Center, although not greatly effective in achieving social change, provided the instruments with which a new generation of DC leaders, men who began their political careers in the party's left wing, would attempt to implement a Keynesian policy of national economic planning—the land reform agencies, the Cassa, and ENI.[37]

All these considerations combined to determine the foreign policy goals of the DC Center. Here again, the attitude of the Church was greatly influential. Pius XII's unflagging support for the cause of European union, although derived in part from his opposition to Communism, was also due to more positive motives. Europe, Pius XII pointed out in 1953, must feel the "need for what one calls the European spirit, the consciousness of internal unity, based not on the satisfaction of economic necessity but on the perception of common spiritual values." Nevertheless, both politically and economically, he saw good reasons for the unification of Europe: "A United Europe is intended to guarantee the existence of each of its members as well as that of the union itself, [and] to favor economic prosperity, so that its political power can be in a position to make itself respected, as is fitting, in the concert of world powers." Such a union would call for short-term sacrifices, "transfer of industries, readaptation of labor, local fluctuations and difficulties in such and such a sector of production"; but they should be made for the long-term good. Pius XII was determined that the Church should act as a stimulus to continuing effort toward this goal. He personally spoke out in favor of European unification whenever the occasion offered—to the European Union of Federalists, to the College of Europe, to the European youth campaign, to the members of the Common Assembly of ECSC, and especially in his radio messages. As he said in 1957, "The statesmen are on the point of creating a united Europe. It is a great work, and We have never stopped saying how much We appreciate the progress made in this direction."[38] Catholic circles were thus encouraged directly to become involved in winning popular support for the European ideal. Apart from the Christian Democratic and ACLI groups, the Church supported the foundation of two militant federalist groups in Italy, the Centro d'Azione Europeistica, founded by the Istituto Cattolico di Attività Sociale, and the very active youth organization, Giovane Europa.[39] When De Gasperi finally decided to make European integration a major goal of DC foreign policy, he was therefore assured not only of Papal backing but of Papal pressure as well.

Until 1949, however, the DC Center showed little support for the practical schemes proposed by the federalists for creating a political union of Europe. The Center could not support the Resistance ideal of a European federation that would include the whole of Europe, once eastern Europe was under Communist control. But the acceptance of Italy as an equal in the Western bloc enabled the Center to consider the possibility of uniting that section of Europe which shared its anti-Communism and its mission of preserving the traditional European values. This stage was reached with Italian participation in the Council of Europe in 1949. A far more significant move, however, was the decision to enter the European Coal and Steel Community in 1950, since it involved some renunciation of national sovereignty. While De Gasperi recognized the long-term economic logic of joining a wider economic unit, he also had to weigh the short-term consequences for Italy. He was given two opposing views—the pessimistic predictions of Senator Falck and the rosy forecast of Finsider President Sinigaglia—and he respected the competence of both. The problem was too complex to be decided by economic logic. Therefore, the decision to enter was made on political grounds. The same desire to achieve political union in Europe impelled De Gasperi later in 1950 to support the European Defense Community and to join with Robert Schuman in 1951 in proposing the formation of a European Political Community.

The determination to maintain power for themselves and their party, however, gave the Center, and especially De Gasperi, the position of political mediators as well as policy-makers. Political expediency, especially the balancing of currents within the government, explained much of the Center's policy. In 1953, just before the national elections, the DC forced the passage of the "legge-truffa," the new electoral law giving a bonus of 85 seats in the Chamber of Deputies to any coalition receiving 50.01 per cent of the popular vote. This touched off a storm of resentment against De Gasperi's methods of governing, and contributed to his downfall. In the elections of June 7, 1953, the DC, in coalition with the Liberals, Republicans, and Social Democrats, won a small majority in the Chamber, but the DC alone no longer held an absolute majority. When the Social Democrats, Liberals, and Republicans refused to join, or even support, a new government headed by him, De Gasperi was refused investiture for his eighth ministry on July 28. The party spent the next five years in the search for an alternative to De Gasperi's Centrism.

THE STRUGGLES AMONG DE GASPERI'S HEIRS, 1953–1958

During the Second Legislature, no premier suceeded in establishing himself in a position of power similar to De Gasperi's, nor in implementing a coherent program of social and economic reform. Giuseppe Pella (August 1953–January 1954) attempted to turn a caretaker government into a durable administration representing the interests of the economic Right and the conservative nationalists, and he was ousted by the old Center led by De Gasperi himself. Mario Scelba (February 1954–July 1955) revived the Center's formula of four-party coalition government, but in spite of passage of a few reform measures for the South and institution of economic planning, he gained a justified reputation for procrastination. His successor, Antonio Segni (July 1955–May 1957), moved slightly to the Left, and during his first year in office he carried through several long-delayed promises—establishment of the Constitutional Court, reorganization of IRI, application of the Vanoni Plan, and passage of the law on mezzadria contracts. During his last year in office, Segni too fell victim to the prevailing political disease of "immobilismo," the incapacity to move; and the Legislature was brought to its close with yet another caretaker government, that of Adone Zoli (May 1957–July 1958).

Meanwhile, within the party, the currents that De Gasperi had labored fairly successfully to keep amorphous and thus more easily satisfied with personal gratifications, became more tightly organized, defined their ideological positions more stringently, and sought to gain the power to implement their beliefs by taking control of the party. While this jostling for influence was taking place, the government pursued an international policy of Atlanticism and Europeanism, supported by almost all elements of the party. But that policy, culminating in Italian membership in EEC and Euratom, merely created the framework within which a new European policy would have to be defined. The outcome of the struggles within the party, which would determine the country's economic and social policy, would also determine the conception of European union that Italy's representatives would attempt to support within the European Community.

For the Christian Democratic left wing, the period of the Pella government was marked by the organization of the more idealistic of Dossetti's former followers into a new current, the Base, while the more practical-minded and ambitious followed Fanfani in preparing the current of Iniziativa Democratica for seizure of the party. In the theory of the Base, the Christian Democratic party was a pyramid, with a wide, popular base and a restricted leadership at the summit, which could only be made democratic by making the leadership responsive to the wishes of the base. This response could only be a program of genuine social reforms brought about in alliance with the other democratic parties of the Left, including the Nenni Socialists. At the same time, the Base current accepted the implication of such an alignment for Italy's foreign policy: a weakening of the commitment to the American Alliance, a partial return to neutralism, and a determination to prevent the movement to European integration from becoming merely an instrument for strengthening one of the blocs in the Cold War.[40] The main strength of the Base lay in Milan, where organizers of the new current found support from old Resistance comrades, Enrico Mattei and Eugenio Cefis, and through them support from ENI.[41]

Fanfani's support came from the so-called "second generation," the DC politicians who had come to maturity under Fascism and were now ready to take over power from the De Gasperi generation of ex-Popolari. Fanfani promised them a program that could bridge the gap between the generations: economic development through detailed state planning, renewed land reform, reorganization of IRI as an instrument of state industrial policy, and a new law on mezzadria contracts. At the Fifth National Congress of the DC at Naples in 1954, Fanfani was elected party secretary, as successor to De Gasperi, thus gaining control of the party organization and the chance to build it into an instrument of his personal power.[42] His followers were in a clear majority in the National Council of the party, while the old Center lost heavily. The current of the Right, Primavera, succeeded only in electing its leader, Andreotti. For the next three years, however, Fanfani was preoccupied with cementing his position of political power; and it was left to Giovanni Gronchi, originally the leader of the party's labor union wing, to attempt to change the orientation of Italian social and foreign policy. His opportunity came when he was unexpectedly elected President of the Republic in April 1955, against the wishes of the government and DC party leadership, whose candidate was Cesare Merzagora, the non-party president of the Senate.

Shortly after the Naples Congress, Gronchi had renewed the current called Concentrazione, an odd mixture of the clerical Right, the industrial Right, and the former members of the trade union Left, united on a policy of neutralism in foreign affairs and of opposition to the Scelba government and the Fanfani party machine.[43] In April, Concentrazione announced that it would vote against Merzagora for the presidency and instead proposed the name of Gronchi. On the third ballot the Communists and Socialists swung their support to Gronchi. Fearing that Gronchi might be elected by the votes of the Communists, the Christian Democratic leadership decided to make him their official candidate also, and he was elected on the fourth ballot by an overwhelming majority.

In the long run, the influence of Gronchi as President was felt most in the encouragement he gave to "neo-Atlanticism." The basis of this doctrine was a desire to reinterpret the Atlantic Alliance, making it an association for economic and political cooperation, rather than simply a military grouping under American domination. An essential part of this new doctrine of independence was the search for a new role for Italy in the Mediterranean and with the Arab countries, and for a preferential position for Italy over its Western allies in trade with the newly independent countries. Enrico Mattei's decision to break the monopoly of the great oil companies by offering a more generous division of profits was an essential part of this new approach.[44] La Pira, too, used his position as mayor of Florence to bring important Arab leaders to Italy and to entertain them at official receptions, even when the central government objected; and in his Convention for Christian Peace in Florence, attended by leading intellectuals from all over the world, La Pira provided a forum for the proclamation of pacifism and for the condemnation of the division of the world into competing power blocs.[45]

In this search for a new foreign policy, Gronchi acted as a leading propagandist, using the presidency for its publicity value. In his speech to the joint session of the parliament on taking office as President, Gronchi attempted to show that a new era was beginning, one in which Italy's policy, both at home and abroad, would be improved by giving greater political power to "that mass of workers and that middle class which universal suffrage has brought to the threshold of the State edifice, without effectively bringing them to the place where the political control of the State is exercised." The government should seek economic and social reforms at home and peaceful coexistence abroad through an increase in understanding between East and West.[46] Speaking before the Congress of the United States on February 29, 1956, he declared that NATO "was no longer adapted to today's reality, now that the imbalance has been largely ended and that the situation in a large part of the world has changed. Today, military solidarity has not lost its importance, but it is necessary to complement it with new and intelligent forms of collaboration."[47] These views found support among the younger officials in the Foreign Ministry, in ENI, in all the left-wing currents of the DC, and from some Republicans and Social Democrats. With Scelba's resignation on June 20, following a new attack on him by Concentrazione, the question was posed whether Gronchi would be able to use his power to nominate a premier who would redirect Italian foreign policy toward neo-Atlanticism. Gronchi's choice, Antonio Segni, had no intention of shifting from a policy of Europeanism and Atlanticism to Gronchi's form of neo-Atlanticism, however, and he at once proclaimed "our unchanged faith in the ideal of a united Europe, our confidence in the Atlantic Alliance, conceived as a defensive organization, and our hope that the policy of relaxing international tension will not be limited to purely symbolic declarations and gestures."[48]

Fanfani had also acted forcefully against the left-wing dissidents within the DC who were pressing for a neutralist foreign policy and strong action at home against the monopolies. Three younger members of the party were suspended for attending the Communist-organized Peace Congress in Helsinki; the editor of the Milanese review *Prospettive*—a voice for those members of the Base who were turning to Gronchi in hopes of forcing the party to adopt a new direction in both internal and foreign affairs—was expelled from the DC; and even *Forze Sociali*, the review of Pastore's syndicalist wing, which had recently become too critical of the party leadership, was "invited" to cease publication immediately. In this way, Fanfani acted to stamp out an incipient revolt in the extreme left wing of the DC, a group that might have found its leader in Gronchi and its principles in neutralism and sweeping social reform.[49] For the next few months the Base remained impotent, while Concentrazione was virtually disbanded.

The debate over neo-Atlanticism was revived at the time of the ratification of the Treaty of Rome, because it was directly related to the internal debate over what form of coalition government the DC should favor: an opening to the Left, with participation of the Nenni Socialists, or the revival of the four-party coalition. The fact that the Treaties of Rome were debated in almost empty Chambers and ratified without difficulty by the Chamber in July and by the Senate in October might well have indicated that all parties except the Communists were united in their acceptance of the principles of the treaties. The debate over neo-Atlanticism revealed that this was not so. It emerged from the debate that members of the Center and Right of the Christian Democratic party, who favored a revival of the four-party formula and a "closing to the Left," wished to maintain the Atlantic Alliance in its old form as a military bloc opposed to Communist expansion; to create the European Community on liberal economic lines as further source of strength of the Atlantic Community; and to continue the internal policy of modifying the expansion program of private industry and agriculture through palliative social reform and restricted state intervention. The left-wing currents favored the opening to the Left because it would de-emphasize the military aspect of NATO in a period when tensions between East and West had eased; give wider scope to relationships with non-Atlantic areas, such as the Mediterranean, the African, or the Arab countries; restrict the liberal concept of the European Community in favor of a more socializing one; and change the balance between state and private economic initiative in Italy in favor of the state.

The debate inside the Christian Democratic party was momentarily stilled with the approach of the elections of May 1958. The party repeated its earlier promises of moderate reforms; and it ignored the neo-Atlanticist debate, merely reaffirming the DC's support of NATO and of the political unification of western Europe.[50] In spite of a polemic over the interference of the Church in state affairs and in the election itself, the Christian Democrats increased their representation to 273 seats in the Chamber. The left-wing currents, especially Forze Sociali and Base, did well, strengthening the demand within the party for an opening to the Left.[51]

AN OPENING TO THE LEFT, 1958–1963

Throughout the Third Legislature, the Christian Democrats moved, though falteringly, toward an opening to the Left, a political alliance with the Nenni Socialists. To achieve this alliance, a coalition of currents favorable to the social reforms demanded by the Socialists had to be formed within the DC; and the Socialists had to learn to stomach the basic tenets of the DC's foreign policy—Atlanticism and European integration.

At the time of the Christian Democratic Congress of Florence in 1959, there were six well-defined currents in the party.[52] On the Left, favoring the Socialist alliance, were the Base (11.2 per cent) and the reorganized trade union current, Rinnovamento (5.7 per cent). On the Right were the conservative business wing, Primavera (13.1 per cent), which opposed the Center-Left experiment for its dangers to the free enterprise system, and the followers of Scelba (5.7 per cent), who distrusted the Socialists for their continuing links with the Communists. In the Center, Fanfani's Iniziativa Democratica had divided, however. Fanfani's second ministry (July 1958–February 1959) had been brief and troubled, and he had earned great distrust by taking into his own hands the positions of premier, foreign minister, and party secretary. Within his own current, a number of young, realistic politicians had turned against him, and they formed their own current, called the Dorotei, after the Convent of Santa Dorotea, where they met from March 1959 on. The Dorotei were led by clever, practical men of moderate reformist opinions—Aldo Moro, a forty-two-year-old lawyer from Bari; Mariano Rumor, a forty-three-year-old political writer and humanities teacher; and Emilio Colombo, another lawyer from the South, who was already, at thirty-eight, one of the party's most brilliant economic administrators. By the time of the Congress, the Dorotei (33.3 per cent) had already exceeded the strength of Fanfani's remaining followers (31 per cent). Future Christian Democratic policy would depend upon an accommodation between the Dorotei and the Fanfaniani.

Fanfani had already sketched out the principles for such an agreement in the program of his second ministry, in which he made a serious attempt to link a multi-faceted development policy at home with acceptance of accelerated political and economic integration. By demanding that the Socialists accept his foreign policy, he made it possible for the Dorotei current to act as the mediator between the party's Right and its Left in moving toward an agreement with the Socialist party. At Florence, Moro, who had become party secretary in place of Fanfani the previous March, accepted the Fanfani program. The entrance of Italy into the Common Market, Moro asserted, by increasing the competitive pressure upon Italian industry and agriculture and offering a vast stimulus to productivity, would aid the achievement of the party's economic goals of increased national revenue and employment. Europeanism, in short, would pay for social reform.

The accession of John XXIII to the Papacy in 1958 helped make the alliance with the Socialists easier. His Encyclical *Mater et Magister* attacked the conception of an uncontrolled capitalist economy; and Catholic Action was advised to devote itself to spiritual affairs. Moreover, John's attitude toward European integration, while favorable, lacked the anti-Communist fervor of Pius XII. To John, European union was one political and economic grouping among many, not the bulwark of Christian values; and he deliberately warned, in the Encyclical *Pacem in Terris*, against the dangers of forming exclusive groupings that would ignore the general well-being. Here again, the Pope's removal of the crusading tone from the Church's endorsement of Europeanism made it easier for the Socialists to give their approval.

The party's move to open acceptance of the Center-Left at the national level took place in its Eighth National Congress at Naples of January 27–February 1, 1962. The forces opposing the opening to the Left were led by Mario Scelba, who argued that the Socialists were still too closely tied to the Communists, both in the administration of local governments and in the trade unions, and were playing the Communist game by retaining their neutralism. Moro himself admitted that "foreign policy is undoubtedly one of the most delicate areas in which the eventual collaboration would be carried out"; and in his report to the Congress he played down the international implications of the opening to the Left. In a finely organized and profound synthesis, he presented to the DC a new ideology, a "third way" between capitalism and socialism, that would make possible a lessening of the political tensions in Italian society through the acceptance of the Socialists in the exercise of political power, and a lessening of social tensions through application of an advanced economic program.[53] Italy, Moro urged, could embark upon a new policy because the economic development of the postwar years had been so rapid. The new role of the state would include direct powers for the economic and social development of certain zones of the country or particular sectors of the economy as well as the power of "orienting and conditioning the economic choices of the private sector." In particular, the state must intervene to correct the tendency of the existing economic system to concentrate capital formation in restricted parts of the country and restricted segments of the population.[54] Such a program, Moro concluded, could be supported by the Socialist party; and, even though a political alliance was impossible as long as the Socialists retained their ties with the Communists and maintained their neutralist foreign policy, such an agreement on specific lines of policy with the Socialists was a highly desirable experiment.[55]

The Congress ended with a victory for the alliance of Base, Forze Sociali, Fanfaniani, and Dorotei, who favored the opening to the Left; and the final motion specifically invited the Socialists to support, though not to participate in, a Center-Left government as a result of agreement on the program to be implemented. Fanfani was at once invited by Gronchi to form a new government on the lines laid down at the Congress. In three weeks of negotiations with the DC currents, Social Democrats, Republicans, and Socialists, Fanfani hammered out the first genuine Center-Left program of meaningful reforms. It included nationalization of the electrical industry; creation of governments for all nineteen regions of Italy; formulation of a plan of national economic planning; implementation of the Green Plan for agriculture and gradual abolition of mezzadria; a well-financed plan of school reform; a tax on stock transactions; and support of the Atlantic Alliance and the Common Market. In the investiture vote on March 10, the government was approved by a vote of 295 in favor (DC, PSDI, PRI) to 195 against (PCI, Monarchists, MSI), and 83 abstentions (PSI).

Fanfani was able to carry out several reforms during his fourth ministry (February 1962–June 1963). The National Commission for Economic Planning was established in August, and the following month the electrical industry was nationalized. The Dorotei, however, after the nationalization of the electrical industry, felt that they had moved rapidly enough against the industrial circles in the country, especially with elections due in 1963; and they forced a postponement of the setting up of regional governments, except in Friuli-Venezia Giulia. The school bill, creating a unified junior high school and making schooling compulsory through the age of fourteen, was passed in January 1963. Thus, the Christian Democrats entered the election campaign with part of the Center-Left program carried out, but, as a party, uncertain whether it was wise to have done so. The election results were a great disappointment both for the Christian Democrats, who saw their percentage of the vote fall from 42.4 per cent in 1958 to 38.3 per cent, and for the Socialists, who saw theirs fall from 14.2 to 13.8 per cent. With both Communist and Liberals making large advances, the Center-Left formula at once came under challenge; and it proved necessary once again to set up a caretaker government, under Chamber Speaker Giovanni Leone. During the ministry of Leone (June–December 1963), the cabinet was completely Christian Democratic, and only day-to-day business was transacted. The principal purpose of this caretaker government was to give time to the Christian Democratic and Socialist parties to re-establish the line they wished to follow, by bringing the warring factions to terms with each other. In August, the Christian Democratic currents agreed to the opening of negotiations with the Socialists for constitution of a Center-Left government after the Socialist Congress in October.[56] On November 5, following the re-establishment of a majority in the PSI Congress in favor of Nenni's policy of collaborating with the Christian Democrats, Leone resigned, and Segni charged Moro with forming a new government.

THE CENTER-LEFT FROM MORO TO LEONE, 1963–1968

Moro's first task was to agree upon a common program with the other parties he proposed to bring into his government—the Socialists, the Social Democrats and the Republicans. On November 25, after detailed discussions among party leaders and experts, the program was accepted. It was twenty-five pages long. The basic reforms, which the four parties had little difficulty in agreeing upon, were creation of the regions, reform of the state bureaucracy, priority to school financing, fiscal reform, aid to the South and to agriculture, and urban planning to prevent profiteering in real estate. The two real problems between Christian Democrats and Socialists were foreign policy and national economic planning. Distrust of the Socialists' continuing coolness toward the Atlantic

Alliance seemed likely to provoke a revolt within the DC by the thirty or so followers of Scelba and Pella, while the left wing of the Socialists, led by Basso and Vecchietti, would not agree to any strong endorsement of NATO or of the multilateral nuclear force proposed by President John F. Kennedy. The Atlantic Alliance was given the most cursory approval—"loyalty to the Atlantic Alliance with the political and military obligations that derive from it." Further study was promised of the multilateral nuclear force. The policy of European solidarity was declared to be one of seeking "space and environment suited to Italy's economic expansion and a significant participation in international policies in relation to its traditions and culture." Foreign policy was thus brushed aside in half a page. Moro's views on national economic planning, which had been moving slightly to the Right, might have caused more difficulties. But, as the agreement on measures for dealing with inflation and the balance of payments difficulties showed, the main task of the new government seemed likely to be a fairly conservative action to drag Italy back from the recession into which it was beginning to plunge.[57]

Dissatisfaction with this compromise program caused problems in the composition of the cabinet. The PSI's leading economic theorist, Riccardo Lombardi, refused to participate, as did Fanfani; and it was generally assumed they felt that the program was going too far to satisfy the Right. The Christian Democratic right wing's insistence on keeping Andreotti at the Ministry of Defense was satisfied only by the counter-concession of giving the Ministry of the Budget, with its primary role in national economic planning, to Antonio Giolitti, a Socialist who had only left the Communist party after the Hungarian uprising. The reappointment of Sullo, whose urban reform law had annoyed real-estate speculators, was blocked by the right wing. The Socialists were unable to bring their dissidents to heel as the DC had; and the twenty-three Socialists who had boycotted the investiture vote withdrew from the PSI to form a new left-wing Socialist party, the Partito Socialista Italiano di Unità Proletaria (PSIUP).

The first Moro cabinet (December 1963–July 1964) was occupied largely with measures to deal with the growing economic crisis through reduction of government expenditures, increased purchase taxes, and credit restriction. It made little progress toward implementation of the Center-Left program; and Moro found himself constantly preoccupied with the confusion in his own party. The clear division in the party between supporters of Fanfani and the Dorotei, which had existed since January 1959 when Fanfani was first ousted, became muddied. Fanfani shifted to the Right, opening relations with the "pure Dorotei" and even demanding a share in the party's decision-making for the Scelba and Pella groups. Moro's followers, now clearly delimited as a separate current (Morotei) moved closer toward Base and Rinnovamento. The DC's coalition partners, already suspicious that the party's commitment to a genuine reform program had been lessened through Fanfani's move to the Right, were outraged when a grant to Catholic schools was slipped into the budget without their knowledge. The Socialists abstained in the vote on this item in the Chamber, put the government in a minority, and Moro thereupon resigned.

After an abortive attempt by a few Christian Democrats to have their leadership propose a Center-Left government without Socialist participation, Moro was again designated by President Segni to form a cabinet on similar lines to that of his earlier ministry. Although all four parties declared themselves in favor, it took twenty-two days of negotiations before a new agreement could be drawn up. This program was specifically based upon the agreement of the previous November, modified by "the necessary clarifications and improvements." The Christian Democrats accepted postponement of the decision on state aid to Catholic schools. The Socialists agreed to harsh anti-recession measures, on condition that the five-year economic program be presented to parliament before the end of the year. They even agreed to the replacement of Budget Minister Giolitti, who had annoyed many Christian Democrats by being overzealous in his conception of state planning. Finally, no mention at all was made of the delicate question of the Atlantic Alliance, while the only reference to Europeanism linked it to the maintenance of a market economy "open to EEC and to the international world," which was held to be compatible with national economic planning. The relative political stability of the second Moro cabinet (July 1964–January 1966) lay in the willingness of the coalition to give Moro a chance to try out the more moderate version of the Center-Left, free from pressure within the government by the more impatient Socialists and from sniping by Fanfani and his followers.

Following the investiture of Moro at the beginning of August, the Christian Democratic party devoted itself to preparation of its ninth National Congress, which had been postponed until September 1964.[58] The divisions within the party were never more clear. At one extreme was Scelba's Centrismo Popolare, with 10 per cent of the delegates, who blamed the party's desire for an understanding with the Socialists for making the DC forget its internal unity, its duty to the electorate, the requirements of economic policy, and the boundary between democracy and antidemocracy. The solution, Centrismo Popolare held, was to re-emphasize the primary role of private initiative in the economy and to press with renewed vigor for the political unification of Europe. At the other extreme was the alliance of syndicalists of Rinnovamento with Base, called Una Forza Nuova per la Politica di Centro-Sinistra. They wanted to put new teeth into the internal programs of the Center-Left government, and to seek an end to the international Cold War confrontation of power blocs, which they felt could be achieved in part by the assertion of the independence of a united western Europe.[59] These two statements of the interrelationship of concepts of internal and foreign policy were clear; in contrast, the muted criticism of Fanfani's group, now called Nuove Cronache, appeared somewhat convoluted. In internal policy, while they accused the government and the party of making mistakes, both politically and economically, the Fanfaniani affirmed their support of a watered-down kind of national economic planning. In foreign policy, while they claimed to support a strengthened EEC, they revived the old neo-Atlanticists' cry for a progressive NATO in search of peaceful solutions, and demanded a positive role for Italy in its relations with "the characteristic zones of the Mediterranean, Europe, the Atlantic Community, and Latin America." Finally, the group of Impegno Democratico, consisting of the re-grouped Moro-Dorotei, offered an imprecise defense of a moderated Center-Left program. National economic planning was conceived as a happy middle course between state centralization and mere guidelines; international policy as a strengthening of the ties between peoples—allies, neighbors, and newly independent countries. Most commentators felt that the party line, laid down by such powerful leaders of the Dorotei as Rumor and Colombo, would be more conservative.[60]

Yet the party continued to be torn apart by the battle among its currents. At the National Council in October, the Fanfaniani even abstained on an anodyne motion denouncing Communism. When Segni's ill health forced his resignation as President, the DC's currents fought a bitter, public battle over the selection of his successor. In opposition to Giuseppe Saragat, the candidate of the other parties in the governmental coalition, the Dorotei nominated Giovanni Leone. When voting began in parliament on December 16, however, many of the Nuove Cronache current voted for their leader, Fanfani, and others, of Forze Nuove, for their leader, Giulio Pastore. Although Fanfani withdrew after the eleventh ballot under pressure from the Vatican, the Dorotei were unable to get the party to support Leone, and they switched their support to Saragat. Saragat was finally elected on the twenty-first ballot, with the help of Communist votes, twelve days after the balloting had begun.

The bickering within the party, and the consequent paralysis of governmental action, continued throughout 1965. The appointment of Fanfani as foreign minister in place of Saragat did not appease the dissenting currents. A significant portion of its left wing was talking of a "dialogue" with the Communists, following the lead of Florence's mayor La Pira, whose earlier neutralism was turning into anti-Americanism under the impact of the war in South Vietnam. The Dorotei were still principally concerned with the struggle against the recession, and, while bringing in a batch of new measures to stimulate the economy in June 1965, they also obtained the postponement for one year of implementation of the state's five-year economic plan. The party made a major effort to pull itself together at its Sorrento conference of October 30–November 3, but it achieved little beyond public statements of harmony. The real disharmony was seen in the pirouetting of Foreign Minister Fanfani, who gave his resignation to Moro four times in the course of the year, most notably for having passed on to President Lyndon B. Johnson messages his friend La Pira had gathered when visiting Ho Chi Minh in Hanoi. After a year of careful maneuvering to keep both his party and the governmental coalition together, Moro was finally voted down in the Chamber on a minor matter, and he resigned on January 21, 1966.

Moro's main problem in forming his third ministry (January 1966–May 1968) was not in reaching agreement with the other three parties, but in achieving unity within his own party. Only by granting governmental positions as ministers or under-secretaries to seventy-two people was Moro able to put together a new coalition; yet the program of the government was in no way different from those of the two preceding ministries.

Having brought all the currents into the government, the Christian Democratic party's leaders attempted, at the National Council of March 30–April 2, to persuade the currents to disband. Rumor argued that "the currents have lost their reason for being," were preventing the party from facing the urgent problems of the country, and should accept "their voluntary and total disbanding with the consequent liquidation of their organization, hierarchies, press organs, headquarters, etc, etc." In the final vote, all currents approved the principle of the Center-Left government, but Forze Nuove, through its spokesman Galloni, refused to support the dissolution of the currents. According to Galloni, " 'Forze Nuove' has ceased to be—if it ever was one—a power group and is seeking to assume the role of an opinion group which should not be repressed or challenged if a dialectic of opinion is to be maintained within the DC."[61]

The characteristics of the new struggle within the DC were to become clear during the two years of the third Moro ministry. Conditions had changed, both nationally and internationally. The permanence of the Center-Left formula had been accepted, and there was a consequent transfer of the emphasis to the means by which the program should be carried out.[62] There was a ferment among Italian Catholics, greatly encouraged by the pontificate of John XXIII, for new relationships with all groups within Italian society, including a dialogue with the Communists. A new generation was coming of age, and in the various organs of the party, CISL and ACLI, and Gioventù di Azione Cattolica, there were demands for real changes in party leadership, organization, and program. It even seemed that international conditions had improved. The Western and Eastern blocs were following a policy of disengagement, and there were signs of dissolution in both blocs.

Under these new conditions, the role of the Christian Democratic party had to be thought out more clearly. This rethinking began at the Convegno di Lucca and in the tenth National Congress, around the theme of the ability of the dominant Dorotei to adapt themselves to the demands of the dissatisfied classes within the country at large, demands which the party's left wing attempted to express inside the DC. At stake was a reconsideration of the basic themes adopted by the DC in both foreign policy and economic policy over the preceding two decades. Challenged in particular were the dominant role given to the workings of the free market economy and to the individual entrepreneur in economic development and thus in the preparation of the Italian economy for entry into the wider market of a unified Europe; the policies of the public companies; the acceptance of liberal economic planning within EEC; and especially a new analysis of the role of the DC, and of the government, in solving the problems of the social discontent within Italy. All these issues came to the head in the crisis following the elections of 1968, and they dominated the negotiations that led to the Leone ministry.

The confusion within the DC's warring currents explains the lack of any major role taken by Italy in EEC during the 1960's. As during the negotiation of the Treaty of Rome, the country's policy tended to fall into the hands of a few experts, like Emilio Colombo, whose permanence in office in the major economic ministries helped assure continuity of policy. The move toward the Center-Left had few major conseqences at the European level. The DC were finally persuaded to accept the representation of the CGIL on the Economic and Social Committee, and even, in 1969, to agree to the representation of all political parties, including Communists and parties of the extreme Right, in the European Parliament. Support was given to the attempts at economic planning at the European level carried on by the EEC Commission, especially in the medium-term program, which was felt to complement Italian national economic planning. But the long-expected battle over the shaping of the liberal or interventionist character of the Community never assumed the proportions that had been expected, largely because the Community did not evolve rapidly toward a genuine economic union; and the primary significance of the Center-Left experiment was that it committed a government dedicated by political agreement to economic and social reforms at home to carry out that program within the framework of an integrated economic Community.

Looking back over the quarter-century of the DC's activity in foreign policy, one can see a clear pattern in the maneuvering of the currents. The basic direction of Italian foreign policy—trust in the Atlantic Alliance and unstinting support of the integration of western Europe—was formulated by De Gasperi and the Center. Once made, this choice was never revised, because its motive force was ideological. The DC Center accepted Europeanism as it was defined by Pope Pius XII, as a union for the defense of spiritual values distinctive to Europe and, indeed, after 1945, distinctive to non-Communist Europe. In the short run, economic integration was regarded as a sacrifice to be made for the strengthening of that union, although the long-term advantages of larger markets, increased competition, and so on, were also recognized. The right wing of the party, while accepting the ideological justification of Europeanism, tended to regard ideology as encompassing economics. It held that the rise of state intervention in the economic system was an infringement on spiritual values, and that therefore European union should by definition be a defense of a liberal economic system both nationally and internationally. The fluctuating left-wing currents challenged the identification of Europeanism with Atlanticism, and sought, through such doctrines as neo-Atlanticism, to make a united Europe into a third and probably a neutral force, and to shift the focus of Italian interest from northern Europe and the Atlantic toward the Mediterranean and the underdeveloped countries. De Gasperi first allied with the right wing, establishing a liberal economic policy at home and a foreign policy based on Atlanticism and Europeanism. After 1950, without altering the essential direction of his foreign policy, he moved toward the Left, accepting social reforms that did not affect the basic structure of the economy. De Gasperi's policies were carried on during the Second Legislature (1953–58) by his successors, and the culminating commitment to Europeanism was made in the Treaty of Rome. The Dorotei, whose dominance was established during the Third Legislature, fought off the attempts of the DC left-wing currents and of the PSI to change this line of foreign policy; but they gradually accepted the need for a reform program at home. Europeanism ceased to be a divisive issue, and the struggle within the DC focused once again on the future of the Italian economic and social structure.

14
Opponents and Allies of Christian Democracy

The evolution of the attitude of the Christian Democratic party toward the major issues of economic and foreign policy was not only influenced by its internal struggles; it was also conditioned directly by the views of its coalition partners and less directly by the opinions of its opponents. In dealing with its partners, the Christian Democratic party had to draw up coalition platforms, hand over important ministries, formulate governmental policy that would be satisfactory to its partners, secure their parliamentary support on crucial votes, and, quite often, negotiate under threat of a vote of no-confidence. The views of the DC's partners on issues affecting Italy's relationship to European integration often differed from those of the DC, and to some extent they were able to force the Christian Democrats to change their policy. It is also evident, however, that the opinions of the opponents of the Christian Democrats, especially those of the Communists and Socialists, were influential. In one sense, this influence was negative, in that Communist-Socialist espousal of any policy was often enough to make the Christian Democrats reject it. (Togliatti once remarked that he could defeat any government bill merely by supporting it!) But the Christian Democrats were competing with the extreme Left for electoral support; and so, whenever the left-wing parties proposed a policy that was favorably received by the electorate, the governmental coalition was compelled to produce competing propositions. Conversely, the success of programs proposed by the government, including its espousal of economic integration of western Europe, compelled the left-wing parties to change their own attitudes, since no opposition can support for long policies that are obviously unpopular. The Communist party, however, could only change its policy toward European integration by breaking from the rigid line adopted by the Soviet-dominated powers and espousing the cause of the national road to Communism. Hence the PCI found itself in the ironic position of justifying the national road to Communism in order to accept the coming of supranationalism.

THE COMMUNISTS—THE LONG ROAD TO CONSTRUCTIVE CRITICISM

When Palmiro Togliatti returned to Italy in March 1944 to take personal control of the Italian Communist party, he found himself in a situation completely different from that of the East European Communist leaders like the Bulgarian Georghi Dimitrov, who was returning from Moscow to a country occupied by the Red Army.[1] Stalin was giving no direct support or encouragement to an attempt to use the Resistance forces controlled by the Communists for a *coup d'état;* and, had an uprising been attempted, the Communist party would have found against it not only the forces of the Italian army and police but also the Anglo-American occupation forces.[2] Togliatti therefore announced the "Salerno policy" of full cooperation in the political and economic reconstruction of the country.[3] The best way to capitalize upon the popularity of the Communist Resistance forces, he argued, was to place great emphasis upon the maintenance of national unity.

Later, in 1958, he tried to explain the party's assumption of the role of nationalist. The workers have no country, Marx had written, but the proletariat must become nationalist to fight against the bourgeoisie whose imperialism is the negation of nationalism. By becoming nationalist the Italian Communist Party would "not only be defending the independence of its own country but affirming and defending the independence of all nations. . . . Fighting against the imperialist and chauvinist fervor of the most reactionary bourgeois groups, it is working and fighting for the coming of an era of security and peace for all peoples."[4] This was the theoretical justification for nationalism. For Italy, he wanted "a democratic and progressive regime," based on representative parliamentary democracy, which would make possible a major change in the economic and social structure of the country. The Communist party must "increase its membership, make itself known, and link up with all the groups of the working population, to give it a positive function in the economic and political action of reconstruction and renewal of the country."[5] Togliatti seems to have believed that it would be possible in this way to bring the Communist party to a position where it could take power through a free election. Foreign policy goals during the period of cooperation played a very minor role.

During the war, therefore, the Comunist party urged collaboration with the Anglo-American armies in the struggle against the Nazis and their Fascist allies. After the war, the party called for the maintenance of Great Power unity, and especially for the avoidance of the division of Europe into two competing blocs. Yet events were moving against the Communists. The party's program, laid down in January 1946, was a last desperate effort to ignore the Cold War. It called for a "foreign policy of peace, of respect for the rights of all nations, of organized collaboration with all peoples and particularly with our neighbors. . . . The Communist party is opposed to a policy of power blocs, because such a policy could not lead to anything other than the direct or indirect subordination of our country in the economic fields."[6] The party thus fell back on proclaiming the rights of Italian nationalism, which in foreign policy meant neutralism, while demanding a policy of social renovation at home that would have to be financed by the United States. Yet the party was unable to make the necessary ideological commitment to the Western bloc to get that financial aid. The PCI was only too well aware that the division of Europe into two opposed alliances had doomed its hope of turning its wartime popularity into peacetime successes; and it was coming under strong pressure from the Soviet Union to drop its moderate or so-called "conservative" line and to work more effectively on behalf of the Soviet bloc inside Italy. Once ousted from the De Gasperi government, the Italian Communists had little choice but to follow the Stalinist line, although they did so in a very lukewarm fashion.[7]

The attitude of the PCI toward the Marshall Plan and NATO was little different from that of the CGIL. Well aware of the difficulty of attacking America for offering economic aid to Italy—"Whoever raises doubts," *Rinascita* remarked, "is simply treated as a strange being, with no common sense, with a tendency to suicide, who for sectarian reasons doesn't want his country to be helped"—the Communist party first attempted to make the problem one of trust in the Soviet Union, which, as a country governed by the workers, would hardly have refused economic aid without a good reason. But since this had little appeal, the PCI asserted that the goal of the Plan was to block measures of internal economic and social reform in western Europe in order to perpetuate the power of the big monopolies and the political dominance of the United States.[8] This argument, as one of the currents inside the Communist party itself asserted, was likely to lose the party the support of the whole middle class in the coming elections.[9] Especially after the *coup d'état* in Czechoslovakia, the PCI's claim that it stood for Italian nationalism and the avoidance of the division of Europe into blocs would not hold water.[10] The overwhelming victory of the DC in April 1948 nevertheless came as a surprise to the Communist party, and the conclusions it drew were far-reaching in their consequences. The party would have to increase its electoral base, by assuming a moderate reformist position on internal matters, even if remaining totally negative on foreign policy issues.

Here, however, the PCI found itself caught in a contradiction. It was easy to denounce those foreign policy decisions of the Italian government that brought Italy within a military alliance directed against the Soviet Union.[11] But attempts to prove that this military grouping was a necessary accompaniment to the plans to form a political federation in western Europe and to raise living standards through economic integration required more ingenuity. The division of Europe into Western and Eastern blocs, and of western Europe internally, could only be avoided, Togliatti asserted, "by the unity of the peoples in all the European countries in the struggle to bring to triumph new regimes and new forms of democracy that will bury forever the capitalistic regime and will lay the foundations for a new civilization."[12] By definition, no form of European federalism that would preserve the capitalist system would be acceptable to the PCI. The West European federalists had identified the American conception of the free enterprise system with the federalist conception of the "idea of Europe," so that the attempts to unite Europe were merely measures to preserve the capitalist system. The Schuman Plan therefore had to be rejected, both to safeguard the possible reform program within Italy and to maintain Italian independence from the monopolistic groups controlling America's political and economic policy toward Europe.

The PCI found it even easier to see through the smokescreen of federalistic propaganda that covered what it considered to be the real aim of the European Defense Community—the rearmament of West Germany. According to Mauro Scoccimarro, Adenauer's Germany was consumed with the desire to intervene in East Germany and to resume the *Drang Nach Osten*, that old dream of a Drive to the East of the industrial and military classes whom Adenauer represented. In West Germany, he asserted, the Americans had helped create a "hotbed of foreign and national reactionary interests, of class egoisms and imperialist appetites, of yearnings for revenge and of aggressive proposals: a turbulent world of self-seekers, speculators, and adventurers."[13] The use of federalist propaganda to cover this rearmament was unimportant, since European federalism was both anti-Communist and pro-capitalist. Western European Union, which permitted the national rearmament of West Germany and its membership in NATO, was naturally interpreted as a last-ditch move by the reactionaries in the Italian ruling classes to defeat the moves of the post-Stalin leadership of the Soviet Union toward a relaxation of international tension.

In short, the PCI's attitude up to Stalin's death and for three years thereafter, was to trumpet the Soviet line in foreign policy, adapting it to Italian circumstances only to the extent of claiming, without much conviction, that their aim was to defend Italian national interests by seeking neutralism.[14]

The shattering events within the Communist world in 1956, from Khrushchev's denunciation of Stalin at the Twentieth Party Congress in February to the repression of the Hungarian uprising in November, shook the Italian Communists out of their complaisant acceptance of the Stalinist line in foreign policy. But it did nothing to make them more sympathetic to the ideals of a united Europe.

Togliatti's first reaction to the Twentieth Party Congress was to ignore the attack on Stalin.[15] As a long-time protégé of Stalin, and as an example himself of the cult of personality, he was not willing to encourage an open attack on Stalin within the PCI that could have had disruptive effects on discipline. But he found himself under strong pressure from the PCI's left-wing current, which was demanding more revolutionary leadership, and from its right-wing current, which was seeking a more independent, reformist approach. Togliatti's strategy, which he expressed in an interview published by the review *Nuovi Argomenti* in its May-June issue, was to side with the Stalinists in his party by blaming the other Soviet leaders and the Soviet bureaucratic system for Stalin's errors, but to appeal to the reformers by indicating his independence from the Soviet line. The consequence of the new direction taken by the international Communist movement, he said, would be "greater autonomy of judgment" for the separate national parties: "The whole system is becoming polycentric, and in the Communist movement itself one cannot speak of a single guide but rather of progress being achieved by following paths that are often different."[16]

Since this apparent declaration of independence from the Soviet line came at the very time when the diplomats were preparing to move to Brussels to write the treaty establishing the Common Market, it might have been expected that Togliatti would moderate his attitude toward Europeanism. At first, he seemed prepared to adopt a more flexible position with regard to changes in the capitalist world. In June he declared that Communist parties in capitalist countries could not take the experience of the Soviet Union as their only guide; and he openly criticized the establishment of the Cominform. He was forced to retreat, however, and was soon reaffirming the correctness of "the battle against the Marshall Plan, against the Atlantic Pact, against the self-styled American-clerical Europeanism, against the Schuman Plan, against the EDC and the WEU. . . . All this is an integral and essential part of our struggle to open and to build an Italian road to socialism."[17]

By the summer of 1956, Togliatti had returned to an intransigent line in foreign policy. The party praised the suppression of the Poznan riots in Poland as a defeat for the imperialist provocateurs; and Togliatti endorsed the Soviet military intervention in Hungary as a necessary step in dealing with the challenge of

White reactionaries.[18] However, a few of the more important intellectuals in the party, led by Antonio Giolitti, spoke out at the Eighth Party Congress in December against the party's acceptance of a whole series of Soviet mistakes, from the condemnation of Tito through the suppression of the Hungarian uprising. Giolitti roused the greatest opposition when he argued that the party had to reanalyze the character of contemporary capitalism: that it had to accept the obvious fact that the system, far from collapsing, was growing in strength and that the workers would move toward socialism through structural reforms in the system rather than by its overthrow.[19] The Communist party's more orthodox spokesmen condemned Giolitti. They believed his ideas would lead to the permanent subjection of the working classes to monopoly capitalism and to the rejection of the role of the Communist party in the struggle between the classes.[20]

The rejection of criticism within the party and the refusal to follow up Togliatti's thesis on polycentrism with concrete action, while restoring inner discipline and quieting the Stalinist forces in the party, encouraged a further revulsion from Communism both within and outside the party. Membership fell by 10 per cent in one year, and Communist activity had to be reduced.[21] Weakened at home, the Italian Communists found themselves under renewed pressure within the world Communist movement to accept Soviet doctrinal leadership. The PCI agreed to conform, and, in Galli's words, it relapsed "into the most complete immobility on the international level."[22] In formulating its attitude to EEC in 1957, then, the Communist party found no reason to change its stand from the uncompromising opposition it had always shown toward Europeanism.

As Togliatti wrote in his book on the PCI, published in April 1958, the Italian Communists were internationalist in linking "Italy's national strength to the great reality of socialism that is growing stronger, rising, conquering, and guiding all humanity on the road to radical economic renovation." But they could have no links with the "Europeanistic movement . . . [which] seeks to maintain and strengthen the capitalist order and thus, in effect, is reduced to being the façade for a new form of organization of the relationships between the great monopolistic associations of national and international capital."[23] The Treaty of Rome, the PCI pointed out in the ratification debate in the Chamber of Deputies, not only reinforced the power of the monopolies but "aggravated the division of the world into two blocs" and, with the blessing of the United States, was "destined to assure a predominant role to the Germany of Bonn over all western Europe."[24] This political analysis merely repeated the basic attitude toward the Common Market of the Soviet Union, which, through 1960, persisted in regarding it as no more than another nefarious American-German invention for perpetuating their political dominance of western Europe.[25] But the Italian Communists, at least three years before the Russians, were aware of the economic implications of EEC. According to Mario Montagnana, the Communists were, in principle, even favorable to European economic integration, "since technical progress, the development of mass production at decreasing cost, and the prospect of automation and the utilization of nuclear energy (both requiring enormous capital investment) indeed pose this problem forcefully."[26] This had been the position taken by the CGIL in its first favorable declaration in July 1957. But the PCI rejected any hope that the Treaty of Rome would produce general economic benefits for Italy.[27] Only the Italian monopolies would profit, the party's spokesmen declared; the rest of the country would suffer. The Soviet analysis of the American recession of 1957, as the beginning of the major crisis in the capitalist world, further encouraged the Communist party in their prognostications of economic doom; and, after pressuring the CGIL to return to a position of intransigence toward the EEC, the Communist members in the Chamber of Deputies cast their 143 votes in opposition to ratification of the treaty.[28]

Within a year, however, the undeniable resurgence of the economy of the United States, coupled with the boom in production and trade in the Common Market countries, forced the PCI to reconsider the wisdom of predicting economic disaster that patently was not going to occur. By making such a prediction they would simply be repeating the mistake they had made over the Marshall Plan. Both at the conference of European Communist parties held in Rome in November 1959 and at the Moscow conference of eighty-one Communist parties from throughout the world, the Italian delegation urged that the productive expansion of capitalist Europe should be recognized and that a new strategy, suitable to this changed situation, should be evolved.[29] In particular, the Italians proposed that the Communists should seek representation within the European Community, so as to be able to meet the challenge of the monopolies from within. The most hopeful result of this economic progress, they urged, was that the Common Market was making western Europe independent of the United States, and hence increasing the significance of the rapid development of European Communism.[30]

The apparent willingness of the Communists to dispute openly the Soviet Union's position was due to the coincidence of internal needs with external opportunity. Inside the Italian party, the further revelations about Stalin and the group of old-time Stalinists made at the Twenty-second Party Congress in Moscow in October 1961 had caused enormous dissatisfaction with the Soviet leadership, which Togliatti feared would reflect upon him. Moreover, the party leaders were worried by events at home. The Christian Democrats were about to conclude the much-feared opening to the left with the Socialists; economic prosperity was being enjoyed by ever increasing levels of the working classes, and was making possible the financing of reforms in the South, in agriculture, and in social welfare. The Communist party therefore felt it essential to stake out a more positive position that would enable it to influence, and take credit for, the economic evolution that was being brought about by the Common Market. The Soviet search for allies in its sharpening confrontation with the Chinese Communist leadership probably gave the Italians the opportunity to press for a new approach in Europe. It was the CGIL, at the Fifth Congress of the World Federation of Trade Unions in December 1961, that first challenged the Soviet view of the Common Market and opposed the use of the WFTU as a means of enforcing the Russian views on the world trade union movement; and these views were repeated even more strongly in the Executive Committee meeting in Budapest in May 1962. By then, however, there were very significant signs of a change of mind within the Italian Communist party itself.

The spokesman for the new assessment of the Common Market was Giorgio Amendola, the leader of the reformist faction that was pressing the party to accept a "gradualist" approach, working within the political and economic system to achieve immediate reforms and seeking to reach power ultimately by peaceful means.[31] In his report to the conference on "Trends in Italian Capitalism," organized by the Gramsci Institute in March 1962, Amendola argued that the workers now held the balance of power against the capitalists, and could themselves protect and better the conditions of the working class. He felt that the mistakes made by the Communists in their economic strategy during the past two decades should be renounced, including the party's evaluation of the coming effects of the Common Market. At first, the party had confused the effects of the American recession with those of the opening of the integrated market. "Our position, which was politically responsible, of criticism of EEC was accompanied, however, by an erroneous overvaluing of the economic difficulties that would be caused by the coming into force of EEC and by an undervaluing of the new possibilities offered by the initial formation of a European market to Italian economic expansion. In reality it is in the interest of the working class to favor economic development that would permit the Italian economy to acquire competitive capacity on the international markets."[32] Evidently, Amendola's comments on EEC, unlike many of his earlier reformist comments, were acceptable to the party's dominant Center; for a month later Vice Secretary General Luigi Longo also admitted that "we failed to predict accurately the consequences of integration provisions on the Italian economic situation. . . . It is a fact that European integration has been a fundamental factor in Italy's economic leap forward."[33]

The Soviet government's own renewed appraisal of EEC was much less positive. Even so, in the Conference on Contemporary Capitalism held in Moscow in August–September 1962, they went some way toward endorsing the view argued by the Italian delegation, that the EEC had made a definite contribution to recent European economic progress, that this progress had increased Europe's independence of the United States, and that the Communist world had to deal with EEC as an objective and permanent reality.[34]

Freed from the outright negatives of the original Soviet attitude, the PCI began to demand a new approach to EEC. The Italian Communists were unwilling to see an open break within the Communist movement, however, and they reverted to the theme of "unity in diversity," a felicitous name for "polycentrism."[35] But diversity would only be possible if greater autonomy were allowed to the individual national parties. The role of the Communist parties in western Europe, in the PCI's view, was to seek greater influence over their own societies by making alliances with the non-Communist Left and by participating in the national economic planning that was being adopted on an ever larger scale. This view was expressed most significantly in the so-called Testament of Togliatti, a memorandum for the Soviet leaders on the problems of the world workers' movement, which Togliatti wrote shortly before he died.

The situation in western Europe as a whole, he felt, was not encouraging. The United States, aided by reactionary European groups, was seeking international aggression as a way out of its internal tensions. The monopolistic concentrations in Europe were being strengthened by the operation of the Common Market, which was thus increasing the power of the reactionary political forces. But certain favorable conditions could be exploited. "To do so the Communists must have much political courage, overcome any form of dogmatism, face and resolve new problems in new ways, and use methods of work that are adapted to a political and social environment in which continuous and rapid transformations are taking place." The Communists must influence economic planning, both nationally and at the EEC level, by coordinating the workers' demands and by preparing a general plan of economic development of their own, which could be applied even before the coming of Communist political control. The trade unions must act internationally and in concert with the non-Communist unions. And the possibility of an understanding with the Catholics must not be hampered by the "old atheistic propaganda."[36] The Communists, Togliatti urged, must seek more successful ways of increasing their political participation within states that were still bourgeois.

The publication of this Testament in *Rinascita* on September 5, 1964, has been generally interpreted as a proof of the determination of Togliatti's successors in the leadership of the party to emphasize, not Togliatti's own desire for an understanding with the Russians, but the Italian party's determination to seek its own Italian way to socialism in spite of the Soviet Union. It is obvious from the later positions of the PCI that there had been considerable pressure from within the party for a far more independent stance. This pressure was evident in the PCI's continuing opposition to the holding of a worldwide conference to denounce the Chinese, in its protest at the manner in which Khrushchev was ousted in 1964, in its anguished outcry against the Soviet invasion of Czechoslovakia in 1968, and in the harshly critical speeches of Enrico Berlinguer when the world conference of Communist parties was finally held in the summer of 1969.

With this new attitude within the party, the PCI's attitude to EEC at last became constructive. The party set itself up as the protector of the democratic character of the Community's institutions. It demanded greater powers for the European Parliament, seeing a strong parliament as a necessary protection against the technocratic character of the European Commission. It claimed that, within the Parliament, democratic representation would only have meaning when the Communist parties of Italy and France were represented. In particular, the PCI poured scorn on the failure of the Italian government to renew the membership of the Italian delegation to the European Parliament after the 1963 elections, when the DC's new ally, the PSI, was demanding Communist representation. This situation was not remedied until 1969, when representatives of the Communist party were finally admitted to the Italian delegation. In the same way, the Communists objected to the exclusion of the major unions, the CGIL and the French CGT, from the Economic and Social Committee; and in 1965, at the moment of the ratification of the treaty on the fusion of the executives of the three Communities, it demanded that the new Commission have direct representation of the workers.[37]

The party admitted that EEC had succeeded in two of its major objectives, abolishing most barriers to free movement of goods and setting up the framework of an integrated agricultural policy, even though the former had stimulated industrial production by the monopolies while the latter had favored the large-scale distributors and processors. It held that the agricultural policy's effects in Italy were negative, since they continued the existing irrational structure of ownership and crop selection, and allowed the forces of competition to further weaken the backward agricultural regions. The concept of increasing the capitalization and hence the mechanization of farming was being applied only in those regions of Italy where it would bring a quick return. Hence the party felt that wide-scale intervention by the state and by the FEOGA was essential to build peasant agriculture on a cooperative basis. Here, in fact, was an illustration of that gradual reform within the existing structures which Amendola was asking the party to espouse.[38] The weakness of the customs union lay in the absence of the other forms of integration that should have accompanied it—freedom of migration of workers, services, and capital. Hence, the Communists joined with the majority of other Italian parties in demanding that the customs union be transformed into an economic union. A common industrial policy was needed "that would integrate whole sectors of activity in a coordinated productive framework, through the installation of a whole series of instruments that would increase the dimensions of the companies, creating European structures, linked to a single capital market for the six countries . . . orienting through economic planning the direction of private as well as public investments."[39] The Commission, however, tended to free private industry of controls while restricting the state-controlled industries to marginal and unprofitable activity. As for social policy, it had simply made Italy the "reservoir of low-cost labor"; and, to remedy this, the party urged the Community to adopt better programs of professional training through the European Social Fund; to have more consultations with the trade unions, especially the Communist ones; and to give higher priority to social betterment than to restrictive measures against inflation. Relations with third countries also had to be changed, especially since EEC's attitude toward the underdeveloped countries was neocolonialist. In the PCI's view, EEC wanted to use the countries of the Near East and Africa as captive sources of raw materials and captive markets for finished products.[40]

The party's final judgment, however, was that the Common Market was becoming outdated. The integration, or at least the interdependence, of Europe's economic structure was being achieved independently of EEC, by such diverse methods as American capital investment and bilateral trading agreements with the East European states, while the process of disengagement of East and West and the weakening of the Atlantic Alliance were making political unification of one section of the Continent a mere remnant of the Cold War days. Here lay the Communist party's ultimate conception of a united Europe:

> In this corner of a Europe which is in the process of transformation, twenty years after the end of the Second World War, the action of the Italian and Western workers' movement can only grow, acting both by economic stimulus and by mass action, trade union and democratic, to encourage the growth of economic relations between the two groups of European countries (socialist and Western) in such a way as to create a sort of economic interdependence that would destroy the barriers of the Common Market, and make possible the development of a more advanced European policy, that would bring our continent from formal to real autonomy, balancing in this way American economic imperialism which still, together with West German desire for revenge, constitutes the major peril for world peace.[41]

In short, the constructive criticisms formed only part of a wider scheme, one in which the PCI found no room for the continued existence of the Common Market. Since it could not accept EEC's political goal, which remained the union of non-Communist Europe, it could hardly be expected to desire EEC's ultimate success.

THE SOCIALISTS—FROM NEUTRALISM TO ATLANTICISM

In 1943, the various Socialist groups that had been operating independently during the years of exile under Fascism were reunited in the Partito Socialista Italiano di Unità Proletaria (PSIUP).[42] From its foundation, the party was sharply divided between a small, extreme Left of young and impatient Socialists, led by Lelio Basso; a large Center, led by Secretary General Pietro Nenni, which was descended from the prewar "maximalists," who sought revolutionary change in Italian society; and a moderate Right, the "reformers" (riformisti), led by Giuseppe Saragat, which wanted gradual social change within a democratic political system.[43]

During the years between the armistice of September 1943 and the coming of peace, the new party made loud demands for internal revolutionary change; but when faced with Allied occupation and Communist moderation, the PSIUP participated in the government and predicted that the changes would be made at the end of the war with the Wind from the North. After 1945, however, the Socialists again put off their deadline for major social changes, saying the reforms could not be made until the party had first achieved a satisfactory constitution and electoral victory in alliance with the Communists. Yet it was not a dispute over the timing of internal reform that split the Socialist party, but the Unity of Action Pacts with the Communists, which were dragging the party into support of the Soviet bloc in the Cold War.

The Pact with the PCI, originally concluded in 1934, had been renewed in 1943 and again in 1946. This third Pact declared that the common goals included "peace with a foreign policy which, permitting us to reacquire as soon as possible the political and economic independence of the nation and thus the liberty to produce, trade, and emigrate, would be based on the principle of the international organization of collective security and the solidarity between peoples and between workers' and democratic associations in all countries." Here, in combination, were the ideal of national independence, which the Communists were making much of, and the concept of class solidarity at the international level. But as early as the National Council of July 1945, Saragat declared that this view had been invalidated by the actions of Russia in eastern Europe and by the totalitarianism of the Soviet state.[44] At the same time, however, Nenni found himself under pressure from the left wing of the party, especially the group around Lelio Basso and the younger members publishing the review *Iniziativa Socialista,* to break off the policy of anti-Fascist unity which later justified Socialist participation in the first three De Gasperi governments. As a result, even the Left of the Socialist party was shattered; and the coherent internationalism of Iniziativa Socialista, which believed that the existing anti-Fascist government alliance was furthering the appearance of Cold War blocs and offered instead a European neutralism based upon a Socialist International and a federal political structure, was temporarily ignored.[45]

The Socialists were too badly divided to profit from their success in the elections for the Constituent Assembly in June 1946, when they obtained 20.7 per cent of the vote to 18.9 per cent for the Communists. Although Nenni decided to remain within the

De Gasperi government, and even became foreign minister from October 1946 to February 1947, he urged closer collaboration with the PCI, and the two parties concluded a new Unity of Action Pact in October. Nenni thereby lost the opportunity of giving his party a clear, individual delineation, separated from the Communists by its democratic methods and competing with the PCI for the votes of the working classes, and he also lost any chance of pressuring De Gasperi to adopt a neutralist foreign policy. If Nenni had not allied so firmly with the Communists after the elections for the Constituent Assembly, the Italian Socialist party, like the French SFIO, might well have remained within the governmental coalition, leaving the Communists to be sent alone into the political wilderness; and the whole Italian government system might have enjoyed a stability denied it by the pro-Communist orientation of Nenni's followers.

During the second half of 1946, Saragat and his followers in PSIUP decided that it was better to split the party than accept the Nenni line of collaboration with the Communists. They believed that the party was threatened directly by the PCI, since they felt the Left of the party was under Communist influence, while former Socialist supporters among the working classes, as the administrative elections of the fall of 1946 showed, were either moving over toward the Communists or abstaining from voting. But the decisive influence was the development of the Cold War. As foreign minister, Nenni had sought "an honest policy of international solidarity, neither supporting the Anglo-Americans against the Soviet Union nor the Soviet Union against the Anglo-Americans." In Saragat's opinion, Nenni was "denying the evidence . . . [of] the parallel development of a democratic socialism and of an authoritarian socialism. . . . It is camouflaging the facts to present Communism as a convert to the democratic notion of Western Socialism, when everything in its organizational structure, in its policy, in its mentality, screams the contrary."[46] He and his followers walked out of the party congress in January 1947, and formed a new party of Social Democrats, called the Partito Socialista dei Lavoratori Italiani. The PSLI was joined by 45 per cent of the Socialist party deputies, but by only about one-quarter of the party membership. The following year it claimed only 200,000 members. The split greatly reduced any hope that the Socialists might have had of influencing the direction of governmental policy in Italy. For the next decade, the Nenni Socialists repeated the Communist line, while the Saragat Socialists, after initially attempting to find an autonomous line, threw their support to De Gasperi. In December 1947, they entered the De Gasperi government. They declared that they were doing so to enable De Gasperi to maintain his centrist concept of government against those in the DC who would swing the party toward a clerical, integralist line.[47]

The years of De Gasperi's hegemony, from 1947 through 1953, saw the Social Democrats justify an almost total adherence to Christian Democratic policy in terms of "democratic solidarity." The Marshall Plan was interpreted as a genuine American attempt to aid the unification of Europe—thus enabling the party to postpone the choice of alignment with one or other of the Cold War blocs. A favorable vote for ratification of the peace treaty was presented as a renunciation of "stupid nationalism" and as faith in the solidarity of the peoples of Europe.[48] Even the Atlantic Pact was justified by Saragat as "scaffolding for the Europe that we want, a provisional barrier that must be demolished one day," but behind which the Social Democrats would attempt to unite Europe as a third force "between the two opposed blocs." Nevertheless, by 1949 Saragat was ready to drop the pretense that the Social Democrats regarded the two blocs as similar. Friendship with the United States, a country that had proved it did not want war, and whose continuing aid was indispensable to Italy's economic recovery and national security, became an axiom of Social Democratic policy from the time of the Congress of Milan, in January 1949.[49] While supporting De Gasperi's foreign policy in its entirety, the Social Democrats found that they were unable to exercise much influence on internal policy, and so they resigned from the government in 1951. They did not return until the Scelba ministry of 1954, when they agreed to participate in return for the specific promise of social reforms.

Following the secession of the Social Democrats in January 1947, the Socialist party, now called the Partito Socialista Italiano (PSI) aligned itself ever more closely with the Communists. The PSI's explanation of its ouster from the De Gasperi government in May 1947 established the principles of the party's action for the next eight years. Internal events were conditioned by international forces, Nenni explained to the party congress in 1952. "Everything was controlled by the cyclopean conflict opened in 1947 by the capitalistic world against the Soviet Union or the Socialist states that it heads."[50] In this struggle, the Socialists must "identify the international sphere as the fundamental area for the class struggle, thus considering the evolution of the internal situation as a variable of the international; accept the division of the world into a Socialist peace camp and imperialist war camp; and identify with the former the position and the fate of the Socialist party."[51]

It followed from these principles that the Marshall Plan was "an instrument for the colonization of Europe"; the *coup d'état* in Prague was a victory of the Czech workers and peasants against counterrevolution; and the Korean War was fought between "the people of the North who represent the double aspiration of the Korean people for the independence of their country and social justice, while the Southerners are a bureaucratic, police-dominated, mercenary group without ties with the living energies of the Korean people."[52] It was the Atlantic Pact, however, that brought out the greatest show of opposition to Italian membership in the Atlantic grouping. The party accepted the Communist position that the internal contradictions inside capitalism, which were responsible for the economic crisis of that time, were pushing the capitalists to prepare for a third world war as "the most convenient solution to their own contradictions."[53] Against such aggression, the PSI posed as the party of peace and of neutrality. Nenni became vice president of the World Council of the Partisans of Peace, and was awarded the Stalin Peace Prize in 1951, while the party declared its official policy to be one of keeping Italy neutral in the event of a war between the two great powers.[54] All the measures tending to the unification of western Europe in these years were dismissed as relevant only to the goal of subjecting Europe to the United States and as worthless in creating a third force. Lelio Basso, speaking in the Chamber on July 12, 1949, attacked the Council of Europe for "hiding, with its federalist, progressive, idealist mask two brutal realities: the economic subordination of Europe to American financial capitalism, and the Western bloc in its anti-Soviet military function."[55]

It was hardly surprising that the Schuman and Pleven Plans

appealed little more than the Atlantic Pact, especially as they clearly stood to strengthen one of the PSI's most denounced enemies, West Germany. The Schuman Plan, according to *Mondo Operaio*, was "an ideal instrument for the execution of American directives and for the rearmament of Western Germany." Its principal aim was the revival of the Ruhr basin, "the German war arsenal as the bulwark of their dominion in western Europe," while the supranational authority would be the direct representative of the capitalistic groups of the Ruhr.[56] The PSI regarded the European Defense Community as no more than an excuse for the rearmament of West Germany, whose twelve divisions were useless as defense but essential for offense in the age of the hydrogen bomb, and could enforce the irredentist claims of Bonn against the East German regime that Nenni still saw, in 1953, as the defender of German liberties. Nenni felt that De Gasperi intended to use the political camouflage of the European Political Community, to lead to "a unification of the European regimes that would be pleasing to the Vatican and a powerful means of social conservation," a "colossal 'cartel' intended to guarantee permanence of profits to capital and stability to the governments, reducing to impotence if not to illegitimacy any demand for social progress."

Thus, throughout the crucial years of the first phase of Europeanism, from 1947 to 1954, the attitude of the Socialist party differed little from that of the Communists—they placed a little greater emphasis on a policy of neutralism between the blocs, and were a little more concerned with the internal implications of Atlantic and European policy as a hindrance to social reform. In 1955, however, there suddenly appeared clear signs that the PSI was willing to move away from its unswerving support of the Communist position in foreign policy. The PSI declared that it would be "ready to consider in a favorable way the policy of a new Government that would follow a rigidly defensive and geographically limited interpretation of the Atlantic Pact and still more of the WEU Agreements." The apparent readiness of the party for a "dialogue with the Catholics" was to change their attitude toward European unification completely.[57]

Encouraged by its success in the 1953 elections, which it had fought without allying with the Communists, the PSI decided, at its Congress of Turin in 1955, to call formally for an "opening to the Left."⁵⁸ Behind this decision was the belief that, following the death of Stalin and the adoption of a policy of disengagement under Malenkov, international events no longer conditioned internal policy, and that therefore the PSI could support a policy of specific reforms without compromising its opposition to capitalism or its links with the Communist party. In this way it seemed possible to have the best of both worlds, avoiding above all the division of the party on the issue of a leftward or rightward orientation.

The events of 1956 in the Soviet world, however, forced the members of the PSI to move further away from the PCI. Nenni opened the debate, in his articles in *Mondo Operaio* on Khrushchev's revelations at the Twentieth Party Congress, by criticizing the whole Soviet system, and the Italian Communist party, for the lack of political liberty: "The monolithic party, carved in a single block, bears in itself the permanent danger of degeneration."⁵⁹ The debate spread deeply through the party, leading to a complete reexamination not only of the errors of the Soviet system, but also of the writings of Marx, Engels, and Lenin, and to a rejection of the traditional interpretations of such ideas as the dictatorship of the proletariat. The Soviet repression of the Hungarian uprising in November 1956 increased the divisions in the PSI that were hindering a full alignment with the Western bloc. A group of about ten deputies on the extreme Left, led by Lussu, upheld the Soviet line in its entirety. The main group on the Left, called the sinistra, led by Tullio Vecchietti and Lelio Basso, were unwilling to endanger their relationship with the PCI by playing the bourgeois game of criticizing Soviet actions, and they attempted to ignore what was happening in Hungary.⁶⁰ The majority of the party, following Nenni, determined to break with the Communist party, and they denounced the party's identification with the "Socialist camp." At the Congress of Venice, in February 1957, the party held one of its greatest debates, undertaking a reevaluation of the whole meaning of socialism and a reconsideration of the party's future policy, internal and international. Nenni's political victory at the Congress led to an outright denunciation of the policy of "frontism," i.e. of alliance with the Communists, because the events in the Communist world from the Twentieth Party Congress to the Hungarian repression "not only raise doubts about a certain number of people but raise doubts about a method and a system." The immediate effect of this reevaluation was to make the PSI again the supporter of the principle of neutralism between the blocs. But in the long run the party's deep reconsideration of the character of political and industrial development, especially that of western Europe, led first to a favorable judgment on West European integration and finally to a moderate endorsement of Atlantic Alliance itself.

The spokesman for a new concept of capitalism was Riccardo Lombardi, who, as early as August 1956, rejected the Marxist-Leninist belief in the inevitable destruction of capitalism by war or economic crisis.[61] The Socialist party could, in Lombardi's view, become the democratic instrument for the transformation of the capitalist state from within. In July 1957 he told the PSI Central Committee that a realistic view of modern capitalism should also be extended to consideration of the European Common Market. Just as the PSI should work within the Italian political system, so the workers' organizations, political and syndical, should counterbalance the employers' organizations within EEC.[62] The left wing, however, refused to accept this optimistic view of EEC. Both Foa and Lussu pointed out that the economic consequences for Italy might be disastrous.[63] In this first major conflict between the currents developing within the PSI, the sinistra and the autonomists, the latter prevailed. The final motion of the Venice Congress declared:

> The Party considers favorably initiatives like that of the single European market and of Euratom, provided that democratic control be guaranteed, provided that the interests of the workers and the needs of the depressed zones be firmly safeguarded, and provided that any complicity in colonial policy be avoided. The party is ready to collaborate in a European policy which, soundly based in the socialist and workers' movement, tends to make Europe into a force for democratic and social progress, mediation, and peace.[64]

The PSI finally decided to abstain on EEC but to support Euratom.[65] The party's attitude was explained in the Chamber on July 22 by Lombardi. Atomic energy represented an entirely new branch of industry, which vested interests had not yet had time to seize; hence the moment was suitable for state initiative through Euratom. As for EEC, the party was favorable on principle to economic integration, which constituted the essential difference between the goal of this Community and that of EDC, which the party still disapproved. The worries of the Socialists were due to the fact that the Treaty of Rome meticulously prepared the customs union but left vague the provision for creation of a Community economic policy, and therefore strengthened the position of those, like the Italian Liberals, who wanted to see EEC as a safeguard of economic liberalism at the international level at a time when it was threatened at home. The Socialists proposed to devote all their energies to the battle over the application of the treaty, seeing in their concept of the Community "not the overturning of the power relationships between the social classes, but a profound modification in those relations."[66]

The PSI thus showed in 1957 an eagerness to participate in orienting the country's rapid economic development, both by national planning and by influencing the character of the European Economic Community. Yet it was still groping ineffectively for its political role. In 1959, the party offered itself as a "democratic alternative" (to both the PCI and the DC); but in 1961, the majority of the party returned to the goal of a "Center-Left" government, within which, as Lombardi stated again, the Socialists, from their position within the governmental majority, could insist upon a program of structural reforms that would move the state in a socialist direction. The Socialists' conditions for coalition were nationalization of the electrical industry, implementation of regional autonomy, school reform, and, especially, adoption of national economic planning. The Christian Democrats accepted these conditions, and the PSI thereupon agreed to abstain on the vote of confidence on Fanfani's fourth ministry.

During the first Center-Left experiment under Fanfani's fourth ministry (February 1962–June 1963), the PSI autonomists felt that the government, through such measures as the nationalization of the electricity industry, was attempting to carry out the type of structural reform that Riccardo Lombardi had been urging within the party for four years;[67] and at the Socialist Congress in Rome, in October 1963, Nenni and the autonomists gained party approval to participate in a Center-Left government whose aims would be national economic planning, agrarian reform, autonomy of the regions, reform of the public administration, education investments, and a foreign policy suited to the new prospects that EEC had created.

> The situation as it is being shaped permits the party, without giving up in any way its principles of internationalism, pacificism, and neutralism . . . to avoid raising the issue of Italian membership in NATO and of the obligations that arise from it. . . .
> The party demands energetic and constant action to create a Europe for the people, founded on democracy, and Italian action in EEC to avoid it being reduced to a closed area. It also requests action within the Community organs of EEC (within which the Socialists intend to participate, working to remove the barriers that have prevented it from doing so up to now), in order that it become the instrument of the forces of European democracy; and, finally, it requests decisive action by Italy to see that the Treaties of Rome are enforced through the election of a European parliament by direct universal suffrage.[68]

In spite of the lack of enthusiasm for Atlanticism evident in this motion, the majority of the DC and the other future coalition partners, the Social Democrats and Republicans, decided it went far enough to permit governmental cooperation. The Socialists named ex-Communist Antonio Giolitti to the crucial Ministry of the Budget, which was given responsibility for drawing up the plans for national economic planning, while Saragat was appointed foreign minister, thus assuring the continuance of a strongly pro-American foreign policy.

Socialist participation in the three Moro governments (1963–68) caused only slight changes in Italian policy toward European unification and the Atlantic bloc. The secession from the PSI in January 1964 of most of the current of sinistra, which formed the Partito Socialista Italiano di Unità Proletaria (PSIUP), cost the party about 20 per cent of its strength, but it removed those leaders who had continually argued that EEC was no more than a means of maintaining the dominance of the conservative economic forces in Europe closely tied to American capital. The Socialists found themselves attacked by their former comrades, such as Vecchietti and Basso, for favoring "a great Western bloc comprising all the capitalist countries and a great Europe politically and militarily united under American leadership."[69] The Socialist party, with its autonomist wing in control, continued to press for neutralism—for example, it demanded the recognition of Communist China and opposed the multilateral nuclear force.[70] But in most other ways the Socialists accepted both Atlanticism and Europeanism. Using their belief that international tensions had eased (they felt this had been proved by the activities of the Twentieth and Twenty-second Party Congresses of the Soviet Communist party), and making Gaullism the new enemy, the Socialists argued that their support of NATO, in Mario Zagari's words, enabled them to "act at the European and Atlantic levels in favor of an authentic peaceful alternative, concretely opposed at every point to the Gaullist position." Within EEC itself, they demanded the election of a European Parliament by universal suffrage; the representation of all groups, including the Communists, in Community organs; and the extension of the Community to include Britain and Scandinavia.

The muting of differences on foreign policy between the PSI and PSDI was a necessary precondition for unification of the two parties. Once that basic obstacle had been removed, more practical considerations—electoral strength, voter appeal, and especially bargaining power in relation to the DC—brought the two parties together. In spite of the opposition of the small Lombardi current, which held that the Center-Left government was failing to achieve real reforms and that unification with the PSDI would merely "Social Democratize" the party, the PSI agreed to unification with the PSDI. In the "Charter of Socialist Unification," agreed on by the two parties in 1966, the new unified party (PSI-PSDI Unificato) stated that its essential role would be to meet the challenge of contemporary capitalism, now no longer the prey of cyclical crises but more dangerous as a result of the concentrations of power produced by new technology and economic progress. From this perspective, foreign policy appeared little more than a well-meaning statement of international solidarity of the working class, and an optimistic acceptance of the status quo in the power relations of the blocs.[71] Nevertheless, as was shown by the party program for the 1968 elections, the Unified Socialist party wished to carry out at the European level many of the goals it had set for itself at home. Recognizing the positive effects of EEC upon Italy, it demanded European economic planning as a means of overcoming disparity of progress between regions and classes, encouraging technological and scientific progress, guaranteeing full employment, and controlling the monopolies. As at home, economic planning was held to possess the magic power of righting economic and social wrongs that were deeply rooted in the system of production.[72] The optimism of election propaganda would, however, have to be backed by effective action if the Socialists were to make up for two decades of lost opportunities. The renewed fragmentation of the party in July 1969, into a revived PSI and a new, largely Social-Democratic PSU (Unitary Socialist Party), was unfortunate proof of the fact that the new proponent of Europeanism was a rather insubstantial champion.

THE ITALIAN LIBERAL PARTY (PLI)

The Liberal Party, which had dominated the Italian state from unification until the Fascist takeover, was suppressed by Mussolini, as were the other democratic parties. Few Liberal party leaders went into exile, however, and opposition remained largely silent. Only in 1942–43 did the Gruppi di Ricostruzione Liberale begin, on a local level, to work at reviving the party. It was officially refounded after the armistice of September 1943. From the start, however, the party was split between the Southern wing, representing the great landowners of the latifondi acting in alliance with conservative business interests, and a more reform-minded Northern wing, led by such intellectuals as Professor Luigi Einaudi and Senator Alessandro Casati.[73] During the last two years of the war, when the Liberals participated in the Committees of National Liberation and in the governments of Badoglio and Bonomi, their principal goal was to prevent the forces of the Left from using their positions in the underground or in the government to purge the representatives of the conservative classes or to prepare the way for a revolutionary takeover by a Socialist-Communist coalition.[74] Their policy was to ignore economic questions for the moment, to seek separation of Church and State, and to demand the safeguard of personal liberties. After the war's end, when the party was reorganized, it spelled out its program more clearly. The emphasis laid on the restoration of order and of firm administration by the state created a sympathy of aim with the Christian Democrats during the period of the Parri government, especially in the desire to disband the Committees of National Liberation and to restrict the purge of former Fascists. Hence, when the resignation of the PLI and the DC brought down Parri, the Liberals were prepared to collaborate with De Gasperi in the work of social and economic reconstruction that dominated his first five ministries.

Until 1950, when the Liberals resigned in opposition to the land reform program of the sixth De Gasperi ministry, their influence lay principally in reinforcing the right wing of the Christian Democratic party in the administration of a conservative economic policy, as laid down by Epicarmo Corbino and Luigi Einaudi. Within the Liberal party, the conservative dominance was contested by various left-wing groups who wished to give the party a more forward-looking policy. They had little success, and many of them left the party. The evolution toward the Right gave the PLI the reputation of being the bulwark of the conservative landowners and monopolistic business interests, reduced its influence within the governmental coalition and in the country at large, and pushed it into closer alliance with the parties of the extreme Right.[75] Thus the Liberals lost their moderate supporters, but failed to attract the extreme right-wing vote.

The desire to save the country from the advances of Socialism and Communism determined the Liberals' foreign policy. During the late 1940's they envisaged Europe as a no-man's-land between two expansionist powers, the Soviet Union and the United States; and, as Francesco Cocco-Ortu pointed out, the official Liberal position was that "between the great Euro-Asiatic imperialism of Russia and the great American imperialism of the United States, the united compact European family should be inserted as rapidly as possible as the third determining element in the destiny of the world." But America's egoistic interests in Europe coincided "with the interest of the free peoples of Europe in not losing their liberty beneath the strength of that great continental military power which is maintaining three hundred divisions" in Europe.[76] Whatever differences the Liberals had with the DC on internal matters, they were willing to support its Europeanism and Atlanticism—in the Marshall Plan, the Atlantic Pact, and the Council of Europe. The measures to integrate Europe economically received the strongest Liberal support, from the liberalization of trade in 1949 to the ratification of the European Coal and Steel Community. During the ECSC debates, Gaetano Martino emerged as the principal Liberal spokesman on European matters; he replaced Piccioni as minister of foreign affairs in the Scelba cabinet in September 1954 and held the position until 1957. It was thus a Liberal who negotiated and guided through parliament the treaties for Western European Union and the Common Market.

Following the defeat of EDC, Martino helped to revive Europeanism in Italy in a way consonant with the more subdued and realistic expectations that had replaced the supranational fervor over ECSC and EDC. In presenting the Western European Union to parliament, he called it "a new form of organization of the solidarity of Europe," and played down the nationalist resurgence that had led to its being substituted for the Defense Community; in defending the EEC treaty, he brushed aside the objections of those who held that supranationalism had been slighted in favor of intergovernmental agreements. For Martino, as for the whole Liberal party, the idea of Europe was a moral reality, implying recognition of liberty as the ideal of social life. As Martino explained in a speech, "The Liberal Idea in Italian Foreign Policy," the Liberals saw Europeanism as the defense of liberty. Its immediate goal was the protection of western Europe from the advance of the Soviet Union, but its long-term goal was the innoculation of European society against the inner germ of Communism. The defense of liberty could not be achieved, as some self-styled Europeanists thought, through nationalization or socialization: "The battle for the construction of Europe is not the battle for a certain amount of state control, but the battle for the realization of liberty as the method of solution of social problems." The weakness of the Treaty of Rome, in its requirements on social policy, harmonization of commercial policy, and so on, cannot be directly attributed to Martino; but it can be said that that weakness agreed with his thinking about the nature of economic integration.[77]

The Liberal party's opposition to "dirigismo," expressed by

Martino at the international level, was reinforced domestically by a secession of the party's left wing following the election of Giovanni Malagodi, in April 1954, to the post of secretary general. Malagodi, a brilliant banker who had served as Italian representative to many international economic conferences after the war, including those of the Marshall Plan and NATO, was regarded by the PLI's Left, and by the country at large, as a spokesman for the interests of Confindustria; and during the first three years of his leadership the main effort of the PLI was devoted to defending the interests of the great landowners in the law on mezzadria contracts. The collaboration of the Liberals in the four-party formula of government lasted only until the fall of Segni in May 1957; and, with the DC flirting with the Center-Left formula, the Liberal leaders turned ever more apprehensively toward outright opposition to such a scheme, holding that it would not only threaten private enterprise at home at a time when it was facing new competition from the EEC partners, but would also lead to a weakening of the now traditional foreign policy of Atlanticism and Europeanism.[78]

From the formation of the first Center-Left government in 1962, the Liberals tried vainly to oppose the various changes imposed as part of the Center-Left program—the nationalization of the electrical industry, the abolition of mezzadria contracts, and national economic planning. Malagodi even hinted that the recession in 1963 was probably due to worry over the policies proposed by the new government.[79] In such a discouraging situation, the Liberals looked with even greater hope to the creation of a united Europe in which all Liberals could act, in Malagodi's words, as "the party of the movement against conservative, paternalistic, socialist, and more or less democratized stagnation."[80] As a member of the Monnet Action Committee and president of the Liberal International, Malagodi himself continued to work for the integration of Europe, to oppose de Gaulle's revival of national powers within the Community, and to press for the inclusion of Britain and the other countries of the European Free Trade Association in EEC. As Malagodi remarked at the tenth National Congress of the PLI in 1966, "In a united Europe certain great Italian problems would be diluted." Yet the path of constant opposition to the Center-Left, while winning over a few of the right-wing DC voters, served little. From 1957 on, the Liberals' opposition was almost totally sterile.

Liberal action did have some lasting effects. In the period of six-party collaboration, from 1944 to 1945, they helped the Christian Democrats preserve the social and economic structure of Italy against the reforming desires of the left-wing Resistance forces; and from 1947 to 1957, they backed the centrist formula of government and shared in the construction of the Western European Union and the Common Market. But after 1957 they relapsed into irritated impotence.

THE MINOR PARTIES

Of all the minor parties in Italian politics, only the Action party, in 1944–46, and the Republican party, later, exercised any real influence on the development of Italian policy toward Europe. Nevertheless, the policy of Europeanism and Atlanticism also found fairly stable support, for somewhat illogical reasons, from the nationalistic parties of the Right, from the monarchists and from the neo-Fascists (Movimento Sociale Italiano).

The first of the right-wing groups to be founded in the immediate postwar years, the Uomo Qualunque (Average Man) party, served to express the frustration of the lower middle classes, especially in the South, with the chaos of the reconstruction period. Its foreign policy, insofar as it had any, was one of aggrieved nationalism. It opposed all of the ideas that had developed within the Resistance, including European federalism. With the demise of the Uomo Qualunque party after the 1948 elections, many of its supporters shifted to the MSI or the monarchists, both of whom claimed to have a coherent goal in foreign policy.

The National Monarchist party (Partito Nazionale Monarchico, or PNM), was created in 1946 by Achille Lauro, a Neapolitan shipowner. It was a coalition of the dispossessed upper classes and the feudal peasantry of the South. Under the parliamentary leadership of Alfredo Covelli, another Southerner, it based its internal policy on a return to national unity through the monarchy and the protection of the social structure through minor social reforms. Its main enemy was Communism, which, "radically mistaken in its theoretical premises in Marxist materialism, can only survive in practice through violence. . . . The only valid antithesis to Communism is the monarchy."[81] If the monarchy was to save the nation from Communism within, the PNM saw that Italy needed allies to save it from Communism from without. It therefore gave enthusiastic support to the Atlantic Pact, and it defended European integration as a necessary safeguard for national prosperity.[82] The party had considerable sympathy for the right wing of the Christian Democrats, and particularly for Pella, whose tough attitude on Trieste greatly pleased it. In the mid 1950's the monarchist movement was torn by internal dissensions that culminated in the formation of a second monarchist party.[83] Although they later reunited as the Partito Democratico Italiano di Unità Monarchica, the monarchists continued to decline, and even as an ally of the DC right wing they exercised little influence.[84]

The neo-Fascists were more vociferous than the monarchists in their support for European unity. They were an extreme nationalist group, which appealed to the admirers of Fascism and especially of the Salò Republic of Mussolini. At the moment of its founding in 1946, the party, rather surprisingly, declared its goal to be a "foreign policy inspired solely by the concrete and immediate interests of the Nation, seeking the formation of a European union on conditions of equality and justice."[85] At first, the party's leaders, finding their inspiration in the ideas of the Italian Social Republic, were sympathetic to state intervention in the economy and to a European union through which a European nationalism could stand against the alien imperialisms of Russia and the United States.[86] In 1951, however, the more moderate and conservative elements within the party brought it into sympathy with the views of the DC's right wing. They declared that the development of the Cold War had made necessary the MSI's "anti-Communist and pro-Western choice." "The struggle against Communism ceases to appear in a purely negative aspect and acquires for us the meaning of a struggle for the defense and the development of a civilization which is no longer represented by the nation, but by Europe: a grouping of human, historical, social, and religious values."[87] In practice, this doctrine implied opposition to EDC because military integration would destroy national feeling, but support for ECSC and for EEC because they would increase the prosperity and thus the strength of the individual nations.[88]

While the right-wing parties regarded Europeanism as a defense of nationalism, the Action party and the Republican party saw Europeanism as an antidote to it. The intellectual roots of the Action party reached back to Mazzinian federalism through the Giustizia e Libertà groups of Carlo Rosselli. Its original program, written in 1942, had called for "promotion of a European federation of free democratic states within the framework of still broader world collaboration."[89] It held that the creation of a United States of Europe was incompatible with the continuance of state-sovereignty, and that "organized economic interests" would resist the limitation of the powers of the national state. However, the Action party's internal program called for the nationalization of the large monopolies, large-scale state intervention in the economy, and land reform; the party believed that through this program the power of the economic groups opposing European federalism would be broken.[90] The Action party thus approached the integration of Europe with a mildly socialist, humanitarian point of view. Had it succeeded in becoming a major party, it is possible that the Italian governments taking Italy into Europe in the first postwar decade would not have laid so much emphasis on the Cold War. The failure of the Wind from the North to revolutionize Italian politics and society, or to put new groups into political and economic power, meant that Italy would only support European federalism when the traditional conservative forces within Italian society had been won over. An entirely different process of persuasion was required to persuade the Christian Democratic elite to support European federalism than would have been needed had the Action party been more powerful.

When the Action party collapsed in 1946, the most dedicated federalists among its members joined the Republican party.[91] The Republicans had stood for federalism within Italy for almost a century. At the end of the war, their party secretary, Randolfo Pacciardi, proclaimed the link of federalism within and without Italy: "The Italian people knows that tomorrow's foreign policy will be indissolubly linked with its internal policy: liberty and association, unity and federalism, within and without. These are Mazzinian conceptions."[92] The most direct influence of the Republicans came during the writing of the Constitution, when they helped win acceptance of the establishment of regional governments within Italy, and with the appointment of Sforza as foreign minister in 1947–51. Pacciardi himself, as minister of defense in 1948–53, was able to exercise some pressure to persuade his ministry and the general staff to collaborate in the negotiation of the EDC treaty. And it was La Malfa, as minister of foreign commerce in 1951–53, who was primarily responsible for the completion of the liberalization of foreign trade. During the years of De Gasperi's hegemony, the Republican party remained a small but constant ally in the ministerial coalition, helping De Gasperi hold off the pressure of the DC conservatives and their allies outside the party and strengthening his growing fervor for Europeanism. In the period of discouragement that followed the French rejection of EDC and the death of De Gasperi, the Republicans again became the federalist vanguard, both in parliament and in the country at large. Western European Union was barely tolerated; the EEC treaty, in spite of many shortcomings that the party found in it, was seen as an essential new beginning.[93] Once EEC was formed, the Republicans saw their role as a goad to compel its conversion into a genuine political union. They persistently demanded the election of the European Parliament by universal suffrage; the realization of an economic union, rather than a mere customs union; and the broadening of the Community to include England and the other applicants. To La Malfa, French President de Gaulle epitomized the dangers facing Europeanism; and La Malfa's support of the Center-Left government within Italy, as he explained in 1964, was due in part to his desire to "keep Italy and European life free of any Gaullist influence." Without a Center-Left government within Italy, La Malfa felt, those forces sympathetic to the weakening of the Community by de Gaulle would triumph; but the Center-Left, with its acceptance of national economic planning within a Community-wide plan, would strengthen the Community in its struggle with de Gaulle. La Malfa himself, as budget minister, took a central role in preparing the national economic plan in 1962. The Republican party, in spite of its size, was able to participate in the planning at ministerial level of most of the decisions concerning European integration; and it sought on every occasion not only to popularize those decisions in the country at large, but also to ensure that they were supported by a forward-looking program of internal reforms. The existence of such a party is one of the few justifications that can be made for the Italian multi-party system of government.

INTEGRATION'S IMPACT ON ITALIAN POLITICS

To what extent did the enemies and allies of the DC affect decision-making on questions of European integration? And, conversely, to what extent were those parties affected by the attitudes of the Christian Democrats? The parties of the extreme Right, the MSI and the monarchists, supplied welcome votes of support for European integration and Atlantic defense, but they received no recompense, except a little patronage. They themselves were compelled to twist their nationalistic doctrines to fit the changed circumstances of Europe—namely, the position of the European nation-states, which had insufficient size and resources to compete with the continental giants, and the advance of Communism in eastern Europe and within Italy itself. These twisted doctrines resulted in foreign policies that were full of contradictions. The existence of the Communist party within Italy and the DC's conception of the Communist threat from without were, of course, the primary factors in persuading the DC to see in a united Europe the safeguard of those Western or Christian values it felt were threatened by Communism, while the need to counteract the appeal of the PCI to the poorer classes of city and country alike strengthened those forces inside the DC who sought to establish a reform program at home that would not only remedy obvious social suffering, but would also lessen the role of free enterprise in the Italian productive system. The impact of the successes of Italian capitalism within the process of economic integration, however, had the more far-reaching effect of compelling the PCI to throw off the Soviet-imposed denunciation of the European Community and, indeed, of western European capitalism, and to act within the world Communist movement as the spokesman of a more collaborative attitude toward European integration. The Republicans and the Social Democrats, although they took a direct part in the cabinet, were never able to push the Christian Democratic party to move faster on European matters than its right wing was willing to go. They were not only too small in parliamentary representation, but their natural allies within the DC, the left-wing currents, too frequently dallied with the neutralism or the Mediterranean orientation that the PRI and the PSDI would not adopt. The Liberal party twice made its wishes felt, but in both cases it was able to do so because its position was akin to that of the Center and Right of the DC. In 1944–47, it sought to preserve the liberal or free enterprise character of the Italian economy, and through the work of Luigi Einaudi it helped provide the financial stability within which the private companies could thrive. In 1955–57, especially through the work of Foreign Minister Gaetano Martino, it was able to press for the imposition of a similar, liberal character upon the European Economic Community.

The Socialists bear the responsibility for the postponement of major social reforms inside Italy. By their unrealistic acceptance of the Communist alliance, with the resultant difficulty in concluding an alliance with the DC, they lost the opportunity to bring about social change in the immediate postwar period. In the 1960's, however, the Socialists recognized the vital contribution of EEC to Italian prosperity, and they joined with the progressive forces in the DC and with the Republicans and Social Democrats in demanding that the new affluence be used in a meaningful program of social reforms. In this sense, the Common Market can be said to have contributed to the coming of the Center-Left governments of the 1960's. Socialist recognition of the value of Europeanism combined with a muted acceptance of a defensive Atlantic alliance was a price they could easily pay when the DC showed its willingness to cooperate in a long-delayed redistribution of the national wealth.

This optimistic situation prevailed in 1963 when the Socialists took part in the first Moro government. The following five years dashed many hopes, and produced the situation of internal crisis that prevailed in Italy after the 1968 elections. Europeanism lost its glamour under the bludgeoning of President de Gaulle. The hopes of broadening the Community to include England and the Scandinavian countries were twice dashed by French vetoes; the Community was paralyzed for half a year by the crisis over agricultural financing; and the agricultural policy, whose formulation preoccupied EEC for more than six years, proved very unsatisfactory to Italian agriculture. The Community officials had lost much of their original élan, and seemed resigned to becoming what de Gaulle had always thought them to be—technocratic administrators. The bitter disappointment felt among Europeans in Italy was paralleled by the disillusionment of many of the original supporters of the Center-Left ideal. The depression of 1963–65, although successfully weathered, delayed the program of social reforms. Quarrels inside both the DC and the Socialist party hampered the effective working of the coalition. Frustrated in their hopes of rapid social change, the trade unions coordinated their demands and their pressure. Italy entered a new period of turbulence, primarily because the government failed to satisfy the aspirations of the working classes which had been aroused by the coming of the new prosperity.

At the time of the 1968 elections Italy was in a state of social and political crisis. No party challenged the value of European union, and most endorsed it strongly. But Europeanism itself was not a major issue. The prosperity that European integration had helped foster had posed major internal questions, but these questions had never been adequately answered. Were the workers receiving a fair share of the wealth they helped produce? Could the gap between agricultural and industrial incomes be tolerated any longer? Could the difference between the wealth of the North and the poverty of the South be overcome? Twenty-five years of extraordinary economic progress had brought Italy to the point where an answer to these problems could be glimpsed; and it was imperative for the country's future that a nationally accepted political authority find the strength to implement those solutions. Italy had indeed chosen Europe; but the choice had helped bring the Italians back to the point where once again they had to decide what kind of an Italy they wanted.

Notes

CHAPTER 1

1. Federico Chabod, *Storia dell'idea d'Europa* (Bari, 1961), pp. 23ff.
2. Luigi Einaudi, *La guerra e l'unità europea* (Milan, 1948), p. 11.
3. Cited in Charles F. Delzell, "The European Federalist Movement in Italy: First Phase, 1918–1947," *Journal of Modern History* (September, 1960), 242.
4. Charles F. Delzell, *Mussolini's Enemies: The Italian Anti-Fascist Resistance* (Princeton 1961), p. 162.
5. Ibid. p. 211; Emilio Lussu, "La ricostruzione dello stato," *Quaderni del Partito d'Azione*, No. 1 (Rome, 1944). This is an article reprinted directly from Giustizia e Libertà, in which Lussu called for a federal Italian state inside a united Europe.
6. Cited in Franco Catalano, "La politica estera del C.L.N.," in Istituto Affari Internazionali, Rome, *La politica estera della repubblica italiana* (Bologna, 1967), II, 422.
7. Centre d'Action pour la Fédération Europeenne, Neuchâtel, *L'Europe de demain* (Neuchâtel, 1945), pp. 35, 47.
8. Reprinted in Einaudi, *La guerra e l'unità europea*, pp. 35-120. Citation from p. 77. These books were smuggled into Italy with a number of other federalist pamphlets.
9. Centre d'Action, *L'Europe de demain*, pp. 74, 78-82.
10. IAI, *La politica estera*, II, 421.
11. Democrazia Cristiana, *Atti e documenti della Democrazia Cristiana 1943–1959* (hereafter cited as DC, *Atti, 1943–1959*), (Rome, 1959), pp. 9, 12.
12. Alfonso Sterpellone, "La politica estera della Repubblica Italiana," in IAI, *La politica estera*, II, 168-69.
13. Altiero Spinelli, *L'Europa non cade dal cielo* (Bologna, 1960), p. 22.

14. Norman Kogan, *A Political History of Postwar Italy* (New York, 1966), p. 29.
15. *Il Popolo*, September 3, 1947.
16. See many Italian books extolling the idea of Europe, especially Chabod, *Storia dell'idea d'Europa;* Guglielmo Rulli, *U.S.E.: Stati Uniti d'Europa?* (Naples, 1945); Carlo Curcio, *Europa: Storia di un'idea* (Florence, 1958).

CHAPTER 2

1. Luigi Salvatorelli, *La guerra fredda, 1945–1955* (Venice, 1956), pp. 126-27.
2. *Politica Estera*, April–May 1945, pp. 89-90; Ferruccio Parri *et al.*, *Europa Federata* (Milan, 1947), pp. 37, 41.
3. *Il Popolo*, July 20, 1947.
4. Giulio Andreotti, *De Gasperi e il suo tempo* (Milan, 1964), pp. 253-56.
5. Giuseppe Mammarella, *Italy after Fascism: A Political History, 1943–1963* (Montreal, 1964), pp. 147-48.
6. Italy, Comitato Italiano per la Ricostruzione, *Lo sviluppo dell' economia italiana nel quadro della ricostruzione e della cooperazione europea* (hereafter cited as CIR, *Lo sviluppo*), (Rome, 1952), pp. 3-8.
7. Ibid. p. 11.
8. Alberto Tarchiani, *Dieci anni tra Roma e Washington* (Verona, 1955), p. 334.
9. Costantino Bresciani Turroni, "Italy's Post-War Economy," *Review of Economic Conditions in Italy: Ten Years of Italian Economy, 1947–1956* (hereafter cited as *Ten Years of Italian Economy*), (Rome, 1957), p. 7.
10. Italy, Presidenza del Consiglio dei Ministri, Servizio delle Informazioni, *Documenti di vita italiana* (hereafter cited as *Documenti di vita italiana*), No. 1, p. 3.
11. Tarchiani, *Dieci anni*, pp. 20-21.
12. Adstans (Paolo Canali), *Alcide De Gasperi nella politica estera italiana* (Milan, 1953), pp. 33-34; James F. Byrnes, *Speaking Frankly* (New York, 1947), p. 141.
13. Adstans, *De Gasperi*, p. 96; Carlo Sforza, *Cinque anni a Palazzo Chigi: La politica estera italiana dal 1947 al 1951* (Rome, 1952), p. 18.
14. Tarchiani, *Dieci anni*, pp. 134ff.
15. Sforza, *Cinque anni*, p. 41.

16. Ibid. p. 43.
17. Minority report of Antonio Pesenti, cited in Luigi Graziano, *La politica estera italiana nel dopoguerra* (Padua, 1968), p. 97.
18. Leo Valiani, *L'avvento di De Gasperi* (Turin, 1949), pp. 149-50.
19. Sforza, *Cinque anni*, p. 51.
20. *Il Popolo*, August 15, 1947.
21. Sforza, *Cinque anni*, pp. 80-81.
22. Ibid. pp. 80-81, 91.
23. Francesco Coppola D'Anna, "L'unione doganale italo-francese," *Rivista di Politica Economica* (November 1948), 98-1008.
24. Sforza, *Cinque anni*, pp. 69-73.
25. Ibid. pp.73-80.
26. George Hildebrand, *Growth and Structure in the Economy of Modern Italy* (Cambridge, Mass., 1965), pp. 5-6.
27. CIR, *Lo sviluppo*, p. 15.
28. Tarchiani, *Dieci anni*, p. 334.
29. CIR, *Lo sviluppo*, pp. 75-126.
30. Ibid. pp. 318-23.
31. *Ten Years of Italian Economy*, p. 162.
32. CIR, *Lo sviluppo*, p. 272.
33. Spinelli, *L'Europa non cade dal cielo*, p. 33.
34. Sforza, *Cinque anni*, pp. 189-96.
35. Tarchiani, *Dieci anni*, pp. 143-44.
36. Text of memorandum in Graziano, *Politica estera*, pp. 106-10.
37. Salvatorelli, *Guerra fredda*, pp. 127-30.
38. Sforza, *Cinque anni*, p. 227.
39. *L'Année politique, 1949* (Paris, 1950), pp. 16-17.
40. Maria Romana Catti De Gasperi, *La nostra patria Europa: Il pensiero europeistico di Alcide De Gasperi* (Milan, 1969), pp. 15-16; Sforza, *Cinque anni*, pp. 91-105.
41. Italy, Camera dei Deputati, *Atti parlamentari: Discussioni* (hereafter cited as Camera, *Discussioni*), (Rome, 1949), July 13, 1949, p. 10,309.
42. Cf. speeches by Togliatti on Council of Europe in Camera, *Discussioni*, July 13, 1949, pp. 10,310-16, and on Atlantic Paçt, cited in Graziano, *Politica estera*, pp. 120-23.
43. Ibid. p. 115.
44. Spinelli, *L'Europa non cade dal cielo*, pp. 43, 55.

CHAPTER 3

1. Pierpaolo Luzzatto Fegiz, *Il volto sconsciuto dell'Italia* (Milan, 1956), pp. 785-89.

2. Council of Europe, Consultative Assembly, *Official Report of Debates* (Strasbourg, 1949–present), August 17, 1949, p. 161.
3. Council of Europe, *Debates*, December 11, 1951, pp. 1118-19.
4. Sforza, *Cinque anni*, pp. 80-81.
5. *L'Année politique, 1950*, pp. 306-7.
6. Sforza, *Cinque anni*, pp. 303-6, 316-19.
7. Paolo Emilio Taviani, *Il Piano Schuman* (Rome, 1953), pp. 9ff.
8. On the negotiations, see William Diebold, Jr., *The Schuman Plan: A Study in Economic Cooperation, 1950–1959* (New York, 1959), pp. 47-77. On consultations with the occupying powers, see F. Roy Willis, *France, Germany, and the New Europe, 1945–1967* (Stanford, 1968), pp. 114-20.
9. Louis Lister, *Europe's Coal and Steel Community: An Experiment in Economic Union* (New York, 1960), p. 65.
10. Taviani, *Piano Schuman*, pp. 90, 38.
11. Italy, Senato della Repubblica, *Resoconto stenografico*, March 1, 1952, pp. 31,641-49.
12. Giuseppe Pella, *La Comunità Europea del Carbone e dell' Acciaio: Risultati e prospettive* (Rome, 1954), p. 25. Every single politician I interviewed said without hesitation that the primary reason for accepting integration was political, and that they all expected harmful economic results.
13. Catti De Gasperi, *Patria Europa*, p. 29; Council of Europe, *Debates*, December 10, 1951, pp. 988-90.
14. Taviani, *Piano Schuman*, pp. 45-46.
15. European Coal and Steel Community, High Authority, *Second General Report on the Activities of the Community* (Luxembourg, 1954), pp. 81-94.
16. ECSC, High Authority, *Fifth General Report*, p. 212.
17. European Coal and Steel Community, High Authority, *C.E.C.A., 1952–1962: Résultats, limites, perspectives* (Luxembourg, 1963), pp. 440-44.
18. See Franco Peco, "L'espansione siderurgica in Italia," *Rivista di Politica Economica*, March 1960, p. 540.
19. ECSC, *C.E.C.A., 1952–1962*, p. 578. See European Coal and Steel Community, High Authority, *Etude sur la situation économique et de l'emploi des entreprises de l'industrie sidérurgique des provinces de Brescia et Udine* (Luxembourg, 1963); European Coal and Steel Community, High Authority, *Programmi di sviluppo e riconversione: Studio sulla zona di Piombino* (Luxembourg, 1963); European Coal and Steel Community, High Authority, *Programmi di sviluppo e riconversione: Studio regionale*

sull'Umbria. Prospettive dell'industria siderurgica in Umbria in relazione al piano regionale di sviluppo economico (Luxembourg, 1964); European Coal and Steel Community, High Authority, Studi regionali sull' occupazione: Liguria (Luxembourg, 1957).
20. ECSC, High Authority, C.E.C.A., 1952–1962, pp. 174, 309.
21. Sforza, Cinque anni, pp. 282, 286-87.
22. Catti De Gasperi, Patria Europa, p. 37.
23. Sforza, Cinque anni, p. 289.
24. Catti De Gasperi, Patria Europa, p. 47.
25. Paolo Emilio Taviani, "Breve storia del tentativo della CED," Civitas, May 1957, pp. 25-26.
26. Sforza, Cinque anni, p. 300.
27. Spinelli, L'Europa non cade dal cielo, p. 115. Interview with Ivan Matteo Lombardo.
28. Council of Europe, Debates, December 10, 1951, pp. 989-90.
29. Catti De Gasperi, Patria Europa, p. 60.
30. Andreotti, De Gasperi, p. 415.
31. Catti De Gasperi, Patria Europa, p. 66.
32. Ibid. pp. 89-91.
33. See L'Année politique, 1953, pp. 603-6 for text of agreements.
34. Catti De Gasperi, Patria Europa, pp. 142-43.
35. Europa Federata, September 1954, p. 218; Chroniques étrangères, Italie, September 10, 1954, p. 13.
36. Spinelli, L'Europa non cade dal cielo, p. 211.
37. Chroniques étrangères, Italie, September 10, 1954.
38. Anthony Eden, Full Circle: The Memoirs of Anthony Eden (Boston, 1960), p. 169.
39. Europa Federata, November–December 1954, p. 245.
40. See Giuliano Pajetta, in Camera, Discussioni, October 16, 1954, pp. 13,211-21; and Pietro Nenni, in Camera, Discussioni, October 18, 1954, pp. 13,269-72.
41. Il Popolo, September 29, 1954, cited Chroniques étrangères, Italie, November 10, 1954, p. 6.

CHAPTER 4

1. Il Popolo, August 4, 1957.
2. Cf. Paolo Rossi in ratification debate on WEU, in Camera, Discussioni, December 20, 1954, pp. 15,555-60.
3. Ibid. December 13, 1954, p. 15,001.
4. Text of Italian memorandum in L'Année politique, 1955, pp. 717-18.

5. See Roberto Ducci's introduction to Achille Albonetti, *Euratom e sviluppo nucleare* (Milan, 1958), p. 4.
6. Text of Messina resolution in *L'Année politique, 1955*, pp. 718-19.
7. *Gazzetta del Popolo*, June 26, 1955, cited in *Chroniques étrangères, Italie*, July 10, 1955, p. 8.
8. IAI, *La politica estera*, II, 499.
9. For text of Spaak Report, see Italy, Presidenza del Consiglio dei Ministri, Servizio Informazioni, *Comunità Economica Europea* (Rome, 1958), esp. pp. 49-65.
10. Camera, *Discussioni*, June 12, 1956, p. 25,821.
11. Ibid. p. 25,824.
12. Ibid. pp. 25,824-25.
13. Interview with Franco Bobba.
14. IAI, *La politica estera*, II, 500.
15. For Italian view of the Community institutions, see the report by Lodovico Montini, in Presidenza del Consiglio, *Comunità Economica Europea*, pp. 267-94.
16. A good short description is given in Michael Curtis, *Western European Integration* (New York, 1966), pp. 155-73.
17. Presidenza del Consiglio, *Comunità Economica Europea*, p. 294.
18. From the government report in parliamentary document No. 2814, reproduced in Ibid. p. 122.
19. Roberto Ducci, "Un mercato comune per l'Europa," *Civitas*, March 1957, p. 23.
20. Duties on these products were settled in intergovernmental negotiations in 1960. Leon N. Lindberg, *The Political Dynamics of European Economic Integration* (Stanford, 1963), pp. 210-16.
21. Interview with Franco Bobba; Curtis, *Western European Integration*, p. 175.
22. Ibid.
23. Ducci, in *Civitas*, March 1957, p. 22. Cf. speech by Colombo in Confederazione Nazionale Coltivatori Diretti, *L'agricoltura e il mercato comune europeo: Convegno di studi, Roma 23–25 gennaio 1958* (Rome, 1958), pp. 14-18.
24. From the important Relazione della Comissione Speciale, Camera document No. 2814A, reprinted in Presidenza del Consiglio, *Comunità Economica Europea*, p. 229.
25. Presidenza del Consiglio, *Comunità Economica Europea*, pp. 136-37.
26. Ugo Munzi, "The European Social Fund in the Development of the Mediterranean Regions of the EEC," *Journal of International Affairs*, 2 (1965), 288. Interview with Ugo Munzi.

27. Ducci, in Albonetti, *Euratom*, pp. 11-15. Interview with Achille Albonetti.
28. Presidenza del Consiglio, *Comunità Economic Europea*, p. 99.
29. Organisation for European Economic Co-operation, *Economic Conditions in Member and Associated Countries of the OEEC: Italy, 1961* (Paris, 1961), p. 29.
30. For figures on gross national product from 1861 to 1955, see Italy, Istituto Centrale di Statistica, *Sommario di statistiche storiche italiane, 1861-1955* (Rome, 1958), p. 210. For postwar period, see *Ten Years of Italian Economy*, p. 98. Industrial indices are given in Organisation for Economic Co-operation and Development, *Industrial Statistics, 1900-1962* (Paris, 1964), p. 4. Agricultural statistics are given in Organisation for Economic Co-operation and Development, *Agricultural and Food Statistics, 1952-1963* (Paris, 1965), p. 28.
31. Italy, Istituto Nazionale per il Commercio Estero, *I quaranta anni dell'ICE, 1926-65* (Rome, 1966), p. 91.
32. *Ten Years of Italian Economy*, p. 6.
33. Hildebrand, *Growth and Structure*, p. 5.
34. Almost all the politicians and businessmen I interviewed began with a glowing praise of the trade liberalization measures. But cf Chapter 11, on Confindustria.
35. Dow Votaw, *The Six-Legged Dog: Mattei and ENI—A Study in Power* (Berkeley, 1964), p. 143.
36. Walter Guzzardi, Jr., "Boom, Italian Style," *Fortune*, May 1968, p. 136.
37. Information supplied by Fiat company.
38. On IRI's views, see the useful summary of industrial opinion reported to the Comitato di studi sul mercato comune europeo, set up by the Milan Chamber of Commerce in 1954, reported in Giulio Bergmann et al., *Europa senza dogane: I produttori italiani hanno scelto l'Europa* (Bari, 1956), pp. 97-99. See also Livio Magnani, "L'Italia di fronte alla Comunità Economica Europea," *Bancaria*, August 14, 1957, pp. 750-53.
39. Article by vice-president of the artisans' federation, Manlio Germazzi, "L'artigianato e il Mercato Comune Europeo," *Rivista di Politica Economica*, March 1958, pp. 240-46; Giuseppe Vedovato, *Mercato Comune Europeo e esportazione artigiana* (Florence, 1963), esp. pp. 86-110; and, for left-wing viewpoint, Giorgio Coppa and Valentino Parlato, "L'artigianato e la piccola industria di fronte al mercato comune," *Politica ed Economia*, July 1958, pp. 17-21.

40. See fine speech by Confagricoltura president Alfonso Gaetani, *L'Italia agricola e il mercato comune europeo* (Rome, 1959).
41. Texts in Presidenza del Consiglio, *Comunità Economica Europea,* pp. 203-58, 295-334, and Chamber Document No. 2814A.
42. IAI, *La politica estera,* II, 502.
43. See speech by Lombardi, in Camera, *Discussioni,* July 22, 1957, pp. 34,225-31, which contains the dispute with Gian-Carlo Pajetta, the first time a Communist had openly criticized a Socialist in the Chamber.
44. Ibid. July 23, 1957, pp. 34,318-27.
45. Ibid. July 30, 1957, pp. 34,783.
46. Ibid. pp. 34,796.
47. Presidenza del Consiglio, *Comunità Economica Europea,* pp. 471-91. On DC's attitude, see articles in *Il Popolo,* August 4, 1957, by principal party spokesmen, including Fanfani, Zoli, Folchi, Piccioni, Pella and Montini.

CHAPTER 5

1. United States, Department of State, Director of Intelligence and Research, *Research Memorandum,* REU-27, REU-41, 1969.
2. European Communities, Statistical Office, *Basic Statistics for Fifteen European Countries* (Brussels, 1962), pp. 90-94.
3. European Economic Community, Commission, *Third General Report on the Activities of the Community* (Brussels, 1960), pp. 238-39; Lindberg, *Political Dynamics,* pp. 215-16.
4. *Comunità Europee,* June 1968, p. xii.
5. Fiat, *Relazioni,* 1956, p. 7; Fiat, *Annual Report, 1968,* p. 12.
6. See articles on Valletta, in *L'Industria Lombarda,* May 1, 1954; *Corriere d'Informazione,* March 14-15, 1956; and *Epoca,* April 15, 1962; May 8, 1966. Description of Fiat's investment program in Ronald Taggiasco, "Italians posed for the tariff-free fight," *International Management,* March 1968.
7. EEC, *Sixth General Report,* p. 45; *Seventh General Report,* p. 44; *Corriere della Sera,* July 18, 1963.
8. *Il Messaggero,* April 13, 1969; *Il Sole 24 Ore,* April 18, 1969.
9. Arrigo Levi, *L'Italia e il Mercato Comune oggi e domani* (Rome, 1966), p. 15.
10. Centro Internazionale di Studi e Documentazione sulle Comunità Europee, "Prospettive dell'artigianato in Italia nel prossimo decennio in rapporto all'integrazione europea," *Incontri di Tribuna Economica* (Milan, 1963), pp. 2-3.

11. Finmeccanica, 20° *Esercizio, 1967–68* (Rome, 1968), p. 41. EEC had pushed these sectors to a much needed reorganization, but the results were still far from satisfactory. See *Corriere della Sera,* October 17, 1964.
12. OECD, *Economic Surveys, Italy,* March 1965, pp. 7, 13; March 1966, pp. 5-6.
13. Centro Italiano di Ricerche e Documentazione, *Annuario politico italiano, 1965* (Milan, 1965), p. 957.
14. Cf also Italy, Senato, IV Legislatura, "Relazione sulla Comunità Economica Europea e sulla Comunità Europea dell'Energia Atomica (1958–1965)," *Disegni di legge e relazioni-documenti,* (hereafter cited as Senato, *Relazione sulla Cee*), No. 92, December 29, 1965.
15. OECD, *Economic Surveys, Italy,* March 1966, p. 8.
16. Mario Bandini, "Parità di concorrenza, progressiva riconversione," *Il Globo,* December 31, 1959. Italy, Ministero dell'Agricoltura e delle Foreste, *Piano quinquennale di sviluppo dell'agricoltura: Relazione al parlamento sul primo periodo di attuazione (fino al 30 giugno 1962)* (Rome, 1962), esp. pp. 55-61.
17. *Il Popolo,* December 22, 1960.
18. IAI, *La politica estera,* II, 525-26.
19. See Colombo's views on integration in Istituto per l'Economia Europea, *L'integrazione economica europea all'inizio della seconda tappa* (Rome, 1962), pp. 3-15.
20. Paolo Albertario, "L'agricoltura italiana nella Comunità Economica Europea," in Istituto per l'Economia Europea, *L'integrazione,* pp. 139-41.
21. *Il Popolo,* January 15, 1962.
22. *Il Messaggero,* January 15, 1962.
23. IAI, *La politica estera,* II, 526.
24. Romualdo Moroni, "La regolamentazione comunitaria per le carni," *Agricoltura,* November 1964, pp. 53-68.
25. Senato, *Relazione sulla Cee,* p. 48.
26. *Il Popolo,* December 23, 1963; EEC, *Seventh General Report,* p. 181.
27. *Corriere della Sera,* September 1, 1964; *Mondo Agricolo,* December 22-29, 1963.
28. *Il Popolo,* December 15, 1964.
29. EEC, *Eighth General Report,* p. 179.
30. *La Bonifica Integrale,* December 1964, pp. 365-69; *Il Popolo,* December 9, 1964; December 17, 1964.
31. *Mondo Agricolo,* December 27, 1964.

32. John Newhouse, *Collision in Brussels: The Common Market Crisis of 30 June 1965* (New York, 1967), pp. 69-71, 108-22; Miriam Camps, *European Unification in the Sixties: From the Veto to the Crisis* (New York, 1966), pp. 61-69; Fanfani's report to the Foreign Affairs Commission in *Il Popolo*, July 22, 1965.
33. Gian Paolo Casadio, *Una politica agricola per l'Europa* (Bologna, 1967), pp. 55-64.
34. Press conference of September 9, 1965, in *L'Année politique, 1965*, p. 438.
35. See Bonomi's remarks in Confederazione Nazionale Coltivatori Diretti, *Documenti di politica agraria, 1961–1966* (Rome, 1967), pp. 203-204; and Gaetani's, in *Mondo Agricolo*, July 11, 1965.
36. *Il Popolo*, October 24, 1965; October 26, 1965; October 27, 1965; October 28, 1965.
37. At this point, a surprising, bitter quarrel erupted over Community preference for Italian oranges, which all Italy's partners considered to be too high and to be keeping out imports of Spanish and North African oranges. In the Comité de Gestion des Fruits et Légumes, the French voted with Germany and the Benelux delegates against the Italians, who were the only nation supporting the higher reference price chosen by the Commission. The Commission refused to change the price, however, unless the decision was overturned by a unanimous vote of the Council of Ministers. *L'Année politique, 1966*, pp. 318-19.
38. *Mondo Agricolo*, February 6, 1966; *Il Popolo*, January 29, 1966.
39. *Mondo Agricolo*, April 3, 1966.
40. Casadio, *Una politica agricola*, p. 87.
41. *Il Popolo*, July 25, 1966; *Corriere della Sera*, July 28, 1966; EEC, *Tenth General Report*, pp. 202-5.
42. *Mondo Agricolo*, October 12, 1969.
43. Munzi, "European Social Fund," *Journal of International Affairs*, 2 (1965), 287.
44. SVIMEZ—Associazione per lo sviluppo dell'industria nel Mezzogiorno, *Le migrazioni-interne nel periodo 1952–1966* (Rome, 1968), p. 4.
45. *European Community*, July 1969, p. 12.
46. Pasquale Saraceno, *La politica di sviluppo di un'area sottosviluppata nell'esperienza italiana* (Milan, 1968), p. 748.
47. Ibid. p. 752.
48. Felice Ippolito, "Dopo il fallimento dell'Euratom," *Nord e Sud*, August–September 1969, p. 32.
49. Italy, Presidenza del Consiglio dei Ministri, *L'Italia e l'integrazione europea* (Rome, 1964), p. 94.

50. Senato, *Relazione sulla CEE*, p. 130.
51. See Felice Ippolito, "La crisi dell'Euratom," *Nord e Sud*, January 1969, pp. 25-35; Franco Maria Malfatti, "L'Italia e l'Euratom," *Mondo Economico*, May 1, 1965, pp. 25-28.
52. Republished as "L'Italia e l'Euratom," *Notiziario del C.N.E.N.*, 2 (1967), 100-109; see also Altiero Spinelli, *Rapporto sull'Europa* (Milan, 1965), pp. 39-50.
53. IAI, *La politica estera*, II, 508.
54. Attilio Cattani, *L'Essai di coopération politique entre les Six de 1960–1962 et l'échec de la négociation sur un Statut politique* (Brussels, 1967; mimeographed). Interview with Attilio Cattani.
55. European Parliament, Political Committee, *Towards Political Union* (Brussels, 1964), p. 7.
56. Cattani, *L'Essai*, p. 5.
57. European Parliament, Direction Générale de la Documentation Parlementaire et de l'Information, *L'Université européenne: Recueil de documents* (Brussels, 1967).
58. *Stampa e Documentazione*, April 1962.
59. Ibid. May 1962.
60. Ugo La Malfa, "La linea di resistenza democratica," in Altiero Spinelli et al., *Che fare per l'Europa?* (Milan, 1963), pp. 149-62.
61. *Il Popolo*, February 1, 1963; February 4, 1963.
62. See the debates in the Chamber in Camera, *Discussioni*, October 19, 1965, pp. 18,188-228, and in the Senate in Senato, *Resoconto stenografico*, April 27, 1966, pp. 22,378-409; April 28, 1966, pp. 22,423-57.
63. *Il Messaggero*, May 17, 1967.
64. *L'Osservatore Romano*, June 1, 1967.
65. The Italian representation to the European Parliament named in January 1969 was made up as follows: PCI, 7; PSIUP, 1; Independent Left, 1; PSI, 6; PRI, 1; DC, 15; PLI, 2; PDIUM, 1; MSI, 1; Mixed, 1.
66. IAI, *La politica estera*, I, 68.

CHAPTER 6

1. *Documenti di vita italiana*, No. 12, pp. 809-12; No. 131, pp. 10,265-68; No. 18, pp. 1,397-98.
2. Ibid. No. 44, pp. 3,487-88; Banco di Roma, *Review of the Economic Conditions in Italy*, November 1957, pp. 506-8; Ernesto Massi, *I fondamenti dell'integrazione economica europea: Il mer-*

cato comune del carbone e dell'acciaio (Milan, 1959), pp. 37-40.
3. Ibid. pp. 66-71.
4. On Italy's supremacy in marble, see *Documenti di vita italiana*, No. 81, pp. 6,449-50; No. 95, pp. 7,553-54; and Italy, Presidenza del Consiglio dei Ministri, *Vita italiana: Documenti e Informazioni* (Rome, 1964), No. 12, 1964, pp. 1,041-44.
5. Unione Italiana delle Camere di Commercio Industria e Agricoltura, *Compendio economico italiano, 1961* (Rome, 1961), p. 76; Banca d'Italia, *Relazione annuale 1951* (Rome, 1952), p. 12.
6. Margaret Carlyle, *Modern Italy* (London, 1957), p. 106.
7. Piero Ferrerio, "Situation and Problems of the Italian Power Industry," *Review of the Economic Conditions in Italy*, November 1955, pp. 523-32.
8. *Compendio economico italiano, 1961*, p. 72; Ibid. *1965*, p. 64.
9. Enrico Mattei, "Ente Nazionale Idrocarburi," *Review of the Economic Conditions in Italy*, May 1960, pp. 243-61; *Documenti di vita italiana*, No. 3, pp. 219-24; No. 51, pp. 4,045-48; and Alfredo Giarratana, "Natural Gases in Italy," *Review of the Economic Conditions in Italy*, September 1956, pp. 440-55.
10. *Compendio economico italiano, 1961*, p. 60.
11. Shepard B. Clough, *The Economic History of Modern Italy* (New York, 1964), p. 60.
12. Glauco Della Porta, "Origins, Evolution, Structure and Prospects of 'Finsider'," *Review of the Economic Conditions in Italy*, November 1955, pp. 553-65; Ernesto Manuelli, "Situation and Prospects of the Italian Steel Industry," *Review of the Economic Conditions in Italy*, November 1958, pp. 567-79.
13. *Documenti di vita italiana*, No. 30, pp. 2,361-68.
14. ECSC, *Fifth General Report*, Annexes, pp. 42-43; *Ninth General Report*, pp. 444-45; *Eleventh General Report*, pp. 642-43; *Fifteenth General Report*, pp. 424-25.
15. Germany's Thomas steel, which usually cost at least 10 per cent less than Siemens-Martin steel, was higher priced than Italian Siemens-Martin steel in 1967.
16. Clough, *Economic History*, p. 89; Italy, Comitato Italiano per la Ricostruzione, *Politica di sviluppo: Cinque anni di lavoro* (Rome, 1958), p. 191.
17. ICE, *Quaranta anni*, p. 95.
18. Franco Garino, "L'industria italiana e la CEE," *Comunità*, February 1966, p. 59.
19. *Documenti di vita italiana*, No. 112, pp. 8,875-80; No. 143, pp. 11,245-48.
20. *Ten Years of Italian Economy*, p. 82.

21. *Documenti di vita italiana*, No. 112, p. 8,878; Rodolfo Biscaretti di Ruffia, "Situation of the Italian Motor Industry in the Middle of 1965," *Review of the Economic Conditions in Italy*, September 1965, pp. 363-73.
22. *Documenti di vita italiana*, No. 35, pp. 2,767-68; No. 38, pp. 3,023-26.
23. Italy, Istituto Centrale di Statistica, *Bollettino mensile di statistica*, January 1967, p. 30.
24. *Vita italiana*, No. 7, 1966, p. 25.
25. Ibid. No. 12, 1964, pp. 1,029-33; No. 7, 1966, pp. 543-46.
26. *Documenti di vita italiana*, No. 78, pp. 6,223-28; CIR, *Politica di sviluppo*, pp. 301-2.
27. Ibid. pp. 284-86; *Documenti di vita italiana*, No. 134, p. 10, 527; No. 139, pp. 10,997-11,000.
28. G. B. Aldo Trespidi, *Realtà e prospettive dell'industria chimica in Italia* (Rome, 1967), p. 28.
29. OECD, *Industrial Statistics, 1900–1962*, p. 254.
30. *Documenti di vita italiana*, No. 69, p. 5,473; CIR, *Lo sviluppo*, pp. 174-76; *Ten Years of the Italian Economy*, pp. 76, 84-85.
31. OECD, *Industrial Statistics, 1900–1962*, p. 158.
32. Ibid. pp. 155, 139, 165. See Giovanni Balella, "The Man-Made Fibres Situation," *Review of the Economic Conditions in Italy*, November 1966, pp. 433-46.
33. *Fortune*, August 15, 1969, p. 107.
34. Clough, *Economic History*, 57ff; Donald S. Walker, *A Geography of Italy* (London, 1958), pp. 238-40; Carlyle, *Modern Italy*, pp. 110-12.
35. *Ten Years of the Italian Economy*, pp. 160-61.
36. Vera Lutz, *Italy: A Study in Economic Development* (London, 1962), pp. 84-85.
37. See CIR, *Politica di sviluppo*, pp. 196-97, on flax; and p. 197, on jute. On silk, see *Documenti di vita italiana*, No. 27, pp. 2,145-46; No. 92, pp. 7,321-22; No. 144, pp. 11,331-34.
38. *Vita italiana*, No. 7, 1966, pp. 535-36.
39. OECD, *Industrial Statistics, 1900–1962*, pp. 128-29, 131.
40. *Review of the Economic Conditions in Italy*, November 1966, pp. 445.
41. *Fortune*, May 1968, pp. 136-45, 236-38, 241-47.
42. OECD, *Industrial Statistics, 1900–1962*, pp. 166-67.
43. CIR, *Politica di sviluppo*, pp. 353-54; CIR, *Lo sviluppo*, p. 260.
44. Ibid. p. 262.
45. European Communities, Statistical Office, *Statistiques de base de la Communauté* (Luxembourg, 1966), p. 147.

CHAPTER 7

1. Lutz, *Italy*, p. 167; *Ten Years of the Italian Economy*, p. 33.
2. Clough, *Economic History*, p. 100.
3. Map prepared by the Istituto Nazionale di Economia Agraria, reproduced in Lutz, *Italy*, p. 160.
4. Lutz, *Italy*, p. 161.
5. Ibid. p. 162.
6. Mario Bandini, "Present Situation of Italian Agriculture," *Review of the Economic Conditions in Italy*, September 1962, pp. 385-86.
7. European Economic Community, Commission, *Documents de la conférence sur les économies régionales* (Brussels, 1963), II, 132-35.
8. Lutz, *Italy*, p. 167.
9. Clough, *Economic History*, p. 100.
10. Carlo Levi, *Cristo si è fermato a Eboli* (Turin, 1945), or, in English, *Christ Stopped at Eboli* (New York, 1947).
11. EEC, *Conférence sur les économies régionales*, II, 126-29.
12. Walker, *Geography of Italy*, pp. 132-39.
13. Organisation for Economic Co-operation and Development, *Regional Rural Development Programmes with Special Emphasis on Depressed Agricultural Areas Including Mountain Regions* (Paris, 1964), p. 242.
14. *Ten years of Italian Economy*, pp. 41-43; *Politica di sviluppo*, pp. 116-17.
15. These classifications were developed by Luigi Cavazzi, in his report to the 22nd Congresso Nazionale della Bonifica in 1965. See Riccardo Argenziano *et al.*, *Bonifica Mezzogiorno ed Europa* (Quaderni di Civiltà degli Scambi; Bari, 1965), pp. 117-33.
16. Italy, Presidency of the Council of Ministers, Information Service, *Italy Today* (Rome, 1962), pp. 155-67.
17. *Ten Years of Italian Economy*, p. 53.
18. Lutz, *Italy*, p. 175.
19. *Ten Years of Italian Economy*, p. 53; ISTAT, *Bollettino mensile*, January 1967, p. 20.
20. For a short summary of the treatment of rye, barley, and oats compared with wheat, and for the development of their use as fodder crops, see European Communities, Information Bureau, Paris, *La Politique agricole commune* (Paris, 1967), pp. 30-34.
21. CIR, *Politica di sviluppo*, pp. 135-36.
22. *Vita italiana*, No. 11, 1964, pp. 914-17.

23. Ibid. No. 11-12, 1965, pp. 947-53.
24. Lutz, *Italy*, pp. 173-75, 180-82; CIR, *Politica di sviluppo*, pp. 137-38; *Ten Years of Italian Economy*, pp. 57-58.
25. *Agricoltura*, October 1964, p. 43; OECD, *Agricultural Statistics, 1952–63*, pp. 235-37.
26. Ibid. pp. 116-18.
27. CIR, *Politica di sviluppo*, p. 138; *Prospettive meridionali*, March–April–May 1959, p. 45.
28. Italy, Istituto Centrale di Statistica, *Compendio statistico italiano, 1956* (Rome, 1956), p. 130; ISTAT, *Bollettino mensile*, January 1967, p. 20.
29. Alessandro Silj, *L'agricoltura italiana nella Comunità Economica Europea: Il ruolo dell'agricoltura in un processo di sviluppo economico* (Milan, 1961), p. 144.
30. Ibid. pp. 144–49. Manlio Rossi-Doria, *Dieci anni di politica agraria nel Mezzogiorno* (Bari, 1958), pp. 25-44.
31. *Review of the Economic Conditions in Italy*, September 1962, p. 379.
32. *Vita italiana*, No. 7-8, 1965, pp. 661-65.
33. Confederazione Nazionale Coltivatori Diretti, *Statistiche agrarie 1961–1966* (Rome, 1967), p. 169.
34. *Vita italiana*, No. 1, 1966, p. 32; *Documenti di vita italiana*, No. 131, p. 10,274.
35. Ibid. pp. 10,276-77.
36. The Institute for Foreign Commerce spent large sums abroad to advertise Italian citrus fruits and, through its offices abroad, maintained a detailed information service on the citrus market. *Vita italiana*, No. 1, 1966, pp. 33-35, gives a strong indictment of the citrus exporters.
37. Ibid. No. 9, 1966, pp. 713-14.
38. *Documenti di vita italiana*, No. 128-29, pp. 10,091-102.
39. Franco Tradari, "L'ortofrutticoltura italiana e il Trattato di Roma," *Prospettive meridionali*, March–April–May 1959, pp. 26-40.
40. *Ten Years of Italian Economy*, pp. 59-60; EEC, *Statistiques de base, 1966*, p. 144.
41. *Mondo Agricolo*, November 6, 1966; Confederazione Nazionale Coltivatori Diretti, *XIX Congresso Nazionale: Relazione del Presidente Paolo Bonomi, 1965* (Rome, 1965), III, 70-77.
42. *Documenti di vita italiana*, No. 3, p. 233; No. 130, p. 10,213.
43. *Ten Years of Italian Economy*, p. 60.
44. Italo Cosmo, "La regolamentazione comunitaria per i viti-vinicoli," *Agricoltura*, November 1964, pp. 99-102.

45. Coltivatori Diretti, *Relazione del Presidente*, 1958, I, 90; Coltivatori Diretti, *Statistiche agrarie, 1961–1966*, II, 138.
46. CIR, *Politica di sviluppo*, pp. 139-40.
47. *Vita italiana*, No. 5, 1965, p. 467.
48. Coltivatori Diretti, *Relazione del Presidente*, 1958, I, 90-92; 1965, III, 52-60.
49. Ibid. *1958*, p. 93.
50. *Bonifica, Europa e Mezzogiorno*, pp. 113-15; *Mondo Agricolo*, April 2, 1967.
51. Confederazione Nazionale Coltivatori Diretti, *Mondo rurale e agricoltura: Convegno nazionale di studio su "Programma di sviluppo economico e Comunità Europea"* (Rome, 1967), pp. 115-16.
52. *Compendio economico italiano, 1961*, p. 55.
53. Silj, *L'agricoltura italiana*, p. 123.
54. *Compendio economico italiano, 1961*, p. 57.
55. *Comunità Europee*, January 1969, p. III.
56. Silj, *L'agricoltura italiana*, pp. 128-29.
57. Coltivatori Diretti, *Relazione del Presidente*, 1957, I, 79-80.
58. Ibid. I, 79-84; *1965*, I, 109-121.
59. Coltivatori Diretti, *Statistiche agrarie, 1961–1966*, pp. 44-46.
60. Coltivatori Diretti, *Mondo rurale*, p. 120.
61. *Compendio economico italiano, 1961*, p. 33; ISTAT, *Bollettino mensile*, April 1961, p. 105; Ibid. April 1969, p. 105.
62. *Review of the Economic Conditions in Italy*, September 1962, pp. 385-87.
63. Lutz, *Italy*, p. 157.
64. Kogan, *Political History*, p. 203.
65. CIR, *Politica di sviluppo*, pp. 144-46. For left-wing opinions on mezzadria, see the report of CGIL President Agostino Novella in Confederazione Generale Italiana del Lavoro, *I congressi della CGIL* (Rome, 1949–present), VII, 28; for the PSI, see Partito Socialista Italiano, *Conferenza agraria nazionale: Atti e resoconto* (Milan, 1958), pp. 143-76.
66. Organisation for Economic Co-operation and Development, *The Position of the Agricultural Hired Worker* (Paris, 1962), p. 78.
67. Danilo Dolci, *Inchiesta a Palermo* (Turin, 1956), published in English as *Poverty in Sicily* (Harmondsworth, England, 1966).
68. OECD, *Hired Worker*, p. 78; European Economic Community, *Etudes: L'Emploi agricole dans les pays de la CEE* (Brussels, 1964), I, 47-50; II, 20.
69. OECD, *Hired Worker*, p. 74.

70. Coltivatori Diretti, *Relazione del Presidente*, 1958, II, 120; 1969, II, 196.
71. Coltivatori Diretti, *Relazione del Presidente*, 1969, II, 206-23.
72. Cf. Gaetani, who suggested in 1969 that "special interests" in EEC countries were blocking Community preference in favor of Italy. *Mondo Agricolo*, March 23, 1969.
73. In 1967, the Community produced 88 million quintals of cereals more than in 1966, an unwanted increase of almost 15 per cent. Production of soft wheat rose 46 million quintals, and hard wheat 9 million. Coltivatori Diretti, *Relazione del Presidente*, 1968, III, 73-76.
74. Ibid. III, 81. See Vincenzo Visocchi, "La politica agricola della Comunità Europea," in Coltivatori Diretti, *Mondo rurale*, pp. 208-9.
75. *Mondo Agricolo*, October 5, 1969.
76. Coltivatori Diretti, *Relazione del Presidente*, 1968, III, 174.
77. Ibid. *1969*, II, 178.
78. In 1966–67, an epidemic of African pig plague wiped out 100,000 pigs, forcing the isolation of the Italian market. Enormous antiparasitic measures were taken. Ibid. *1968*, III, 177.
79. Ibid. III, 142-46.
80. *Mondo Agricolo*, October 5, 1969.
81. Ibid.
82. *Comunità Europee*, April 1968, p. 10.
83. See the preliminary study, European Economic Community, Commission, Direction Générale de l'Agriculture, A. De Leeuw and P. Vicinelli, *Certains aspects de l'amélioration des structures agraires en Italie* (Brussels, 1963).
84. *Comunità Europee*, April 1968, p. 10.
85. Casadio, *Una politica agricola*, pp. 217-23; European Economic Community, Spokesman's Bureau, *Note d'information: Programmes communautaires pour la section orientation du FEOGA* (Brussels, June 1967), described the ten programs laid down as basis for future action.
86. European Communities, *Journal officiel des Communautés Européennes: Communications et informations*, March 15, 1968, pp. 1-17; October 16, 1965, pp. 2,701-704; July 25, 1966, pp. 2,556-60; August 4, 1967, pp. 9-18.
87. *Mondo Agricolo*, October 12, 1969; *Comunità Europee*, January 1969, pp. I-XII.
88. *Mondo Agricolo*, April 27, 1969.
89. ISTAT, *Compendio statistico italiano*, 1967, p. 315; 1968, p. 263.
90. Coltivatori Diretti, *Relazione del Presidente*, 1958, II, 17; 1969, II, 55.

CHAPTER 8

1. Hildebrand, *Growth and Structure*, pp. 107-9.
2. *Ten Years of Italian Economy*, p. 24.
3. Italy, Comitato dei Ministri per il Mezzogiorno, *Studi monografici sul Mezzogiorno* (Rome, 1966), pp. 70, 73. In 1965, the death rate in the South was 8.6 per thousand, compared with 10.5 in the North, but the death rate of infants in their first year of life was 45.0 in the South compared with 28.2 in the North.
4. *Documenti di vita italiana*, No. 3, pp. 227-30.
5. For full report, see Italy, Camera dei Deputati, Commissione parlamentare di inchiesta sulla disoccupazione, *La disoccupozione in Italia* (Rome, 1954); and Italy, Camera dei Deputati, *Atti della commissione parlamentare di inchiesta sulla miseria in Italia e sui mezzi per combatterla* (Rome, 1953).
6. Ezio Vanoni, "Development of Employment and Income in Italy," *Review of the Economic Conditions in Italy*, July 1955, p. 315.
7. Presidenza del Consiglio, *Comunità Economica Europea*, p. 235.
8. Vittorio Badini Confalonieri, *La Comunità Economica Europea* (Rome, 1957), p. 23.
9. Presidenza del Consiglio, *Comunità Economica Europea*, pp. 482-83; Confederazione Italiana Sindacati Lavoratori, *La politica sociale della Comunità Economica Europea: Atti del terzo convegno di studi di economia e politica del lavoro* (Rome, 1959), pp. 70-71.
10. Hildebrand, *Growth and Structure*, pp. 185-88.
11. Lutz, *Italy*, p. 63-75.
12. In 1958-62, 721,728 emigrated, and 398,571 returned.
13. ISTAT, *Statistiche storiche*, p. 65; *Vita italiana*, No. 9, 1966, p. 710.
14. *Documenti di vita italiana*, No. 45, pp. 3,517-28; No. 70, pp. 5,533-44; No. 82, pp. 6,491-502; No. 120-21, pp. 9,501-10; No. 123, pp. 9,661-66; *Vita italiana*, No. 7-8, 1965, pp. 615-20; No. 9, 1966, pp. 705-12. On Southern migration, see Comitato dei Ministri per il Mezzogiorno, *Studi monografici*, pp. 81-91.
15. For regulations, see EEC, *Journal officiel*, August 26, 1961, Reg. No. 15, plus directives; and *Journal officiel*, April 4, 1964, Reg. 38-64. For comment, see Senato, *Relazione sulla CEE*, pp. 13-15. Interview with Angelino Macchia.
16. Interview with Leo Crijns. On free movement of labor in EEC, see the annual reports of European Community, Commission, *La*

libera circolazione della manodopera e i mercati del lavoro nella CEE (Brussels, 1966–present) which give the areas and professions where free movement was not permitted, or where there was Community priority in employment. On the social security of migrant workers, see European Economic Community, Commission administrative pour la sécurité sociale des travailleurs migrants, *Sixième et septième rapports annuels sur la mise en oeuvre des règlements concernant la sécurité sociale des travailleurs migrants* (Brussels, 1967).

17. Mario Di Leo, "L'emigrazione meridionale nelle regioni del Centro-Nord dal 1955 al 1959," *Realtà del Mezzogiorno,* April 1963, pp. 424-36.
18. Francesco Compagna, *L'Europa delle regioni* (Naples, 1964), pp. 162-63.

CHAPTER 9

1. Francesco Compagna, *Mezzogiorno d'Europa* (Rome, 1958), p. 84, cited Sergio Barzanti, *The Underdeveloped Areas within the Common Market* (Princeton, 1965), p. 40.
2. Clough, *Economic History,* pp. 11-27.
3. On effects on South of government policy after 1861, see Alberto Benzoni, "Il Mezzogiorno nello stato italiano," in Achille Parisi and Goffredo Zappa (eds.), *Mezzogiorno e politica di piano* (Bari, 1964), pp. 5-34.
4. Note the collection by a High Authority member, Enzo Giacchero, of a series of opinions in favor of integration of Italy itself by leading Italians, *Il Mezzogiorno nel mercato italiano: Raccolta di testimonianze* (Luxembourg, 1957).
5. Pasquale Saraceno, *La mancata unificazione economica italiana a cento anni dall'unificazione politica* (Milan, 1968).
6. Rodanò, *Mezzogiorno,* p. 292.
7. Cited by P. Giani, "Recent Italian Works on Theories of Economic Development," *Banca Nazionale del Lavoro Quarterly Review,* March 1960, p. 79.
8. Ibid. p. 80.
9. Friedrich Vöchting, *Die italienische Südfrage: Entstehung und Problematik eines wirtschaftschaftlichen Notstandsgebietes* (Berlin, 1951).
10. See criticisms of Vöchting in Rodanò, *Mezzogiorno,* pp. 345-51.
11. *Banca Nazionale del Lavoro Quarterly Review,* March 1960, p. 81.

12. See Di Nardi's article, "Precettistica intuitiva," and Vito's Introduction to Francesco Vito et al., *Problemi di sviluppo economico con particolare riguardo alle aree arretrate* (Milan, 1956).
13. Lutz, *Italy*, p. 132.
14. CIR, *Politica di sviluppo*, p. 17.
15. Lutz cites the Di Fenizio model for Italian development, "I fattori essenziali dello sviluppo economico," presented to the eighth study conference of Confindustria on Problems of Industrial Economics and Policy, in *Rivista di Politica Economica*, October–November 1956, pp. 838-63.
16. Lutz, *Italy*, p. 299; SVIMEZ, *Effetti economici di un programma di investimenti nel Mezzogiorno* (Rome, 1951).
17. See Mario Bandini's justification of the reform, including its economic return, in "Six Years of Italian Land Reform," *Banca Nazionale del Lavoro Quarterly Review*, June 1957, pp. 169-213.
18. Gabriele Pescatore, *L'intervento straordinario nel Mezzogiorno d'Italia* (Milan, 1962), p. 5.
19. See Professor Glauco Della Porta's contribution in EEC, *Conférence sur les économies regionales*, I, 414.
20. CIR, *Politica di sviluppo*, pp. 46-47. See also Giuseppe Di Nardi, "Italy's Development Policy," *Ten Years of Italian Economy*, pp. 123-27.
21. Hildebrand, *Growth and Structure*, pp. 67-68, 70.
22. *Review of the Economic Conditions in Italy*, November 1964, p. 417. This whole issue is devoted to the Southern question during the debate on the new law for the Cassa.
23. *Ten Years of Italian Economy*, p. 125.
24. Ibid. p. 126.
25. See Pescatore's two reports in European Economic Community, Commission, *Rapports de groupes d'experts sur la politique régionale dans la Communauté Economique Européenne* (Brussels, 1964), pp. 109-17, and EEC, *Conférence sur les économies régionales*, I, 379-98.
26. Italy, Comitato dei Ministri per il Mezzogiorno, *Relazione sulla attività di coordinamento* (Rome, 1966), pp. 7-8.
27. *Review of the Economic Conditions in Italy*, November 1964, p. 426.
28. Ibid. p. 434; Confindustria, *Annuario*, 1966, pp. 280-88. Southern per capita income *had* increased by 4.65 per cent annually, compared with 5.65 per cent in the Center-North, and industry accounted for 33.2 per cent of income in 1951, compared with 28.3 per cent in 1951. According to Confindustria, it called the gov-

ernment's attention to the fact that the Cassa began to run out of funds in 1963, just when private industry was getting interested in investing in the South.
29. Vera Lutz, "Italy as a Study in Development," *Lloyd's Bank Review*, October 1960, pp. 31-45, and "Some Structural Aspects of the Southern Problem: The Complementarity of 'Emigration' and Industrialization," *Banca Nazionale del Lavoro Quarterly Review*, December 1961, pp. 367-402. Gardner Ackley and Luigi Spaventa replied in "Emigration and Industrialization in Southern Italy: A Comment," *Banca Nazionale del Lavoro Quarterly Review*, June 1962, pp. 196-204.
30. *Review of the Economic Conditions in Italy*, November 1964, pp. 416-17.
31. Comitato dei Ministri per il Mezzogiorno, *Relazione, 1966*, pp. 19-27, 49-61, 69-118, 141-47.
32. Ibid. p. 119.
33. Finsider, *Esercizio, 1966*, pp. 20-21; IRI, *Esercizio, 1965*, pp. 114-15.
34. EEC, *Conférence sur les économies régionales*, II, 146-47; European Economic Community, *Studio per la creazione di un polo industriale in Italia meridionale* (Brussels, 1966), I, 9-10.
35. EEC, *Conférence sur les économies régionales*, II, 135-38.
36. On economic development of Syracuse, see Eugenio Peggio, Mario Mazzarino, and Valentino Parlato, *Industrializzazione e sottosviluppo: Il progresso tecnologico in una provincia del Mezzogiorno* (Turin, 1960).
37. *Review of the Economic Conditions in Italy*, May 1960, pp. 254-55.
38. Alfonso Falzari, "Caratteristiche e prospettive dell'area di sviluppo industriale di Cagliari," *Sardegna Economica*, October 1963, pp. 573-95; Oscar Puddu, "L'area di sviluppo industriale di Cagliari, prime realizzazioni e prospettive," *Sardegna Economica*, January, February 1967, pp. 691-94.
39. Comitato dei Ministri per il Mezzogiorno, *Relazione, 1966*, pp. 193-52; Ibid. *1967*, pp. 159-83. The report of the Sardinian experts was: Sardinia, Commissione Economica di Studio per il Piano di Rinascita della Sardegna, *Rapporto conclusivo sugli studi per il Piano di Rinascita* (Cagliari, 1959). The plan for 1965–69 is published as: Sardinia, Regione Autonoma della Sardegna, *Piano di rinascita economica e sociale della Sardegna, piano quinquennale, 1965–1969* (Cagliari, 1966).
40. EEC, *Tenth General Report*, p. 175.

41. Interview with Giandomenico Sertoli.
42. Francesco Compagna, "La concezione meridionalista dello sviluppo italiano," *Nord e Sud,* October 1969, p. 7.
43. Saraceno, 1967, in *La politica di sviluppo di un'area sottosviluppata nell'esperienza italiana,* pp. 746-48. See also his requirements for governmental policy to the South in the second five-year plan, in Pasquale Saraceno, *Obiettivi della politica di sviluppo del Mezzogiorno alla vigilia del secondo piano quinquennale* (Rome, 1969).

CHAPTER 10

1. Jean Meynaud, *Rapport sur la classe dirigeante italienne* (Lausanne, 1964), p. 312.
2. Italy, Ministero dell'Industria e del Commercio, *L'Istituto per la Ricostruzione* (Turin, 1955), I, 11-12. The enterprises controlled are described in Vol. I, pp. 218-88. The third volume is a valuable historical survey by Professor Pasquale Saraceno.
3. Joseph LaPalombara, *Interest Groups in Italian Politics* (Princeton, 1964), p. 123.
4. Giuseppe Petrilli, *Lo stato imprenditore: Validità e attualità di una formula* (Bologna, 1967), p. 50. See criticism of this concept by the PCI in Partito Comunista Italiano, Centro Studi di Politica Economica, *Bolletino CESPE,* May 1967, pp. 26-27.
5. Petrilli, *Stato imprenditore,* pp. 40-41, 72-74.
6. Giuseppe Petrilli, "Sviluppo del Mezzogiorno e integrazione economica europea," speech to Consiglio Regionale del Movimento Europeo, Taranto, October 24, 1966.
7. Giuseppe Petrilli, "La nuova industrializzazione," speech to Istituto Italiano di Cultura in Paris, November 15, 1966.
8. Rotary Club of East Rome, *La programmazione economica in Italia: Conferenze tenute al Rotary Club di Roma Est* (Rome, 1966), pp. 17-22.
9. Giuseppe Petrilli, "L'impresa pubblica in una politica di piano," speech to CISMEC, Milan, January 19, 1967.
10. Giuseppe Petrilli, "Un disegno operativo per il rilancio della battaglia federalista," in Movimento Europeo Consiglio Italiano, *Documenti* (Rome, 1965), pp. 101-6.
11. Ente Nazionale Idrocarburi, *L'Italia e l'ENI: Situazione e problemi dell'intervento pubblico nell'industria petrolifera* (Milan, 1968), I, 12.
12. *Review of the Economic Conditions in Italy,* May 1960, pp. 245-

48; P. H. Frankel, *Mattei: Oil and Power Politics* (New York, 1966), pp. 179-81.
13. Alfredo Pieroni, *Chi comanda in Italia* (Milan, 1959), p. 99.
14. Frankel, *Mattei*, pp. 95-96.
15. Charles R. Dechert, *Ente Nazionale Idrocarburi: Profile of a State Corporation* (Leiden, 1963), p. 28-47.
16. Votaw, *The Six-Legged Dog*, p. 129.
17. ENI, *L'Italia e l'ENI*, p. 31.
18. Votaw concludes: "The absence of a genuine audit made it possible for Mattei to do things which could not otherwise have been done . . . and protected him from governmental supervision and control. . . . The dangers of domination of the state by irresponsible state enterprise are too great to be outweighed by any conceivable benefits that might be obtained. Mattei and ENI will long be the paramount examples of the truth of this simple doctrine." Votaw, *The Six-Legged Dog*, p. 149.
19. ENI, *Esercizio, 1968*, pp. 8-9.
20. ENI, *Annual Report, 1966*, p. 62.
21. Protocol of Düsseldorf. See also *Avis du Centre Européen de l'Entreprise Publique sur les lignes directrices d'une politique énergétique commune* (Brussels, July 1968). It is worth noting that Mattei, in spite of his opposition to the foundation of EEC, had suggested in 1958 that it was essential for the Community to adopt such an energy policy. ENI, *Annual Report, 1958*, pp. 216-17.
22. *Fortune*, August 15, 1969, pp. 107-10.
23. Edison, *Esercizio, 1956*, p. 15.
24. Enrico Caperdoni, *Lo sviluppo italiano del dopoguerra* (Florence, 1968), pp. 63-66.
25. Montecatini, *Esercizio, 1956*, pp. 6-7.
26. Montecatini Edison, *Esercizio, 1967*; Montecatini Edison, *The Montecatini Edison Group and Europe* (Milan, 1967); Montecatini Edison, *Il Gruppo Montecatini Edison: Struttura, attività e produzioni* (Milan, 1968).
27. In 1968, IRI and ENI carried out a financial coup by purchasing a small but influential block of shares. The management mustered the small shareholders against them, and entered a continuing battle for control of company policy.
28. *Fortune*, May 1968, p. 136.
29. Valletta felt the need to defend this privileged position in the Annual Report for 1955, by pointing out that the French and British were applying even greater protection. Fiat, *Relazioni, 1955*, p. 18.

30. Fiat, *Relazioni, 1956,* pp. 5-6.
31. *International Management,* March 1968, pp. 28-30.
32. Fiat, *Annual Report, 1968,* p. 12; Roger Priouret, "Face à face avec Giovanni Agnelli," *L'Expansion,* May 1969, pp. 161-65.
33. Fiat, *Historical Notes* (Turin, 1969), pp. 8-9.
34. Giovanni Agnelli, *L'impresa e le sue responsibilità* (Ischia, 1969; mimeographed.)
35. Giovanni Agnelli, "Le relazioni economiche internazionali: Problemi e prospettive dell'industria italiana," in Scuola di applicazione d'arma, *Giovedí culturali,* March 14, 1968; and Giovanni Agnelli, "Gli operatori privati di fronte alla programmazione economica e alla integrazione europea," in Movimento Europeo, *Programmazioni regionali e nazionali e programmazione europea* (Turin, 1968; mimeographed).
36. Pirelli, *Esercizio, 1956,* pp. 18-19; *1957,* p. 14.
37. Pirelli, *Société Internationale Pirelli* (Lausanne, 1965); Pirelli, *Esercizio, 1967,* p. 7.
38. Bruno Caizzi, *Camillo e Adriano Olivetti* (Turin, 1962).
39. Ibid. pp. 45-68.
40. Olivetti, *Esercizio, 1957,* p. 7.
41. Caizzi, *Olivetti,* p. 162.
42. Ibid. p. 309.
43. On Olivetti-General Electric, see Sergio Deschovich, "Interrelazioni tra scienza, tecnologia, industria, università e pubblica amministrazione a livello nazionale e supranazionale," *Tempi Moderni,* Winter 1966–67, pp. 444-48.

CHAPTER 11

1. I have deliberately avoided entering the quarrel between the use of the concept "interest group" and "pressure group," and have used the two phrases interchangeably. For a theoretical distinction, see LaPalombara, *Interest Groups,* pp. 19-20.
2. Ibid. pp. 184-85.
3. Coltivatori Diretti, *L'agricoltura e il mercato comune; Sardegna Economica,* October 1963; *Rivista di Politica Economica,* June 1952.
4. Henri Gironella *et al., La funzione dell'impresa pubblica nell'economia del mercato comune* (Rome, 1962).
5. On patterns of group communications and interaction, see LaPalombara, *Interest Groups,* pp. 173-98.
6. Ibid. pp. 217-18.

7. Ibid. p. 245. On "legislative interaction," see ibid. pp. 199-251.
8. Ibid. pp. 201-7, 275-84.
9. Caperdoni, *Lo sviluppo italiano*, p. 17.
10. Renato Giordano, *Il Mercato Comune e i suoi problemi* (Rome, 1958), p. 30.
11. Confindustria, *Relazione, 1950*, pp. 105-6.
12. On Pella Plan, see ibid. pp. 109-10.
13. *Rivista di Politica Economica*, June 1952, pp. 938-44.
14. Ibid. pp. 944-48.
15. Taviani, *Piano Schuman*, p. 39.
16. Caperdoni, *Lo sviluppo italiano*, p. 66-68.
17. Confindustria, *Annuario, 1957*, p. 296.
18. Cf. Norman Kogan, *The Politics of Italian Foreign Policy* (New York, 1963), p. 138.
19. Confindustria, *Annuario, 1958*, pp. 511-13, and especially De Micheli's comments, pp. 326-28. For specific demands of Italian industry on the government, see the article by Confindustria Vice President Quinto Quintieri, "L'industria italiana nel mercato comune," *Mondo Aperto*, June–August 1957, pp. 185-91. For general survey of business attitudes, see Confindustria's Ninth Convegno di Studi di Economia e Politica Industriale, on The European Economic Community and Third Countries, in *Rivista di Politica Economica*, January–February 1959.
20. Confindustria, *Annuario, 1960*, p. 322.
21. Ibid. *1962*, pp. 308-9.
22. Ibid. *1966*, p. 7; *Tempi Moderni*, Winter 1966–1967, p. 171. Study on pressure groups in EEC is scarce. The article by Orazio M. Petracca and Riccardo Petrella, "La politica europea dei dirigenti industriali," *Tempi Moderni*, Winter 1966–67, pp. 167-75, is just a suggestion of where work might begin.
23. Confindustria, *Annuario, 1961*, p. 436.
24. Lindberg, *Political Dynamics*, p. 211.
25. Confindustria, *Annuario, 1960*, pp. 485-86.
26. Ibid. pp. 442-47; Curtis, *Western European Integration*, pp. 180-83.
27. Confindustria, *Annuario, 1960*, pp. 488-91.
28. Ibid. *1963*, pp. 367-69.
29. Ibid. *1959*, p. 493.
30. Caperdoni, *Lo sviluppo italiano*, p. 110.
31. *Documenti di vita italiana*, No. 82, pp. 6,503-6; No. 86, pp. 6,859-62; No. 88, pp. 7,017-19.
32. Ibid. No. 56, p. 4,417; *Vita italiana*, No. 11, 1964, pp. 894-95.

33. CIRD, *Annuario politico italiano, 1965*, pp. 748-52.
34. Jean Meynaud and Claudio Risé, *Gruppi di pressione in Italia e in Francia* (Naples, 1963), p. 38.
35. LaPalombara, *Interest Groups*, pp. 287-88.
36. Speech to Camera di Commercio Internazionale, March 16, 1957.
37. Confcommercio, *Annuario, 1956*, pp. 5-17.
38. Speech to Assemblea-Convegno della Camera di Commercio Internazionale, March 16, 1957.
39. Confcommercio, *Relazione, 1959*, pp. 19-20.
40. Speech to Assemblea Confederale, February 5, 1964.
41. Meynaud, *Gruppi di pressione*, pp. 90-95; Ernesto Rossi et al., *La Federconsorzi* (Milan, 1963), pp. 28-33; LaPalombara, *Interest Groups*, pp. 235-46.
42. Coltivatori Diretti, *Relazione del Presidente, 1957*, pp. 493-514.
43. Coltivatori Diretti, *L'agricoltura e il mercato comune*.
44. Ibid. p. 164.
45. *Mondo Agricolo*, April 2, 1967.
46. Alfonso Gaetani, *Italia, Europa, e Kennedy Round* (Rome, 1966), pp. 8-9; Coltivatori Diretti, *Relazione del Presidente, 1968*, I, 452-56.

CHAPTER 12

1. Joseph LaPalombara, *The Italian Labor Movement: Problems and Prospects* (Ithaca, 1957), p. xvi.
2. On historical origins of the Italian trade union movement, see Maurice F. Neufeld, *Italy: School for Awakening Countries* (Ithaca, 1961), esp. pp. 90-104; and Daniel L. Horowitz, *The Italian Labor Movement* (Cambridge, Mass., 1963), pp. 10-23.
3. Delzell, *Mussolini's Enemies*, pp. 249-51.
4. Hildebrand, *Growth and Structure*, pp. 189-212.
5. Lutz, *Italy*, pp. 320-21.
6. Horowitz, *Italian Labor*, p. 209.
7. CGIL, *I congressi*, II, 363.
8. Horowitz, *Italian Labor*, p. 212.
9. LaPalombara, *Italian Labor Movement*, pp. 109, 111.
10. Giuseppe Di Vittorio et al., *I sindacati in Italia* (Bari, 1955), pp. 97-103.
11. Horowitz, *Italian Labor Movement*, p. 251.
12. Ibid. p. 260.
13. Ibid. pp. 238-42.
14. CGIL, *I congressi*, VI, 19.

15. Neufeld, *Italy*, pp. 509-10.
16. OECD, *Economic Survey, Italy, 1965*, pp. 12-13, 30.
17. CGIL, *I congressi*, VII, 15-52.
18. Ibid. IV-V, 172-74, 220-21.
19. Ibid. IV-V, pp. 200-209, 471-72.
20. Ibid. VI, 26, 452.
21. Italy, Consiglio Nazionale dell'Economia e del Lavoro, *Parere sul progetto di programma di sviluppo economico per il quinquennio 1965–1969* (Rome, 1965), Allegato A, 107-8. Novella repeats the criticism almost identically in CGIL, *I congressi*, VII, 21-27.
22. Ibid. p. 22.
23. See the position of the PCI, in *Bollettino CESPE*, May 1967, pp. 3-7.
24. Giorgio Galli, *La sinistra italiana nel dopoguerra* (Bologna, 1958), p. 3.
25. CGIL, *I congressi*, III, 17-27; 89-90; Galli, *Sinistra italiana*, pp. 243-55.
26. LaPalombara, *Italian Labor Movement*, pp. 167-68.
27. See Giorgio Galli, "La politica internazionale del Partito Comunista Italiano," in IAI, *La politica estera*, III, 950-57.
28. Bruno Trentin, *La minaccia del Piano Schuman* (Rome, 1952), pp. 5-8, 22-24, 35, 71-74, 138-39.
29. *Rassegna Sindacale*, February 15, 1956, p. 70; July 15, 1956, p. 414.
30. Ibid. July 31, 1957, pp. 420-21.
31. Kogan, *Italian Foreign Policy*, pp. 92-93.
32. *Rassegna Sindacale*, August 15–September 15, 1957, p. 463.
33. Ibid. February–March 1958, pp. 48-49; Gabriele Baccalini and Bruno Di Pol, "Potere sindacale e dimensioni sovranazionali," *Tempi Moderni*, Spring 1967, pp. 17-20.
34. *Rassegna Sindacale*, January 1959, pp. 517-18.
35. Ibid. June 1960, pp. 1,485-89; October 1961, pp. 2,272-76.
36. Donald L. M. Blackmer, *Unity in Diversity: Italian Communism and the Communist World* (Cambridge, Mass., 1968), pp. 282-83.
37. *Rassegna Sindacale*, January 1962, pp. 2,494, 2,514.
38. Ibid. June 1962, pp. 2,872-73.
39. Ibid. January 12, 1962, p. 18.
40. Ibid. February 9, 1963, p. 24.
41. Ibid. March 9, 1963, p. 24.
42. CGIL, *I congressi*, VII, 618-27.
43. See Amedeo Grano, *Mercato Comune e movimento operaio* (Rome, 1963).

44. LaPalombara, *Italian Labor Movement*, pp. 108-9; Horowitz, *Italian Labor*, p. 303.
45. Meynaud, *Gruppi di pressione*, p. 64.
46. LaPalombara, *Italian Labor Movement*, p. 84.
47. Bruno Manghi, *La dinamica della CISL: Dal moderatismo ad una nuova coscienza politica?* in Fabrizio Cicchitto et al., *La DC dopo il primo ventennio* (Padua, 1968), pp. 114-19.
48. LaPalombara, *Interest Groups*, pp. 292-93.
49. Confederazione Italiana Sindacati Lavoratori, *Documenti ufficiali dal 1950 al 1958* (Rome, 1959), p. 237.
50. CISL, *Documenti, 1950–1958*, p. 142.
51. Cicchitto, *La DC*, p. 108.
52. Executive motion, February 27–28, 1951, Rome.
53. Horowitz, *Italian Labor*, pp. 241, 293.
54. CISL, *Documenti, 1950–1958*, pp. 250-54, 122-23.
55. Ibid. pp. 149-53.
56. Meynaud, *Gruppi di pressione*, p. 64.
57. Colin Beever, *European Unity and the Trade Union Movements* (Leiden, 1960), p. 24; Lewis L. Lorwin, *The International Labor Movement: History, Policies, Outlook* (New York, 1953), pp. 258-61.
58. Beever, *European Unity*, p. 29.
59. Lorwin, *International Labor*, p. 296.
60. On ERO, see Beever, *European Unity*, pp. 35-55, and Jean Meynaud, *L'Action syndicale et la Communauté Economique Européenne* (Lausane, 1962), pp. 9-13.
61. Beever, *European Unity*, pp. 170-74.
62. Meynaud, *L'Action syndicale*, pp. 27-41.
63. Ibid. p. 45.
64. Ibid. pp. 53-61.
65. Taviani, *Piano Schuman*, p. 50.
66. CISL, *Documenti, 1950–1958*, p. 370.
67. Ibid. p. 136.
68. Ibid. pp. 396-97.
69. Beever, *European Unity*, pp. 245-46.
70. Confederazione Italiana Sindacati Lavoratori, *Documenti ufficiali dal 1959 al 1961* (Rome, 1962), p. 219.
71. *Conquiste del Lavoro*, April 30–May 6, 1967, p. 13.
72. Ibid. p. 11.
73. Speech of Livio Labor, "Il potere economico nella realtà italiana," in *Quaderni di Azione Sociale*, September 1966, p. 560.
74. Associazioni Cristiane Lavoratori Italiani (ACLI), *Le ACLI: Prin-*

cipi, attività, struttura (Collana Organizzazione, No. 1; Rome, n.d.), pp. 48-59.
75. Associazioni Cristiane Lavoratori Italiani, Ufficio Rapporti Internazionali, *Document on the activity of ACLI in the fields of adult education and the democratic and social training of working people* (Rome, 1964).
76. Ibid. p. 103.
77. Associazione Cristiane Lavoratori Italiani, *Le ACLI per lo sviluppo della società italiana (1945–1963)* (Rome, 1963), p. 33.
78. Ibid. p. 38.
79. *L'Osservatore Romano*, July 1, 1948, cited in Horowitz, *Italian Labor*, pp. 263-64.
80. Associazioni Cristiane Lavoratori Italiani, *The ACLI: What They Are and What Their Purpose Is* (Rome, 1964).
81. Di Vittorio et al., *I sindacati*, pp. 267-72.
82. ACLI, *The ACLI: What They Are*, p. 12.
83. ACLI, *Per lo sviluppo*, p. 275.
84. Ibid. p. 265.
85. Ibid. p. 297.
86. Associazioni Cristiane Lavoratori Italiani, *Le ACLI per lo sviluppo della società italiana (1963–1966)*, pp. 182-83; Meynaud, *Gruppi di pressione*, pp. 54-55.
87. LaPalombara, *Italian Labor Movement*, p. 110; Horowitz, *Italian Labor*, p. 225.
88. Ibid. pp. 234-37.
89. Horowitz, *Italian Labor*, p. 236.
90. Ibid. pp. 236-37, 240-43.
91. *Il Lavoro Italiano*, March 28, 1965.
92. Ibid. January 9, 1966.
93. Ibid. April 2, 1967.
94. Ibid. May 1, 1968.
95. Ibid. March 26, 1957.

CHAPTER 13

1. Giorgio Galli and Paolo Facchi, *La sinistra democristiana: Storia e ideologia* (Milan, 1962), p. 13.
2. Thierry Godechot, *Le parti démocrate-chrétien italien* (Paris, 1964), p. 65.
3. Richard A. Webster, *The Cross and the Fasces: Christian Democracy and Fascism in Italy* (Stanford, 1960), p. 151.
4. Ibid. p. 102.

5. Galli, *La sinistra democristiana*, p. 295.
6. Ibid. pp. 295-300.
7. Webster, *The Cross and the Fasces*, pp. 158-59.
8. Ibid. pp. 9-10, 14; Michael P. Fogarty, *Christian Democracy in Italy and France* (Notre Dame, Ind., 1952), pp. 8-13.
9. DC, *Atti, 1943–1959*, pp. 1-12.
10. Ibid. pp. 12-13.
11. Galli, *La sinistra democristiana*, pp. 34-38.
12. DC, *Atti, 1943–1959*, p. 51.
13. For Communist account, see Marcella and Maurizio Ferrara, *Cronache di vita italiana, 1944–1958* (Rome, 1960), pp. 128-32.
14. Mammarella, *Italy After Fascism*, p. 114.
15. Peter Nichols, *The Politics of the Vatican* (New York, 1968), p. 207.
16. On the character of the Church as a pressure group, see Meynaud, *Gruppi di pressione*, pp. 103-29, and the study by Carlo Falconi, *La Chiesa e le organizzazioni cattoliche in Italia (1945–1955): Saggi per una storia del cattolicesimo italiano nel dopoguerra* (Turin, 1956), esp. pp. 76-77, 81-82. See also the special number of *Il Ponte* of June 1950 devoted to the Church and Democracy.
17. Nichols, *Politics of the Vatican*, p. 100. On the excommunication see Domenico Settembrini, *La Chiesa nella politica italiana, 1944–1963* (Pisa, 1964), pp. 222-29. See also Lucio Libertini, "Pio XII: appunti per la storia di un periodo della politica vaticana," *Mondo Operaio*, September 1958, pp. 42-51, esp. pp. 46-47.
18. Mammarella, *Italy After Fascism*, p. 114.
19. Settembrini, *La Chiesa nella politica*, p. 91.
20. Banca d'Italia, *Relazione, 1946* (Rome, 1947), pp. 239, 252-54.
21. Andreotti, *De Gasperi*, pp. 277-79.
22. Godechot, *Le Parti démocrate-chrétien*, p. 251.
23. See Luigi Somma, *De Gasperi o Gronchi* (Rome, 1953).
24. Cf Gabriele De Rosa, "I partiti politici dopo la Resistenza," in *Dieci anni dopo, 1945–1955* (Bari, 1955), pp. 153-54.
25. Galli, *La sinistra democristiana*, p. 85.
26. Ibid. p. 89.
27. Democrazia Cristiana, *I congressi nazionali della Democrazia Cristiana* (Rome, 1959), pp. 315-18.
28. Galli, *La sinistra democristiana*, pp. 94-96, 106-7.
29. Ibid. p. 126.
30. Muriel Grindrod, *The Rebuilding of Italy* (London, 1955), p. 66.
31. Vito G. Galati, *La Democrazia Cristiana* (Verona, 1956), p. 103.
32. Mario Einaudi and François Goguel, *Christian Democracy in Italy and France* (Notre Dame, Ind., 1952), p. 28.

33. See De Gasperi's oblique reference to freedom from too close ties with the Holy See, written to Fanfani and published in *Il Popolo*, August 21, 1954. See also Arturo Carlo Jemolo, *Chiesa e stato in Italia negli ultimi cento anni* (Turin, 1948), pp. 689-98.
34. Palmiro Togliatti, *L'opera di De Gasperi: Rapporti tra stato e chiesa* (Florence, 1958), p. 9.
35. DC, *I congressi*, p. 27.
36. Togliatti, *L'opera di De Gasperi*, p. 36.
37. Cicchitto, *La DC*, pp. 28-30.
38. For Papal messages in support of integration, see European Communities Press and Information Office, Rome, *La Chiesa e l'Europa* (Rome, 1967), pp. 8-14; Carlo Ramaciotti, *I Cattolici e l'unità europea* (Quaderni del Centro di Azione Europeistica, No. 3; July, 1954), pp. 22-30, 85-108.
39. Centro di Azione Europeistica, *Notiziario Europeo* (Rome, 1950–present), and *I Cattolici e il federalismo: Atti del IV congresso di studi del C.A.E.* (Rome, 1961); Giovane Europa, Centro d'informazione e di studi, *Il congresso di "Giovane Europa" e la parola di Paolo VI* (Rome, 1965). *Giovane Europa*, July–September 1963, gives a summary of the propaganda work of the organization.
40. Galli, *La sinistra democristiana*, pp. 401-8.
41. Ibid. p. 137.
42. DC, *I congressi*, pp. 556-62.
43. Galli, *La sinistra democristiana*, pp. 158-59.
44. Kogan, *Political History*, pp. 133-34.
45. Pieroni, *Chi comanda*, pp. 38-39.
46. *Chroniques étrangères, Italie*, June 10, 1955, p. 17.
47. Ibid. April 10, 1956, p. 4.
48. Ibid. August 10, 1955, p. 16.
49. DC, *Atti, 1943–1959*, pp. 917-19; Galli, *La sinistra democristiana*, pp. 184-85.
50. Democrazia Cristiana, *Programma della Democrazia Cristiana per il quinquennio 1958–63* (Rome, 1958), p. 89.
51. Kogan, *Political History*, pp. 123-25.
52. *Tempi Moderni*, July–September 1961, p. 13.
53. Cicchitto, *La DC*, pp. 37-38.
54. Ibid. p. 43; Democrazia Cristiana, *Atti dell'VIII Congresso Nazionale della Democrazia Cristiana* (Rome, 1963), pp. 69-98.
55. Ibid. pp. 120-21.
56. Democrazia Cristiana, *Atti e documenti della Democrazia Cristiana 1961–1964* (Rome, 1964), pp. 706-10.
57. Ibid. pp. 804-6.

58. Democrazia Cristiana, *Atti del IX Congresso Nazionale della Democrazia Cristiana* (Rome, 1965), pp. 24-32.
59. Ibid. pp. 33-47.
60. Ibid. pp. 48-58.
61. Democrazia Cristiana, *Una Democrazia Cristiana unita* (Rome, 1966); Giorgio Galloni, *Una politica nuova per la Democrazia Cristiana* (Rome, 1966).
62. Ibid. p. 3.

CHAPTER 14

1. On early history of the PCI, see Giorgio Galli and Fulvio Bellini, *Storia del partito comunista italiano* (Milan, 1953), pp. 57-202.
2. Togliatti, *Partito comunista*, p. 101.
3. William E. Griffith (ed.), *Communism in Europe: Continuity, Change, and the Sino-Soviet Dispute* (Cambridge, Mass., 1964-66), II, 305.
4. Togliatti, *Partito comunista*, p. 90.
5. Ibid. p. 89.
6. Ibid. pp. 103-7.
7. Togliatti later testified (in *Rinascita*, July 1956 cited in Galli, *Sinistra italiana*, p. 6) that great pressure was put on the PCI at the founding meeting of the Cominform.
8. Paolo Alatri (ed.), *Rinascita, 1944-1962: Antologia* (Rome, 1962), I, 223-27.
9. Galli, *Sinistra italiana*, p. 22.
10. Yet the PCI insisted upon the official Soviet interpretation of the coup as the "victorious resistance to the attempt of internal reaction and foreign imperialism to bring about . . . a *coup d'état* against the people." *Rinascita*, July 1948, cited in Galli, *Sinistra italiana*, p. 56.
11. When the party mounted a marathon attack on NATO in the Chamber in March 1949, it found considerable support for a return to neutralism from both the left and the extreme right. Ferrara, *Cronache*, pp. 234-35.
12. Alatri (ed.), *Rinascita*, I, 330, 363-69.
13. Ibid. II, 502-3.
14. Ibid. II, 768-73, 803-8.
15. Palmiro Togliatti, *Problemi del movimento operatio internazionale, 1956-1961* (Rome, 1962), pp. 27-72.
16. Ibid. pp. 85-118; Blackmer, *Unity in Diversity*, p. 116.
17. Alatri (ed.), *Rinascita*, II, 865. See also Fabrizio Onofri, *Classe operaia e partito* (Bari, 1957), pp. 107-34, 201-22.

18. Blackmer, *Unity in Diversity*, pp. 90-93; Togliatti, *Problemi del movimento*, pp. 203-7.
19. Blackmer, *Unity in Diversity*, pp. 107-8.
20. See Giolitti's reply to Sereni, in Alatri (ed.), *Rinascita*, III, pp. 1,010-13.
21. Kogan, *Political History*, p. 102.
22. IAI, *La politica estera*, III, 958.
23. Togliatti, *Partito comunista*, pp. 142-43.
24. Mario Montagnana, in Camera, *Discussioni*, July 18, 1957, p. 34,018.
25. Zbigniew Brzezinski, "Russia and Europe," *Foreign Affairs*, April 1964, pp. 429-30.
26. Camera, *Discussioni*, July 18, 1957, p. 34,018.
27. Montagnana's version rests upon the official directive of the party of March 24, 1957: "Sul mercato comune," *Comunicato della Direzione del PCI*, March 24, 1957, cited in Blackmer, *Unity in Diversity*, p. 153.
28. Marshall D. Shulman, "The Communist States and Western Integration," *Problems of Communism*, September–October 1963, p. 48.
29. Blackmer, *Unity in Diversity*, pp. 173-75.
30. Brzezinski, in *Foreign Affairs*, April 1964, p. 430.
31. Blackmer, *Unity in Diversity*, pp. 185, 189.
32. Istituto Gramsci, *Tendenze del capitalismo italiano: Atti del convegno di Roma 23–25 marzo 1962* (Rome, 1962), I, 203.
33. *L'Unità*, April 22, 1967, cited in Blackmer, *Unity in Diversity*, p. 305.
34. Ibid. pp. 312-19.
35. Ibid. pp. 375-76.
36. CIRD, *Annuario politico italiano, 1965*, pp. 1,217-20.
37. Speech by Mario Alicata, in Camera, *Discussioni*, October 18, 1965, pp. 18,191-92.
38. *Bollettino CESPE*, April 1967, p. 23-28.
39. Ibid. pp. 28-29.
40. Ibid. pp. 35-37.
41. Ibid. p. 64.
42. See Partito Socialista Italiano, *Il Partito Socialista Italiano nei suoi congressi; Vol. IV, I congressi dell'esilio* (Milan, 1963).
43. Alberto Benzoni and Via Tedesco, *Il movimento socialista nel dopoguerra* (Padua, 1968), pp. 9-13.
44. Umberto Righetti, *Contributo ad una storia della socialdemocrazia italiana* (Rome, 1962), pp. 12-13.
45. Benzoni, *Movimento socialista*, p. 22. Cf. Basso's explanation of

where the Socialists went wrong in the postwar period, in speech to PSI Congress in 1948, in Alberto Benzoni and Via Tedesco, *Documenti del socialismo italiano, 1943–1966* (Padua, 1968), pp. 24-26.

46. Giuseppe Saragat, *Quaranta anni di lotta per la democrazia: Scritti e discorsi 1925–1965* (Milan, 1966), pp. 296, 306.
47. Righetti, *Contributo*, pp. 21-22; Benzoni, *Movimento socialista*, p. 44.
48. Ibid. p. 46; Saragat, *Quaranta anni*, pp. 355-56.
49. Ibid. pp. 360-61; Righetti, *Contributo*, p. 27.
50. See Nenni's report to the 29th Congress, in Partito Socialista Italiano, *Il Partito Socialista Italiano nei suoi congressi; Vol. V, Il socialismo italiano di questo dopoguerra 1942–1955* (Milan, 1968), pp. 304-5.
51. Benzoni, *Documenti*, pp. 59-60.
52. PSI, *Congressi*, V, 298, 305; Benzoni, *Documenti*, pp. 68, 71-72.
53. *Avanti*, August 3, 1949; July 7, 1949.
54. PSI, *Congressi*, V, 247-48.
55. *Avanti*, July 13, 1949; July 14, 1949.
56. *Mondo Operaio*, May 17, 1950; June 15, 1950.
57. PSI, *Congressi*, V, 435.
58. Nenni's report, in Ibid. V, 404-7.
59. Benzoni, *Documenti*, p. 115.
60. Ibid. pp. 117-18.
61. Ibid. pp. 116-17.
62. Ibid. p. 126.
63. PSI, 32° *congresso*, pp. 203-4, for Foa, and p. 259 for Pertini.
64. Ibid. pp. 303-4.
65. See esp. Lucio Libertini and Dario Valori, in *Politica ed economia*, July 1958, pp. 23-24, 26-27.
66. Camera, *Discussioni*, July 22, 1957, pp. 34,225-31. See also the long technical discussion in Fernando Vasetti, "L'industria italiana e il mercato comune," *Mondo Operaio*, July–August 1957, pp. 13-22; September 1957, pp. 17-20.
67. Benzoni, *Movimento socialista*, p. 152.
68. Partito Socialista Italiano, 35° *Congresso Nazionale* (Milan, 1964), pp. 589-90.
69. Vecchietti, in the Foreign Affairs committee of the Chamber, cited in Piero Ostellino, *L'Italia tra Atlantismo e neutralismo* (Turin, 1964), p. 16.
70. Ibid. p. 90.
71. Benzoni, *Documenti*, pp. 153-56.

72. Movimento Europeo, *Per un comune impegno di politica europea* (Rome, 1968).
73. Delzell, *Mussolini's Enemies*, pp. 219-20.
74. Arnaldo Ciani, *Il Partito Liberale Italiano* (Naples, 1968), p. 17.
75. Ibid. pp. 64-65.
76. Camera, *Discussioni*, September 27, 1948, pp. 2,514-15; July 13, 1949, pp. 10,317-18.
77. Gaetano Martino, *Verso l'avvenire* (Florence, 1963), pp. 131-32, 137, 145-47.
78. Ciani, *PLI*, pp. 140-41.
79. Partito Liberale Italiano, *10° Congresso Nazionale, Roma, 1966* (Rome, 1966), p. 21.
80. Ibid. p. 134.
81. Cesare Degli Occhi and Piero Operti, *Il Partito Nazionale Monarchico* (Milan, 1957?), pp. 128, 132.
82. See Roberto Cantalupo, in Camera, *Discussioni*, July 30, 1957, pp. 34,783-87.
83. Francesco Leoni (ed.), *Annuario dei movimenti politici* (Rome, 1961), pp. 169-74.
84. In the 1968 election platform, the PDIUM declared, "We believe in European unity and we fight for it because we are convinced that only from the union of all the forces of the continent can come the salvation of the supreme values of Western civilization." *Comunità Europee*, May 1968.
85. Movimento Sociale Italiano, *Venti anni del M.S.I. al servizio della Patria: Idee, programmi, battaglie del M.S.I. nella raccolta degli atti ufficiali* (Rome, 1966), p. 10.
86. See program for the 1948 elections and the founding document of the Fascist trade union CISNAL, in ibid. pp. 23-24, 31.
87. Ibid. p. 37.
88. See speech by Augusto De Marsanich, in Camera, *Discussioni*, July 30, 1957, pp. 34,796-98.
89. Delzell, *Mussolini's Enemies*, p. 211.
90. *L'Italia Libera*, November 1, 1943, cited in Centre d'Action, *L'Europe de demain* (Neuchâtel, 1945), p. 103.
91. Valiani, *L'avvento*, pp. 48-50; Roberto Battaglia, "Note sul congresso del Partito d'Azione," *Il Ponte*, March 1946, pp. 221-31.
92. *La Voce Repubblicana*, February 18, 1945; April 18, 1945.
93. Ugo La Malfa, *Contro l'Europa di de Gaulle* (Milan, 1964), pp. 35-38.

Bibliography

DOCUMENTS

Assider, Ufficio Studi. *Lineamenti strutturali della siderurgia e confronti con i paesi della C.E.C.A.* Milan, 1956.
Associazioni Cristiane Lavoratori Italiani. *Le ACLI per lo sviluppo della società italiana (1945–1963).* Rome, 1963.
———. *Le ACLI per lo sviluppo della società italiana (1963–1966).* Rome, 1966.
———. *Le ACLI: Principi, attività, struttura.* Collana Organizzazione, No. 1; Rome, n.d.
———. *The ACLI: What They Are and What Their Purpose Is.* Rome, 1964.
Associazioni Cristiane Lavoratori Italiani, Ufficio Rapporti Internazionali. *Document on the Activity of ACLI in the Fields of Adult Education and the Democratic and Social Training of Working People.* Rome, 1964.
Banca d'Italia. *Relazione annuale.* Rome, 1946–67.
Benzoni, Alberto, and Via Tedesco, (eds.). *Documenti del socialismo italiano, 1943–1966.* Padua, 1968.
Confederazione Generale dell'Industria Italiana. *Annuario.* Rome, 1950–67.
Confederazione Generale Italiana del Lavoro. *I congressi della CGIL.* Rome, 1949–66.
Confederazione Italiana Sindacati Lavoratori. *Documenti ufficiali dal 1950 al 1958.* Rome, 1959.

———. *Documenti ufficiali dal 1959 al 1961.* Rome, 1962.

———. *La politica sociale della Comunità Economica Europea: Atti del terzo convegno di studi di economia e politica del lavoro.* Rome, 1959.

Confederazione Nazionale Coltivatori Diretti. *L'agricoltura e il mercato comune europeo: Convegno di studi, Roma 23–25 gennaio 1958.* Rome, 1958.

———. *Documenti di politica agraria, 1961–1966.* Rome, 1967.

———. *Mondo rurale e agricoltura: Convegno nazionale di studio su "Programma di sviluppo economico e Comunità Europea."* Rome, 1967.

———. *Relazione del Presidente.* Rome, 1957–67.

———. *Statistiche agrarie, 1961–1966.* Rome, 1967.

Council of Europe, Consultative Assembly. *Official Report of Debates.* Strasbourg, 1949–50.

Democrazia Cristiana. *Atti dell'VIII° Congresso Nazionale di Napoli.* Rome, 1962.

———. *Atti dell VII° Congresso Nazionale della Democrazia Cristiana.* Rome, 1961.

———. *Atti e documenti della Democrazia Cristiana, 1943–1959.* Rome, 1959.

———. *Atti e documenti della Democrazia Cristiana, 1959–1961.* Rome, 1961.

———. *Atti e documenti della Democrazia Cristiana, 1961–1964.* Rome, 1964.

———. *Consiglio Nazionale D.C. del 15–18 marzo 1959.* Rome, 1959.

———. *I congressi nazionali della Democrazia Cristiana.* Rome, 1959.

———. *Programma della Democrazia Cristiana per il quinquennio 1958–63.* Rome, 1958.

———. *Una Democrazia Cristiana Unita.* Rome, 1966.

European Coal and Steel Community, High Authority. *C.E.C.A., 1952–1962: Résultats, limites, perspectives.* Luxembourg, 1963.

———. *Etude sur la situation économique et de l'emploi des entreprises de l'industrie sidérurgique des provinces de Brescia et Udine.* Luxembourg, 1963.

———. *General Reports on the Activities of the Community.* Luxembourg, 1953–67.

———. *Programmi di sviluppo e riconversione: Studio regionale sull' Umbria. Prospettive dell'industria siderurgica in Umbria in re-*

lazione al piano regionale di sviluppo economico. Luxembourg, 1964.

———. *Programmi di sviluppo e riconversione: Studio sulla zona di Piombino.* Luxembourg, 1963.

———. *Studi regionali sull'occupazione: Liguria.* Luxembourg, 1957.

European Communities. *Journal officiel des Communautés Européennes: Communications et informations.* Brussels, 1965–68.

———. Commission. *First General Report on the Activity of the Communities in 1967.* Brussels, 1968.

———. European Parliament, Direction Générale de la Documentation. *L'Universite européenne: Recueil de documents.* Brussels, 1967.

———. European Parliament, Political Committee. *Towards Political Union.* Brussels, 1964.

———. Press and Information Bureau, Paris. *La Politique agricole commune.* Paris, 1967.

———. Press and Information Bureau, Rome. *La Chiesa e l'Europa.* Rome, 1967.

———. Statistical Office. *Basic Statistics for Fifteen Countries.* Brussels, 1962.

———. Statistical Office. *Bulletin général des statistiques.* Brussels, 1962–69.

———. Statistical Office. *Sidérurgie, Annuaire 1966.* Luxembourg, 1966.

———. Statistical Office. *Statistiques de base de la Communauté.* Luxembourg, 1966.

European Economic Community

Commission. *Etudes: L'emploi agricole dans les pays de la CEE.* Brussels, 1964.

———. *Documents de la conférence sur les économies régionales.* Brussels, 1963.

———. *General Reports on the Activities of the Community.* Brussels, 1959–67.

———. *La libera circolazione della manodopera e i mercati del lavoro nella Cee.* Brussels, 1966–68.

———. *Rapports de groupes d'experts sur la politique régionale dans la Communauté Economique Européenne.* Brussels, 1964.

———. Commission administrative pour la sécurité sociale des tra-

vailleurs migrants. *Sixième et septième rapports annuels sur la mise en oeuvre des règlements concernant la sécurité sociale des travailleurs migrants.* Brussels, 1967.
———. Direction Générale de l'Agriculture, A. De Leeuw and P. Vicinelli. *Certains aspects de l'amélioration des structures agraires en Italie.* Brussels, 1963.
———. Spokesman's Bureau. *Note d'information: Programmes communautaires pour la section orientation du FEOGA.* Brussels, June 1967.
Ente Nazionale Idrocarburi. *Esercizio.* Rome, 1957–68.
———. *L'Italia e l'ENI: Situazione e problemi dell'intervento pubblico nell'industria petrolifera.* Milan, 1968.
Fiat. *Relazioni del Consiglio d'Amministrazione e dei sindaci.* Turin, 1955–57, 1966–68.
Finsider. *Annual Report.* Rome, 1946–68.
Istituto per la Ricostruzione Industriale. *Esercizio.* Rome, 1955–68.

Italy

Camera dei Deputati. *Atti parlamentari: Discussioni.* Rome, 1949–68.
———. *Atti parlamentari: Documenti.* Rome, 1949–68.
Comitato dei Ministri per il Mezzogiorno. *Relazione.* Rome, 1966–67.
———. *Studi monografici sul Mezzogiorno.* Rome, 1966.
Comitato Italiano per la Ricostruzione. *Lo sviluppo dell'economia nel quadro della ricostruzione e della cooperazione europea.* Rome, 1952.
———. *Politica di sviluppo: Cinque anni di lavoro.* Rome, 1958.
Istituto Centrale di Statistica. *Bollettino mensile di statistica.* Rome, 1962–69.
———. *Compendio statistico italiano.* Rome, 1956–69.
———. *Sommario di statistiche storiche italiane, 1861–1955.* Rome, 1958.
Istituto Nazionale per il Commercio Estero. *I quaranta anni dell'ICE, 1926–1965.* Rome, 1966.
Ministero dell'Agricoltura e delle Foreste. *Piano quinquennale di sviluppo dell'agricoltura: Relazione al parlamento sul primo periodo di attuazione (fino al 30 giugno 1962).* Rome, 1962.
Ministero dell'Industria e del Commercio. *L'Istituto per la Ricostruzione.* Turin, 1955.

Presidenza del Consiglio dei Ministri. *L'Italia e l'integrazione europea.* Rome, 1964.
———. Servizio delle Informazioni. *Comunità Economica Europea.* Rome, 1958.
———. Servizio delle Informazioni. *Documenti di vita italiana.* Rome, 1952–63.
———. Servizio delle Informazioni. *Italy Today.* Rome, 1962.
———. Servizio delle Informazioni. *Vita italiana: Documenti e informazioni.* Rome, 1964–69.
Senato della Repubblica, IV Legislatura. "Relazione sulla Comunità Economica Europea e sulla Comunità Europea dell'Energia Atomica (1958–1965)," *Disegni di legge e relazioni-documenti*, No. 92, December 29, 1965.
Montecatini Edison. *Esercizio.* Milan, 1967.
Movimento Europeo Consiglio Italiano. *Documenti.* Rome, 1965.
Movimento Sociale Italiano. *Venti anni del M.S.I. al servizio della Patria: Idee, programmi, battaglie del M.S.I. nella raccolta degli atti ufficiali.* Rome, 1966.
Olivetti. *Relazione del Consiglio di Amministrazione.* Ivrea, 1956–57, 1966–68.
Organisation for Economic Co-operation and Development. *Agricultural and Food Statistics, 1952–1963.* Paris, 1965.
———. *Industrial Statistics, 1900–1962.* Paris, 1964.
———. *Regional Rural Development Programmes with Special Emphasis on Depressed Agricultural Areas Including Mountain Regions.* Paris, 1964.
———. *The Position of the Hired Agricultural Worker.* Paris, 1962.
Organisation for European Economic Co-operation. *Economic Conditions in Member and Associated Countries of the OEEC: Italy.* Paris, 1961.
Partito Liberale Italiano. *10° Congresso Nazionale, Roma, 1966.* Rome, 1966.
Partito Socialista Italiano. *Conferenza agraria nazionale: Atti e resoconto.* Milan, 1958.
———. *Congresso Nazionale.* Milan, 1957–61.
———. *Il Partito Socialista Italiano nei suoi congressi; Vol. IV, I congressi dell'esilio.* Milan, 1963.
Partito Socialista Italiano di Unità Proletaria. *1° Congresso Nazionale, Roma, 1965.* Milan, 1966.
Società Edison. *73° Esercizio.* Milan, 1957.
Sardinia. *Commissione Economica di Studio per il Piano di Rina-*

scita della Sardegna. Rapporto conclusivo sugli studi per il Piano di Rinascita. Cagliari, 1966.

———. Regione Autonoma della Sardegna. *Piano di rinascita economica e sociale della Sardegna, piano quinquennale, 1965–1969.* Cagliari, 1966.

Unione Italiana delle Camere di Commercio Industria e Agricoltura. *Compendio economico italiano.* Rome, 1956, 1961.

United States, Department of State, Director of Research and Intelligence. *Research Memorandum, REU-27, REU-41,* Washington, D.C., 1969.

BOOKS

Adstans (Paolo Canali). *Alcide De Gasperi nella politica estera italiana.* Milan, 1953.

Alatri, Paolo (ed.). *Rinascita, 1944–1962.* Rome, 1962.

Albonetti, Achille. *Euratom e sviluppo nucleare.* Milan, 1958.

Amendola, Giorgio. *Classe operaia e programmazione democratica.* Rome, 1966.

———. *La democrazia nel Mezzogiorno.* Rome, 1957.

Andreotti, Giulio. *De Gasperi e il suo tempo.* Milan, 1964.

Argenziano. Riccardo, et al. *Bonifica Mezzogiorna ed Europa.* Quaderni di Civiltà degli scambi; Bari, 1956.

Badini Confalonieri, Vittorio. *La Comunità Economica Europea.* Rome, 1957.

Banco di Roma. *Review of Economic Conditions in Italy: Ten Years of Italian Economy.* Rome, 1957.

Barzanti, Sergio. *The Underdeveloped Areas within the Common Market.* Princeton, 1965.

Beever, Colin. *European Unity and the Trade Union Movements.* Leiden, 1960.

Benzoni, Alberto, and Via Tedesco. *Il movimento socialista nel dopoguerra.* Padua, 1968.

Bergmann, Giulio (ed.). *Europa senza dogane: I produttori hanno scelto l'Europa.* Bari, 1956.

Blackmer, Donald L. M. *Unity in Diversity: Italian Communism and the Communist World.* Cambridge, Mass., 1968.

Bo, Dino Del. *La crisi dei dirigenti.* Florence, 1964.

Byrnes, James F. *Speaking Frankly.* New York, 1947.

Caizzi, Bruno. *Camillo e Adriano Olivetti.* Turin, 1962.

Camps, Miriam. *European Unification in the Sixties: From the Veto to the Crisis.* New York, 1966.

Caperdoni, Enrico. *Lo sviluppo italiano del dopoguerra.* Florence, 1968.
Carlyle, Margaret. *Modern Italy.* London, 1957.
Casadio, Gian Paolo. *Una politica agricola per l'Europa.* Bologna, 1967.
Cattani, Attilio. *L'Essai de coopération politique entre les Six de 1960–1962 et l'échec de la négociation sur un statut politique.* Brussels, 1967.
Catti De Gasperi, Maria Romana. *La nostra patria Europa: Il pensiero europeistico di Alcide De Gasperi.* Milan, 1969.
Centre d'Action pour la Fédération Européenne, Neuchâtel. *L'Europe de demain.* Neuchâtel, 1945.
Centro d'Azione Europeistica. *I Cattolici e il federalismo: Atti del IV congresso di studi del C.A.E.* Rome, 1961.
Centro Informazione e Studi sul MEC. *Il Mercato Comune visto dalla Comunità dalle amministrazioni dello stato e dagli operatori economici italiani.* Milan, 1960.
Centro Internazionale di Studi e Documentazione sulle Comunità Europee. *Incontri di Tribuna Economica.* Milan, 1962–63.
Centro Italiano di Ricerche e Documentazione. *Annuario politico italiano, 1965.* Milan, 1965.
Chabod, Federico. *Storia dell'idea d'Europa.* Bari, 1961.
Ciani, Arnaldo. *Il Partito Liberale Italiano.* Naples, 1968.
Cicchitto, Fabrizio, et al. *La DC dopo il primo ventennio.* Padua, 1968.
Clough, Shepard B. *The Economic History of Modern Italy.* New York, 1964.
Curcio, Carlo. *Europa: Storia di un'idea.* Florence, 1958.
Curtis, Michael. *Western European Integration.* New York, 1966.
Dechert, Charles R. *Ente Nazionale Idrocarburi: Profile of a State Corporation.* Leiden, 1963.
Delzell, Charles F. *Mussolini's Enemies: The Italian Anti-Fascist Resistance.* Princeton, 1961.
Diebold, William, Jr. *The Schuman Plan: A Study in Economic Cooperation, 1950–1959.* New York, 1959.
Dolci, Danilo. *Poverty in Sicily.* Harmondsworth, England, 1966.
Einaudi, Mario, and François Goguel. *Christian Democracy in Italy and France.* Notre Dame, Ind., 1952.
Einaudi, Mario (ed.). *Communism in Western Europe.* Ithaca, 1951.
Einaudi, Luigi. *La guerra e l'unità europea.* Milan, 1948.
———. *Lo scrittoio del Presidente 1948–1955.* Turin, 1956.

Falconi, Carlo. *Gedda e l'Azione Cattolica.* Florence, 1958.
———. *Il Pentagono vaticano.* Bari, 1958.
———. *La Chiesa e le organizzazioni cattoliche in Italia (1945–1955): Saggi per una storia del cattolicesimo italiano nel dopoguerra.* Turin, 1956.
Ferrara, Marcella, and Maurizio Ferrara. *Cronache di vita italiana, 1944–1958.* Rome, 1960.
Fogarty, Michael P. *Christian Democracy in Western Europe, 1820–1953.* London, 1957.
Frankel, P. H. *Mattei: Oil and Power Politics.* Milan, 1959.
Gaetani, Alfonso. *Italia, Europa, e Kennedy Round.* Rome, 1966.
———. *L'Italia agricola e il mercato comune europeo.* Rome, 1959.
Galati, Vito G. *La Democrazia Cristiana.* Verona, 1956.
Galli, Giorgio, and Paolo Facchi. *La sinistra democristiana: Storia ed ideologia.* Milan, 1962.
Galli, Giorgio. *La sinistra italiana nel dopoguerra.* Bologna, 1958.
Galli, Giorgio, and Fulvio Bellini. *Storia del partito comunista italiano.* Milan, 1953.
Galloni, Giorgio. *Una politica nuova per la Democrazia Cristiana.* Rome, 1966.
Gasperi, Alcide De. *Discorsi politici.* Rome, 1956.
Giacchero, Enzo (ed.). *Il Mezzogiorno nel mercato italiano: Raccolta di testimonianze.* Luxembourg, 1957.
Giordano, Renato. *Il Mercato Comune e i suoi problemi.* Rome, 1958.
Godechot, Thierry. *Le Parti démocrate-chrétien italien.* Paris, 1964.
Grano, Amedeo. *Mercato comune e movimento operaio.* Rome, 1963.
Graziano, Luigi. *La politica estera italiana nel dopoguerra.* Padua, 1968.
Grindrod, Muriel. *The Rebuilding of Italy.* London, 1955.
Hildebrand, George. *Growth and Structure in the Economy of Modern Italy.* Cambridge, Mass., 1965.
Horowitz, Daniel L. *The Italian Labor Movement.* Cambridge, Mass., 1963.
Istituto Affari Internazionali. *La politica estera della Repubblica italiana.* Milan, 1967.
Istituto Gramsci. *Tendenze del capitalismo europeo: Atti del convegno di Roma organizzato dall'Istituto Gramsci, 25–27 giugno 1965.* Rome, 1966.
———. *Tendenze del capitalismo italiano: Atti del convegno di Roma, 23–25 marzo, 1962.* Rome, 1962.

Istituto per l'Economia Europea. *L'integrazione economica europea all'inizio della seconda tappa.* Rome, 1962.

Jemolo, Arturo Carlo. *Chiesa e stato in Italia negli ultimi cento anni.* Turin, 1948.

Kogan, Norman. *A Political History of Postwar Italy.* New York, 1966.

———. *The Politics of Italian Foreign Policy.* New York, 1963.

L'Année politique. Paris, 1946–68.

LaPalombara, Joseph. *Interest Groups in Italian Politics.* Princeton, 1964.

———. *The Italian Labor Movement: Problems and Prospects.* Ithaca, 1957.

Leoni, Francesco (ed.). *Annuario dei movimenti politici.* Rome, 1961.

Levi, Arrigo. *L'Italia e il Mercato Comune oggi e domani.* Rome, 1966.

Levi, Carlo. *Christ Stopped at Eboli.* New York, 1947.

Lindberg, Leon. *The Political Dynamics of European Economic Integration.* Stanford, 1963.

Lister, Louis. *Europe's Coal and Steel Community: An Experiment in Economic Union.* New York, 1960.

Lorwin, Lewis L. *The International Labor Movement: History, Policies, Outlook.* New York, 1953.

Lutz, Vera. *Italy: A Study in Economic Development.* London, 1962.

Luzzatto Fegiz, Pierpaolo. *Il volto sconosciuto dell'Italia.* Milan, 1956.

Malfa, Ugo La. *Contro l'Europa di de Gaulle.* Milan, 1964.

Mammarella, Giuseppe. *Italy After Fascism: A Political History, 1943–1963.* Montreal, 1964.

Martino, Gaetano. *Foi en l'Europe.* Florence, 1967.

———. *Verso l'avvenire.* Florence, 1963.

Meynaud, Jean. *L'Action syndicale et la Communauté Economique Européenne.* Lausanne, 1962.

———. *Rapport sur la classe dirigeante italienne.* Lausanne, 1964.

Meynaud, Jean, and Claudio Risé. *Gruppi di pressione in Italia e in Francia.* Naples, 1963.

Nichols, Peter. *The Politics of the Vatican.* New York, 1968.

Neufeld, Maurice F. *Italy: School for Awakening Countries.* Ithaca, 1961.

Newhouse, John. *Collision in Brussels: The Common Market Crisis of 30 June 1965.* New York, 1967.

Occhi, Cesare Degli, and Piero Operti. *Il Partito Nazionale Monarchico*. Milan, 1957(?).
Onofri, Fabrizio. *Classe operaia e partito*. Bari, 1957.
Ostellino, Piero. *L'Italia tra Atlantismo e neutralismo*. Turin, 1964.
Parisi, Achille, and Goffredo Zappa (eds.). *Mezzogiorno e politica di piano*. Bari, 1964.
Peggio, Eugenio, Mario Mazzarino, and Valentino Parlato. *Industrializzazione e sottosviluppo: Il progresso tecnologico in una provincia del Mezzogiorno*. Turin, 1960.
Pella, Giuseppe. *La Comunità Europea del Carbone e dell'Acciaio: Risultati e prospettive*. Rome, 1954.
Pescatore, Gabriele. *L'intervento straordinario nel Mezzogiorno d'Italia*. Milan, 1962.
Petrilli, Giuseppe. *Lo stato imprenditore: Validità e attualità di una formula*. Bologna, 1967.
Pieroni, Alfredo. *Chi comanda in Italia*. Milan, 1959.
Ramaciotti, Carlo. *I Cattolici e l'unità europea*. Quaderni del Centro d'Azione Europeistica, No. 3; July, 1964.
Righetti, Umberto. *Contributo ad una storia della socialdemocrazia italiana*. Rome, 1962.
Rodanò, Carlo. *Mezzogiorno e sviluppo economico*. Bari, 1954.
Rossi, Ernesto. *Elettricità senza baroni*. Bari, 1962.
Rossi, Ernesto, et al. *La Federconsorzi*. Milan, 1963.
Rossi-Doria, Manlio. *Dieci anni di politica agraria nel Mezzogiorno*. Bari, 1958.
Rulli, Guglielmo. *U.S.E.: Stati Uniti d'Europa?* Naples, 1945.
Salvatorelli, Luigi. *La guerra fredda, 1945–1955*. Venice, 1956.
Saraceno, Pasquale. *La mancata unificazione economica italiana a cento anni dall'unificazione politica*. Milan, 1968.
―――. *La politica di sviluppo di un'area sottosviluppata nell'esperienza italiana*. Milan, 1968.
―――. *Obiettivi della politica di sviluppo del Mezzogiorno alla vigilia del secondo piano quinquennale*. Rome, 1969.
Saragat, Giuseppe. *Quaranta anni di lotta per la democrazia: Scritti e discorsi 1925–1965*. Milan, 1966.
Settembrini, Domenico. *La Chiesa nella politica italiana, 1944–1963*. Pisa, 1964.
Sforza, Carlo. *Cinque anni a Palazzo Chigi: La politica estera italiana dal 1947 al 1951*. Rome, 1952.
Silj, Alessandro. *L'agricoltura nella Comunità Economica Europea: Il ruolo dell'agricoltura in un processo di sviluppo economico*. Milan, 1961.

Somma, Luigi. *De Gasperi o Gronchi.* Rome, 1953.
Spinelli, Altiero. *L'Europa non cade dal cielo.* Bologna, 1960.
———. *Rapporto sull'Europa.* Milan, 1965.
Spinelli, Altiero, et al. *Che fare per l'Europa?* Milan, 1963.
SVIMEZ. *Effetti economici di un programma di investimenti nel Mezzogiorno.* Rome, 1951.
———. *Le migrazioni interne nel periodo 1952–1966.* Rome, 1968.
Tarchiani, Alberto. *Dieci anni tra Roma e Washington.* Verona, 1955.
Taviani, Paolo Emilio. *Il Piano Schuman.* Rome, 1953.
———. *Solidarietà atlantica e Comunità Europea.* Florence, 1958.
Trentin, Bruno. *La minaccia del Piano Schuman.* Rome, 1952.
Trespidi, G. B. Aldo. *Realtà e prospettive dell'industria chimica in Italia.* Rome, 1967.
Togliatti, Palmiro. *Il partito comunista italiano.* Milan, 1953.
———. *L'opera di De Gasperi: Rapporti tra stato e chiesa.* Florence, 1958.
———. *Problemi del movimento operaio internazionale, 1956–1961.* Rome, 1962.
Valiani, Leo. *L'avvento di De Gasperi.* Turin, 1949.
Vedovato, Giuseppe. *Mercato Comune Europeo e esportazione artigiana.* Florence, 1963.
Vito, Francesco, et al. *Problemi di sviluppo economico con particolare riguardo alle aree arretrate.* Milan, 1956.
Vittorio, Giuseppe Di, et al. *I sindacati in Italia.* Bari, 1955.
Vöchting, Friedrich. *Die italienische Südfrage: Entstehung und Problematik eines wirtschaftlichen Notstandsgebietes.* Berlin, 1951.
Votaw, Dow. *The Six-Legged Dog: Mattei and ENI—A Study in Power.* Berkeley, 1964.
Walker, Donald S. *A Geography of Italy.* London, 1958.
Webster, Richard A. *The Cross and the Fasces: Christian Democracy and Fascism in Italy.* Stanford, 1960.

Index

ACLI (Associazioni Cristiane Lavoratori Italiani), 245–49
Action party, 4, 10–11, 314, 316–17
Adenauer, Konrad, 34, 46, 96, 290
Agnelli, Giovanni, 195
Agriculture, Italian: and negotiation of Treaty of Rome, 61–62; EEC's future impact assessed, 69–70; and Stresa conference, 77–78; and Mansholt Plan, 78–79; negotiation of EEC market regulations, 79–81; and EEC agricultural financing, 81–82; and common cereals price, 83–84; and "empty chair" crisis, 84–86; and concluding agricultural negotiations, 86–87; first effects of common agricultural policy, 88–89; agricultural zones analyzed, 119–24; cereals, 124–26; livestock, 126–28; dairy products, 128–29; fruit and vegetables, 129–32; industrial crops, 132–33; wine, 133–36; olives, 136–37; fragmentation of ownership, 137–39; structural deficiencies, 139–40; mezzadria, 141–42; braccianti, 142–43; commerce in EEC, 143–44; EEC's effects on crop choice, 145–47; FEOGA's influence, 147–48; unsatisfactory results of EEC, 148–49; in South, 160–61. *See also* Coltivatori Diretti; Confagricoltura
Albertario, Paolo, 61, 78
Albonetti, Achille, 56, 65
Allied Control Commission, 8–9, 13
Amendola, Giorgio, 294–95
Andreotti, Giulio, 203, 256, 279

Badoglio, Pietro, 7–8
Badini Confalonieri, Vittorio, 153
Bandini, Mario, 141, 218
Basso, Lelio, 279, 299, 300, 303, 305, 309
Benvenuti, Lodovico, 32, 46, 56
Berti, Giuseppe, 70
Beyen, Johan Willem, 53–54
Bidault, Georges, 21, 46
Bitossi, Renato, 224, 231
Bobba, Franco, 56, 59, 64
Boldrini, Marcello, 188
Bonato, Corrado, 137, 218
Bonomi, Ivanoe, 10, 13
Bonomi, Paolo, 136, 217–18
Buozzi, Bruno, 222

Cantalupo, Roberto, 71
Casaltoli, Sergio, 215–17
Cassa per il Mezzogiorno: founded, 24, 263; and European Investment Bank, 91; and agrarian reform, 128; development theory

Cassa per il Mezzogiorno (*cont'd*) of, 162–65; second cycle, 168–74; and DC, 267

Catholic Church: and DC, 7, 9–10, 14, 255, 266–67, as decision-maker, 178; and ACLI, 245–49; and Communists, 257–58; and DC Right, 264–65; and DC Center, 265–68; and federalism, 267–68, 276, 283

Cattani, Attilio, 56, 95, 199

Cefis, Eugenio, 188, 271

CGIL (Confederazione Generale Italiana del Lavoro): and Treaty of Rome, 70; wartime organization, 221–22; interconfederal wage agreements, 223; tensions within, 223–24; and Marshall Plan, 224, 231; splits up, 224–25; size, 225–26; as pressure group, 226; relations with PCI and PSI, 226–27; long-term goals, 227–28; and Piano del Lavoro, 228; supports economic planning, 229–30; opposes ECSC, 232; position paper on EEC, 233; denounces monopolies in EEC, 234; seeks influence in EEC, 234–36; and WFTU, 235–36. *See also* Novella, Agostino; Vittorio, Giuseppe Di

Christian Democratic party: wartime goals, 7, 9, 11; and postwar political planning, 13–15; economic policy of, 15–16; and peace treaty, 16–18; victory in 1948 elections, 20–21; and NATO, 28; and EDC, 52; relations with CISL, 223–24, 237–38, 245; currents formed, 252–56, 260; break with PCI, 257–59; current of Gronchi, 260–61; syndical current, 261; Dossettiani, 261–64; currents of Right, 264–65; current of Center, 265–69; power struggles within, 269–71; Fanfani's rise, 271; debate over neo-Atlanticism, 272–73; and opening to Left, 273–74; and 1958 elections, 274; strength of currents (1959), 275; Dorotei founded, 275–76; influence of John XXIII, 276; debates relations with PSI, 276–77; accepts PSI participation in cabinet, 278–79; approves first Moro cabinet, 278–80; continuing battles of currents, 281–82; role re-considered, 283–85; postwar policy reviewed, 285. *See also* Gasperi, Alcide De

Churchill, Winston S., 7, 8

Cicogna, Furio, 209–10, 212

CISC (International Confederation of Christian Trade Unions), 238, 245

CISL (Confederazione Italiana Sindacati Lavoratori): and Treaty of Rome, 59; founded, 224–25; relations with DC, 237–38; anti-Communism of, 238–39; conception of union's role, 239–40; supports economic planning, 241; relations with ICFTU, 241–43; favors integration, 243–45

Colitto, Francesco, 58

Colombo, Emilio: and Treaty of Rome, 61–62; and agricultural negotiations, 79, 82–83; and vacant chair, 86; and British application, 97; and Dorotei, 275, 282, 284

Colorni, Eugenio, 4–5

Coltivatori Diretti: and EEC negotiations, 77–89, 134, 137, 139; as pressure group, 202–3, 217–20

Communist party, Italian: wartime policy, 7, 9, 11, 287–88; in De Gasperi governments, 14–15; and NATO, 28; rejects ECSC, 36, 290; 1953 elections, 47; and WEU, 52, 290; and Treaty of Rome, 70, 291–93; and labor movement, 222–27; postwar goals, 288–89; de-Stalinization, 291–92; and EEC, 293–99; and PSI, 299, 305–6

Compagna, Francesco, 159, 160, 177

Confagricoltura (Confederazione Generale dell'Agricoltura Ital-

Confagricoltura (cont'd)
iana): and agricultural negotiations, 77–89; and mezzadria, 142; and EEC, 147–48; as pressure group, 202, 217–20

Confcommercio (Confederazione Generale del Commercio e del Turismo), 213–17

Confindustria (Confederazione Generale dell'Industria Italiana): opposes ECSC, 36; and EEC negotiations, 59; influence of, 178, 202, 204; early history, 204; postwar goals, 204–5; views on trade liberalization, 206; debates ECSC, 206–7; intervenes in politics, 207–8; seeks liberal basis to EEC, 208–9; collaboration in EEC, 210–11; and concentrations policy in EEC, 211; demands completion of economic union, 211–12; and wage agreements, 223, 227–29, 250

Corbino, Epicarmo, 16, 311

Costa, Angelo, 204–7, 210

Council of Europe, 27–31, 44

Council of the Communes of Europe, 31

Croce, Benedetto, 17

de Gaulle, Charles: and Val d'Aosta, 16; and Kennedy Round, 82–83; and political union, 94–96; vetoes Britain, 97–99; ousts Hallstein, 98; summit conference, 99; criticized, 216–17, 244, 248, 317–19

Democracy of Labor party, 10

Diana, Alfredo, 148

Dorotei, 275, 277–78, 280, 285

Dossetti, Giuseppe, 260–62, 270

Ducci, Roberto, 56, 59, 60, 97

Economy, Italian: effects of ECSC, 38–41; and Treaty of Rome, 57; boom, 66–71; effects of EEC, 72–73, 143–49; industrial resources, 102–6; iron and steel, 106–7; engineering, 108–11; chemicals, 111–12; textiles, 114–16; cement, 116–18; agricultural zones, 119–24; crop choice, 124–37; agricultural problems, 137–43

ECSC (European Coal and Steel Community): and sectoral integration, 30; proposed, 33; Italian reaction, 33; negotiation of treaty, 34; Italian demands, 34–36; attitude of Italian political parties to, 36–38; effects on Italian coal mines, 38–39; and ore supplies, 39; and scrap, 39; effects on Italian iron and steel industry, 40–41, 106–7; and Confindustria, 206–7; and CGIL, 232; and CISL, 243; and PSI, 304

EDC (European Defense Community): proposed, 41–42; Italian reaction, 42; Italian role in negotiations, 43–45; and political union, 44–45; difficulties in ratification, 46–47; linked to Trieste question, 48; debated in Italy, 48–49; De Gasperi's anguish over, 49–50

Eden, Anthony, 50, 51

EEC (European Economic Community): proposed, 53–54; Martino memorandum on, 54; Messina conference, 55–56; Spaak Committee, 56–57; Spaak Report, 57–58; negotiation of Treaty of Rome, 57–62; Venice conference, 58; Italian representation in negotiations, 58–60; Italian demands, 62–64; treaties signed, 65; Italian economic miracle and, 66–69; fears of Italian agricultural circles, 69–70; ratification debates, 70–71; effects summarized, 72–73; success of Italian industry in, 73–75; and recession of 1963-65, 76–77; negotiation of agricultural policy, 77–88; effects of agricultural policy, 88–89, 143–49; negotiations for free trade area, 93–94; Fouchet committee, 94–95; European University, 95; British application

EEC (cont'd)
for membership, 96–98; summit conference (1967), 99; and Italian emigration, 155–57; and Italian unemployment, 157–58; intervention in South, 174–77; public companies, 178–89; private companies, 189–201; and Confindustria, 207–13; and Confcommercio, 213–17; and agricultural federations, 217–20, and labor unions, 227–8, 232–37, 242–45, 248–49; and DC currents, 271–74; and PCI, 70, 291–99; and PSI, 306–7; and Italian politics, 318–20

Einaudi, Luigi, federalist views, 3, 5–6; and Liberals, 10, 310–11; budget minister, 19, 22–23, 66, 259

Emigration, 150–59

ENI (Ente Nazionale Idrocarburi): economic role, 67, 105, 178–79; and South, 173–74; history, 184–85; under Mattei, 185–87; and EEC, 188–89

EPC (European Political Community), 144–50

Euratom (European Atomic Energy Community): negotiations, 54–66; treaty appraised, 66–71; effects, 92–93

European Investment Bank, 64, 90–91, 175

European Social Fund, 63–64, 89–90, 174

Fanfani, Amintore: on EDC, 50; and agricultural negotiations, 84–86; on Euratom, 92; and political union, 94–96; and European University, 95; law for mountain areas, 123; and mezzadria, 142; and neovolontarism, 254; minister of labor, 262; and Iniziativa Democratica, 263–64, 270–71, 275; party secretary, 271–73; and Center-Left governments, 275, 277–81; seeks presidency, 282; foreign minister, 282

Federalism, European, in Resistance, 6, 12; First Hague Congress, 27; Second Hague Congress, 48

Federalism, Italian, proposals, 3–4; wartime activity, 4–6; postwar goals, 6–11; and Atlantic alliance, 12; popularity, 31–32; and EDC, 50; European Movement, 183–84; and ACLI, 248–49

Federconsorzi, 217–18

Ferlesch, Giuseppe, 78

Ferrari Aggradi, Mario, 82–83

Fiat Company, 68, 74, 107–8, 193–95, 202

Fouchet, Christian, 94–95

France: peace negotiations, 16–17; customs union with, 21–22; and ECSC, 31–39; and EDC, 41–46; and Treaty of Rome, 55–62, 69; and EEC, 74–75, 77–89; and political union, 93–99

Franco-Italian Customs Union, 21–22

Galloni, Giorgio, 283

Garosci, Aldo, 6

Gasperi, Alcide De: restoration of pre-Fascist state, 13–15; economic policy, 15–16, 22–23, 258–59, 267–68; and peace treaty, 17–18; visits U.S., 18–19; ousts PCI from cabinet, 19, 257–58; welcomes Marshall Plan, 19–20; victory in 1948 elections, 20–21; frees trade, 23–24; reform program, 24–25; and NATO, 25–27; and Germany, 30, 42; and ECSC, 37; welcomes EDC, 42, 44; relations with Schuman, 42–43; proposes European political authority, 44–45; Charlemagne prize, 45; eighth ministry rejected, 47; and Gronchi, 260–61; and Dossettiani, 263; and DC Right, 263–64; criticized by Togliatti, 266, 267; attitude to Church, 266–67; formulation of foreign policy, 285

Germany: occupation of Italy by, 5–7, 32; and ECSC, 30–31, 33–34; and Council of Europe, 32; and

INDEX

Germany (cont'd)
  EDC, 41–50; and WEU, 51–52; and EEC, 55, 74; and Italian migration to, 155–59; and ENI, 188
Giacchero, Enzo, 31
Giolitti, Antonio, 279, 280, 292, 308
Giovane Europa, 268
Gonella, Guido, 253, 259
Grandi, Achille, 222, 239
Great Britain, 7–9, 27, 32, 50–52, 93–99
Green Plans, 78, 126, 140
Gronchi, Giovanni, 187, 256, 260–61, 264, 271–73, 277

ICFTU (International Confederation of Free Trade Unions), 238, 241–42, 245, 249
Industry, Italian: economic miracle, 66–71; in EEC, 73–77; resources, 102–6; iron and steel, 106–7; engineering, 108–11, chemical, 111–14; textiles, 114–16; cement, 116–18; and unemployment, 151–55; in South, 162–65; IRI, 180–84; ENI, 184–89; private companies, 189–200; and pressure groups, 202–13; distribution system, 213–14
IRI (Istituto per la Ricostruzione Industriale): Marshall aid to, 24; and ECSC, 39, 106–7; weak sectors, 111; in South, 173–74; role in economy, 178–80; history, 180–82; formula, 181; and EEC, 182–84

John XXIII, 246, 247–48, 276, 283

Labor, Italian: and EEC, 62, 89–90, 156–59; and overpopulation, 150–55; and unemployment, 151–55; and unions, 221–51
Land reform, 165–66
LaPalombara, Joseph, 202–3, 221, 226, 238
Leone, Giovanni, 278, 282, 284
Levi, Carlo, 122
Levi Sandri, Lionello, 99

Liberal party: goals, 6, 10, 310; and WEU, 52; and Confindustria, 208; and De Gasperi, 310–11; and integration, 311–14
Lombardi, Riccardo, 10, 70, 279, 306–7, 309
Lombardo, Ivan Matteo, 44
Longo, Luigi, 295
Lutz, Vera, 115, 120, 163–64, 170

Malagodi, Giovanni, 70, 208, 313–14
Malfa, Ugo La, 10, 23, 51, 53–54, 70, 97, 317
Malvestiti, Piero, 253, 255–56
Marsanich, Augusto De, 71
Marshall Plan, 15, 18–23, 222–23, 230–31, 242–43, 288
Martino, Edoardo, 70, 99
Martino, Gaetano, 51–52, 54–55, 312–13
Mattei, Enrico, 185–87, 271–72
Mendès-France, Pierre, 47, 49
Merzagora, Cesare, 19
Meynaud, Jean, 178, 179
Micheli, Alighiero De, 207–8, 212
Monarchist party, National, 314–15
Montecatini Edison Company, 114, 190–93
Moro, Aldo, 253, 275–85, 319–20
Movimento Federalista Europeo, 5, 31
MSI (Movimento Sociale Italiano), 50, 71, 225, 315–16
Mussolini, Benito, 3, 7, 107, 124, 161, 189, 315

Nardi, Giuseppe Di, 162–63
Nenni, Pietro: and PSIUP, 299–300; foreign minister, 300–301; neutralism of, 302–4; on de-Stalinization, 305; and Center-Left government, 307–10
Neo-Atlanticism, 187, 272–74, 281, 285
Nitti, Francesco, 161–62
Novella, Agostino, 226, 228–30, 234

Olivetti, Adriano, 197–99
Olivetti Company, 173, 197–99
Olivi, Bino, 66, 93

Pacciardi, Randolfo, 43–44, 50, 316–17
Parliamentary Group for European Union, 31–32
Parri, Ferruccio, 11, 13–16, 31
Pastore, Giulio, 238, 241, 261, 273
Paul VI, 99, 253
Pella, Giuseppe: on ECSC, 36–37; and EDC, 43–45; premier, 47–48, 269; and Treaty of Rome, 71; and labor in EEC, 153–54; and industry, 203; budget minister, 263; and Center-Left government, 279
Pescatore, Gabriele, 166
Petrilli, Giuseppe, 181–84, 203
Piccioni, Attilio, 49, 265, 312
Pira, Giorgio La, 253–54, 262, 272, 282
Pirelli Company, 195–97
Pius XII, 247, 258, 267–68, 285
Popular party, 4, 254–55
PSIUP (Partito Socialista Italiano di Unità Proletaria): in 1944-47, 9, 299–302; in 1964, 279, 308–9

Republican party, 10, 52–53, 316–18
Restivo, Franco, 86–87
Roosevelt, Franklin D., 7–8, 16–17
Rosselli, Carlo, 4, 316
Rossi, Ernesto, 4–5, 206–7
Rossi-Doria, Manlio, 10
Rumor, Mariano, 275, 282, 283

Saragat, Giuseppe: wartime goals, 9; and EEC, 96; president, 282; in PSIUP, 299–302; foreign minister, 308
Sardinia, 36, 104, 121–22, 174, 203
Salvatorelli, Luigi, 12, 26
Santi, Fernando, 235–36
Saraceno, Pasquale, 91, 166, 176, 218
Scelba, Mario, 48–49, 269–70, 273, 275–76, 279, 281
Schuman, Robert, 21–22, 27, 32–33, 42–46
Segni, Antonio, 59, 65–66, 265, 270, 273, 280
Sforza, Carlo: federalism of, 4; vetoed as foreign minister, 8; and peace treaty, 18; and Marshall Plan, 19–22; and NATO, 25–29; and Council of Europe, 27; on Germany, 32; and ECSC, 33–37; and EDC, 41–45; as foreign minister, 259
Sicily, 54–55, 105, 121–22, 163, 173–74, 185
Silone, Ignazio, 13
Sinigaglia Plan, 36, 107, 182, 268
Snia-Viscosa Company, 114, 199–200
Social-Democratic party, 52, 301–2
Socialist party: and De Gasperi, 14; and NATO, 28; pacts with PCI, 30, 305–6; rejects ECSC, 36; 1953 elections, 47; and Treaty of Rome, 70; and opening to Left, 274–85; neutralism, 302–4; and de-Stalinization, 305–6; and EEC, 306–7; and Center-Left governments, 307–10
South, Italian: and Treaty of Rome, 57, 63; and EEC, 80–81, 90–91, 174–77; agriculture of, 119–24, 129–31, 135–36, 141; labor in, 142–43; overpopulation, 151; unemployment, 152–53; and Vanoni Plan, 153–54; origins of problem, 160–62; development theory in, 162–64; Cassa, 164–75; industrialization, 185
Soviet Union, reparations demand, 16, 18; and Marshall Plan, 230–31; and PCI, 287–89; and EEC, 295–96; de-Stalinization, 290–92, 294
Spaak, Paul-Henri, 32, 55–65, 96, 208
Spinelli, Altiero, 4, 6, 8, 11, 25, 28, 50, 100
Stalin, Josef, 7, 287, 290–91
Storti, Bruno, 241, 244
Sturzo, Luigi, 4, 50, 254
SVIMEZ (Associazione per lo Sviluppo dell'Industria nel Mezzogiorno), 164–66

Taranto, 40, 107, 174–75
Taviani, Paolo Emilio, 11, 33, 43, 52, 254
Togliatti, Palmiro: and Badoglio, 7; wartime goals, 9, 287; assassination attempt on, 224; and De

INDEX

Togliatti, Palmiro (*cont'd*)
  Gasperi, 266–67; and DC, 286; and de-Stalinization, 291–92; and EEC, 292–94; Testament, 296–97
Trentin, Bruno, 232
Trieste, 8, 48
Truman, Harry S, 16–17, 18–19

UIL (Unione Italiana del Lavoro), 59, 225, 249–51
United States of America: and liberation of Italy, 7–8; forms Atlantic bloc, 12–18; Marshall aid, 18–25; and NATO, 25–29; and EDC, 40–42

Uomo Qualunque party, 314

Valletta, Vittorio, 195
Vanoni Plan, 63, 153–54, 246, 250
Vecchietti, Tullio, 279, 305, 309
Vito, Francesco, 163, 218, 254
Vittorio, Giuseppe Di, 221–23, 231, 233–34
Vöchting, Friedrich, 163

Western European Union, 25–26, 50–52
WFTU (World Federation of Trade Unions), 234–36, 294

Zoli, Adone, 270

WIDENER UNIVERSITY-WOLFGRAM LIBRARY

CIR   HC305.W48
Italy chooses Europe

3 3182 00308 4453